The
HEART GARDEN

Sunday Reed and Heide

Janine Burke

V
VINTAGE

A Vintage book
Published by
Published by Random House Australia Pty Ltd
Level 3, 100 Pacific Highway, North Sydney, NSW 2060
http://www.randomhouse.com.au

Sydney New York Toronto
London Auckland Johannesburg

First published in Australia by Knopf in 2004
This Vintage edition first published 2005

National Library of Australia
Cataloguing-in-Publication Entry

Burke, Janine, 1952– .
The heart garden.

Bibliography.
Includes index.

ISBN 1 74 051 330 4.

1. Reed, Sunday, 1905–1981. 2. Women painters – Australia – Biography. 3. Art, Modern – 19th century – Australia. I. Title

759.994

Cover illustration Australian Picture Library
Cover photograph courtesy of the La Trobe Australian Manuscripts Collection, State Library of Victoria
Cover design by Greendot Design
Internal design by Greendot Design
Typeset in KaatskillH 13/17pt by Midland Typesetters, Maryborough, Victoria
Printed and bound by The SOS Print + Media Group

10 9 8 7 6 5

To Jean

CONTENTS

✎

Introduction

I'M LOOKING AT TWO PHOTOGRAPHS of Sunday Reed. In the first, it's 1923 and she is seventeen years old. It's a summer afternoon and Sunday is sitting on the terrace at Merthon, the family holiday house at Sorrento, facing the sea. Her shoulder-length hair is loose and she is wearing a long white frock, white stockings and shoes. She has been posed by society photographer Pegg Clarke for a spread on Merthon in the fashionable Sydney magazine, *The Home*. She smiles but it's more a grin, as if she can't quite keep a straight face.

Surrounded by her parents, younger brother Everard and cousin John, Sunday appears her family's shining member: handsome, tanned, energetic and, with her legs crossed on the rail, casually imperious, mistress of all she surveys. Yet Sunday is seated at a slight remove from her family, and in profile. Closer together, the family forms a unit. From her position, it is as though Sunday observes the group but is not quite part of it.

In the second photograph, Sunday is milking a cow. It's a cool evening sometime in 1942 and she is at Heide. She stares directly at Albert Tucker, who is taking the photograph, with the unstudied freshness of the spontaneous moment. She is wearing a pullover tied with a belt and trousers turned up at the cuffs. Her hair is shorter and brushed back from her face. She radiates confidence and vitality as if milking a cow in the Yarra Valley is to be blissfully content at the centre of the universe.

Two photographs. Two lives. The first displays a girl at the core of Melbourne's establishment elite and on the cusp of womanhood, a member of the class who is born to rule, who is expected to make a dynastic marriage, bear children and not rock the boat. The second photograph reveals a very different energy: mature, earthy and individual, the result of a choice about needing to live without grandeur or the expectations that privilege bestows.

By quitting the first life, Sunday gained the second, a complex and at times brilliant endeavour that saw her become one of the most significant women in Australian cultural life, an enterprise that included risk, defeat and tragedy as well as hard work, satisfaction and respect. How did Sunday invent her life at Heide, a life unimaginable from the terrace at Merthon that summer's day? What personal odyssey enabled a woman destined for a life of leisure to transform herself into an influential and committed modernist who drew around her a circle of artists who remain central to Australian art history? What were the strengths, and flaws, that made it possible for her to abandon all that Merthon symbolised, and not return?

This biography explores Sunday's creative work by emphasising her greatest single creation — her home, Heide, where she lived from 1935 until her death in 1981. She shared that home with her husband, John, and while this book does not seek to exclude John from Heide's various projects, or from his pivotal role in Sunday's life, it focuses on the areas Sunday made her own: the design and atmosphere of both Heide I and II, and the Heide garden.

More contentiously, it argues that Sunday was the engine behind Heide, the ideas person, the critical, seeing eye, an inspiring, quickening force that enthralled, and infuriated, many. Sunday developed a vision of Australian modernism that she sought to explore, guide and disseminate through art, literature, publishing, landscape design and architecture. Once she had defined her taste, she followed it unswervingly and never doubted its veracity. This book traces the arc of that taste.

It takes its name from a garden Sunday made after her affair with Sidney Nolan had ended, when she returned from Europe in 1949. Jean Langley was present when Sunday 'created this little garden with chamomile and little herbs and things all in the shape of a heart. It had a sentimental beginning, it was like a private love letter.'[1] Sunday arranged it on the lawn, in an enclosed area, not far from the dining room window, the room where Nolan had painted the Ned Kelly series. Facing north in its protected spot, it would have received sun all day, and thrived. It was also a secret garden, its meaning communicated only to Langley. 'We exchanged some sort of intensity — without words — a sort of femininity . . . I don't know whether she told anyone else about the making of the Heart Garden. She knew I liked things to be sacred, as she did.'[2]

As garden historian Jane Brown writes, the secret garden, 'a hidden place of enchantment and peace, where all our ills can be cured, is one of the most powerful ideas in cultural history'.[3] The garden as refuge, as a place of beauty and magic, of revivification and as a symbol of childhood's promise, all played their part in the creation of the Heide garden.

The Heart Garden is a *hortus conclusus*, an enclosed garden, its high brick walls on two sides offering protection from harsh northerlies, making a sheltered place for the heart itself, a site where growth and change were possible. It provides the template of Sunday's aesthetic. Deeply sentimental, she manifested her feelings in ways that were at once practical, imaginative and aesthetic and nature often had a strong role to play in her creative impulses.

The Heart Garden was a memorial to a great love gone wrong. In a way, it was Nolan's tombstone, the place where Sunday could grieve and honour him. She was not an artist but peopled her life with artists, making them her inspiration and her instruments. Nolan lived with her and loved her. She nourished him with food, money, ideas, books, painting materials, all the passions of the mind and the body. But she could not bind him to her.

The Heart Garden was not an entirely private matter. Langley, as Sunday's confidante, was audience to the garden's intent, the female companion to its meaning and construction. What Sunday created she was impelled to share, and intimate dialogues with male and female friends contributed to the shaping of her aesthetic.

At Heide, Sunday's highly personal project was to bestow on her select circle gifts of nurture and encouragement in an exquisite and stimulating environment that was wholly her own. But Sunday was no saint and Heide could also be a dangerous place, where resentment, anger, betrayal and manipulation could damage and poison the very friendships Sunday sought to secure. That she succeeded more than she failed and was loved more than reviled is probably a testament to her determination and loyalty, her ability to renew and transform herself, to commit herself to new art, new friends, new dreams.

Sunday's genius was eclecticism. She translated her vision of modernism into the Australian vernacular and surrounded herself with it in the art she collected. The Heide garden was a fusion of French formalism, English romanticism and eucalypts, Heide I's interior a mix of exquisite antiques and dazzling modern art. It was the same with friends. She excelled at attracting diverse characters from Tucker to Charles Blackman, Joy Hester to Hal Porter. Part of Heide's spectacular history of fights and friction came from Sunday's need to hear dissenting voices, and to give her own opinion, to be heard. She was never afraid of an argument, or of strong characters and big egos. She sought out creative people who could identify and articulate the Australian idiom: not only did she want to see modern Australian culture triumphant, she sought to assist at its birth. Over several decades at Heide, Sunday combined figurative with abstract painting, French style with Australian natives, old friends with youthful arrivals. The overriding desire was to privilege Australian culture within an international context. To Sunday, art was a fundamental expression of an Australian identity that she constructed as complex, volatile and mutable – rather like her own.

Finally, Sunday abandoned the Heart Garden.[4] Perhaps it had achieved its healing purpose, a release from melancholy through work, through the consolations of beauty and the cycles of nature. Equally for Sunday, as a modernist, creativity was synonymous with destruction, with leaving the past behind and aggressively embracing the new. It was a process she maintained all her adult life. Sunday might have been sentimental but a gardener must be destructive as well as creative, and nostalgia has no place in a thriving garden.

Sunday was an excellent gardener, energetic and organised, and she recognised that a garden, no matter how great, is transitory. So despite how much Nolan meant to Sunday, and how often she brooded on the bonds between them, in real terms her life continued to grow at Heide. There was always a new garden to make.

· I ·

Troubled Princess

Money (or the lack of it) was never mentioned in polite conversation, let alone the
price of anything. It was considered vulgar. Life was very peaceful, very leisurely.
It was certainly very quiet. No trams ran on Sunday because their noise would
have disturbed the church services.

JAMES PAXTON, TOORAK AS I KNEW IT[1]

I always think the men in our family regard their women in much the same light
as a nicely arranged bowl of flowers or a nice meal!

SUNDAY REED TO JOHN REED[2]

WHEN LELDA SUNDAY BAILLIEU WAS BORN on 15 October 1905,
her family had not assumed its legendary prominence and status.
In fact, the Baillieus had both a whiff of new money and an odour

of scandal about them. William Lawrence Baillieu's ability to survive the crash of the 1890s, the bust of Melbourne's mighty landboom, meant he was regarded with opprobrium by those who had done their money and lost the lot. When he built Collins House in 1910, a massive building devoted to fifty Baillieu enterprises in the centre of Melbourne's financial district, it was known in some quarters as Glenrowan House – a snide reference to the site of Ned Kelly's siege: the place was full of robbers.[3]

W.L., as he was called, created the family fame and fortune and he drew his siblings along in his wake. He was Sunday's uncle, the older brother of her father Arthur, a visionary mercantile adventurer whose career encompassed real estate, mining and a stint in parliament. But W.L. also set the family tone: there were no grand mansions built in the wilderness like other rich Edwardian families, no ostentatious behaviour, no flagrant displays of wealth. 'Great achievements *sotto voce*' could have been the family motto.[4] Privacy was a Baillieu characteristic, one that Sunday inherited. As Michael Cannon observed, despite W.L. exerting tremendous influence over Australian economic and political affairs, his life remained shrouded in mystery for decades.[5]

The family history is certainly a romantic tale. The Baillieus were embroiderers and mercers from Liège, Belgium, who settled in Bristol in the late eighteenth century. The artistically inclined Lambert Baillieu taught music and dancing. His son James, Sunday's grandfather, opted for the new world. He was a twenty-one-year-old sailor when he dived off the *Priscilla* in January 1853 while it was anchored at the Portsea quarantine station inside the Port Phillip heads. He must have not only been desperate but a strong swimmer: the currents are fierce and the water freezing, but he managed to swim the five kilometres to Queenscliff. He said he was escaping the bullying of a drunken captain who may have been a bad commander or a fancier of young men but it was not unusual for poorly paid seamen to jump ship at a port of call.

James avoided arrest for desertion by hiding in William Buckley's cave, the former convict who was befriended by local Aboriginal tribes.[6] The goldrush was at fever pitch in Victoria but James liked the slower pace of Queenscliff. He found work as a boatman for the Customs Department and later worked as assistant lighthouse keeper at Point Lonsdale. As soon as he was settled, he married Emma Pow who had arrived on a ship loaded with other young women immigrants, eager for their chance at life in the colonies. She was a fine seamstress and used her skills to make all her children's clothes from offcuts and scraps. The couple lived first in a tent on the beach, then in a government cottage where they had ten sons and four daughters.

It was not a comfortable childhood and elder son W.L.'s relentless determination to succeed was probably generated by the early years of poverty. James rose to prominence as a solid burgher and became councillor and mayor of Queenscliff though he was 'not what was known as a sharp businessman'.[7] By 1881, W.L. had arranged sufficient backing from the Commercial Bank for his father to leave the Customs Department and build the Ozone Hotel, originally called Baillieu House, premises lavish enough to lure the governor of Victoria to holiday there. It was a gift from a devoted son. Indeed, family loyalty became a tradition among the Baillieus, regarded as the highest duty of all.

Meanwhile, W.L. trained in a local bank. Like many of the Baillieu men, he was tall, blue-eyed and handsome. He was also charming, ambitious and athletic. Through a shared interest in yachting, he developed a close bond with Edward Latham, founder of Carlton brewery, who would become his friend, mentor, investor and father-in-law. In 1885, W.L. moved to Melbourne and started an estate agency with Donald Munro, another adventurous young man – it was backed by the Federal Bank and a personal guarantee from Latham. In a short time, the dashing W.L. became 'the greatest auctioneer of them all'.[8] In 1887, Munro & Baillieu trounced their rivals in an extremely competitive industry, selling land worth more than three million pounds. W.L. literally left the onlookers gasping.

When the crash came six years later, Victoria swooned as the banks in Collins Street closed their doors. An overinflated property market accompanied by dizzying levels of borrowing and speculation both here and in England had lead to the economic demise and, as each business collapsed, others were dragged down with it. The nightmare of unemployment that followed was accentuated by epidemics of influenza, typhoid and measles.[9]

But the Federal Bank obligingly wrote off the thousands W.L. owed them and he convinced his investors to accept sixpence in the pound as compensation for their losses. It was a shrewd strategy. He managed not only to disguise the truth about his finances but he never faced the ignominy of the Insolvency Court. Donald Munro, W.L.'s partner, was shattered and retired to suburbia but W.L. did not flinch. He opened a new estate agency and busily began making his second fortune. In 1897, he appointed Arthur, Sunday's father, to run the business for him while he pursued his Australia-wide mining ventures, the most lucrative being the formation of BHP. Arthur's previous job had been to liquidate several of W.L.'s companies after the crash.

There seemed to be two classes of Baillieu men: stalwarts, like Arthur, and W.L. His brothers may have been bright, hard-working fellows but W.L. was the head of the family and no-one challenged his authority. Essentially, everyone at Collins House was working for him. There were so many men in the family, W.L. had nothing short of a squadron to command. He was the eldest surviving son, then there was George, Robert, Charles, Edward, Arthur, Richard, Norman and Maurice. There seem to be no historical records of the four daughters. Not all the Baillieus made fortunes, even if they followed W.L.'s lead, but all did well. W.L. saw to that.

The band of brothers, and their sons, created the stifling, male, mercantile atmosphere in which Sunday grew up and which she abhorred. Once, crossing Swanston Street, she saw 'a big black car coming round the corner and as she looked into [it], she thought, "What awful men!" Then she had another look and she said, "They were all my cousins and uncles."'[10] She was also aware of the decorative role women were expected to play in her world, reflecting that 'the prejudice is so strong and I quite understand that I'm never expected to say anything worth listening to and it would cause great annoyance if I did so that now I feel I never want to!'[11] The years of feeling trivialised and silenced lead Sunday to both cherish and encourage freely expressed opinions, even though such frankness often lead to argument and discord at Heide.

Australia was a masculinist society. Despite the tragedies of the First World War, with its killing fields of young, dead men, patriotism remained fervent. None of Sunday's immediate family enlisted though three of W.L.'s sons – Clive, Harry and Tom – served with distinction in France and Britain. The heroes of the day were all men, either soldiers or sportsmen like aviator Charles Kingsford Smith, tennis ace Gerald Patterson or swimmer Andrew 'Boy' Charlton. England was home, even more so for the wealthier Australians who could afford to visit. The focus was on King and Empire and the best Australians could hope for was to imitate the customs and the culture of their betters. The higher the family's social rank, the more likely it was to slavishly model itself on British manners and style.

Sunday may not have been born a rebel but as she grew up, she reacted against a male ethos that was as much the product of her time as it was symbolised by the Baillieus' dynastic conquests. Men ruled Sunday's world and when she came to create her own at Heide, her personality and ethos would dominate. Not only would her family be banished, so would the conventional definition of 'family' itself.

Tellingly, Sunday emphasised the Baillieus' romantic history, rather than its recent rude wealth. When Jean Langley first met Sunday, Langley 'used to do a lot of sewing for babies . . . and [Sunday] would send me little packets of lace, whole cards of them and she'd say, "This is from my Belgian lacemaker ancestors" . . . She liked to go back to that Belgian connection rather than the Australian Baillieus.' Sunday also affectionately remembered 'the old lighthouse keeper Baillieu . . . She didn't like the Baillieu uncles at all. Despised them.'

But life was not all chafing constriction. Arthur and Ethel doted on their children and Sunday was definitely daddy's girl. She adored her father and he worshipped her. 'She loved her father deeply and dearly.'[12] Arthur, sedate, kindly and dignified, epitomised a type of masculinity different from other Baillieu men. He was not a bullish leader but a gracious follower, a man without the hubris of W.L. Home life was of paramount importance to him and his marriage to Ethel was a contented one. Arthur was also gently protective of his vital, highly strung daughter.

Sunday may have needed it. She was the only girl in a family of boys. She had two older brothers, Jack Kingsbury (known as King) and Darren, who were respectively four and two years older than she, and Everard, seven years her junior. King was her favourite. She felt close to him and he was a fond childhood companion, but with Darren and Everard she established no firm common ground and, in adult life, the gulf between Sunday and these two brothers widened.

Ethel was the youngest child of David and Maria Ham. An enterprising Englishman who had arrived in Australia in 1849 at nineteen, David based himself at Ballarat where he launched into a series of successful careers first as a goldminer and shopkeeper, then a stock and share broker. In 1886, he was elected to the Victorian Legislative Council. A freemason and a devout Wesleyan, he also had business interests in Queenscliff and the Bellarine Peninsula. The Baillieu family may have known him from there. In 1893, David donated a pair of marble lions which are situated inside the gates of Ballarat Botanical Gardens. Sunday was fond of the lions and proud of her grandfather's munificence.

Like Sunday, Ethel grew up in the lap of luxury. She became an amateur painter and an arts patron, attending Victorian Artists' Society exhibitions. When Fred McCubbin needed cash to underwrite his 1914 monograph, Ethel was one of the many society figures who provided financial support.[13] In 1916 she and Arthur bought McCubbin's *The Rabbit Burrow* (c.1910, Private Collection) which Sunday inherited, a whimsical study of two children at play in the bush. More importantly, Ethel and Arthur became friends and collectors of Arthur Streeton's, buying *The Grand Canal* from Streeton's highly successful 1914 exhibition at the Victorian Artists' Society and several of his studies of the Mornington and Bellarine Peninsulas.

Typically, it was W.L. who forged the connection. In 1907, after meeting Streeton at his patrons' country retreat, W.L. commissioned him to paint aspects of Queenscliff's coastline and put him up at the

Ozone Hotel. Streeton had grown up in Queenscliff where his father was headmaster at the local state school and where he had known Arthur Baillieu when both were lads.

On his return to Australia in 1923, Streeton's ties with the Baillieus strengthened. Not only did he become a regular guest at Merthon but he also rented an apartment-studio on the top floor of Fairlie House in Anderson St, South Yarra, which was owned by Arthur. Streeton described the latter as 'delightful premises . . . overlooking the Botanic Gardens and my big studio windows are the Highest in South Yarra.'[14]

Sir Arthur Streeton was a leading member of the club of grand old men who dominated the Australian art world and exercised a deadening effect on the local scene. Opposed to modern art, their taste dominated gallery acquisition's policies, prizes, criticism and the art market, and they were lionised by the establishment. Their vision of Australia was typified not by the sparkling brilliance of the Heidelberg School but a preference for the pastoral calm and banality of Hans Heysen, Ernest Buckmaster and W.B. MacInnes. Streeton's glory days as a member of the Heidelberg School when, together with Roberts and McCubbin, he invented a fresh image of the landscape, were over. As art critic for the *Argus* from 1929–1935, Streeton's was a loud, brisk, conservative voice. He represented the forces of reaction that Sunday and the Heide circle would stand against.

Merthon was Sunday's special world and Streeton homaged it in art. He painted *Nocturne* (c.1920, Private Collection), a blue-toned study of Sunday dancing in the moonlight at Merthon. On the same visit, he completed *Point King, Sorrento* (1920, Private Collection), a sparkling watercolour that illustrates Merthon's commanding position. The larger coastal properties had private jetties, reached by steep stairs from the cliffs, and the Baillieus constructed their own sea baths as well. *Point King* shows figures descending the stairs to the jetty: Everard Baillieu speculated it was him in his red dressing-gown accompanied by his nanny.[15] While it was a status symbol for a wealthy family to have a famous artist as a house guest, it also gave Sunday the opportunity to watch Streeton work in her own home. Watching an artist create was one of her greatest pleasures. She could not get close enough. 'I miss your work. I miss watching you work,' she once told Joy Hester.[16]

Sunday may have associated Streeton with the Baillieu world but she did not dismiss his art or the significance of the Heidelberg School. They were factors that lead to the purchase not only of two excellent early Streetons, but of Heide itself. Streeton's presence at Merthon was another influence, more subtle but equally potent. Streeton could entertain his hosts with 'myriad memories', fond reminiscences of a stimulating artistic fraternity, of get-togethers with Roberts and McCubbin 'in the cool evenings after the hot dry days and our work – the walks from Box Hill on Sunday evenings . . . and the long afternoons and evenings at Heidelberg.'[17] He also provided an example of an artist who lived and worked in Sunday's ambience, making the creative act a direct, intimate and accessible experience.

Ethel painted watercolours and took lessons from Streeton. While Ethel's *Still Life* (1930, Heide Museum of Modern Art) may be stodgy and unadventurous in form and touch, nonetheless it gave Sunday another chance to see art being produced and discussed in her environment. The home as studio, as a conflation of domestic and artistic space, was a key element in Sunday's project at Heide.

Merthon had been built in 1897 by the prolific boomtime architect and politician William Pitt, who designed several of

Melbourne's most sumptuous buildings including the Princess Theatre and the Rialto. Pitt named his holiday home after Captain Merthon, commander of the first transport ship that passed through the heads and anchored near the property. Arthur bought Merthon on Pitt's death in 1918. For the Baillieus, nearby Portsea had special significance: it was where the dynasty began, where James fled the *Priscilla* and swam to freedom across the bay.

Unlike Pitt's public projects, Merthon's architecture was unadorned, simple and airy. Made of local pale-gold limestone, it was a big one-storey house set in six and a half acres of garden that included tea-tree and pines. The living room – where Streeton painted Sunday – was a large room facing the sea, designed for parties and gatherings. It had a flat roof and was open on three sides but could be closed off in cooler weather by sliding shutters that disappeared into the floor. Furnished with comfortable cane furniture, it had a specially sprung dance floor and panoramic views of the bay.

The rest of Merthon's main living area was arranged with Windsor chairs and an oak dresser that held a collection of rare pewter, while the walls were hung with prints and a mellow-coloured Chinese embroidered tapestry. It was tasteful, not starkly modern but not cluttered in the Edwardian manner either. Ethel directed Merthon's interior design, giving it clarity, simplicity, openness and light, qualities lacking in the grand homes of Toorak.

Sunday 'loved Merthon very much'.[18] When she took Nadine Amadio there in the 1960s, Sunday 'sat in a chair at the end of the table, that dining room at the end of the house where you could see right down the hall to the water. She said, "This was one of my favourite aspects. This was like a screen that the visual world passed by."'[19] The views of Port Philip Bay are one of Merthon's best features and Arthur had chosen a spectacular site. Standing on Merthon's lawn – or sitting on its terrace – would offer a thrill of power and beauty as the eye surveys the vast, glittering, blue sweep of the bay and the steep green rise of Arthur's Seat to the right. Beyond that, the arc of the coastline rims the south-eastern suburbs reaching, in the distant haze, the city of Melbourne.

Summer holidays were long, leisurely affairs. Families left Melbourne around Cup Day, early in November, and often did not return until Easter. There were few shops in the Sorrento village, so families would bring a cow, chickens and whatever foodstuffs and comforts they required. As most came down on the paddle-steamer from Melbourne, there was plenty of room. A thriving vegetable garden was necessary for the table and it may have been at Merthon, rather than at the family home in Toorak, Balholmen, where Sunday learned to enjoy gardening.

Sunday divided her time between swimming, sunbathing and sailing with her father who was a keen yachtsman. It was why Sunday was delighted to inherit her mother's jewel box, probably decorated by Streeton with a bevy of mermaids (c.1920, Private Collection). Merthon was a refuge for Sunday, a retreat from the restrictions of Toorak, a place of beauty and pleasure where she felt free and healthy. Importantly, it was an introduction to a life lived close to nature, the life she would fashion at Heide.

Ethel was a beautiful, elegant woman, affectionate, imaginative and sensitive, who bequeathed to her daughter a sense of style, an appreciation of art and music and a mastery of the French language. Sunday treasured Ethel's copy of *Lettres completes d'Abelard et Heloise*, the passionate correspondence between the twelfth-century star-crossed lovers, philosopher Peter Abelard and his pupil Heloise.[20] At home Sunday was also taught piano which she greatly enjoyed.

She was especially fond of her mother's baby Bechstein which she installed at Heide.

Such skills, together with lessons in watercolour painting and embroidery, were regarded as essential for a well brought-up young lady. They were meant to enhance her decorative, 'feminine' qualities in the home of her father and then of her husband. It was exactly why Sunday felt she was treated merely as 'a nicely arranged bowl of flowers or a nice meal' by the men in her family. The skills she learned were meant for show, not for a greater purpose or even her own pleasure.

Instead, Sunday herself was an object on display, contrived to look suitably attractive, like the flowers, or to be served up and consumed, like the food. The passivity inherent in these images, coupled with the deliberately bland adjective 'nice', was at odds with Sunday's vigorous and critical reaction to her place as a woman within her family and her society. It is also telling that Sunday chose the metaphors of flowers and food to condemn what she regarded as Baillieu male boorishness. It was precisely the cultivation of flowers and the preparation of food, linked by her garden, that would become two of Sunday's consummate skills, symbols of Heide itself.

Such clarity and resentment regarding her role meant Sunday's feelings towards her mother were not undiluted. She confided to one friend that 'the only thing I ever saw my mother do was wash her silk stockings' but when Joy Hester's mother died in 1949, Sunday was distraught.[21] It brought back Ethel's death in 1932, when 'my own gentle little mother died ... crying and I would like to speak of it but it is painful for me'.[22] Sunday's reservations about her mother came from an awareness that Ethel's accomplishments could never be more than the credentials expected from a woman of her class and having no bearing on the wider world. It was 'the grandiose, bourgeois existence' that irked Sunday and the way Ethel 'never worked at anything'.[23]

Sunday's world as a child was pampered and protected. She was born at Bringa, the family home in Broadway, Camberwell. But the family moved up in the world when Sunday was five, when Arthur bought Enmore in Struan St, Toorak, renamed Balholmen. Aside from holidays at Merthon and four overseas trips, Sunday would stay close to Toorak until the move to Heide in 1935. It was the splendid tower from which John, her prince, would finally help her to escape.

Toorak was a village until the 1920s. After the First World War, the new money crowd of tycoons and magnates moved in and either built, or bought, their palaces. It was the first property boom in Toorak since the 1880s, making it Melbourne's most desirable and snobbish suburb. Older Toorak residents were aghast and 'there remained an inner core of the old school who kept aloof, their social boundaries barricaded against the onslaught by refusing to receive the newcomers'.[24]

But around the turn of the century, the Baillieu real estate barons had accurately sniffed out the prime locale for Melbourne's up and coming elite. The crash was but a memory and the Baillieus were positioning themselves as respectable members of the establishment, moving from the margins, where W.L.'s business activities had nudged them, into a central position.

Clive, W.L.'s eldest son, lead the way by settling in St George's Road, and Arthur followed suit. Clive bought two acres of land and commissioned Walter Butler to design Kamillaroi, an opulent thirty-room Federation Arts and Crafts-style mansion where Dame Nellie Melba was a regular visitor. It was an advertisement that the

Baillieus had arrived. Sir John Monash lived nearby as did Theodore Fink, a business partner of W.L.'s. As for W.L., he played it his own way, as usual, by staying in Hawthorn. He wasn't one for chasing convention. Some years later, when W.L. was offered a knighthood, he turned it down.

When Sunday was a child there were only two houses in her street, so numbers were unnecessary. The name of a house and the street was enough for the delivery of goods and mail. This was true for most of Toorak.[25] The family shared Struan Street with the property of solicitor T.C. Alston. Local roads were unsealed and motor cars were a novelty. Streets were gaslit and each night the lamplighter did his rounds, armed with a long pole, and returned in the morning to extinguish them. Though many streets were not tree-lined, the number of trees in private gardens and open spaces gave an impression that was green, lush and semi-rural.

Balholmen no longer exists but the larger Toorak houses usually contained a ballroom, billiard-room and conservatory. They had high ceilings with elaborate plaster mouldings made by master craftsmen and exquisitely carved marble fireplaces. Until the '20s, they were often over-furnished in the high Victorian manner which meant paintings, mirrors and prints were crammed on the papered walls and every other surface was covered with statues, vases, photographs and other bric-a-brac. Tables were festooned with lace or tasselled cloths while plumply upholstered chairs, couches and chaise-longues were draped with shawls or anti-macassars. Thick drapes hung from the windows. Polished wood floors were scattered with rugs or carpets and halls were marble-paved or tiled.

The Victorian upper classes used the *horror vacui* to full advantage to display their wealth, revealing their homes as a cornucopia of possessions. But the interior was not only a blatant show of materialism. It also emphasised elements that were sentimental, sensual and feminine. The Victorian era prized keepsakes, mementos and the very notion of childhood itself. It was a decorative taste that delighted in patterns and fabrics, in the glittering surfaces of glass, china and brass. High and low art, the exotic and the local, the precious and the manufactured were combined in the visual panoply of the domestic interior.

In the late nineteenth century, the domestic interior became what Walter Benjamin described as 'the universe of the private citizen'. It was also a time when interior design became a form of self-expression practised by women and interior design magazines flooded the market. Sunday, strongly sentimental, would furnish Heide with a mix of treasured familiar objects, contemporary art, antique heirlooms and modern furniture.

A bevy of servants was needed to keep such houses pristine and even though girls who came to the colonies preferred working in factories to the drudgery and isolation of domestic service, in Toorak it was always easy to find help. Housework and cooking were unnecessary skills for Sunday to learn. Indeed it would have been frowned upon had she tried. Gardens in the big houses were usually maintained by a head gardener and one or two assistants. As a girl, Sunday liked gardening (though she was not permitted to do the heavy work) and both Merthon and Balholmen had extensive, beautifully kept gardens. In 1920, the Balholmen garden was quite formal. It had wide paths, a large vine-covered trellis at the side of the house and a substantial pergola in the backyard. The back garden also contained a swimming pool.

Sunday was brought up with the finest clothes and toys. It was more than an indulgence: it was to remind her that the home, and everything related to it, was her concern. Though Sunday was physically active, hardy and strong, stamina was not encouraged in girls of her class. Her life was meant to be restricted, constrained, and that applied to her body as well. When English writer Beatrice Webb visited several leading Australian families, she noted the girls were 'nicely mannered but idle and empty-headed young women ... seedy from lack of exercise'.[26]

For the wives of the wealthy, home could be a busy place and Sunday was expected to assist her mother, though not to take responsibility for, the smooth running of the house. She was learning to equip herself with the skills neccesary to manage her own home. The time-consuming etiquette of visits, receptions and dinners was relegated to women as, behind the scenes, they oiled the wheels of high society.

The daily routine was as rigid as the social order. Meals were punctual, formal and large. Breakfast was at 8.15, lunch was at one and dinner was at seven sharp. The gong was rung gently so as not to startle the ladies and it was deemed rude to arrive even a few moments late. Everyone changed into formal attire for dinner though this was relaxed on Sunday evenings when it was correct to remain in casual or sports clothes. Meals were served on white damask tablecloths. Wine was served only with dinner and to get drunk was an appalling infraction of decorum.

Each day there were 'morning calls' which were always made in the afternoon. A dozen or more callers could be expected, though each call was limited to twenty minutes. In that time, tea would be offered, gossip exchanged and further appointments arranged. Etiquette demanded calls must be returned within a few days or at least a visiting card left. There was also an At Home Day, held each month, where newcomers could call on their neighbours. The lady of the house was obliged to return the call but if she decided to 'drop' the new neighbours, a second call could be ignored.

Dinner parties were lavish affairs and a success meant a family edged a little higher up the social scale. The lady of the house planned everything, in consultation with her staff, from the items on the menu to the colour of the flower arrangements. The best silver, china and crystal were polished immaculately. The seating plan was crucial: seating was a display of social hierarchy and a lesser mortal could not be seated next to a grander one. Whom each guest accompanied from the drawing room to the table was decided beforehand and strictly adhered to.

Rather than reject such domestic order, Sunday was impressed by it and remained a stickler for schedules all her life. She transformed and modernised what was pompous, superfluous and overly formal about the etiquette and household rules she had been taught but in principle she obeyed them. Heide ran like clockwork, meals were served promptly and Sunday took pride in keeping her kitchen clean and neat. In that sense, she remained a daughter of her class.

Home was the centre of Sunday's life and, like other Toorak girls, she spent most of her time there. Her brothers boarded at Geelong Grammar, leaving Sunday alone for much of the year. She was tended by a nurse, then tutored by a governess until she was fifteen when she attended St Catherine's School in Williams Road, Windsor. This was not unusual. School meant finishing school for rich young women before they took up their true purpose in life: marriage. School meant the end of Sunday's childhood and her first step into a larger world. It was a place she hated so much that, later in her life, friends believed, 'she didn't go to school' or if she did it was just 'for a short period and she was very unhappy and didn't fit in at all'.[27]

St Catherine's, started in Castlemaine, had just opened in Melbourne with Ruth Langley as principal and Flora Templeton as co-principal.[28] It was a small school with only forty-eight pupils. By 1922, the year Sunday left, it had grown to eighty students and moved to 17 Heyington Place, Toorak, where it is today.

For Sunday, childhood was a precious, magical time of safety, innocence and promise. A key feature in the art she later favoured was a joyful, tender, childlike naïveté found in the works of Nolan, Danila Vassilieff and Charles Blackman. Sunday always responded well to children and never stood on ceremony where they were concerned. She loved games and gifts and special occasions like birthdays and Christmas. She longed to have her own family. She was always attracted to youth in the artists and intellectuals of her circle because youth promised fresh ideas, excitement and change.

Childhood complimented Sunday's 'reverence for equality' and helped to fashion an aesthetic that was opposed to institutional or codified learning. For Sunday, art 'sprang into being', untutored and spontaneous, with a child's freshness and fervour.[29] Her own childhood was fruitful and rewarding, a time that she did not leave behind so much as carry into the future, using it as the base for her sensibility as an arts patron.

For example, Sunday was an omnivorous reader, a habit that began as a child, and one of her favourite childhood books was *The Arabian Nights*. Scheherazade's tales were designed as an entertainment for an emperor. Betrayed by his wife, whom he had beheaded, the emperor swore that at each dawn another woman would die. For one thousand and one nights, the intelligent and educated Scheherazade so beguiled the emperor that he did not fulfil his threat.

Perhaps one reason Sunday was captivated by *The Arabian Nights* was because Scheherazade's storytelling takes place in the exquisite walled garden of a palace, a Middle Eastern paradise garden, where the ponds were surrounded with 'sweet basil, lilies and narcissus in pots of inlaid gold', with 'thickly intertwined branches . . . heavy with ripe fruits' and 'couches of sandalwood covered with silver'. Jane Brown suggests that, due to *The Arabian Nights*, 'such gardens, and their pleasures, hang suspended in our imaginations'.[30] *The Arabian Nights* are tales of enchantment, of flying carpets and genies, of talking animals and treasure-filled caves, generating Sunday's lifelong fascination with Islamic art and architecture which she transferred to artist Peter Hobb and that influenced him in the 1970s.

Sunday told such arresting stories about herself as a child that her friends seemed to find these images in contemporary reality. At Bondi beach in 1948, when Hester and Nolan caught sight of 'a little girl with long hair and brown skin and a white frock and a pink bow', it made them think of Sunday as a child. Hester wondered if it was because the child gazed so intensely at the ocean, making her seem deeply connected to it, with her 'lovely seaweed green hair'.[31] Both Nolan and Hester were moved by the sight.

But this is an image of Sunday on the beach at Sorrento, captivated by the natural world and at peace within it. Sunday needed to be in her own domain to flourish. The larger world was never that and she loathed the experience of school so much that, for a time, she decided to tutor Sweeney, her adopted son, at home. Sunday's preferred method of learning was generated by individual preference and choice.

Intellectual demands were not Sunday's problem at school: she had a swift, original, questioning mind. Ethel had taught her to read and speak French. She enjoyed studying the piano and continued to learn at St Catherine's. She was also strong and athletic, like the men in her family, and excelled at calisthenics and hockey. Her natural grace meant she coped ably with deportment classes and dancing lessons. What she disliked were the rules and regulations. Worse still, she was painfully shy.

The confidence Sunday drew from the safe, private worlds of Balholmen and Merthon evaporated in the playground. At school, she was Sunday Baillieu, heiress, whose family was the envy of Melbourne. Exclusive girls' schools were hotbeds of snobbery as Laura Rambotham discovered, to her pain and humiliation, in *The Getting of Wisdom*. Henry Handel Richardson based Laura's experiences on her own at Presbyterian Ladies' College in the late nineteenth century. Her name – Ethel Florence Lindesay Richardson – was greeted with ridicule, her appearance was mocked and she survived by masking her embarrassment and the rebuffs she suffered with haughtiness. 'About me everything was wrong,' she recalled.[32]

Sunday's unusual name might have also produced sniggers. But it was better than Lelda, her given first name at birth. Sunday insisted on using her second name. She hated Lelda and vigorously scratched it off her girlhood jewel-case, symbolically erasing it from her identity.

Education for girls of Sunday's class was hardly designed as an arena for rigorous intellectual development. Girls were warned to avoid undue displays of emotion or curiosity in public. Probing or 'impertinent' questions in general conversation were similarly prohibited.[33] Conversation was polite and touchy subjects never raised. It was unthinkable for a young woman to disagree with a man, let alone her father. Expressing herself and using her brain were discouraged. Manners were crucial, the mark of a lady, and if a girl wished to successfully graduate into her desired career and marry her socially engineered match, she obeyed the rules. In fact, the rules were taken for granted to such a degree that no-one even considered them.

Melbourne was a solidly conservative town. The old money was in the Western District and, even after the First World War, Western District pastoralist families were still regarded as the social leaders, the pinnacle of Melbourne's establishment elite. Next came the lawyers and doctors, followed by the businessmen. The Baillieus had arrived, they had won their place even though Dame Mabel Brooks, a grande dame of Melbourne society, opined that 'for years the Baillieus were on the outer'.[34] Nor had the business world forgotten how W.L. escaped the crash. Now that his fortunes were on the rise again a joke did the rounds that the motto of Collins House was 'when on thin ice skate fast'.[35] The Baillieus were no longer new money. They were a rich, powerful family among other rich, powerful families. It was a competitive world with bruisingly distinct hierarchies and expectations. Sunday was expected to become a leader in that world, not just a princess but a queen.

The '20s were a great decade for the Baillieus: Collins House became an international player and in 1929 Clive was dispatched to London to manage the family's burgeoning operations. There were philanthropic projects, too. With his brothers, W.L. donated twenty-five thousand pounds – the largest single gift – to the Australian Soldiers' Repatriation Fund as well as buying a Brighton mansion which, as Anzac House, was a hostel for disabled veterans. The brothers also set up the Baillieu Educational Trust to assist the children of dead or wounded soldiers. Such examples of generosity and compassion must have impressed on Sunday the idea that there were better things to do with money than shore up one's social position or throw lavish dinner parties.

Sunday attracted envy all her life and she probably had her first taste of it at school: the effect was abrasive. Sunday could be imperious and distant but she often used hauteur as a shield: she became withdrawn in social situations not of her choosing. With a lithe, elegant frame, fair hair and forget-me-not blue eyes, Sunday had grown into a strikingly attractive young woman but at fifteen she probably felt as tender and self-conscious about her appearance as any adolescent. She spoke softly in a quavering voice, especially when nervous, creating the impression that she was affected and ethereal. Sunday was not a loner. Sharing and companionship were fundamental needs, making her isolation at school even more onerous. 'For Sunday, fun didn't come alone – she needed someone to share it with.'[36]

Sunday had no idea what she wanted to do with her life. It certainly wasn't to study at university. St Catherine's must have convinced her of that. The rules she had learned about running a house had some application but she could see none in the regulations of school. It meant that home, where she had been tutored by her mother and a governess, was a far more productive learning environment. It was a dilemma that took Sunday another decade to resolve: how to find surroundings that were stimulating and expansive, a stage for her abilities, yet sensitive and sympathetic enough to balance her delicate temperament.

Sunday longed for female friendship. She was 'very interested in relationships between females. She was sorry she didn't have a sister'.[37] Her two best friends were both outsiders. Valerie Fairfax attended St Catherine's and was also part of the Sorrento crowd.

She was known as Mud because of her unconventional behaviour. After a social gaffe, Valerie would declare, 'My name's mud in that quarter!'[38]

Sunday's other friend was Clare Pitblado, nicknamed Doodie. She had started work at Balholmen as a housemaid, then became Sunday's companion before marrying John Pitblado, a Toorak plumber. Girls of Sunday's class were required to have chaperones for all occasions. Traditionally, lady's maids were the confidantes of their charges and often ostracised by other household staff as a result. Sunday changed the arrangement into a close friendship that would last the rest of Doodie's life. While it indicates Sunday's ability to transform socially proscribed relations into lasting and mutual friendships, it was a lonely girl whose best friend was her maid.

In 1923, standing on the terrace at Merthon, Sunday may have felt quietly triumphant but it was rivered with unease. She had escaped the hated school-yard and she was preparing to 'come out'. That meant a trip to London where she would be presented at Court. She still wore her hair loose with a ribbon. After her debut, she would wear it up. She could also wear make-up, attend parties and the theatre. Girls were not encouraged to spend time with boys until their debut.

Sunday was on the brink of adult life: attractive, healthy, rich and loved. Her future was mapped out. She would never work or have a career, she would probably never cook a meal. She might raise money for charitable institutions, like a hospital or an orphanage, but she would need to ask her husband's permission first. She would take tea with the other ladies and host formal occasions. Regularly she would appear in the society gossip columns as she attended this ball or that function as an ornament on her husband's arm. She would not argue or raise her voice. One of her chief problems would be to find good staff to mind her children and run her homes.

Sunday was brought up to be, and thoroughly disgraced herself as, a lady. In that sense, Sunday's model was not her kindly father or her 'gentle' mother but the relentless, buccaneering W.L. who paid scant attention to society's niceties and would follow his own star come what may. Much as she may have despised all that W.L. represented, he also provided an enviable image of freedom and originality, a dreamer of big dreams, the successful architect of his own life who inspired and directed others. As far as the Baillieu family went, Sunday became, after W.L., the one who contributed the most to Australian life. Such a notion would probably have her 'cousins and uncles' spinning in their graves.

* 2 *

The Wide World

The Australian girl has no equal in London, Paris or New York.
The golden-skinned, long-haired girl of the surf beaches, strong and vital in her
shapely semi-nudity, exultant and unashamed is, to my thinking, as beautiful
a thing as may be found under the blue arch of the sky.

DULCIE DEAMER[1]

For my part, I was scarcely sane, I think, the year that I found Europe!

NINA MURDOCH[2]

SUNDAY'S FIRST MARRIAGE WAS A TRAGEDY that shaped her life.
It also constituted her first act of rebellion against her family and
her class.

Leonard Quinn was a dashing, handsome, dark-haired Irish-

American born in Boston, Massachusetts, where his father Charles was a businessman. Little has ever been known about him and even some of those facts are contradictory. Sunday's information was so meagre she believed Leonard was related to the actor Anthony Quinn. In 1943, when Sunday was staying with Nolan at Nhill, she saw a newspaper photograph of Anthony and was convinced he was Leonard's brother Paul, using a stage name. Sunday felt 'quite sure . . . I recognised his face' and it gave her 'a funny feeling'.[3] In fact, Anthony Quinn was born in 1915 in the *barrio* of east Los Angeles to an Irish father and a Mexican mother before appearing in movies in 1936. But Sunday continued to entertain the idea, canvassing it with friends over the years, indicating the engima that Leonard presented to her.

Two photographs of Leonard remain. Significantly, both are blurred, so Quinn's features are foggy, unclear. In one he is absorbed in a game of chess. The other shows him stripped down to a singlet that may be part of a swimming costume, holding a cigarette in his right hand. His body is taut and muscular, a man who liked to play sport and who is fit, agile and lean. His hair is slicked back in the '20s style and his face, cast in shadow and sunlight, is pensive, watchful, alert. Perhaps it was his fine, dark features that lead Sunday to speculate Anthony Quinn was his brother. Leonard appeared, brutally altered Sunday's life and then vanished, never to be seen again. But Sunday, who conserved objects that held meaning for her, kept the two photographs of Quinn, fugitive mementos of a terrible first love.

In 1924, Sunday sailed first-class to England with her family for the great colonial ritual of being presented at Court. They stayed at 11 Eaton Square in exclusive Belgravia, not far from Buckingham Palace itself, in a Georgian terrace house with generously proportioned rooms and a balcony that overlooked a private garden. With international markets opening up for the Baillieus, there were plenty of family connections in London. Applications from Australian families to be presented at Court were handled by the Colonial Office in London, which ensured that only suitable people received the sought-after invitations.

Before the event, an expensive flurry of outfitting was necessary. For men, the process was comparatively simple: they hired formal Court dress from Moss Bros., consisting of knee breeches, silk stockings, tunic, lace ruffles, sword and gloves. Women had to undergo endless fittings for their new evening dress, long white gloves and twelve-foot train. A married woman's Court plume consisted of three white feathers and yards of tulle; a single woman's of two feathers and tulle. Wealthy women often wore huge amounts of jewellery, even diamond tiaras. Lavish bouquets of roses were usually carried on one arm.[4]

Sunday looked the part but she adapted the style's more rigid aspects to suit current taste. The white feathers are bunched behind her head and her tulle train is fastened by means of a glittering, fashionable 'headache band' veil. She wears a discreet string of pearls, an exquisitely embroidered, straight '20s shift and probably the most make-up she ever applied in her life. Her expression is still, contained and serious as if she knows her duty and is about to do it but without any great enthusiasm. Perhaps she was simply nervous. She had good reason.

Protocol was strictly observed. Australian traveller Nina Murdoch was in Pall Mall at six o'clock 'to see the debutantes going to their presentation at Court. The ceremony does not commence until 9pm but as the first to arrive are the first presented, the wise ones sit in their carriages for three hours, sooner than in the precincts of the Court where even to powder their noses would be an impertinence.' The hoi-polloi enjoyed the show 'sometimes flattening their very noses on the carriage windows and frequently commenting in cheerfully loud tones on the merits of the dazzling ones within, the debutantes' cheeks getting rosier and noses shinier [as they] await their splendid ordeal'.[5]

Inside the great Throne Room, King George V and Queen Mary sat immobile and received the tense young women in virginal white. Each girl had been instructed beforehand in the difficult art of curtseying while holding a bouquet in one trembling hand and manipulating her train with the other. She was aware that the eyes of the British aristocracy were critically assessing her grooming and self-possession. It was hardly a situation Sunday would have relished and it did nothing to increase her confidence. When the family visited Paris, 'Sunday was so shy none of the boys asked her to dance, she was hiding away so much. When a handsome young man asked her to dance, she was thrilled. She found out later her father had paid him to dance with her.'[6]

Being presented at Court was a ritual that gave colonial, moneyed families the sense they had established an honourable position in society and in the empire. Otherwise the experience of being an Australian in London could be deflating. 'To the English we are little more than a curious antipodean people with nice eyes and appalling voices, and an annoying habit of expecting people to be impressed when we say we are from Australia.'[7]

'Doing the season' involved a schedule of socialising for Sunday, though she was not in the limelight like the aristocratic London debs whose attendance at parties and balls was eagerly tracked by

Fleet Street. The season was purely a hunting exercise transformed by the twentieth-century media into a celebrity event: at its end the prettiest, richest, luckiest girls were expected to announce their engagements.

But 1920s London was a great city to explore and experience. It was the largest and most cultured city Sunday had visited and its sheer size, energy and splendour usually left colonials astonished. There were historic sites to inspect like The Tower, London Bridge and the Houses of Parliament. Then there were the theatres of the West End, the opera at Covent Garden and the seedy glamour of Soho. Despite proverbial English stuffiness, the Jazz Age had arrived and London's nightlife included clubs like The 43 where Bright Young Things gathered and where the Prince of Wales could be seen sipping cocktails.

Though London was Sunday's introduction to Europe, she never felt comfortable there. Paris had a more profound impact on her. She visited several times, lived there briefly with Quinn and underwent one of her life's most distressing events there. In the '20s, Paris was the pre-eminent cultural centre for art, literature, design and fashion. It was the *Ville Lumière*, the City of Lights, the home of modernism, that drew and absorbed every aspect of creativity in one of the most exciting periods of the twentieth century. As modernist writer and art collector, Gertrude Stein, declared, 'Paris was where the twentieth century was.'[8]

The weight of European culture oppressed Sunday. 'I . . . am always in search of the newborn,' she declared to Jean Langley. 'I love history in some kind of context and everything is history in the end but antiquity as such rather frightens me and smells funny. In Florence I used to wander around holding a handkerchief soaked in dettol under my nose. I remember my skin grew quite red and sore and I began to hate the miles of christianity and all the Jesus paintings too and saints and tormentors. In the end I got a dreadful Jesus-tomb-and-old-age complex and standing in the Forum in Rome watching the little brown birds pecking the wild sweet thyme between those monstrous B.C. pillars and stones all falling over and standing up, I would feel great panic and pray to be delivered by some angel – some bright modern angel.'[9]

There were plenty of bright modern angels in Paris, the most cosmopolitan city in Europe. In the interwar years, it welcomed American expatriates who mythologised its charms, a largely literary community that included Scott and Zelda Fitzgerald, Ernest Hemingway, bookseller and publisher Sylvia Beach, and Gertrude Stein who had been living in Paris since 1903. For them Paris provided an escape from a restrictive and puritanical American society. It was Hemingway's 'moveable feast', a site of personal and cultural experimentation, where inhibitions were relaxed and identity reconfigured. The European avant-gardes of Dada and Surrealism were also based there as were Picasso, Braque, Matisse, Chagall and virtually every major School of Paris artist.

In 1926, Australian artists Grace Crowley and Anne Dangar settled in Montparnasse to study at André Lhote's modernist art school. As far as Crowley was concerned they were 'the happiest years of my life. Why? . . . The "woman's role" was reduced to a minimum. I could work every day at my painting and there was the joy of discovering Paris in our own way. From the first we rejected guided tours . . . which was part of the fun . . . Soon we learned more about Paris than the richer people who took guided tours or taxis. The restaurants were a puzzle at first, so we took turns to order something different every day . . . flying blind so to speak.'[10]

Sunday did not share Crowley's sense of adventure. She did not embrace the bohemianism of the left bank nor is there evidence that museums and galleries, let alone modern art, made an impression on her. That would come later, on her own soil. But French culture and French style impressed her and shaped future aesthetic choices. Sunday's interest in modernism began with French fashion design and its insistence on freedom, quality and style. For women, fashion can be a primary mode of self-expression, an exercise in discernment and an education in aesthetic judgement.

Not only was Paris incontestably the centre of fashion in the '20s but it was where artists and designers worked together, blurring the boundaries between high and applied art, between style and stylishness. Gertrude Stein pointed out 'it was important that Paris was where the fashions were made ... and it is always in the great moments when everything changes that fashions are important.'[11] Previously clothing had been an expression of social conformity or a way of advertising financial success. But the best designers like Paul Poiret and Coco Chanel revolutionised the social role of dress and liberated women's bodies.

Chanel was friendly with Picasso and the abstract patterns of cubism decorated the newly fashionable woollen jumpers and separates she designed. Chanel's dictum was a ruthless elimination of inessentials. In 1924 Chanel designed costumes for Les Ballets Russes' production of *Le Train Bleu*, a ballet about the smart set on holidays on the Riviera that showed the influence of sport and the '20s obsession with the tanned, ultra-thin, ultra-fit body. Chanel also designed clothes that, while extremely expensive, deliberately did not advertise wealth. Never mind your diamonds, Chanel said, as long as they look fake.

Poiret designed lavish costumes for the Folies Bergère where *La*

Revue Nègre, starring African-American dancer Josephine Baker, scandalised and entranced Paris and that Sunday could have seen at the Théâtre Champs-Elysée. Further connections between fashion and art were explored by Sonia Delaunay and Jacques Heim when they opened a boutique in 1925. Sonia and her husband Robert had developed an abstract style based on colour and Sonia created jazzy, patchwork, 'simultanist' fabrics based on Robert's paintings which were the hit of the 1925 Arts Décoratifs exhibition.

Fashion had changed dramatically since Ethel's day when the corseted S bend figure of the wealthy woman, decked with jewels, lace and embroidery, made her a monument to conspicuous consumption, in Poiret's words, 'a decorated bundle'.[12] In the '20s fashion, design, art and architecture shared a streamlined aesthetic that echoed the sharp geometry of cubism and abstraction. Line, not decoration, was the emphasis and the new ideal was functionalism.

Sunday had the perfect figure, slender, boyish and athletic, for the style of the day: short, straight tunics with dropped waistlines, cloche hats, neat, short skirts, tight pullovers and low-heeled shoes. Breasts and buttocks were out in the skinny '20s and women bound and flattened their bosoms to achieve the right look.

The subtle, flattering colours of the time – white, cream and pale blue – suited Sunday and were her favourite colours. She chose delicate, natural fabrics like silk and cashmere, together with well-tailored shirts and comfortable, elegant shoes. When trousers became fashionable she adopted them, too, and from then on, rarely wore skirts. Sunday's fastidiousness was matched by French couturiers who delivered impeccable quality combined with deceptive simplicity. All her life Sunday remained faithful to the chic, tailored style and the colours she discovered in Paris. But she incorporated a very feminine note, relating to her childhood. Hair ribbons, usually blue or decorated with red or pink roses, were not only worn and treasured by Sunday but given as gifts to friends. She wore them exactly as she had as a fifteen-year-old, looped beneath her hair and tied in a bow on the crown.

The new fashions registered fresh expectations and obligations for women. The First World War had shifted women's social roles and women entered the workforce in large numbers. After the war, following the deaths or injuries of husbands and fathers, many women had to find jobs to support themselves and their families – though this was less true of Australia than Europe. Suddenly women were out in the world, participating in the daily life of the city and a visible presence on the streets. Few, however, were in the position to pursue highly paid careers and most worked as typists, shop assistants and in factories. The New Woman, also known as 'the flapper', 'the career girl', 'advanced woman' or 'bachelor girl', was popularised by fashion and the media, particularly the new Hollywood 'talkies' and by gamine movie star Clara Bow, known as the 'It' Girl. ('It' was a euphemism for sex appeal.)

The '20s was an optimistic, racy, hedonistic decade, pulsating with dance crazes and the syncopated rhythms of jazz, and its emblem was the thin, youthful female form. Movement and speed were hallmarks of design. Travel conferred modernity and the New Woman was imaged as a sophisticated world traveller. In 1929 Thea Proctor celebrated her on the cover of *The Home*. A young woman perches on her suitcase in front of a map of the South Pacific, knees crossed, cloche hat firmly in place, looking airily confident. Perhaps most importantly, she is alone. No chaperone or husband in sight.

'The flapper ... goes her blithe twentieth century way,' wrote Dulcie Deamer. 'The world is her oyster ... She is sleekly or fluffily shingled, well-groomed, well-fed and fairly complacent unless Reginald phones to say he has the flu and can't take her to that studio party where there will be wine cocktails and a jazz saxophonist.'[13]

By the time Sunday returned to Australia in 1925, she had cropped her hair and raised her hemlines. She started smoking (still considered 'fast' for women) and learned to drive. In short, she was the New Woman incarnate. But there was one thing missing.

If Sunday had wanted to offend and infuriate her family she could not have chosen better than Leonard Quinn. He was an adventurer, a petty criminal and, perhaps worst of all, a Catholic. It would not have taken long for the astute, worldly Baillieu men to estimate Quinn's worth as a man and a marriage prospect. The family was against the match from the start and desperately tried to dissuade Sunday.

The Baillieus had only recently established themselves in Melbourne society after their fall from grace in the 1890s and Sunday's reckless choice might take some of the gloss off their prestige. To make a bad marriage was regarded as the worst thing a girl could do. It reflected not only on her but on her family, a fact of which Sunday would have been all too well aware.

Quinn gave differing accounts of himself. Born on 6 November 1905, he was actually three weeks younger than Sunday but on the marriage certificate declared he was two years older. He listed himself as a business manager. Elsewhere, he said he was involved in journalism. It is likely he had no career, no job at all. He certainly didn't have any money but 'behaved like a rich young man'.[14] *Herald* art critic Basil Burdett knew an unsavoury story about Quinn passing bad cheques in Barcelona. Maybe Australia offered greener pastures because by the mid-1920s, Quinn had settled in Greycliffe Avenue, Vaucluse, a well-heeled suburb in eastern Sydney. It is unknown where Quinn and Sunday met.

Leonard was American and, in the '20s, that symbolised modernity, glamour and otherness. Perhaps it was his glamorous aura that made Sunday associate him with Hollywood. The talkies, ushered in by Al Jolson's *The Jazz Singer* in 1927, generated a wider audience for American film accompanied by stars who popularised the new fashions and an enviable lifestyle. In Australia, Leonard would have seemed positively exotic. His background also meant that his past could have remained shadowy. Sunday visited Leonard in Sydney and together they enjoyed browsing through stylish shops such as Lyster Ormsby's in Hunter Street for antiques or Costa's, the Italian shop, or Hunt's for the best men's wear.

Leonard's hometown of Boston was a prosperous, cultured harbourside city.[15] It was also a bastion of Catholicism after it became a recipient of the Irish diaspora after the Great Famine of the 1840s.

Henry James spent his youth in mid-nineteenth century Boston and set his novel *The Bostonians* there. It is the tale of a seduction by Basil Ransom of the beautiful, talented Verena Tarrant. James had no illusions about what the contract of marriage could mean to members of his class: love is constructed as a quest for power. Ransom believes that 'the essential was to show [Verena] how much he loved her, and then to press, to press, always to press'.[16] When Ransom finally achieves his goal, Verena bursts into tears. James observes 'it is to be feared that with the union so far from brilliant, into which she was about to enter, these were not the last [tears] she was destined to shed'.[17]

Sunday was smitten and defied her family. There was more to it than passion. 'She said she ran away with him just to get away from her family. Her family was very oppressive. She just found them terribly oppressive . . . She was a bit infatuated. She said she was quite excited by him. But mainly she just wanted to get away from her family.'[18] It was the classic case of rebellion: the more the family tried to talk Sunday out of it, the more she clung to Leonard, heightening the romance with its illicit pleasures and sense of desperation and persecution. Leonard was going to help her escape from her gilded cage and make good all that Europe had offered.

As the arguments went on during 1926, something so dreadful happened that the whole family was left stunned and bereft. On 21 April, King, Sunday's beloved older brother, died from typhus. He had been ill for only four days, before dying at his home in Grange Road, Toorak. At twenty-five, King had joined his father's firm as an accountant. Two years earlier he had married Grace Lavers. There were no children. The following day he was buried at Brighton Cemetery.

Sunday was devastated by the loss of the one man in her family, aside from her father, whom she admired and with whom she had some degree of intimacy. Jean Langley recalled 'the only brother she really, really loved died. She stuck by that story always, that he was the one . . . She repeatedly told me how much she had loved him and how sad it had been.'[19]

It is not difficult to see, given these circumstances, how attractive a proposition Leonard appeared to Sunday as he supported her during her sadness and shock. If Leonard was chasing Sunday's fortune, it certainly made her an easy target as the grief-stricken heiress turned to him for solace.

Sunday was an extremely emotional woman and her nervous sensitivity brought her close to collapse. She never witheld emotion and if she was sad, or angry, or happy, then those close to her knew it. Indeed the closer they were, the more likely they were to bear the brunt of her feelings. When Sunday was upset, she became ill and literally took to her bed. Nurturing and healing were two of her strongest drives but when she was sick or miserable, she expected others to tend her.

Her behaviour is perhaps not as self-indulgent as it first appears. In the upper-class Edwardian home, a young, unmarried woman was powerless to control her own space: the domestic environment was dominated first by her father and then her mother. Rules, routines and manners were meant to prevent, or quash, outbursts. A girl could not leave the house without permission or unchaperoned. Retreating to her room, 'taking to her bed', in order to inhabit her own space was one of the few recourses a woman could legitimately employ to gain privacy, or 'breathing space', if she felt distressed or simply desired solitude. It was a pattern Sunday followed all her life.

Leonard was handsome and charming, two things to which Sunday was particularly susceptible. She liked romance, flattery and the games of love, a man who could flirt with her, be witty, clever, seductive, tell tall tales, amuse and provoke her. Sunday had a taste for irrepressible rogues, the kind of man who represented a light, breezy playfulness, a capriciousness that promised infinite possibilities, a type of masculinity that subverted the stolid, materialistic conservatism of the Baillieu men. Leonard was not an artist but he defined a type to whom Sunday would be attracted in her artist lovers, Sam Atyeo and Sidney Nolan.

For Sunday, love – and love affairs – provided the fire of creative activity, engendering passion as well as pain. Until the late 1940s, sexual intimacy instigated new cycles of energy and productivity no matter what the personal cost. It gave another dimension to her need to share fully with those close to her. By giving deeply of herself, Sunday gained enormously – though often it would be at the expense of both her own, and her lover's, equilibrium.

As a high society adventurer, Leonard may have been skilled in the arts of seduction. Sunday was a sensual woman: to her love meant sexual pleasure as well as emotional commitment. When Sunday lost her virginity to Leonard, she came alive. The difference between the dressed-up doll at her Court debut and the sexy, commanding young woman photographed at Sorrento in 1926, confident in her body and her beauty, is startling.

Another reason the Baillieu men were against the marriage was because Quinn was a Catholic and they were staunch Masons. Many businessmen joined the Masonic brotherhood: it was simply a wise career move. Albert Tucker's grandfather, the canny, enterprising Albert Lee, was a landbooming property developer, a mayor of Fitzroy and a government minister. He was also a Mason and it helped his career. But for the Baillieu men, Freemasonry was not just another business opportunity. It defined both spiritual and civic identities. The Masonic antipathy towards Catholicism was profound and centuries old.

Freemasonry is a secret society, probably formed in late sixteenth-century Scotland, whose membership was initially the craft guilds of masons – the men responsible for building all the great public monuments – but it soon broadened to include local gentry and middle-class businessmen.[20] They developed formal and elaborate initiation ceremonies, meeting places known as Lodges and a particular handshake. Gradually the Masons became a very special kind of men's club: it was clannish and secretive, upheld a code of good citizenship and civic duty, was a superb networking opportunity for the captains of industry and it was a brotherhood – all of which suited the Baillieu men.

But the Masons' intense privacy lead to fear and speculation. Catholics were anxious that the Masons were running Australian business and politics and they were being systematically excluded. Discrimination in the workforce was rife and in the 1920s Catholic secret societies were formed to combat the Masons.[21] Most of Australia's politically conservative prime ministers up to the early 1970s were members of the Masonic Lodge, including Stanley Bruce, prime minister from 1922–29.[22] Bruce was a silver-tail, born into Melbourne's mercantile elite and connected by marriage to a Western District pastoral dynasty. Even today, Masonic rituals and membership are cloaked in secrecy. For the Baillieus, Leonard's religion (and his Irishness) would have confirmed his disreputable, outsider status.

Religion demarcated Australian society in the '20s and the mistrust and dislike between Catholics and Protestants was tribal and fierce. 'Foreign-Irish-Catholics' were viewed as a threat to the empire. 'This is a Protestant country,' declared E.K. Bowden, the minister for defence, in 1922.[23] Organised religion meant nothing to Sunday and, though she believed in God, her faith was a private and deeply felt pantheism. Arthur, as a Mason, would have attended a church of Protestant denomination while Ethel was a Christian Scientist.

Founded in Boston in 1879 by Mary Baker Eddy, Christian Science was based on Baker Eddy's 'discovery' of a mystical science of healing underlying Biblical texts. She espoused that prayer could cure any illness, no matter how grave. By definition, Ethel's faith had to be extremely strong to embrace such a creed. Perhaps it was the eccentric spiritual atmosphere created by Arthur's secret male bonding and Ethel's zealous faith healing that made Sunday wary of organised religion but she remained a believer all her life.

The Baillieu family's reservations about Leonard would have come as no surprise to him. Perhaps it was one of the reasons he positioned himself in Sydney, away from from their scrutiny. Protestant Boston had resisted the Irish-Catholic influx and discrimination against the newcomers had been more virulent than in Melbourne. Boston, too, had rigid society codes. Part of Sunday's attraction to Leonard was that he subverted those rules and helped her to do the same.

It was not the first scandalous marriage in the family. In 1920 Merlyn Baillieu, Sunday's young cousin, married Sidney Myer, founder of the Myer department store and twenty-two years her senior. Not only was Myer estranged from his first wife, worse still he was Jewish. The couple wed in Nevada to escape opprobrium and Myer converted to Christianity to please his new in-laws. After several years, the couple returned to Melbourne and Myer's immense wealth, power and charm managed to soothe the dismay the union had caused. Perhaps Merlyn's example encouraged Sunday to defy her family, too.

Once Sunday turned twenty-one, she was her own woman and, two weeks before her twenty-first birthday in October, the engagement was announced. She knew Arthur, no matter how disapproving, would not cut her off without a penny and even if Leonard was without funds, Sunday had enough money for them both. In 1926, that was probably around five hundred pounds a year, a very comfortable income. In the same year, John Reed was earning three hundred and fifty pounds a year as an articled clerk.

The situation was highly irregular. The suitors of Toorak girls had to be well-established financially and good prospects were essential before a young man dared propose marriage. A man was expected to maintain his bride 'in the style of living to which she had been accustomed' by his own efforts, even if she possessed independent means.[24] Sunday's wedding would not be held in Toorak (St John's was the preferred choice of the well-to-do) or feature in the pages of *Table Talk* or *The Home*. It would be a quiet affair at St Mary's Star of the Sea, the little Catholic church in Sorrento.

Sunday had two choices. She could convert to Catholicism, an arduous process that meant taking instruction from the local priest, learning her catechism, being baptised and receiving her first communion. Then she could be married in full splendour before the altar and her family and friends. If she chose not to convert, her marriage would take place in the sacristy, a small room at the side of the church where the priest prepared himself for mass, and where sacred vessels and vestments were kept. The marriage would still be performed according to the rites of the Roman Catholic Church and Sunday would also be expected to undergo some form of instruction. It was the quicker, more low key alternative and most likely Sunday's choice.

But being married in the sacristy was a slight, designed to remind non-Catholics of their lesser status. 'Mixed marriages' were frowned on by the Church. It was seen as moving outside the caste and polluting the faith. 'Mixed marriages are spreading wider and wider amongst us,' lamented Sydney's Archbishop Kelly in 1923. 'The dark shadow of culpability falls on a large and growing number of our rising generation.'[25]

On New Year's Eve, 1926, Sunday got her wish and married her beau. Mary Quinn, Leonard's mother, arrived for the wedding and Sunday was nervous about meeting her. Charles, almost as elusive as his son, did not attend. The reception was held at nearby Merthon, the place Sunday felt most content. But if Sunday had hoped for a night of romantic bliss, she was disappointed. Leonard got completely drunk and fell asleep.[26] Perhaps the strain of dealing with the assembled Baillieus was too much for him.

In November 1927, Sunday and Leonard set sail for Europe. Over the next two years, they lived the life of the peripatetic rich in Paris, Provence, London, Cambridge and the Cotswolds. Arthur hoped Sunday would soon find some work 'after your own heart'. Perhaps his sporty daughter would become a champion golfer or tennis player. Life, he advised her, would be more compelling if Sunday committed herself to a profession rather than just 'chasing butterflies'.[27] But for the moment, chasing butterflies — perhaps a snide reference to Leonard's casual attitude towards earning a living — was exactly what she did. Tellingly, in the many letters and telegrams Arthur and Ethel sent to Sunday as she travelled, Leonard is mentioned once or twice in passing. Arthur encourages Sunday to put on weight and to drink plenty of milk while Ethel fusses over her daughter, telling her how much she misses her and sends her money to buy the best clothes. Both Arthur and Ethel seemed to be trying to erase their son-in-law from their minds.

Travelling through Europe, searching for a new sense of home and identity, Sunday and Leonard symbolised 'a lost generation', Gertrude Stein's famous epigram to Hemingway's *The Sun Also Rises*. The young were heading 'to the sidewalk cafés of Paris, escaping . . . provincialism, searching for a degree of sophistication' unavailable in their own countries, registering 'the disequilibrium of life [that] gave rise to a romantic sensibility'.[28] Scott and Zelda Fitzgerald were also following the same path from Paris to Provence, renting houses on the Riviera and 'vaguely floating about on the surface of fancy French apartments' with Zelda speculating 'it looks as if we will never stay anywhere long enough to see how we like it'.[29]

Sunday glimpsed Hemingway 'misbehaving publicly' in Paris and did not care for *The Sun Also Rises*.[30] Published in 1926, the novel made Hemingway an overnight success and became a bible for the young and the restless. But its plangent mood of dislocation and alienation and its spare, muscular prose did not appeal to Sunday's poetic and lyrical sensibility. Her pantheon included Rimbaud, Jules Supervielle and American expatriate Julien Green, whose writings she may have discovered while living in Paris. Sunday's response to Rimbaud would prove influential to Nolan while Supervielle and Green would be inspirational to Hester.

If you were young and rich, there was plenty to do in Paris in the late '20s. Sunday, eager for experience, no doubt took her fill. In 1929, Diaghilev's Ballets Russes were performing at the Théâtre Sarah-Bernhardt with music composed by Stravinsky and Prokofiev. Jean Cocteau's *Les Enfants Terribles* had recently been published to acclaim, while Radclyffe Hall's lesbian novel *The Well of Loneliness*, though banned in New York and England, was printed by a local press. There were the great cafés to visit like Aux Deux Magots and Café Flore on Boulevard St Germain and Le Dôme and La Coupole in Montparnasse. Sunday's fluency in French gave Paris a depth for her that tourists did not often enjoy.

Paris offered more than entertainment. Even if Sunday did not penetrate to the city's salons and studios she was impressed by French cultural traditions which served to stimulate her intellect. In France, artists and writers were respected and admired, their achievements lauded and, even if new art or literature garnered criticism, nonetheless it was assessed as a contribution to vital and ongoing cultural debates. Art mattered.

When the Quinns moved to the south of France, with its blistering summers, hard, bright light, eucalypts, scrubby soil and brilliant seascapes, Sunday revelled in an environment similar to Australia's. The Riviera was arguably the most fashionable and beautiful watering-hole on earth, the playground of western Europe. Originally Cannes and Nice were invalid resorts but 'the world, the flesh and the devil . . . have come into the province where ministering angels once held sway'.[31] It was where Scott Fitzgerald finished *The Great Gatsby* and set his last great novel, the tragic *Tender is the Night*. It was also the summer retreat of many artists, not only Paris-based artists such as Picasso and Matisse, but English modernists like Vanessa Bell and Duncan Grant.

Zelda recalled passing through 'the white romance of Avignon into the scent of lemon, the rustle of black foliage, clouds of moths whipping the heliotrope dusk – into Provence, where people don't need to see unless they are looking for the nightingale'.[32] The Riviera was 'a seductive place' with 'the blare of the beaten blue and those white palaces shimmering under the heat' where 'a small horde of people wasted their time being happy'.[33]

Though similar to Australia in climate, Provence was a far more dramatic setting than Sorrento. Sunday 'liked winter well enough for its firesides and warm beds and how it gave you energy, but what she liked best was summer and sun'.[34] In Provence Sunday could indulge one of her chief pleasures, beach life, and spend days swimming, suntanning and boating, wearing the local brightly coloured cotton swimsuits and espadrilles.

Suntans became fashionable in the '20s and Sunday was a true sunworshipper, who always tried to keep up a tan. Seen as a sign of health and vigour, before anything was known about its harmful effects, tanning was also associated with leisure, pleasurable pursuits and the ability to afford summer holidays. In earlier decades, upper-class women prided themselves on their

pallor and wore elaborate hats and veils to protect themselves
from the sun. Tanned skin was synonymous with the working
classes and manual labour. The democratic '20s changed that.
Pale skin that once epitomised a woman who did not have to
sully herself in the rude, everyday world was rejected by a generation of young women who valued their physicality, sex appeal
and energy. Tanning was part of a cult of the body that swept
Europe in the '20s. In northern Europe and Scandinavia, it was
also expressed through 'healthy' nudism, naturism and a frank,
non-sexual appreciation of the body. Sunday's preoccupation with
health, diet and devotion to nature meant that she, too,
responded to these influences.

Aside from the beaches, there was plenty of entertainment on
the Riviera. In the larger towns like Nice and Cannes, clubs and
restaurants competed for nightly custom with the big hotels that
had their own orchestras. Further along the coast were the gambling
dens of Monte Carlo which Somerset Maugham famously described
as 'a sunny place for shady people'. In picturesque villages like St
Raphaël, Antibes and Juan les Pins, villas could be rented cheaply.
Near St Tropez was Hyères and the island of Porquerolles, which
Sunday revisited with John in 1949. She wrote, 'here in this azure
Méditerranée where there are no sharks and no tides you cannot
imagine such bliss and we have never loved the water more – one
floats infinitely in pale crystal'.[35]

Provence was a gardener's delight, sensual and sweet-smelling.
Aside from lavender, nasturtiums and iris, there were 'kaleidoscopic
peonies massed in pink clouds, black and brown tulips and fragile
mauve-stemmed roses, transparent like sugar flowers in a con-
fectioners' window'.[36] The landscape was dotted with vineyards,
eucalypts, pencil pines and groves of olive, fig, lemon and peach

trees. Local food was fresh and delicious. In Marseille, Sunday learned to cook bouillabaise.

Perhaps a fondness for Provence was a reason Sunday later considered buying a Van Gogh though she was unable to raise sufficient funds.[37] Van Gogh lived the last two years of his life at Arles and St Rémy, the core of Provence, producing his greatest works. Interestingly, he went there to found an artists' commune, which he described to his brother Theo as 'the studio of the future'. Van Gogh wanted to make 'an artist's house – not precious, on the contrary nothing precious but everything from the chairs to the pictures having character'.[38] *Provençale* style also inspired Sunday's choices about Heide's interior: rush-bottomed chairs, pale colours (especially white and blue) and a feeling for earthy simplicity were incorporated into her design schemes. Heide 'looked like a French farmhouse'.[39] Lavender and roses, features of Provence gardens, were also favourites of Sunday's.

In Sunday's embrace of French life it is possible to discern a pattern of dissatisfactions: the restrictions of her adolescence and the constraints of her Australian upbringing that insisted on social success and decried intellectual pursuits. In the '20s, Australia was a country steeped in secondhand and second-rate British traditions, struggling to define its identity. France, supremely confident in its own traditions, offered a rich, sophisticated alternative to immaturity and dependence on a dominant 'mother country'.

Nor could have Sunday ignored French attitudes towards marriage. Edith Wharton, a product of aristocratic Old New York, ended up in Boston courtesy of her banker husband. She dispensed with her husband and fled to Paris in 1906, where she wrote novels criticising the false values of American parlour society. In Wharton's opinion the Anglo-Saxon heritage kept women childlike, irresponsible and socially segregated. The root of the problem was the link between 'fidelity' and 'family responsibility' and Wharton praised the French for separating these components: 'the French marriage is built on parenthood not passion'.[40]

It meant that husbands and wives could pursue sexual freedom without jeopardising marital unity. It was the norm for a married Frenchman to keep a mistress and it was expected that he would behave discreetly in the circumstances. Such unconventional yet stable arrangements gave French society its peculiar character. Despite the surface glitter of Parisian life, it was utterly bourgeois and solidly Catholic yet, at the same time, frankly and flamboyantly sexual. What seemed shocking and licentious had socially observed and widely accepted rules. It was a combination of order and personal freedom that proved attractive to Sunday. The *ménage-à-trois* would become a feature of her second marriage and of her life between 1933 and 1947.

In 1928–29, the Quinns also stayed in London, Cambridge, and the village of Broadway in the Cotswolds.[41] The latter was a sentimental journey. Sunday had first visited Broadway with her parents years before and this time she stayed at the Lygon Arms, the same hotel, much to Ethel's delight.

Situated in central England, the Cotswolds are characterised by green, rolling uplands interspersed with shallow meandering valleys where modest streams wind in a leisurely fashion. Broadway is recognised as the Cotswold village par excellence with its immaculately maintained buildings, many dating back to the sixteenth century, made of mellow Cotswold limestone with steeply pitched rooves and bow windows. Not only was it similar to Merthon's limestone but the name Broadway was also the name of Sunday's first home in Camberwell.

It was the wealth of exquisite, untouched early architecture that attracted William Morris to the area in 1871. Morris, an internationally influential designer, initiated the Arts and Crafts movement as a reaction to the ornate, mass-produced goods of the Victorian era. The movement emphasised craftsmanship and quality of materials, producing goods that were simple, subtle and superbly executed. Morris persuaded other Arts and Crafts designers like C.R. Ashbee to move to the Cotswolds and it was impossible to see much of the area without coming across examples of their work and influence.

Landscape design was an important part of the Arts and Crafts movement where house and garden, created from local materials, blend with their surroundings. In the Cotswolds, Morris had the chance to develop these ideas for the first time. 'The flat, reedy river landscape was ideal for a dreamer . . . [Morris] loved the landscape not just for its quiet beauty, but for the materials that could be brought back into the house . . . he collected reeds, grasses, roots, flowers and willow twigs for making dyes and studied the plants and birds which were favourite designs for his textiles.'[42]

Sunday chose a similar gentle, river landscape for her home at Heide and shaped a garden from it. The Cotswolds' natural beauty suggested an ideal environment in which to live, it was a place of inspiration for artists and it had a wealth of fine gardens. Further, finely crafted handmade objects available in local shops offered stimulating possibilities for interior design. No doubt Sunday wanted to establish her own home and start a family, though with all the travelling she would have agreed with Zelda Fitzgerald that she and Leonard seemed to 'never stay anywhere long'.

There was only one exhibition from Sunday's travels that left an impression. In June 1929, she saw D.H. Lawrence's erotic paintings at the Dorothy Warren Gallery in London's Mayfair.

The show was a scandal. Lawrence, dying from his long battle with tuberculosis, stayed in Italy while Frieda Lawrence attended the exhibition's opening and the furore that followed. While Gwen John praised the paintings' 'stupendous gift of self-expression', critics condemned their bold sensuality. Around 13,000 people visited the gallery, mainly to gawp. The *Daily Express* thundered, '*Spring,* a study of six naked boys is revolting. *Fight with an Amazon,* [which] represents a hideous, bearded man holding a fair-haired woman in his lascivious grip while wolves with dripping jaws look on expectantly, is frankly indecent. *Boccaccio Story,* another of these works of art, is better not described.'[43]

A lacklustre draughtsman and mediocre colourist, Lawrence was certainly a better writer than artist. The males in his paintings are egocentric self-portraits, even including a dead Christ. Herbert Read described it best. 'When in the autumn of 1926, [Lawrence] found he was confident enough to embark on his own compositions he became a typical expressionist, like Nolde or Soutine. But without the sensuous harmony of the one or the pulsating rhythm of the other. But Lawrence did achieve the quality that he himself most desired, vitality, despite his literary approach and technical inadequacy.'[44]

There were complaints to the Home Secretary, then police raided the gallery and removed thirteen of the twenty-five works – anything with a penis or pubic hair. Though Sunday later dismissed the merit of these paintings, Lawrence's situation provided her with an example with which she would become familiar in the 1930s and '40s: the embattled modernist fighting a hostile and philistine public.[45] The promotion and protection of the artist would soon become Sunday's role and the unfair criticism and treatment of Lawrence must have registered with her. She became a keen admirer not only of Lawrence's novels but his philosophy that prized spontaneity and the intuitive nature of creativity.

Art, however, was far from Sunday's mind during late 1929. The Quinns were living in Paris and strains in the marriage were starting to show. A woodpecker used to peck at the pine tree outside their bedroom window and Sunday 'became friends' with it. Quinn said he wished he could become the woodpecker and peck Sunday to her marrow.[46] Leonard was often out. In London that July, which Sunday recalled as 'the hottest month', she used to sit 'in the twilight . . . waiting for Leonard to come home and he never did'.[47]

Sunday was growing increasingly ill. At first her symptoms were slight: pain and burning on urinating, an increase in vaginal discharge. Gradually, it became worse until her lower abdomen was wracked by pain. Her periods became irregular, she had fevers, chills and attacks of vomiting.

Finally Sunday went to a Catholic hospital where, after an examination, the doctor told her the diagnosis. She had contracted gonorrhea. Because it had gone untreated for so long, it was extremely serious: the disease had spread from her cervix to her fallopian tubes which were infected. She needed to have a hysterectomy immediately, otherwise the disease could prove fatal.

Sunday 'felt . . . very devastated and almost as if her life was ending'.[48] 'It was a terrible shock. She said it was the first time in her life she was blushing so much. She felt she would never stop blushing when the doctor came along and said, "I'm sorry but I'm afraid you won't be able to have children after this operation." She just lay there and blushed and was quite overcome.'[49]

Leonard 'just pissed off. He wasn't going to stay and help her through that.'[50] After the operation and Leonard's hasty departure, Sunday moved to London. Langley recalled that Sunday 'went and lived in a bedsitter all by herself and just locked herself in and cried and I don't know how long [for] but she made it sound like an enormous amount of time because she told it in that way.'[51]

Sunday's marriage had ended in the worst possible circumstances. She had been abandoned by Leonard who had given her a venereal disease, which meant he had been unfaithful to her during their marriage. Not only did she have the shock of undergoing the hysterectomy but, after the loss of her womb, she would have experienced the turmoil of premature menopause. Symptoms could include hot flushes, insomnia, anxiety and depression. Further, she lost most of the hearing in her right ear. The gonococci circulating in the blood can attack any organ in the body. Ethel had bad hearing, Sunday had inherited it and now the disease made it worse.

When the family discovered what had happened, Arthur and Everard set off for London to bring Sunday home. She was a physical and emotional wreck. Arthur, horrified at Leonard's behaviour and Sunday's condition, took care of everything: he simply wanted to erase the whole ghastly business. 'Sunday dearest,' he later wrote, 'to recall anything . . . would revive pain in all our hearts' and Arthur abjured her to 'abstain from reflections'. Despite the rupture, family unity had not been damaged and 'the great love between us all still binds us as strongly as ever . . . Providence has been with us and brought you safely from the very edge of the rocks of disaster.'

But Arthur's warmth and kindness could not absolve all wounds. For Sunday there was the humiliation of having defied her family to marry Leonard only to be forced to admit that their assessment of him was correct, especially demeaning for a woman as proud and strong-willed as she. Nor did Arthur refrain from gently chiding her. 'However the lesson (which I could never go through again) subscribes I think to the old saying, "Once bitten twice shy."' Arthur urged Sunday to 'accept that' and then 'caution and sound judgement' would 'prevail' for the future.[52]

Sunday returned to recuperate at Balholmen and Merthon, to be cared for by Doodie and the family. Inevitably, the gossip went around Toorak about the awful thing that had happened to Sunday Baillieu Quinn.

In June 1930, when Sunday had recovered, she left once more for Paris. Perhaps the sadness and embarrassment at home was too much to bear. But it indicates that Sunday had enough pluck to try her fortune in the wide world again. If the family thought she was cowed by the experience and that she would now dutifully fulfil her designated role, they were mistaken. She might have been wrong about Leonard but she was not wrong to choose a larger life than her birth predicted.

Sunday was a different woman. She had lost her innocence, her husband and her fertility. She longed for children and that desire did not cease, merely created an ache within her. The intimacy of lovemaking had been turned into a public disgrace and Sunday's sense of her own sexuality, just awakened, was stained by a disgusting and shameful disease. In fact, sex had nearly proved fatal.

The 1929 Wall Street crash had signalled a worldwide depression that had brought massive business failure, unemployment and social and political tensions. Though Sunday's wealth inured her to its effects, she would have seen a tougher, grimmer, more unequal society than the one she had left a few months earlier. Paris itself no longer offered the promise of pleasure: it harboured memories of distressing events. Whatever she had prized as alluring about an expatriate life had also ended and she never again wished to live overseas. In fact, she became a bad traveller, longing for home and grumbling about small discomforts.

While in Paris, Sunday sat for her portrait at the studio of Australian expatriate painter Agnes Goodsir. In 1930, Goodsir was sixty and lived at 18 Rue de l'Odeon in the Latin Quarter with her American lover Rachel Dunn, known as Cherry. It was the same apartment building where Sylvia Beach lived. The intrepid publisher of James Joyce's *Ulysses*, Beach also ran Shakespeare and Company, a bookshop that was a hub of expatriate intellectual life. Goodsir and Beach were part of a network of lesbian intellectuals who had fled America, Australia and England and made their home in Paris.

Aside from her portrait commissions (Goodsir also completed a portrait of society matron Ruth White, Patrick White's mother) and sensuous studies of Cherry, Goodsir painted women dressed as men, the cool, cross-dressing look favoured by the Paris gay crowd whom she could have observed at Le Monocle, the lesbian bar, where Brassai photographed women in tuxedos dancing with girls in frocks.

Goodsir had left Australia to study in Paris but modernism did not shape her art as the portrait of Sunday shows. Goodsir handles colour and pattern with an expert touch but without the bold formal disjunctions that signified modernism. Goodsir's is a 'feminine' art celebrating fabrics, surfaces, interiors and the quiet, reflective moments of women.

Sunday is imaged as immaculate, beautiful and frozen. A photograph shows Goodsir putting the finishing touches to the painting, observed by Sunday and the elegantly attired Tom Cochrane, London correspondent for *The Home*. Goodsir did not like the photograph, complaining that 'in a frightful light' the painting 'looks all wrong'.[53] In the portrait Sunday's still and lifeless face is bleached by the 'frightful' light, making her look ghostly, ethereal. She wears the same fashionable striped jumper in both photograph and painting, the kind created by Chanel. As Sunday rests her elbow on the easel, her eyes are downcast, her expression remote, unfathomable. She hardly looks the picture of happiness.

Goodsir emphasises Sunday's best features – her large eyes and the clean, strong lines of her face. *Portrait of Mrs Leonard Quinn* (c.1930, now lost) was regarded highly enough to be selected for the July 1930 Salon, together with four other works by Goodsir who was described as 'perhaps the best known Australian artist in Paris'.[54]

Sunday probably enjoyed her sittings in Goodsir's studio-apartment, nestled in the heart of the Latin Quarter. Agnes was a spirited and modest woman, cheerfully settled in Paris where her career may not have been illustrious but was successful enough, together with a private income, to guarantee a comfortable life with Cherry.

Sunday was not brave enough to carve out her destiny in Paris. Her great need was to secure male protection through love and intimacy. Sunday's life had to be shared. She could not cope with the solitude that Goodsir had endured during her apprenticeship. But in Goodsir's studio, chatting with her during the sittings for the portrait, Sunday may have felt the longing for such a studio-home of her own, one that was shared with a sympathetic companion where artistic activity, lively conversation, books, paintings and modern decor, all contributed to a stimulating ambience, redolent with French style. In that house, she would hang her portrait: an image of Sunday the wanderer facing the living image of Sunday, settled and content.

* 3 *

John

Perhaps because I am not an 'ideas' man myself I am always drawn
to those to whom ideas come quickly.

JOHN REED, 'AUTOBIOGRAPHY'[1]

JOHN WAS AN UNAWAKENED MAN when he met Sunday in 1930. On the edges of an artistic circle, to whom he was introduced by a sophisticated older woman friend, John worked steadily and quietly at one of Melbourne's most conservative law firms. He lived in a series of boarding houses and apartments around Toorak and South Yarra, his only companion Karel, his German shepherd. John seemed, and admitted he was, 'hopelessly immature', a case of delayed development.[2]

John's background and upbringing were even more patrician and, in some respects, even worse than Sunday's. Unlike Sunday, whose passionate sense of home was shaped by her attachment to Merthon, John did not have a stable home-life from the time he was ten until 1935 when he and Sunday moved into Heide. But, also unlike Sunday, John was not at war with his family. His personality was impressively controlled, tranquil and strong. Tradition did not temperamentally offend John, as it did Sunday, and, as a young man, he did not feel oppressed or alienated by the privileges of his class. John sought for solutions, not rebellion, balance not strife. Until his marriage to Sunday, he was respectful of authority and both unambitious and unclear in regard to his life's vocation.

While John was growing up, he was constantly on the move, an occasional visitor to Tasmania, a boarder at ghastly English public schools, a university student at Cambridge and, finally, a young man kicking around town in Melbourne. It was with Sunday that John first encountered both the concept and the reality of a stable and happy home.

John grew up at Mt Pleasant, near Launceston, one of the grandest houses in northern Tasmania. It was dubbed Mt Unpleasant by younger sister Cynthia's malicious wit. He had moved there in 1909, when he was eight years old, from his birthplace at Logan, a Reed family property near Evandale. The family dynasty had been founded by John's grandfather Henry Reed who landed in Hobart Town in 1827 before tramping to Launceston on foot.

Rather like W.L. Baillieu, Henry Reed was a driven and imaginative businessman, a combination of rapacious mercantile industry, tub-thumping evangelism and unstinting philanthropy. Henry's was a big life, encompassing two marriages and sixteen children, together with hugely successful shipping, whaling, grazing and banking interests, as well as a sincere commitment to the Wesleyan Church. In 1847, he took the family home to England where he preached the length and breadth of the country for the next twenty-five years.

Returning to Tasmania, Henry bought Mt Pleasant in 1874 and renovated it to accommodate his vast entourage. A commanding, gracious Georgian-style mansion reached by a long, winding drive, Mt Pleasant sits atop a hill just outside Launceston where Reed property once stretched as far as the eye could see. Henry Reed was conscious of founding a dynasty. By planning and building for posterity, he was creating a home fit for aristocracy.

Cynthia, in her autobiographical novel *Daddy Sowed a Wind!*, titled the house Worthness and recalled

> the big house in its surrounding gardens, with its lake on which floated white swans, with its orchards, its stables and farmhouses and cottages, its bloodmares somnolent in the little sheltered paddocks, its coachmen and stable boys, grooms and gardeners and croquet lawns; the big house so English, so utterly un-Australian, so foreign in the midst of the eucalypt-covered, wild mountain land, where chained convicts toiled upon the dusty roads . . . At Worthness all was cultivated, schooled, watered, green and flowery.[3]

Henry also had a beautiful, classically inspired chapel constructed at the rear of the house, reached by passing an enormous oak and a small, romantic arbour. Henry preached there on Sundays. On either side of the front door were glass panels, decorated with the family crest – a sheaf of wheat over the stern admonition, 'Nothing without the cross'.

Henry junior, John's father, inherited Mt Pleasant but not his father's vision, only his religious fervour. Apart from Dick (Henry Richard) and John, there were four girls in the family: Margaret, Barbara, Coralie and Cynthia, the youngest. Though John grew up in a feminine environment surrounded by a bevy of lively, intelligent sisters, Mt Pleasant was not a cheerful place. Henry was 'a very difficult man who sired very difficult children'.[4]

Henry had been demoralised by the corruption he had seen while serving in the Red Cross during the First World War. Packages meant for wounded men went astray, pilfered by a chain of theft and bribery. Henry returned home and had a breakdown. Even after he recovered, he remained withdrawn and lugubrious. Lila, his first wife, suffered from ill-health, a condition that seemed in equal parts physical and mental, adding to Henry's personal unhappiness. 'Mother is not at all well,' Henry told John, 'a nasty cold sticks to her and a return of the blood pressure causes great depression. I am at a loss to know what to do, barring every reasonable comfort and convenience in the House there does not seem much to do.'[5]

There was no joking or tomfoolery at Mt Pleasant, nor much entertaining, making it a gloomy and severe place for children, controlled by a stuffy etiquette, where they were expected to be seen and not heard. It grated on the fragile, intense Cynthia who imparted to Patrick White a bitter sense of the 'Tasmanian Gothic gloom' of her childhood.[6]

A patriarchal but not unkindly man, Henry strictly followed the rules of his society. It meant his grasp on a changing world, and his questioning children, grew increasingly slender. He tried to explain to John that, 'I was always so sure of my Duty in Life . . . it was up to me to take hold of the Estate and manage things for Granny and your Aunts . . . I'm afraid the bigger questions never bothered me very much ... "Do justly, love mercy and walk humbly with thy God". There is no finer motto than that to adapt for one's guide in life.'[7]

As well as the six children, Henry, Lila and old Mrs Reed, the household also included eleven staff – three gardeners and a groom, a cook, a lady's maid, two housemaids, a scullery maid and a butler together with the fearsome Holmes who had accompanied Henry to war as his batman. Holmes was the chauffeur but after the war became the house's major domo and governing spirit. Each morning all the staff joined the family in prayer.

Mt Pleasant was a self-contained, formal world where the evening meal meant a dinner suit. After the gong was struck, the family seated itself in the huge dining room where Henry said grace and carved the roast. 'And if you were late, you didn't sit down.'[8] Six paintings graced the room. Four were by John Glover – three European landscapes and one Tasmanian study – none of which, John recalled, made any impression on him.[9] Portraits of Henry Reed senior and his second wife Margaret gazed down on the assembled company.

Downstairs the house was spacious. Across the hall from the dining room were the drawing rooms whose elegant proportions and fine furniture were kept for best. Behind them was the sun-drenched, north-facing library, its shelves stacked from floor to ceiling with copies of the Bible and religious tracts as well as the *English Art Journal* plus works of history, geography and a collection of Tasmaniana. It was the inspiration for the library at Heide.

The first floor was rather more crowded with half-a-dozen bedrooms of varying sizes. Perhaps the grandest room was the bathroom which faced the drive. It was expressly installed for the Prince of Wales who was touring Australia in 1920 and was to honour Mt Pleasant with his presence. He didn't arrive. 'Half the servants wept,' John told his sister Margaret, 'and the other half swore when they heard he wasn't coming.'[10] Also on the first floor, a narrow corridor lead to the rabbit warren of staff living quarters. It was not a comfortable home. Peter Holyman, whose family bought Mt Pleasant from the Reeds in 1961, found it unbearably cold and impossible to heat.

The children were not allowed to run riot through the house. As Henry packed them all off to school as soon as he could, it was rare for the family to be there together. Outside there were more adventurous prospects. The family tomb, tucked away at the east end of the property, was an atmospheric place. A crypt was built into the side of the hill, staunched with a bluestone wall and surrounded by a holly hedge. It is where several Reed relatives, including Henry senior, are buried.

John's calm, meditative personality could always find benefits, even in difficult situations. John loved country life, seeking refuge in the wilderness and the mountains and he became a keen bird-watcher and bushwalker, pursuits encouraged and shared with Dick. Barrett Reid suggested that 'unknowingly [John] developed in the need for stillness and accuracy of observation that bird-watching demanded . . . a sensibility which was to serve him well when later he turned his eyes from birds to look at paintings.'[11] His sisters were not especially thrilled with John's birdwatching activities. When Cynthia accompanied John, she was made to sit stock still for an hour while John managed to inveigle Barbara into climbing trees, raiding the nests and descending with the eggs held delicately in her mouth.

Not long before their marriage, John wrote to Sunday that, 'Mt Pleasant . . . certainly seems to hold a wonderful beauty and attraction for me not only the house and garden but everything I see in every direction.'[12] The large, expertly maintained garden also grew vegetables and fruit for the table including grapes, tomatoes, figs and asparagus. Henry, an active gardener, ordered his seeds from England and they would be sent out in small packets of tin foil. Each day, Henry would check the garden and advise the gardeners what was required for the cook. There were also cows to be milked and eggs to be gathered from the henhouse. While John would not have performed these chores himself, they were routines he chose to replicate in his own life, the complement to a home in a beautiful rural setting, a practical life lived close to nature.

Mt Pleasant was also an inspiring place because of Henry senior's commitment to the greater good, to practising philanthropy not as a random gesture but on a systematic basis, even if self-sacrifice was involved. Shocked by the poverty of his congregations in northern England, Henry senior provided housing, food and other forms of assistance for them, while in his native Doncaster, he bought cottages for the elderly and indigent. It was a fine tradition of *noblesse oblige* and John was stirred by his grandfather's example.

Summer holidays were spent at Wesley Dale, near Deloraine, a sheep and cattle station of over 3000 acres. Built in 1876 by a Scotsman for Henry senior, the imposing house is Victorian rustic Gothic and unique to Tasmania. Set on a rise facing a lush green valley with the magnificent backdrop of the Western Tiers, it was dear to Henry who had the bricks shipped out from England. Ever the good Christian, he also built a chapel. The stables housed Henry's favourite draught horse, Peter the Great, whose grave on the property he marked with a tombstone.

Visiting Wesley Dale in autumn 1931, John had 'that feeling of irresistible attraction to a place without being able to explain altogether satisfactorily because there are many things about Wesley Dale that don't get many marks, particularly the lack of trees about the house but the soil is rich and there are hawthorn hedges everywhere, great big ones now all red with berries and willows along the little creeks, and cattle, and occasional poplar trees and old cottages in the distance and, on either side, mountains of ever-changing blue, which I suppose one couldn't really go on looking at indefinitely but one feels as if one could.'[13]

John's Tasmanian childhood ended in 1911 when the family travelled to England to place Dick and John at Pinewood School at Farnborough, near London. Among wealthy colonials it was the done thing to send their children to English schools for a proper education, no matter how much the children loathed the process. Mrs Staughton in *Daddy Sowed a Wind!* reflects, 'It is sad to be parted from our children but . . . we must do our duty and educate them in a country with tradition and among gentlefolk.'[14]

John was at Pinewood a year before moving to Cheltenham College in the Cotswolds. He never recovered from the brutishness of Cheltenham which he described as 'ghastly and primitive'.[15] Patrick White, who followed him there, felt exactly the same. The College, which looked like a toy Gothic monastery, was an undistinguished school that fed half its young men into the British Army and 'turned out good chaps who believed in honesty and fair play'.[16] John's developing masculinity – gentle, quietly confident and self-contained – was at odds with the machismo of Cheltenham.

Sensitive and bookish, John learned stoicism and independence from his schooldays as well as a distaste for the forms and hierarchies of upper-class life. Once more, he found release in the countryside.

Saved from Cheltenham by the outbreak of the First World War, John returned to Australia. Not to Tasmania but to Geelong

Grammar outside Melbourne where he finished his education. Geelong Grammar was the choice for the sons of the ruling class. Darren and Everard, Sunday's brothers, also attended.

John boarded at Manifold House and became a sergeant in the cadet corps and a member of the school choir. It cannot have been too gruelling an experience as John decided to send Sweeney, his adopted son, there in 1954, but it is telling that no friendships survived from that time. John, shy and sensitive like Sunday, was also finding it difficult to connect with like-minded souls. School was followed by 'three beautiful years at Cambridge from which I emerged with a law degree and the sense of at least the freedom to be myself, something I had never known before.'[17]

There were strong ties between Geelong Grammar and Cambridge and major Melbourne families like the Fairbairns, Sargoods and Clarkes followed that pattern.[18] At Caius College, John's friends included Harold Abrahams and Robin Roberts. Abrahams, who was also reading law, was the Olympic runner on whom the film *Chariots of Fire* was based. John shared his love of the outdoors with Abrahams and went on mountain-climbing expeditions with him. *Chariots of Fire* chronicles Abrahams' athletic exploits and the discrimination he encountered at Cambridge – not only anti-Semitism but also his driven individualism which was at odds with Cambridge's *esprit de corps*. John dismissed the film version of his friend's Cambridge years as 'a hopeless failure, with Cambridge almost unrecognisable, and Harold completely so'.[19] Yet it is conceivable Abrahams did not fit the mould and suffered for it among the blue-bloods.

But for John the notion of *esprit de corps*, of bonding and belonging to a larger group of sympathetic souls, of acting not alone but in concert with others, was not just an ideal: it became a way of life where the elective affinities of friendship replaced the inherited network of family. John dispensed with his family, rather as Sunday did, though for slightly different reasons. The ethos of sacrificing oneself for the greater good further provided John with a maxim consonant with the rectitude of his own personality.

Robin Roberts, who became a don and Dean of College at Corpus Christi, fell in love with John. In 1924, after John graduated and was returning home via South America, Roberts mourned John's departure. He was 'so glad' that John liked Joseph Conrad's *Victory*, declaring that John 'appeared like the principal figure out of a possible Conrad novel; to me anyway and now that you have gone the stage is empty'. John's friends at Cambridge (though one suspects Roberts means himself) 'obviously devoted such a lot of thought to understanding and appreciating your personality' and John could not guess 'how keenly the people you knew in England have missed you'.[20]

Such caring and intelligent attention was probably welcome to John. Dick had chosen not to attend university but remained in Australia where he went on the land, establishing farms first in New South Wales, then Tasmania. John had increasingly little contact with his parents. His older sister Margaret had successfully opposed Henry's disapproval and was studying medicine at nearby Newnham College but Cynthia was the sibling to whom John felt closest. She was boarding at The Hermitage, Geelong, the sister school to Geelong Grammar.

John's adolescence had been a lonely and restless time with no firm sense of home or of purpose. Perhaps Roberts' affection for John was one of the reasons he found Cambridge 'beautiful'. Roberts went on to admit, 'I cannot bear to think of you unhappy – I wish I could see you for even a day – an hour. Dear John – You know how I have loved you! and the stage is terribly empty.'[21]

While there is no evidence that John reciprocated Roberts' affection, the friendship continued. When Cynthia visited London in 1929 she met Robin, and liked him. Robin, still missing John, sent his love and remarked that Cynthia resembled John, which Cynthia took as a compliment.

Roberts puzzled over John's personality. What was it about John that reminded Roberts of a character from Conrad? Axel Heyst is the complex and enigmatic protagonist of *Victory*, arguably Conrad's greatest novel. Heyst was a wanderer, 'invariably courteous' but 'invulnerable because elusive'. Heyst's father was an 'uneasy soul', filled with 'disillusion and regret', who bequeathed to his impressionable son 'a profound mistrust of life'. It meant that Axel became 'a waif and a stray . . . It was the very essence of his life to be a solitary achievement, accomplished not by hermit-like withdrawal with its silence and immobility, but by a system of restless wandering, by the detachment of an impermanent dweller amongst changing scenes.'[22]

At Cambridge, an antipodean among the English upper classes, an outsider to the prevailing system and a young man who had been on the move since he was ten, John appeared to Roberts, and perhaps felt within himself, that he was a wanderer on the face of the earth, 'a waif and a stray'. He had no destination, no goals in sight. His years at boarding school, then university, unmoored him, and his home was far away, both geographically and emotionally. Axel's difficult, depressive father could also symbolise the effects of Henry Reed's dour personality on John.

John grew into an austerely handsome and restrained man. He was dignified and patrician, without snobbery or calculated charm, eager to listen and, unless roused by a cause or an issue, relatively subdued. There was a strain of passivity in John which welcomed domination by stronger characters, either male or female, the 'ideas' people to whom he was attracted. He had spent years being ordered about by his superiors – first his father, then a stream of principals, teachers, tutors and older boys. Perhaps John had found the path of least resistance was the most appropriate, both for his personality and the circumstances in which he found himself. But Roberts perceived the hurt that lay behind John's reserve, the self-sufficiency hard won by a gentle boy in the brutish dormitories and playing fields of his long education.

No doubt there was frustration for Roberts, too, if John's 'elusiveness' meant he did not respond to Roberts' love. John was not homosexual though Roberts was the first of a number of clever, articulate, dynamic men with whom he enjoyed intimate friendships. Adolescence is a time of sexual awakening and experimentation and John may have been aroused by his own sex. It is not an uncommon experience.

When John returned to Australia, it was not to Tasmania, but the University of Melbourne where he studied Arts/Law for a year. His love of the outdoors made him want to go on the land, like Dick, but Henry was against it. Concerned that John had arrived at 'your stage in life without any definite goal before you', Henry pointed out that John's hayfever meant farming was 'right out of Court for you'.[23] Correctly, his father also assessed that 'with your mental outlook, you would have found [farming] very trying'.[24] While Henry 'could very easily pitchfork you into something either in the Law or on the Land . . . that would be no good to you, you are of an age now when it is your Duty to make up your own mind about things.' Finally, Henry suggested 'if you really want to get into Blake and Riggall's I think something can be done'.[25]

John followed his father's guidance and Henry organised a position for his son as an articled clerk at Blake and Riggall's, 'one of the biggest ... [and] probably the most conservative [law firms] in the southern hemisphere'. John was not bored by the work. On the contrary, he found it 'stimulating and satisfying', working his way up to junior partner over the next eight years.[26]

It was the friends John made outside the office that quickened him, introducing him to the pleasures of art and the gregarious, bohemian art crowd. Clarice Zander was a confident and attractive woman who managed the New Gallery in Elizabeth Street. It had been opened by *Herald* art critic James MacDonald, an outspoken champion of traditional art and a future director of the National Gallery of Victoria. It was probably at the New Gallery that Zander met Will Dyson, one of Australia's most popular cartoonists, and later became his lover.

John credited Zander with 'leading him' to art.[27] He met her through Sylvia Rodmell, his landlady, at her boarding-house in Caroline St, South Yarra. Through Zander, he got to know a diverse and interesting group including Dyson, MacDonald, Jimmy Bancks, Harold Herbert and, more importantly, Fred Ward and Reg Ellery.

Zander was a woman of many talents. She had earned her living as a commercial artist before the war and was a proficient journalist and occasional short story writer. Charles, her husband, had been injured in the First World War, leaving him a troubled man with a fondness for drink. Like many others, he tried to make a living on the land from the soldier settlement scheme. When it ended in disaster, Charles set off for America. Clarice and Sylvia Rodmell, who were in similar straits, had come to Melbourne to find work, Clarice bringing her daughter Jocelyn.

John was impressed by the elegant, enterprising Clarice and may have been a little infatuated with her. She was the kind of woman — worldly, competent, intelligent and stylish – to whom he responded.

The notion of her 'leading' him into art implies a willing submission on his part. Clarice was the stronger character to whom John was temperamentally attracted, who was taking charge of him and taking him forward. To know Clarice, and Dyson, meant being swept up in a social whirl.

Dyson, recently returned from England in 1926, had a tremendous reputation as a political cartoonist. In London, he had revitalised the *Daily Herald* with his brilliantly acerbic cartoons and moved in circles where Bernard Shaw, G.K. Chesterton and H.G. Wells were friends and admirers. Despite the adulation, Dyson was despondent. His wife Ruby Lindsay had died in 1919 and his years as a war artist had made him painfully aware of war's brutality and waste. Brought back by the *Herald* to work on *Punch*, his return made front-page news.

Dyson was a man of extremes: his wit, charm and hilarious hijinks meant he was in demand at Melbourne's fashionable gatherings but his bitterness and despair surfaced, alienating friends like Vance and Nettie Palmer. Dyson was critical of postwar Australia. It was crassly materialistic, dominated by the anti-Labor Bruce-Page coalition which governed the nation according to its doctrine of 'men, markets and money'. In particular, Dyson blamed the intellectuals who 'had let the country become a backwater, a paradise for dull boring mediocrities, a place where the artist or the man of ideas could only live on sufferance'.[28] Clarice tried to smooth the ruffled feathers Dyson often left in his wake, spiriting him away for quiet weekends in the country.

Dyson lived in fine style at Mirrool in Wallace Avenue, Toorak, with his fifteen-year-old daughter Betty whom John recalled as 'very attractive and precocious'.[29] John had left the boarding house in Caroline Street and rented a flat at 94 Mathoura Road before sharing a house at 24 Douglas Avenue, around the corner from Mirrool, where he was a frequent visitor.

John was not impressed with Dyson's work. Populist art or art that employed scathing satire never appealed to him. But it gave John the opportunity to see a commercially successful artist at work, for in his day Dyson was not regarded as merely 'a cartoonist' but a serious artist. John also observed that while Dyson could be 'a very funny man', especially in the company of Jimmy Bancks, creator of the internationally syndicated Ginger Meggs cartoons, their antics had a note of hysteria, making John feel Dyson was 'unhappy and rather lost'. But Dyson's articulate and trenchant pronouncements on the state of Australian culture and society must have been both stirring and welcome to John who was searching for his own direction in such matters.

Through Dyson, John came into contact with artist Harold Herbert and James MacDonald, both frequenters of the Savage Club, an exclusively male haunt for artists, writers and other members of bohemia. It gave John a taste of mingling with the powerbrokers of the Melbourne art world, ironically, in this case, with two men who would become his sworn enemies in the coming battles over modern art. Herbert would declare to John, 'There are only two things I hate, modern art and communism and you stand for both of them!'

Herbert was no great shakes as an artist. A technically competent watercolourist in the Heidelberg School tradition, he became the *Argus*'s waspish art critic, taking pot shots at the modernists. John 'could never pretend to have any feeling' for his work but he liked the man who was a bon vivant, 'fat and cheerful, a good companion, who enjoyed having people around him'. MacDonald, appointed as director of the National Gallery of Victoria in 1936, was an arch-conservative artist and critic. Both Herbert and

MacDonald were admirers of Dyson's work and heaped unqualified praise on his 1926 exhibition.

Also close to Dyson was Dr Reg Ellery, a firebrand psychiatrist
and follower of Freud's. He inspired Dyson to make Freud the
subject of several etchings and cartoons. As John reflected, 'in those
days psychiatry was regarded as a sort of first cousin to the devil'
and Ellery had no qualms about putting forward his views: he was
a 'born controversialist and stirrer of muddy waters'.[30] Ellery had
already been the centre of notoriety when a Royal Commission of
inquiry examined his work at the Victorian Lunacy Department.
Ellery was then transferred to work at the Sunbury asylum where
he took up residence with his wife Mancell, a gifted musician.
Dyson and Clarice visited the Ellerys there. Later, Ellery would
become a member of the Heide circle and an author published by
Reed & Harris. An enthusiastic admirer of D.H. Lawrence and
James Joyce, Ellery recommended these authors to John, as writers
of psychological insight.

But it was a struggling cartoonist who would have the most
pertinent effect on John, connecting him not only with a vital
appreciation of art but of modernism itself. Dyson, Herbert,
MacDonald and Bancks were all older men, highly successful in
their chosen fields and prominent in the art world. They were also
virulently anti-modernist. In 1929, Dyson had completed a series
of etchings illustrating 'the pretensions and affectations of the intelligentsia . . . the extravagances of social life and the sterile gropings
of the impotent modernists in art, music and literature'.[31]

Fred Ward's talents were nascent. He was working unhappily
at the *Herald* while devoting himself to his true calling – furniture
design – when time allowed. For John, Ward (a year older than he)
was a kindred spirit, prefiguring the type of artist who would be

welcomed at Heide. Nor was it Ward's cartoons that appealed to John, 'it was rather that he and Puss [Ward's wife Elinor] seemed to let fresh air into my life; relatively they were uninhibited, unconventional, ready to talk . . . about anything.' After years of regimentation and discipline at home, school and university, John was captivated by his new friends and 'at once felt at home in this atmosphere'.

John briefly shared a house in Toorak with Ward and Geoffrey Thomas, a friend of Ward's, before Ward married in 1925. It prefigured the domestic arrangements that characterised Heide, where the Reeds were in daily, intimate contact with their chosen artist-friends. John needed to be encouraged and motivated and Ward 'was always coming up with what seemed to me fresh thoughts about the world, about art, about our daily activities . . . and there was always a good deal of laughter'.[32]

In those days Ward regarded John as a straitlaced fellow who wore a bowler hat to work 'and did not utter at breakfast except to chide me for wearing my pyjama top for a shirt'.[33] John also read the *Times* and turned out for rugger practice on Saturday mornings. But as the friendship developed, so did discussions: there was the serious issue of furniture design that Ward felt 'needed a complete overhaul'.[34]

Ward was a pioneer industrial designer who, in the early '30s, started his own small factory to produce his furniture: simple, elegant objects made from Australian timbers and influenced by the clean functionalism of the Bauhaus. A former student at the National Gallery School, Ward had studied engineering and worked in engineering shops to master manufacturing processes. He had also worked at E.L. Yencken's designing stained glass where his immediate boss was Jock Frater.

In 1932, Ward set up his own shop at 52a Collins Street, two doors from the Melbourne Club, which Robin Boyd believed displayed Melbourne's most innovative design.[35] It proved popular, at least with a discriminating section of the public, and in the mid-'30s Ward was invited to set up his own studio in the furniture department at Myer department store where he designed the UNIT line of modernist timber furniture. He proved to be an important catalyst for the core group of modernists who surrounded Sunday and John, which included Sam Atyeo and Cynthia Reed.

Ward did not look back. Later, he not only designed furniture for the National Library and the Australian National University but collaborated with Robin Boyd.

What was it about Ward's furniture that appealed to John? As an ardent naturalist, he could relate to the simplicity and lustrous appearance of the natural timbers. John admired Ward as a pioneer in his field who 'horrified the conservatives'.[36] The clean, undeco-rated lines and plain wood of Ward's furniture was considered to be extremely modern and he used Australian timbers whose beauty had not yet been recognised. Ward believed Australians were surrounded by 'so much unoriginal, poverty-stricken design' that it amounted to a 'lack of national style'.[37] He also believed his own training in manufacturing was the right one for 'a new and very efficient kind of designer' who would disregard the 'almost endless copying of the styles of the past' and create something fresh and exciting.[38]

Most of the furniture of the day was unattractive and frequently shoddy. Much use was made of veneer, particularly in walnut, and although there was furniture manufactured in Queensland maple and other Australian woods, this was invariably stained to imitate imported woods. Ornamentation was coarse and heavy varnish was used. But Ward's furniture was built for the modern house: it was not too large, it was easily carried or moved yet it was as solid as furniture could be.

Ward provided John with an introduction to an emphatically Australian creative expression, one that implied a criticism of the heavy, ornate, English furniture that dominated Australian interior design and notions of good taste. Even art deco, under the purist Bauhaus critique, was fussy and decorative. Lastly, for John (and Sunday), friendship and empathy often came first in the creative alliance, and the art followed. The 'bright spark', an animating force which initiated cultural and personal change in John's life, disrupting the previous order and challenging his beliefs and certainties – and there would be many over the years – was also prefigured by Ward.

The Bauhaus, a revolutionary art school founded by architect Walter Gropius in 1919, was at its peak in the late 1920s. The school had moved from Weimar to Dessau and Gropius had attracted key exemplars of modernism to teach there including Paul Klee, Wassily Kandinsky, Lazlo Moholy-Nagy and Lyonel Feininger. The influential Bauhaus aesthetic was determined by functionalism and the hard-edged imperatives of cubism. It became an international movement shaping every aspect of design and architecture. 'The nature of an object is determined by what it does,' Gropius stated.[39] But there was more to the Bauhaus than design.

The art school was meant to be an ideal community where skills were shared in a democracy of learning. 'Art cannot be taught,' Gropius believed.[40] The Bauhaus also abandoned distinctions between the arts, so fine art and crafts were not regarded as fundamentally different but aspects of the same creative and formal impulse. Further, the Bauhaus was committed to a program of social responsibility that included designing cheap housing equipped with affordable, mass-produced household objects. The Bauhaus stood for internationalism, radicalism and change. No wonder the Nazi government made it an early target and closed it down in April 1933, the first tangible evidence of Nazi cultural policy.

For John, Bauhaus ideals about the function and standard of contemporary design, disseminated by Ward, were a valuable starting point for his discovery of modernism both as a cultural expression and as a way of life. In Ward's furniture he could see the practical results of those ideas and in Ward's vivid personality, he found a man he could follow. Admiring Ward's furniture perhaps made John aware of what he did not have: his own home where such beautifully made objects could take their place.

· 4 ·

Together

Let me not to the marriage of true minds
Admit impediments. Love is not love
Which alters when it alteration finds,
Or bends with the remover to remove.
SHAKESPEARE, SONNET CXVI

Darling Fiancé I am so happy — you have — made me so happy — Johnny Johnny
isn't it exciting — I'm going to marry you & you can't get out of it.
SUNDAY REED TO JOHN REED, 22 OCTOBER 1931[1]

'IT WAS NOT A DRAMATIC MEETING,' John remarked with typical understatement.[2] The tennis party where Sunday and John were first introduced, late in 1930, was in Toorak where the two were neighbours: Douglas Street was just around the corner from Balholmen.

Sunday's version of the meeting, as recounted by her friend Jean Langley, is a little more romantic. '[Sunday] was at her cousin's place in Toorak, she was washing her hair and drying it in the sunlight and all the young people were playing tennis downstairs. Somebody said, "Come down and meet this beautiful young man called John Reed." She said, "I'm drying my hair. I'm not interested." And they said, "He's very nice." She finally went down and met him and after they got to know each other, she said, "You'd better marry me!" '3

Since the break-up of her marriage, Sunday had had an unsettled existence, staying with friends at 8 Glyndebourne Avenue, Toorak, and with her parents at Fairlie House, 38 Anderson St, South Yarra. In 1928, Arthur and Ethel had sold Balholmen and moved into one of the splendid apartments at Fairlie House. Darren and his wife Diana, and Everard, also had apartments there. Sunday had not long returned from Europe and she had healed, physically at least, from the ordeal with Quinn.

In a photograph from 1930, John looks quite the dandy in his superbly cut suit, colour co-ordinated vest and tie, the outfit completed with immaculately polished shoes. His body language is uncomfortable, stiff and restrained. Holding Karel, his German shepherd (named after the Czech writer Karel Capek), he seems equally to be holding himself in. He does not look like a man of the world, like the louche Leonard Quinn, but a properly brought-up young fellow, virginal and impeccably polite.

Sunday had a charismatic presence and for those who fell under her spell, meeting her for the first time was usually a memorable event. She was 'stunningly beautiful in the most original and different way. Different to anybody else I'd ever seen. Most beautiful, most inspiring face. She just stood out.'⁴ In fact, John and Sunday's features were not dissimilar: both had long, strong jaws, wide mouths and deep-set eyes. They were of the same height, both lean, olive-skinned and vigorous, but John was dark where Sunday was fair. They could have been brother and sister, a fact that was not lost on Cynthia.

Once Sunday got over her shyness, she could be charming, personable and flirtatious. She was also inspiring, as the artists she attracted would discover. Sunday challenged John 'in a way no-one else had ever done . . . She in effect forced me to get to grips with what I had so far only tentatively approached. It was not enough just to talk vaguely about modern art. I had to identify my thoughts and to involve myself more closely. None of this was expressed explicitly; but it was the unavoidable conclusion to be drawn into her own clear and direct approach to anything we talked about.'⁵

John told Michael Keon that 'Sunday had taught him not just to have confidence in his own emotions and thoughts – and he had needed that damned near all his life before Sunday – but also to have no fear of receiving as much as giving. Sunday had recognised the fear of receiving he had in him because she had the same fear in herself.' What also impressed John was Sunday's magnificently cavalier attitude – 'rules came afterwards and were other people's business'.⁶

That might apply to parking tickets, or life's larger issues. Neil Douglas recalled 'Sun . . . was one of the early women drivers. She used to have great battles with policemen and parking attendants. She parked where she bloody well liked and would imperiously call the parking attendants "Bores!"'⁷ When she got parking tickets, which she called 'bluies', she tore them up.

Sunday set her cap at John and he happily submitted to a woman who seemed to offer both the worldly sophistication he lacked and a type of sensitivity he not only understood and respected but could expertly protect. John remained in awe of Sunday's 'high degree of sensibility, [her] personal integrity and moral courage'. Sunday was an individualist who 'always responded to her own truths', who reacted 'to people and situations out of some natural and intuitive sense of understanding within herself'. He stood back and admiringly observed Sunday's direct confrontations, unalloyed by 'the usual subterfuges which blind the edge of human relationships'. Though John was adamant 'Sunday did not "change my life"', he also recognised that 'she has, however, made it so far as it is able to be made'.[8] That same could be said for John's impact on her.

John and Sunday seemed an ideal couple not only because of what they shared – a wealthy, privileged background – but because of the wounds that heritage had administered. For Sunday, it was the Baillieu clan's oppressive mercantile masculinity. For John, it was the cold comfort of his Tasmanian home followed by the miserable years at boarding school. Both felt they had to escape from their families and create a freer, more independent existence and both were trying to do exactly that. John was succeeding rather better than Sunday for, as a man, he could control his life in a way she could not.

Was Sunday John's first lover? Gentlemanly and reserved, John seemed a candidate for seduction and it is possible that Sunday lead the way. Within a short time, John and Sunday were regularly staying together at Douglas Street or Fairlie House. Sexuality was a crucial and fully realised expression of Sunday's life, with all the pitfalls and problems that can accompany passion. John's ardour appeared not of the same order and intensity. While their dissonant sexualities created problems in their marriage, it did not diminish their love for one another. The tenderness and loyalty between Sunday and John was never in doubt and, all their lives, they slept in the same bed, enjoyed physical closeness and chafed when separated from one another. Indeed, Sunday could become extremely anxious when John was out of her sight.

During one separation, not long after they were married, Sunday wished she was 'Elizabeth Barrett Browning and could write you straight away all sorts of intelligent things', impressing John with

what a wonderful wife you had – but I'm not Elizabeth. I'm just Sunday and really dont feel particularly intelligent this morning or particularly inclined to say anything at all except put me in your jama pocket tonight and [hold?] me 'gainst your heart and in the morning dont forget to take me out because I dont want to be packed away all day in your suitcase – I think I'm just small enough to fit in your waistcoat, tho it would be more fun for me to be in your Trousers!!!!!! so if I'm not in the way you must leave me there when you dress in the morning. Come back quickly Johnny – Kisses – Goodnight – Kisses Sunday Kisses – Goodnight.[9]

When John visited Sydney for a legal conference, Sunday fretted.

It will be so odd not to have you with me tonight. I shall truthfully miss you and need you terribly – even in two days. Of course we've been away from each other before but somehow Sorrento is different . . . and just the thought – Sydney – strikes a note of fear – what if – I dont know – you wont get run over – meet bill collectors or fall into the blue blue harbour (which I really do love the look of) or be unfaithful – and yet – and yet.

She rallied to instruct John to 'find some time darling – just a little teeny bit of time, in which to bring me back some good feeling – see something, do something, feel something, that I've never even thought of, so that when we go to Sydney we can see or do or feel it together – and it will all be new and lovely'.[10]

In the early days of their courtship, Sunday introduced John to a language of the heart that was emotional, ardent and emphatic. For Sunday, love had to be spoken, written, visualised, celebrated and recorded. She was a gift giver, enjoying (and expecting) tokens and mementos. John responded gallantly, sending her a stream of flowers, ribbons, presents and affectionate notes.

Sunday particularly responded to flowers, telling John 'the primroses are so marvellous. I wonder if you know – primroses, real ones, with long long stems and a fist full of red rose buds looking very wild and wet – and the first lilac Johnny and the last hyacinth . . . Isn't lilac good John; such fun to bury your face in its smell.'[11] Sunday's sentimentality also made her a conservator and she kept their early exchanges, no matter how casual or small, even a piece of wrapping paper on which John had scrawled 'Happy Christmas'.

Sunday's first letter to John was addressed both to him and Karel. She was off to Brisbane for a brief trip and enclosed 'a small piece of blossom for Carol's [sic] dinner – a sort of special parting present'.[12] John advised that 'it's really "Karel" and he's very particular about it too.' Unctuously, he told Sunday there would be a present awaiting her on her return 'and then, if you're very good, I'll take you out'.[13]

But Sunday's moodiness and sensitivity soon surfaced. Though it seemed 'awfully mean upsetting arrangements at the last minute', she wondered if she could cancel their dinner plans? 'I want to go to bed.' She felt that 'this realization business – which includes you is making me terribly tired in an inside secret sort of way and today I feel as if my hair is standing on end'. She needed 'an opportunity to have a quiet think all to myself or perhaps a good sleep'. If John came to dinner with Darren she 'would just sit about quite useless – and – oh! no more explanations – please Johnny, understand – don't be cross. I would have rung the office but I thought it might be too difficult to say what I wanted to say on the phone.'[14] Perhaps the 'realization business' meant coming to terms with her future with John.

In his reply, John characterised the role he would play in their marriage: caring, empathetic and self-sacrificing.

> Darling sweet, how could I be cross? I only love you all the more and feel very sad I can't do something to help. I try to make myself exactly as you feel, but of course I can't do it or I would ever be so much more use to you. But I do understand a little and I will think of you tonight in our big bed . . .
>
> All my love little one
> John[15]

Despite a robust system, Sunday's health could be delicate, a state often influenced by her emotions. But ongoing ailments included her deafness, back problems, poor digestion (which she cured by diet) and her teeth.

Not long after they were engaged, a bad case of mouth ulcers, dyspepsia and back-ache meant a recuperation period at Merthon with Doodie. An almost daily exchange of letters between Sunday and John reveal Sunday's struggle with the fluctuations of her own moods and John's loving and, at times, baffled attempts to understand, counsel and sympathise. Sunday declared she was 'trying to be strong' for John's weekend visit, 'eating an apple a day, drinking lots of milk and resting and doing all the things that at my age I am ashamed to think about'.[16]

But when the men of her family were present, her spirits drooped. 'The prejudice . . . [is] so strong I quite understand that I'm never expected to say anything worth listening to and it would cause great annoyance if I did, so that now I feel I never want to – and mostly fall into long silences . . . I always hope to harden myself against all the vibrations . . . but somehow it never quite works – if one was sufficiently equipped one wouldn't be so influenced – and it's absurd to worry and to mope on about it as I do.'[17]

Merthon's chief benefit was the solace of nature where Sunday could stand beneath 'a clear cloudless lavender coloured sky . . . watching the stars come out and smelling the wood of the trees and the rosemary hedge and listening to the folding noise of the sea and losing the moon behind a tree and finding it again in the birds' pool like a silver dish lying on the grass . . . and feeling as quiet as the sleeping birds and as wild as a tiger.' It was as if nature, and the environment of Merthon, gave Sunday the clarity to recognise twin needs and personal qualities: a sense of repose and, equally, a fierce, innate power that was awaiting release.

But 'what is the use of feeling like a wild tiger if you can't do anything about it?' Sunday mused. Her illness and convalescence symbolised some of the frustrations life had offered Sunday so far. John – her promising new life – was at a remove while she was constrained by sickness and solitude, and felt daunted and helpless, 'stupid'.[18]

Anxiety could suddenly engulf Sunday assailing her with 'awful thoughts somewhere in the back of my mind, of a parting – as if we had experienced a parting or were going to experience it. An ending. I know the thought is unreasonable but it hangs on. You are coming back to me but not in the same way, the old fun has gone – Why can't I think the new fun commencing ... of even better things for us. Johnny I suppose it's partly nerves & partly your absence that makes me so depressed. I fear the future for us as I fear the pain in my body.'[19]

John, worried about the depression into which Sunday was sinking, advised her to 'think happy thoughts'.[20] 'You are made so essentially for such a wonderful life and so much happiness.'[21] On a practical note, John also suggested she 'take a little notebook round with you ... so that you won't forget to tell me everything that is happening in the garden ... not to mention all the birds and their goings on. I will expect the fullest particulars' – which she dutifully transcribed in her letters.[22] She also included some sketches of sea birds which later encouraged John, the keen birdwatcher, to hatch a plan (which came to nothing) to produce a bird book – 'OUR BOOK' – which Sunday would illustrate and he would write.[23]

Sunday was a voracious reader and no amount of ill-health could stop that. She recommended novels to John including W.H. Hudson's *Green Mansions* and *Faraway and Long Ago* together with John Cowper Powys' *Wolf Solent*, popular books of the day rather than literary masterpieces.

Hudson, an early conservationist and naturalist, had grown up on the Argentine pampas in the 1840s before moving to England where he became a novelist. John correctly described *Green Mansions* as Hudson's 'masterpiece' but *Faraway and Long Ago*, Hudson's autobiography that focused on his childhood in Argentina, had special meaning for Sunday: she referred to it as her 'book of dreams'.[24] 'God, it's good!' John enthused, 'I had no idea how good. Full of knowledge, full of wisdom, the wisdom of the true philosopher of nature, with a simplicity and directness of style that absolutely captures me.'[25]

Hudson's prose is suffused with an intense and spiritual nature worship, 'the wonderfulness and eternal mystery of life itself; this formative, informing energy' which emerged during his childhood and shaped his sensibility.[26] He was opposed to the destruction of the environment and to the practice of nineteenth-century orthinologists who killed birds in order to study them. His philosophy mirrored Sunday's own rapport with the natural world which developed during her adolescence. When asked why she became a vegetarian in later life, she replied, 'I don't like to eat my friends.'[27] Respect for nature, a vital sense of kinship with all living things, was an inspirational force, leading to the purchase of Heide as the site of her creative work.

In *Wolf Solent*, (a novel Sunday would later recommend to both Atyeo and Hester) Cowper Powys wanted to chart 'the whole mysterious essence of human life upon earth, the mystery of consciousness'.[28] Solent is a yearning young man grappling with relationships with the women in his life – his mother, his wife and his mistress. Turgid and overstated, it reads as an amalgam of Virginia Woolf's heightened states of consciousness and D.H. Lawrence's vigorous sensuality. For Sunday, it defined the seeker who plots an individual course against the odds, who privileges sensuality alongside intellectuality and who disrupts convention. It symbolised the trajectory of her own life and also the artist-type to whom she would be attracted.

Both Hudson and Cowper Powys picture relationships as romantic, highly emotional, even melodramatic. Engagements with nature or with the beloved are passionate, poetic, troubling and consuming. There are no half measures and tragedy can result. Able, the protagonist in *Green Mansions*, is abandoned by the bewitching Rima, a personification of the forest, and is left to wander to his doom. Wolf Solent can find no relief, either in sex or love, and registers his sense of alienation by a restless inner questioning, a profound dissatisfaction with all life offers. Sunday could identify with such qualities, both on a personal level – as one who yearned for closeness but encountered stress in intimacy – and on a more abstract level, as an example of the modern, alienated personality who searches for but cannot find equilibrium.

While Sunday continued to recuperate at Merthon, John insisted she keep 'regular hours and eat your food properly and take just the right amount of exercise'.[29] Rest was particularly important. 'You must go to bed very early every night and must only read a very little in bed and then go to sleep and keep on sleeping until it's time to give the birds their breakfast.'[30]

Monitoring Sunday became John's task and vocation. It is a role reminiscent of that in Leonard and Virginia Woolf's marriage where Leonard committed himself to managing Virginia's febrile disposition. Though Sunday did not suffer from manic depression as Virginia did, nor from any clinical condition, her acute sensitivity made John her watcher and keeper. Virginia reflected on Leonard's 'divine goodness', observing that 'after 25 years [we] cant bear to be separate . . . you see it is an enormous pleasure, being wanted: a wife. And our marriage so complete.'[31]

But friends like Ottoline Morell often lamented Leonard's control. 'We had just begun to talk when Leonard came in, which

I felt she felt as a bore – as I did but it's important not to offend him. He is her Guardian – and if I offended him I should never see her.' Virginia confided to her sister Vanessa Bell that 'she found Leonard absolutely dependable & like a rock which was what she badly wanted . . . & that he was also very unselfish – & always ready to plunge into any enterprise she suggested.'[32]

Nadine Amadio recalls, 'John had this guardian feeling about Sun at various times . . . She was always someone I felt that he felt he had to guard . . . John could get very stern – he really did have this big daddy aspect about him. It was as though he was afraid to let himself go. But I think he saw his role in life as a protector.' John's attitude could earn the ire of friends, especially if they were homosexual. 'They felt he was repressing Sun.' While Amadio also felt 'he loved her more than she loved him – if you could quantify these things,' she observed the Reeds' was a 'true marriage of minds, the real meaning of the word, in fact the sum total of them together was more than either of them separately.'[33]

Slowly Sunday recovered her health and well-being at Merthon and she was 'so glad because I have felt beastly for a long time'.[34] John was part of that healing – 'it seems as if my whole spirit flows naturally to you and with you'.[35] Even after their marriage and despite John's protestations, Sunday knew she was an unconventional marriage partner and her remark – 'if only I was a better wife!!' – carries a charge of self-recrimination.

No doubt Arthur Baillieu breathed a sigh of relief when Sunday brought John home. He seemed the perfect match. She had done exactly what Arthur had advised after the debacle with Quinn. That was a case of 'once bitten twice shy'. Now Sunday needed to set her position. It was, Arthur advised, like the navigation of a voyage– 'the Captain must understand the compasses and take his bearings accurately'.[36] In many ways, Sunday had chosen a man like her father: kindly, protective, patrician, balanced, steadfast and indulgent of her whims and needs.

But Henry Reed was horrified. His son was marrying a divorcee, damaged goods who could not have children. Breeding was regarded by Henry's class as marriage's prime benefit – the continuity of the line. As a strictly religious man, divorce was out of the question. The gulf between father and son only widened when, a year after Lila's death, Henry remarried. 'I can quite understand that none of you wanted me to marry again,' Henry wrote testily to John, 'but . . . I have to live my own life . . . I do hope the Family will now adopt a more natural attitude to Daisy.' Henry was annoyed with his children's 'stiff stand off attitude as if you were doing us a favour by having anything to do with us at all'.[37]

In 1931, John and Sunday were making plans for their wedding and their future. It was a happy and exciting period, marred only by the tricky business of the divorce which Arthur was negotiating. Divorce in the 1930s was complicated and rare. Because it was a fault-based system, one party or the other had to admit blame so grounds could be established and the matter proceed. The grounds were stringent, either desertion or cruelty. Though Quinn qualified on both counts, the matter remained difficult because he lived overseas and, if he had proved unhelpful, it could have been held up interminably. For Quinn as a Catholic there was no divorce and, under Church law, he could not remarry. That did not apply to Sunday. Perhaps Quinn finally got the cash he was after because in June 1931, Arthur wrote to Sunday with 'indescribable relief' that 'our dreadful nightmare is ended'.[38] Arthur had received a cable confirming the divorce and on 15 June, Sunday was a free woman.

During that time, Sunday and John were regularly visiting the

Yarra Valley to take Karel for walks. It was all open country, low lying with green rolling fields, reminiscent of the Cotswolds, which both were familiar with. There was also the area's strong artistic connection – it was the place that gave its name to the Heidelberg School.

There was another reason to visit the area. Fred and Puss Ward had moved to an English-style cottage in Glenard Drive, Heidelberg, where Fred was making simple, well-proportioned furniture for the rooms. Puss recalled, 'we painted the walls with kalsomine. One attic bedroom . . . was in pale gold with furniture painted in deep Madonna blue; another was in palest green with grey furniture.' It proved so popular with friends that Fred made more, specifically for sale. 'As Christmas came they came out in droves and bought things right and left, bought our seats from under us, until no more could be spared.'[39]

The Wards were among the guests invited to Sunday and John's wedding reception. Once again, Sunday's marriage would be slightly unconventional: this time because she was divorced. The wedding took place on 13 January 1932 at St Paul's Cathedral, Melbourne's grandest neo-Gothic Anglican church, in what John described as 'our special chapel'. To the left of the nave's main altar, the small, beautiful Ascension Chapel is decorated with richly coloured stained glass windows and a glittering mosaic that shows Christ's ascension into heaven after his death. It was donated by the Clarkes, another illustrious Melbourne family. That day John wrote, 'Darling Sunday . . . it's going to be marvellous being married to you.'[40]

Though Richard Sherwood, the presenter at St Paul's, married Sunday and John 'according to the rites and the ceremonies of the Church of England' and signed their marriage certificate – which he had to do by law – there is no record in St Paul's register of the wedding. It was not removed. It was never there. While divorce was allowed by the Church of England – indeed Henry VIII had created the Church of England in order to divorce his first wife and marry Anne Boleyn – it was viewed as shameful, unholy. To include Sunday's divorcee status in the church archive would have been a smudge on church sanctity. As far as the clergy of St Paul's were concerned, such a marriage never occurred in their hallowed grounds. Perhaps Sunday was not even aware of the hypocrisy.

The bad spirit of Leonard hovered. When Sunday signed the marriage certificate, she wrote Sunday Baillieu Quinn in her flamboyant handwriting, then frantically crossed out 'Quinn', making Arthur Baillieu and Richard Sherwood witness the change with their signatures.

Once again, Sunday had chosen to be married in summer, her favourite season, and just two weeks after the anniversary of her first marriage. Her outfit was deliberately modern, unadorned and elegant. She wore a long, white, fitted gown with short sleeves and a diaphonous bodice. John was resplendent in a morning suit. In a photograph taken at the reception, Sunday clasps John's hand, radiating happiness. It was the height of the Depression but Arthur spared no expense on the reception which was held outside under white marquees. A good time was had by all, including Karel who disgraced himself by eating the wedding cake. Then the Reeds set off on their European honeymoon.

· 5 ·

The First Circle

In choosing [friends] . . . there is no doubt that those in your own Social Position are more likely to prove permanent and to have more in common with you than those in another Social Scale [who are] much less likely to be acceptable or agreeable to one's family and other friends when you have a Home of your own.

HENRY REED TO JOHN REED, 27 JUNE 1926[1]

Relationships [are] just as essential as marriage [and] without them we would be incomplete.

JOHN REED TO SUNDAY REED, 1934[2]

THE REEDS' FIRST CIRCLE OF ARTISTIC FRIENDS comprised those John had met through Clarice Zander (Fred and Puss Ward, Reg and Mancell Ellery, Vivian and Sunny Ebbott) and those they met through Sam Atyeo and Cynthia Reed (Moya Dyring, Edward Dyason, H.V. and Mary Alice Evatt). Nor did the first circle congregate at Heide but in South Yarra where the Reeds lived after they married. By the time the Reeds moved to Heide in 1935, the group had virtually dispersed.

For the Reeds, the first circle signalled the start of a culturally committed, communally oriented life, shared with artists and those interested in modern art. It also revealed the tensions rife in such intimate friendships. For Sunday, the first circle marked the beginning of her commitment to modernism. Equally, it was a time of growing self-confidence for her as an aspiring artist, a patron and a collector, and as a sexually independent woman embarking on her first affair.

When Sunday and John returned from their honeymoon, they moved to 4 Stonnington Place, Toorak, before settling in fashionable South Yarra. They rented 27 Marne Street while looking for a permanent home. The two-storey house, built around 1910, was divided into two maisonettes in a street graced by Fawkner Park at one end and the Royal Botanic Gardens at the other.[3]

Sunny, comfortable and attractive, it included a large living room and a dining room downstairs, together with a smallish kitchen, while upstairs was a big bedroom with an ensuite, a second bedroom that Sunday used as her studio, and the maid's quarters. The entrance had a fanlight over the door and glass panels on either side, as did Heide. The backyard was cobbled with bluestone. It was probably the most modern place in which either Sunday or John had lived. As they were renting, they could not make structural changes but they could assemble their burgeoning art collection.

The Reeds had already started buying modern art. It was one of their earliest acts as a couple and it was Sunday who lead the way. In December 1930, they visited Adrian Lawlor's first exhibition at Joshua McClelland's Little Gallery in Collins Street. It was John's first recollection of a modern art show in Melbourne and 'it drew so little public attention that I cannot even remember anyone writing an abusive letter to the press about it'.[4]

Born in London in 1889, the son of domestic servants, Lawlor emigrated to Australia in 1910. By 1922, he was reviewing Nietzsche for the *Bulletin*, extolling the German philospher's writings as 'the bible of my visionary youth'.[5] In 1916, Lawlor made a marriage of convenience with Eva Nodrum, a woman twenty years his senior, who had substantial holdings in her family's tannery business. The impecunious Lawlor's economic freedom was now secured. After an unhappy stint of working in the tannery office, Lawlor set out with the grand ambition to be a voice that mattered in Australian cultural life.

He became a champion for modernism's cause as a painter and a critic, emerging in the Melbourne art world as a literate and cultured commentator on the arts, a satiric and independent writer who eloquently described the battle between the conservatives and the moderns in the late 1930s. Lawlor's artistic career charts the history of that battle with military precision.

In a series of spectacular exhibitions between 1930 and 1940, Lawlor produced over five hundred paintings that explored modernism through landscapes, still lifes, portraits and abstracts. If, on the final count, Lawlor's paintings amount less to a satisfying and original oeuvre than to a series of set-pieces on modernism's formal problems, the effort was heroic. Lawlor was forty-one when he began to paint.

The Reeds got to know Lawlor through Fred Ward who had met him at Yencken's. William Frater, head of the stained-glass department, was Ward's boss: he was also Lawlor's friend and painting companion. Visiting his show the Reeds 'were both excited by the whole lively atmosphere, not the least of which was Adrian Lawlor himself from whose mouth words poured in a continuous stream ... We felt immediately involved and wanted to buy something; but neither of us had much money ... we hesitated until Sunday took the plunge and *Enjoying Life* became our first modern painting.' But its fate was due to the Reeds' generosity. 'Unfortunately it is lost – we lent it to a friend and it disappeared.' The subject, 'a scene in a Paris street café', no doubt had fond memories for Sunday. The work was 'charming, gay and free ... the very opposite of academicism'. The Reeds admired Lawlor, as a man and an artist, who 'blasted the forces of reaction'.[6]

Lawlor's exhibition was hailed by George Bell, the *Sun's* influential critic, as 'the first one man show by a local artist' of modern art and Lawlor 'earns many congratulations on his bravery in doing the unpardonable'. The work had technical limitations but Bell was prepared to overlook that because Lawlor communicated some of 'the exciting possibilities of modernism'.[7] But as far as Arthur Streeton was concerned, there was nothing over which to enthuse and 'nothing that is new and hardly anything that is beautiful or of artistic intent'. He damned the show as 'a dull exposition of how one may waste time'.[8] Lawlor, no stranger to self-promotion, claimed his 1930 show was 'the wildest thing that Melbourne had so far seen, and there were some shocking battles fought in celebrating the event ... after all this was Melbourne's first "modern" show'.[9]

For the first time, Sunday had the opportunity to identify her taste with modern art and to see it in a critical context as Bell lauded the show and Streeton dismissed it. The differences between Bell and Streeton in their reviews marked the start of the bloody battle between the moderns and the conservatives for art world dominance that would be fought out during the 1930s and '40s and in which Sunday would be actively engaged.

Enjoying Life was hung at Marne Street, its very title celebrating the Reeds' new-found happiness as a married couple. They also formed a friendship with Lawlor and with his lover Connie Smith, another advocate of modern art.[10] They bought several more of his paintings including *Still Life* (1933, Heide Museum of Modern Art), a touching *Portrait of John* (c.1938, Heide MoMA) and an astute *Self Portrait* (1938, Heide MoMA) that details Lawlor's remarkable features and keen intelligence. Lawlor's big, balding head is covered by a rakishly angled hat: his eyes are watchful, the mouth set and unsmiling as he discloses a face of character, depth and sculptural form. Lawlor, nearing fifty when he painted his portrait, did not trivialise his self-image with superficial flatteries. He presents himself – with tremendous self-consciousness and more than a whiff of bohemian panache – as an intellectual, a man of the mind. In 1938, John opened Lawlor's exhibition at Riddell's Gallery, titled 'Abstract Paintings', that earned praise from Bell and enlightened *Herald* critic Basil Burdett.

What did Sunday find in Lawlor's early work that encouraged her to 'take the plunge'? Because Lawlor suffered the tragic loss of the bulk of his oeuvre in 1939 when the Black Friday bushfires destroyed his Warrandyte home, few of his paintings remain. But Bell's review offers the crucial impact of Lawlor's show: it looked new, different and provocative – modern. Discerning what was fresh, unusual and original in an artist's vision, and thereby discerning cultural change, was Sunday's project and it began with Lawlor.

Nor can Lawlor's personality be excluded from the equation. Sunday was attracted to vitality, exuberance and confidence, both in an artist's temperament and in their artwork. In that sense it could be said she was easily seduced.

Lawlor had discovered his talents as a modernist painter courtesy of Frater and Arnold Shore. They 'took to tramping about the Parnassian hills of Warrandyte in the company of a congenial spirit from the south of France named Paul Cézanne . . . and covering thousands of yards of posh canvas with impasto, gusto and good intentions'.[11] Cézanne's emphasis on form and structure, on the abstract scaffolding of art, also directed Bell and Arnold Shore when they started their art school in 1932.

Cézanne's post-impressionism emerged as the first clear statement by Melbourne's early modernists. It was an art of reduction, where the form was subjected to a rigorous analysis that ignored painting's traditional three-dimensional pictorial illusion, privileged the brush-stroke and emphasised the flatness of the picture plane. It eschewed narrative, symbolism, romanticism and literary qualities. Modernism could not be understood without appreciating the revolutionary nature of Cézanne's work.

Enjoying Life, from John's description, sounds cheerful and decorative. Lawlor was a good colourist if a rather heavy-handed painter. Due to his lack of training – he abandoned classes at the Gallery School – Lawlor's grasp of the human form could be clumsy and unsure. But he made up in boldness for what he lacked in control and tuition. Sunday was particularly responsive to artists who had abandoned formal art training and Lawlor, as well as Vassilieff, Nolan and Hester, fitted that category. She had found the regimentation of school destructive to her own creative sensibilities and the rebels who were temperamentally at odds with academic expectations, who were by personality or choice outlaws of the system, who sought spontaneity and freedom of expression, were her artistic ideals and desired companions.

But the man who meant most to the Reeds, who disrupted their lives, who challenged, instructed, seduced and abandoned them was Sam Atyeo. He was the 'catalyst' and John recognised that meeting Atyeo was 'crucial to my whole life and, I believe, to Sunday's'.[12] Years later John told Atyeo, 'Our lives then took on a new dimension, which has persisted ever since.'[13] Atyeo returned the favour. 'I suppose you two have had the biggest influence on my life of all.'[14]

Atyeo, like Lawlor, was a gifted, working-class lad busy pulling himself up by his boot straps. The son of a chauffeur, Atyeo had grown up in Coburg, an industrial suburb in Melbourne's west. Lawlor married money to end his penury while Atyeo attracted a series of illustrious patrons including the Reeds, Edward Dyason, Louise Hanson Dyer and H.V. Evatt – none of whom, unfortunately, helped his art in the long run. Atyeo's was to be a brief but brilliant moment in Australian art and by the time he reached Paris in 1936, his extraordinary confidence evaporated and he went on to pursue two unlikely careers, first as an international diplomat, under Evatt's wing, and then as a rose-grower in Provence.

In 1932 Atyeo was a star pupil at the Gallery School and had carried off a swag of prizes. He was an ebullient and argumentative larrikin, 'perpetually restless and active, articulate and never satisfied to passively accept authority'.[15] Dark-haired and thickset with a large nose and protruding ears, Atyeo's unprepossessing looks were more than compensated for by his overwhelming charm, hubris and energy.

Atyeo also proved inspiring to George Johnston who based the character of Sam Burlington, the artist in *My Brother Jack*, on him.

'Sam Burlington adored talking; he handled words with the comic skill of a vaudeville juggler tossing Indian clubs; he loved to play with puns and flowery phrases and ludicrous images; he had that overflowing confidence in words, in verbal sleight-of-hand.'[16]

Not only did Atyeo educate the Reeds in the syncopated rhythms of jazz and the latest art and criticism but he initiated them as patrons, revealing what it meant to fully commit themselves to an artist's needs and dreams. Atyeo would be, like Nolan, an animating force in their marriage, bringing illumination and pain. With Atyeo the Reeds were introduced to, and accepted, a bitter-sweet equation: that the price of a deep, fulfilling, collaborative relationship with an artist would include jealousy, anguish and turmoil.

Atyeo got to know the Reeds just as his star was on the rise. He had upset the judging panel for the School's 1932 Travelling Scholarship competition by his painting A Gentle Admonition (Lot admonishing his daughters). Cocking a snook at authority, Atyeo had portrayed the naked Lot as Bernard Hall, director of the Gallery and its school. Hall was outraged. A forbidding personality with deeply conservative tastes, Hall refused to allow Atyeo's painting to be hung.

In December 1932, Fred Ward and Cynthia Reed came to Atyeo's rescue when Atyeo arranged to display Lot in the front window of Ward's Collins Street shop for all of Melbourne to see. Ward knew Atyeo through Yencken's stained glass where Atyeo was designing leadlights and it was Ward who introduced Atyeo to Cynthia and the Reeds. Bell wanted to rub Hall's nose in the scandal and reviewed Lot, commending Atyeo on his 'courage of individual thought and action against the odds'.[17]

The incident caused a media outcry, exactly the kind of fracas Atyeo welcomed. One of Atyeo's supporters was Clarice Zander

who wrote a letter to the press querying Atyeo's exclusion, defending modern art and remarking, 'Mr Atyeo's intention seems . . .
serious.'[18] The enterprising Zander had returned from London with
an exhibition of British Contemporary Art that would open in
Melbourne in March before travelling to Sydney. Already Zander,
Ward and Cynthia were making plans for the exhibition's installation and display.

Cynthia, nicknamed Bob, had returned from Europe early in
1932, probably for John and Sunday's wedding. She had wandered
from London to Germany trying to find work and a niche for her
mercurial personality. Her European sojourn made her believe she
could never make a permanent home in Australia. Unlike Arthur
Baillieu, Henry Reed had no intention of supporting his difficult
daughter and Cynthia, independent and unchaperoned, made her
way alone. Seven years younger than John, she was bright, witty
and unpredictable with a sharp tongue and a consummate sense of
style. Patrick White dubbed her 'a kingfisher of the spirit' but
admitted 'Cynthia was difficult.'[19]

There was an agonised undercurrent to Cynthia's personality.
The Tasmanian years had cut deep into her psyche, making her feel
both wounded and bitter about the politics of family life: the depth
of her hurt and desire for revenge would find its expression in her
novel *Daddy Sowed a Wind!* (1947), a grotesque portrait of her family.
In caustically frank and occasionally abject letters to John and
Sunday, Cynthia described lonely peregrinations, terrifying mood
swings and masochistic love affairs. In darker moments, she hinted
at the possibility of suicide. Cynthia mused that her relationships
failed because 'there's too much smell of hell about me'.[20]

Settling in Melbourne, Cynthia soon established close and affectionate bonds with Sunday and John. When she was sufficiently

amused and relaxed, Cynthia could be excellent company. But John and Sunday remained anxious about her temperament and sought psychiatrist Reg Ellery's opinion. Ellery advised John that Cynthia was 'a pretty difficult case and, like all of us, thinks she has first got to come to earth and face realities before she can hope to be really happy'.[21]

The quest for Cynthia, as for Sunday, was how to manage her talents. Though Cynthia had literary ambitions, she had not yet published, perhaps due to fierce self-criticism as much as a lack of confidence. Nor did she, in her many European letters to John during the late 1920s, display any interest in art. It makes her partnership with Fred Ward, and her brief excursion into promoting, making and studying modernist art and design, a surprising one.

In 1932, Cynthia worked in Ward's shop where she organised an exhibition of prints by Sydney modernists Thea Proctor and Margaret Preston. Cynthia cut a dash. She not only looked 'very slim and chic' but proved an 'an excellent mistress of ceremonies' at gallery openings. Her flat at Alcaston House in Collins Street (where Basil Burdett also lived) was 'the most intriguing place. Terribly modern, but with a restfulness which comes from having masses of books and flowers everywhere ... Hand-stamped and woven linens form the curtains and brightly covered felt covers the floor.'[22]

Early in 1933, she opened Cynthia Reed's Modern Furnishings at 367 Little Collins Street, which she ran irregularly for the next two years. Sam Atyeo, Adrian Lawlor and Ian Fairweather exhibited there and Cynthia also showed the fabrics of Michael O'Connell. It seemed the stimulating atmosphere created by Ward, Atyeo and the Reeds had a fertile effect. Cynthia had only a small income to invest in her shop – money was always a problem for her and she scraped by. While Mary Alice Evatt believed that Cynthia and John had 'put part of their inheritance' into the shop, it is more likely that Sunday, after receiving an inheritance from her mother's will late in 1932, helped fund the enterprise.[23] It was not until Henry Reed's death in 1956 that John received an inheritance.

Cynthia insisted she had 'kicked Atyeo out of the gutter' but the voraciously ambitious Atyeo did not need Cynthia's help to make his way in the world.[24] He was, however, grateful to show *Lot* and gain attention for it in Ward's shop. It marked the beginning of his complex relationship with Cynthia and the Reeds. Through Atyeo, Sunday also met Gallery School graduate Moya Dyring, Atyeo's girlfriend. Other friends from that time included dentist and art collector Vivian Ebbott and his wife Sunny.

Late 1932 was an exciting time for Sunday as her new life began to take shape. She found herself surrounded by a group of restless, gifted, articulate people who were keenly following the latest developments in international contemporary culture, who were united in their criticism of conservative art, politics and lifestyle and who were firing one another's ambitions.

But it was also a period undercut with mourning and loss. In November, Sunday's mother Ethel died from cancer. It was not sudden. She had been ill for three years. What had started as breast cancer spread to her spine and throat. As Ethel's health deteriorated, she and Arthur quit Balholmen and moved into a smaller, more manageable apartment at Fairlie House. One of the reasons Sunday and John moved to Marne Street may have been its access to Fairlie House, which was virtually around the corner.

Sunday was with her mother at the end and confided to Hester her trauma when 'my own gentle little mother died . . . crying and

I would like to speak of it but it is painful for me'.[25] It widened the gap between Sunday and the men in her family: Ethel's ameliorating feminine presence was no longer there to act as a buffer. Alone with the men, Sunday could feel trapped and sought John's protection. 'I adore Dad and the boys,' she wrote, 'but they do so often depress me. I need you as a lightning conductor . . . I miss you. I will be glad in so many ways to be with you again.'[26] Ethel's death marked another step away from her family and her class.

Sunday's commitment to modern art encompassed more than being a collector. She wanted to be an artist and, soon after its foundation, she joined the Bell-Shore School.

The school, started in February 1932, was housed in the Salisbury Buildings at the corner of Bourke and Queen streets in two large, light, airy, top-floor rooms. Maie Casey recalls, 'there was an unstable coke stove to keep pupils and the occasional model warm, and an unstable lift, fortunately circled by a wooden stairway'.[27]

A competent academic painter, Bell had not only discarded his traditional style, he had become a crusader for modern art. As Bell announced dramatically, he saw the light.[28] Through his activities as a critic, teacher, painter and organiser in the '30s, Bell did his best to tear asunder the smug success and hidebound assumptions of the art establishment. He was well-fitted for the job. Highly principled, authoritative and eloquent, Bell achieved a quiet revolution in the Melbourne art world, one that eventually overtook and discarded him.

Bell and the gentler, less combative Shore were running the only school in Melbourne that taught the principles of modernism. Bell provoked strong feelings and many of his students adored him. During the '30s the best were a diverse group including Russell

Drysdale, Sali Herman, Yvonne Atkinson, David Strachan, Maie Casey and Peter Purves Smith. Drysdale, Bell's favourite student, believed that it was Bell's knowledge of abstract composition, derived from Cézanne, together with the technical craft of painting that made him such an inspiring teacher.

Bell's attitude was critical, detached and bracing. He despised dabblers. The school was a dedicated community of modernists where all shared in the aesthetic excitement. 'No-one knew the game as thoroughly [as Bell] – others were glorified amateurs.'[29] Bell wasn't called 'the Boss' for nothing. Even Bell's most admiring students admitted that he could be overbearing. 'He didn't like you to argue or talk back.'[30] Students either 'followed him or went under, with no compromise. "Will you discipline yourself or shall I do it?" Bell asked.'[31]

Maie Casey recalled that at first 'Bell had little to do with me. He was concerned with the serious talent that came to the school.'[32] But when the school opened, there was not much serious talent around. Drysdale was there for two months in 1932 but, baffled by modern art and Bell's dictums, hastily departed. He would return three years later. Bell himself only knew modernism from reproductions. In 1934, he travelled to London to study at Iain McNab's Grosvenor School of Modern Art. But by then, Sunday had left the school and relinquished painting.

Between 1932–34, Sunday's co-students were a mixed bunch that included Casey, Eveline Syme, Yvonne Atkinson, Joan Yonge, Jessie Mackintosh and Alan Sumner together with a gaggle of socialites and 'a lot of old ladies'.[33] All were at varying levels of competence.

Yvonne Atkinson was only sixteen when she started and 'dreadfully self-conscious'. She 'slogged away for a year' at drawing before 'touching a painting'.[34] Joan Yonge was eighteen and, during her first term, she waited for the awful moment each day when she must cross the room to where 'miles away, was a little sink where we took our brushes to wash. Every footstep I took I felt I was going to trip.'[35] Alan Sumner was an ambitious young man recommended by Frater, his boss at Yencken's, a stone's throw from the school. Sumner became a faithful follower of Bell's for the rest of his life, promoting Bell's principles as director of the Gallery School in the 1950s. Elegant and talented Maie Casey was married to federal treasurer R.G. Casey and attended the school on visits from Canberra.

Due to the school's small size, the atmosphere was relaxed and comradely. Students could attend whenever they liked and, apart from weekly composition sessions, there was no set routine, no course as such. But Sunday made no lasting connections or friendships. More tellingly, she did not buy paintings by Bell, Shore or any of the artists associated with her teachers or their principles. It was a clear-cut rejection of Bell and Shore's attitudes towards art, one that shaped her taste, finding expression in the artists she drew around her and in the collection she built. School had never suited Sunday, even a school of modern art. But for her to attend and subject herself to other people's rules indicates how much the study of art meant to her.

What did Bell teach Sunday? Bell was eminently practical and his students received an excellent grounding in their craft. First, they drew from the model, emphasising three-dimensional form and volume. The untutored started with conte, charcoal and crayon and Bell decided when they could pick up the brush. He guided students in 'how to use the tools of the trade, how and what to draw and paint with, how to glaze, how to build up, how to discard and reject. Form was the base of his teaching and colour was used to reinforce form.' But there was more to Bell's teaching than mere practicalities. 'He taught us to be brave.'[36]

For those who did not wish to submit to Bell's rules, the school was also a lively meeting-place and a centre for ideas. While Sunday was a pupil, both Atyeo and Dyring were regular visitors, so were Basil Burdett and also John Reed. Mary Alice Evatt was an occasional student in 1936–37 and H.V. Evatt would arrive for vigorous discussions with Bell.

Bell's patrician, Toorak background was similar to Sunday's – he had previously run classes at his Selborne Road home – and the women who attended his school were often the nicely brought-up ladies from Sunday's world. The influx of socialites looking for amusement at the start of each term was a direct result of Bell's Toorak profile. At a costly four guineas for a term's tuition, the school was not for the impoverished.

Bell had scant respect for women students though his classes, like those of the Gallery School, overflowed with them. Sunday, who was distancing herself from Toorak and the proper, polite roles for women enshrined by her class, must have felt uncomfortable surrounded by such women. Bell himself was another big, opinionated, upper-class male, like those in her family, the kind of man who made her feel silenced and diminished. Though Sunday finally left the school and abandoned art, personal animosity and class irritations were not the only factors.

Sunday did not believe she was sufficiently talented. The impatient struggle to succeed to her own standards was too great and she destroyed all her work, except for one small drawing. Even that was screwed up, ready to be thrown out, before being saved and carefully smoothed, perhaps by hands other than her own. Nor did

Sunday ever discuss her art training with friends of later decades. None knew she had studied art because she never told them and no examples of her work were seen at Heide. It's as though she were ashamed of both her effort and her failure. Sunday, the meticulous conservator, who treasured mementos from all periods of her life, did not choose to similarly honour her own work. Uncharacteristically, and deliberately, she ditched the lot.

Sunday's tough choice meant that, in later years, she had no qualms about delivering brutally frank opinions on an artist's work. If she felt that John Perceval was missing the mark or that Neil Douglas was better suited to activities other than painting, she would not hesitate to say so. She had been as harsh on herself.

Landscape (c.1933, Private Collection) was probably an exercise set by Bell and based on a plein air sketch by Sunday. It is a controlled, strongly realised drawing with a clear sense of design and structure and a lively, balanced tonal range of greens and blues. It is both a modernist statement and a perfectly adequate accomplishment for an art student early in her training. Interestingly, Sunday takes as her subject a beautiful landscape, exactly the kind of gentle, verdant countryside of rolling hills, water and tended fields that attracted her to the Yarra Valley and Heide.

Sunday has drawn the landscape from a bird's-eye perspective and subjected it to the principles of form and structure she learned at Bell's. That is, the whole was more important than the details, an overall rhythmic design must dominate and unify all elements and colour becomes an integral, harmonious part of the composition, aiding the structure. Sunday flattened the perspective, reduced fussy details to a minimum and composed the design in terms of interlocking semi-circles. The eye is lead into the drawing from the road at the bottom which snakes up to the house in the middle left and from there to the yellow fields and beyond, along a rank of serried trees, to the lake and the sky in the distance.

Landscape may not be a great work of art but it is certainly not a failure. A deliberately realised exercise in shape and form, its best quality is its sensitive use of colour. By arranging the lighter shades in the centre, Sunday centralised the composition, distributing darker areas to the sides to achieve an impression of space, depth and airiness. Sunday studied the natural world for its hues, then quantified colour to convey a sense of abstract pattern. In the smooth, undulating terrain, with its folding s-shaped hills echoing into the distance, she captured the earth's curve. Such close observation of the landscape would stand her in good stead when she came to design the garden at Heide.

Landscape's decorative qualities link it less to Cézanne's 'classical modernism' and more to the schematised designs of printmaker Claude Flight who taught at Iain MacNab's Grosvenor School of Modern Art. Eveline Syme, a co-student of Sunday's, a friend of Bell's and a member of his Contemporary Group, had studied under Flight in 1929. In the same year, she attended André Lhote's school in Paris where a palatable form of realistic, geometric cubism was taught. When Syme returned to Melbourne, she exhibited her modernist linocuts at Everyman's Library in Little Collins Street, winning the attention of Bell. Her co-exhibitors included Eric Thake, Nutter Buzacott, Michael O'Connell and Fred Ward.[37] Sunday visited the show: it was held in the same month, and at the same end of town, as Lawlor's first exhibition, plus it was the only time that the multi-talented Ward exhibited art.

Flight's pictorial aim was to build geometric patterns of opposing rhythms by 'combining and simplifying [form] after very careful analysis and [by] the suppression of unnecessary details'.[38] Syme, and her close friend Ethel Spowers who studied with her in London and Paris, explored modernism's decorative possibilities in their prints. Bell, aware of Flight due to Syme's evangelical zeal, decided to study at MacNab's when he went London at the end of 1934. Jessie Mackintosh was another painter-printmaker alongside Sunday at Bell's who was influenced by Flight's principles. It would have been difficult for Sunday not to have been aware of the effect of Flight's work and teachings on Syme and Mackintosh.

Flight, MacNab and Bell were, however, all teaching the same principles: abstract pattern based on form. All had been influenced by Roger Fry, instigator of the pioneering post-impressionism exhibition at London's Grafton Galleries in 1910. Fry was modernism's effusive apologist. His soothing interpretation of modern art in *Vision and Design* was nothing more threatening than 'a return to the ideas of formal design'. It was a diplomatic position that suited Bell. Indeed *Vision and Design* is one long plea for situating modern art as the saviour of 'a whole lost language of form'.[39]

When Sunday went searching for books and reproductions of modern art, they were not difficult to find in the hub of bohemian inner Melbourne. Gino Nibbi's Leonardo bookshop at 170 Little Collins Street was more than just a place to browse. A refugee from Mussolini's Italy, the genial, tubby, moon-faced Nibbi was a sophisticated commentator on cultural issues. In Rome, Nibbi had been familiar with a circle of artists and intellectuals that included de Chirico, and he arrived in Australia with paintings by de Chirico, Severini and Moise Kisling under his arm. The Reeds became good friends with Nibbi. The Leonardo wasn't the only place to find modern art prints and books in Melbourne – there was Primrose Pottery and the Bookshop of Margareta Weber – but it was by far the liveliest.

At Marne Street, Sunday set up her studio in a small, south-facing room she dubbed the playroom, a name redolent with connotations of the nursery, childhood games, fun and creativity. Indeed, childhood *meant* creativity to Sunday so while her studio's name light-heartedly poked fun at the serious business of making art, symbolically it linked art with the freshness and spontaneity of a child – a source Sunday sought to tap in her art studies, and that eluded her. Sunday was experimenting with watercolours and, by mid-1933, had begun to paint with oils. When she did, it proved a major hurdle.

Also, the kind of instruction, and the forms of modernism itself, available in Melbourne in the early 1930s were not consonant with the aesthetic vision that most intrigued Sunday. Art that was expressionist, poetic, raw, hallucinatory, spontaneous, allusive, humanist and touchingly emotional captivated her in the late 1930s and early 1940s in the work of Arthur Boyd, John Perceval, Joy Hester, Sidney Nolan and Albert Tucker. But the tenor of early Melbourne modernism was much more formal: an inability to discover an adequate means of expressing such fundamental interests was perhaps another reason for quitting art.

Art seemed an all or nothing exercise for Sunday. She didn't choose to dabble, as her mother had, as did many women of her class who had been taught to draw by governesses and who continued to enjoy art as a pleasurable hobby. The Bell School and the Gallery School were full of such dilettantes but Sunday had no intention of being an amateur. She wanted to be an artist. If she could not do that, then she must apply her talents elsewhere.

John lost his taste for Bell, too, perhaps encouraged by Sunday. Unwillingly he visited the school, on Sunday's instructions, to advise Shore that Sunday was interstate. He reported that 'the studio was full of frightful looking women with hair all over their faces — I mean moustaches & things — & simpering girls, with old George looking on as sour as a sack of onions & not even bothering to recognise me. Arnold hopped up from the table where he & Jock Frater & some more women were feeding and greeted me very cheerfully ... & said he was quite sure you wouldn't be able to help doing some work while you were away.'⁴⁰

But the person who gave Sunday the most encouragement and who, ironically, did more to alienate her from her artistic ambitions was Atyeo. He had fallen head over heels in love with Sunday and, in a torrent of advice, ideas and praise, incited her to greater endeavours. They began a complicated affair, conducted with John's knowledge and Moya Dyring's acceptance. Later, Dyring and John would have an affair. Cynthia, who also admired Atyeo and was a friend of Dyring's, became jealous of Sunday's dominance of their small group. The claustrophobic intimacies of the first circle presaged a way of life for the Reeds that continued for the next fifteen years.

The very quality of Atyeo's work must have shown Sunday the difference between the competent hobbyist and the gifted professional. In an early letter Atyeo assured her, 'I'll be a tremendous painter ... You must work too Sun and we'll be sitting on the top rung together.'⁴¹ Not only did he tell her 'how much I wanted her to paint and how to laugh at all the terrible horribleness she is sure to commit at the start' but, on a practical level, also advised where to get the best easel — 'at the National Gallery from Mr Roberts gallery carpenter it will cost thirty shillings'.⁴² He planned painting excursions for the two of them — 'I know we'll have a lovely time in the Mallee, paint all day and get marvellously tired and sit by a whopping fire' — and gave her detailed exercises to complete.⁴³

'Paint the sky blue, the tree green, the house blue grey (or cream) the fence yellow grey – the road warm ochre, the patch in the bottom right hand corner green. Hill behind blue, paint it simply and try to make the colours sing in harmony, decide what is to be your darkest colour and which is to be your lightest. That is a very important thing Sun to have enough dark in your picture to give significance to your light.'[44]

Atyeo told Sunday his reservations about Bell's school which was 'good for grey people to learn to paint – like they would go somewhere to learn to ride a bike . . . there is something of which you have (and if I were not writing this) I have, and you know and I know, these bloody grey people will never be able to realise never be aware of.' Atyeo continued, 'I hope you have painted, though I suppose the limitations are tremendous. Grey people asking you what you have done and why you have done and how you have done and can't you have done [better] . . . I want to show you lots about colour, and am looking forward to seeing you paint in oils – people don't live until they paint.'[45]

The problem, Atyeo recognised, was that while he and John 'have got tremendous faith in you, you haven't got any faith in yourself at all . . . you must have faith in yourself.' Sunday was 'a very fragile flower'.[46] But Atyeo believed 'Sun has to work, Sun has got to . . . and work with her teeth feet hands body and the first few attempts will make her cry, she'll get terribly depressed and then things will be easier. If Sun doesn't, I have to go along by myself. That will be a lonely business.'[47]

Such words must have been tremendously heartening. Sunday admired Atyeo as Melbourne's best modern painter and he was offering her a compact: they were a team, they were artists together. Sunday told Atyeo to 'go into the playroom & breathe on all my brushes & canvas – they must be lonely without me.' That wasn't all. She instructed John to 'tell Sam to *paint*' – and underlined the word seven times.[48] Sunday may have needed an artist at the centre of her life but, equally, Atyeo needed her by his side as a fellow painter of comparable abilities with whom he could share his life and work, his talented and sensitive companion. Yet despite Atyeo's protestations – 'I'm terribly sorry to hear of your repeated failures in paint Sun don't give in now for God's sake' – Sunday ceased making art.[49]

Between 1933 and 1936, Atyeo was Melbourne's most inventive and spirited modernist, experimenting with a number of different styles and settling for none of them. He had no time for the Bell School and had the independence of mind to create a separate arena for his version of modernism. It was a stand that influenced the Reeds and was another factor drawing them away from Bell. The Gallery School had proved too narrow a stage for Atyeo's talents and he, like so many other ambitious young moderns, was teaching himself via reproductions. Until Clarice Zander's exhibition of British Contemporary Art there was very little modern art to see.

After following Will Dyson to London, Zander got a job as manager at Rex Nan Kivell's Redfern Gallery. Zander's show announced itself as the first attempt to provide Australia with a comprehensive coverage of modern English art and it attracted over 5000 people in Melbourne. It was a fine array of major talent that included Augustus John, Matthew Smith, Vanessa Bell, Duncan Grant, Paul Nash, Ben Nicholson, Walter Richard Sickert and sculptor Jacob Epstein.

Displayed at Newspaper House in Collins Street in March 1933, Zander, Ward and Cynthia devised ingenious ideas for installation. Not content with a conventional display, paintings were hung in front of Ward's furniture or, in the case of an Epstein bust, resting on a Ward table made from Australian timber. It cleverly showcased modern art by relating it to modern design, seeking to identify a unified aesthetic. Fabric designer Michael O'Connell, who had exhibited with Ward at Everyman's Gallery along with Eveline Syme, hung his sumptuous hand-printed curtains at the windows. Cynthia contributed, too. She had designed a corner cupboard, influenced by Ward's clean, simple lines. All the furniture was available from her new shop at 367 Little Collins Street.

Zander's exhibition also provided the Reeds with an opportunity to buy, for the first and only time, international works for their collection: Epstein's watercolour *Sunita* (c.1925, National Gallery of Victoria) and a cubist etching by Ben Nicholson, *Still Life* (1928, Heide MoMA). As works on paper neither were especially expensive and John and Sunday, putting their money aside to buy their first home, were watching their pennies. While daringly voluptuous, *Sunita* is a graceless, clumsy work, lacking a coherent sense of form or colour. It was a bad choice. John reflected tactfully that 'though [*Sunita*] does not often see the light of day, I am still happy to see her when she does.'[50] Why did the Reeds choose these works?

Epstein was a controversial artist, his sculptural works receiving praise and damnation in equal measure from the English press. The public monument for which he attracted the most attention, and that was vandalised several times, was the 1925 statue of Rima in Hyde Park. Rima was the heroine of W.H. Hudson's novel *Green Mansions*, Sunday's 'book of dreams'. Sunday would have known of the public debates surrounding the statue. Perhaps it was a reason for buying *Sunita*, a way of supporting the embattled Epstein. In April 1932, to learn more about the artist, they bought Epstein and Arnold Haskell's *The Sculptor Speaks* (1931).

Sunita Peerbhoy, the model for the work, is rather more interesting than the many works Epstein produced of her. In the mid-1920s Sunita, her sister and her son Enver lived with Epstein and his family. A tall, strikingly beautiful young woman from Kashmir, Sunita had left her husband and run away to England where she and her sister joined a troupe of magicians called the Maysculine Brothers. Her act involved sitting in a glass tank completely immersed in water for five minutes, a trick performed with the aid of a translucent macaroni tube. Another sideline in survival was selling exotic trinkets at a stall which the sisters set up at the Wembley International Exhibition and it was there that Epstein met, and was entranced by her.[51]

Ben Nicholson was exploring abstraction, the same direction Atyeo would follow later that year in *Organised Line to Yellow* (c.1933, National Gallery of Australia), and it may have been Atyeo's excitement about Nicholson's fine, geometric abstraction that encouraged the purchase. Whatever the enthusiasms that lead the Reeds to buy these two works, it did not encourage them to commit themselves to international modernism. Quite the reverse. The Heide collection would be a determinedly Australian one, comprising the artists Sunday and John felt were conveying a uniquely Australian modernism.

The influence of the English exhibition on Atyeo was apparent in his first solo show at Modern Furnishings in June where colour and energy are hallmarks. But Atyeo was his own man and refused to be overwhelmed even if Matthew Smith's luscious palette may have enticed a more sensuous tonal range in his paintings. Writing about Zander's show, Burdett noted Smith was 'the most vital of "the moderns" . . . whose conception of colour showed a separate outlook from the rest of the show'. He was 'the finest English colourist of his day'.[52] But for Atyeo the real spur was to see English art and measure himself against it. For his efforts, Bell congratulated him as 'an artist brave enough to work out his own salvation'.[53]

Norfolk Island Pine (1933, NGA) was painted at Metung in Gippsland where Atyeo was holidaying with Dyring. He provided the Reeds with a sketch, saying 'this is a picture I painted on Saturday of a big pine tree on a cliff, against the sea, with you and John in the foreground, you are reading and John is looking out to sea. John should be well satisfied with himself, as I am sure it is his only way to posterity.'[54] The tree, created in a whirl of brushstrokes and sharp angles, dominates the composition which also includes the figures of John and Sunday in a sentimental 'luncheon on the grass', a staple of impressionist painting.

Later in the year, Atyeo honoured a promise made to Sunday when he took the Reeds camping in the Mallee and the result, *Wyperfeld National Park* (1933–34, Heide MoMA), is a work of greater energy, confidence and modernist intent. The light impressionist brushstroke has changed to dense painterly marks and a stronger, more turbulent composition, reminiscent of Wyndham Lewis' Vorticist paintings and the 1920s landscapes of Paul Nash. Naturalistic depth is abandoned as Atyeo forces sky, trees and earth into a flatter, more pictorial space.

Atyeo made the break with *Organised Line to Yellow* (c.1933, NGA) which he showed in Bell's 1934 Contemporary Group exhibition. It was the first abstract work exhibited in Melbourne, and Sunday snapped it up. Taking such a risk was a perilous exercise and Atyeo unburdened himself to the Reeds. 'I have risked everything, burnt my bridges. I have painted a very big abstract thing. It is nearly very good. It may be a terribly good painting. Christ I hope it is. I am going to be a big big painter when I paint I feel something very big.

So big I don't care about anything, my body, money, anything &
when I come to I think of you. I can't say anymore than that.'[55]

Atyeo told Basil Burdett *Organised Line to Yellow* had been inspired
by a variety of sources including Bach's Double Fiddle Concerto
and Atyeo's reading of Hegel and Schopenhauer.[56] But surrealism
appears the core influence. From a labyrinth of delicate black lines,
against a yellow ground, two gentle creatures with bird-like heads
arise, the forms flowing in dual, asymmetrical rhythms. A brave and
tender painting with echoes of the playful abstractions of Paul Klee
and Joan Miró, it would have been at home in a French surrealist
show. In 1932 Atyeo had painted *Surrealist Head* (now lost) and
Herbert Read, his favourite art critic, promoted surrealism in his
book, *Art Now* (1933).

Art Now also reproduced several examples of the art whose sensibility matched Atyeo's — the elegant, geometric, transparent
constructions of Nikolaus Pevsner and Naum Gabo. Atyeo's *The
Thinker* (1933–35, Heide MoMA) elicits from the human body a
sculptural sense of form, even if the gigantic legs owe a debt to
Picasso's 1920s classical period. A controlled and contemplative
study, it counterpoints nicely the forceful emotion of its inspiration, Rodin's *Thinker* (1889). After *Organised Line to Yellow*, *The
Thinker* is Atyeo's best and boldest painting.

Herbert Read was another shared experience for Atyeo and the
Reeds. Together, they read *Art Now* which, John recalled, came as
'a bombshell to us'. The book had brought Atyeo into contact with
cubism and abstraction, causing him 'the most enormous excitement' which John was 'privileged to share as his friend'.[57] It 'gave
us the first comprehensive insight into the world of art.' Herbert
Read became the unflagging guiding spirit for John's theoretical
thinking, a 'sort of god father of modern art in Australia'.[58]

Aside from Read, John and Sunday were reading extensively about modern art, ploughing through Clive Bell; Roger Fry; Wyndham Lewis; *Savage Messiah* (1931), H.S. Ede's biography of Henri Gaudier-Breska; and R.H. Wilenski's *Outline of French Painting* (1932). It was the beginning of the Reeds' vast art library which would entrance their artist friends.

Sunday did not choose to express herself in writing as John did in the numerous articles, reviews and speeches he produced from the mid-'30s on. She was also a dismal correspondent, to the despair of her friends, choosing to write only to her intimates – Nolan, Hester and Jean Langley. It was John who dutifully answered the letters and maintained the Reeds' vast network of friendships by post. Nor was Sunday a theoretical thinker: immediacy and spontaneity were hallmarks of her sensibility. She read widely but privileged poetry and literature's primary texts rather than academic or critical commentaries.

Sunday 'always has a book of poems in her hand' though John 'very rarely' picked one up. He admitted, 'I have never, in any real sense, been able to read poetry.'[59] For Sunday 'the idea of original-ity was high on the agenda' but that rarely involved the exposition of theoretical positions.[60] What Sunday desired of her artists, and herself, was a creative expression that was well informed but authentically one's own.

Read, an effusive and learned English poet and critic, was breaking new ground in criticism. Aside from Roger Fry, whom he quoted extensively in *Art Now*, no other critic was attempting to formulate modernism's place in art history. *Art Now* is a carefully argued and moderately worded case for modernism as the contin-uation of culture. Read, like the Melbourne modernists, recognised that powerful conservative forces in the art world were primed to attack modernism's disruptive, confronting formal explorations, and he tried to assuage them. 'Everywhere is the same lack of unity, the same absence of authority, the same break with tradition.'[61] He contextualised modern art by drawing parallels with modern music and literature, and with philosophy. Art was not isolated: it was part of a new movement embracing all the arts.

Art's 'organic' quality – a concept borrowed from Fry – was a central idea of Read's, and one adopted enthusiastically by John and Sunday. Constructed as a positive way of measuring art's intention and success, a work's 'organic' quality meant its parts related well to the whole. Good art showed 'the rhythm expressive of organic life . . . the pervading sense of creative purpose [that] informs and animates the design'.[62] Slightly ridiculous though the notion of 'organic' art now seems, it is telling that the Reeds, whose lives were connected to the earth through Heide, were inspired by a word defining the interconnectedness of living things and one that also suggests what is natural, fundamental and instinctive – Sunday's idea of art exactly.

Three-dimensional work was a key influence for Atyeo in 1934–36, perhaps because he was forced to survive by designing furniture and textiles for Cynthia, Ward and Minna Schuyler and, under the auspices of Edward Dyason, architecture as well. While his work in this area was stylish and well-made, Atyeo regarded such jobs as blood money, complaining to Sunday, 'I'm making money helping Minna in Bob's shop. I hate making money. Oh I hate money Sunshine. See I have to put my painting away until I've made enough. I know you won't like that, still, Sun, understand.'[63] Schuyler wanted him to 'design some mats for her and she'll weave or needlework them'. But Atyeo preferred to work with Sunday. 'Can I design some things for you to do in needle colours on chairs and things? Do you want to?'[64]

Atyeo's solo show at Cynthia's had also provided him with the opportunity to meet patrons, including Dyason and the Evatts, who would shape his destiny.

H.V. Evatt arrived at the shop, probably on his wife Mary Alice's advice. At thirty-six, Evatt was the youngest man ever apppointed to the High Court which sat for six-week sessions in Melbourne. 'Doc' Evatt was a hugely intelligent man, an adventurous thinker already ambitious for his country and its culture. He and Mary Alice embroiled themselves in Melbourne's heated art politics, staunchly defending the moderns.

Evatt was also a hypochondriac who loathed the big, draughty hotel where he was installed during his Melbourne visits so Mary Alice found a comfortable apartment at Ardoch in Dandenong Road, Malvern. She was impressed by Cynthia's shop with its Van Gogh prints hanging in the window, and by Cynthia herself. Cynthia nicknamed Evatt 'Judgie' and treated him with a warm and friendly impertinence, while he dubbed her 'Skin-thia'.

Atyeo recalled 'in walks this old guy in butterfly collar, cravat, lavender waist coat, black tails, striped pants, button up boots and black Derby hat . . . He looked at me and said, pointing to one of the paintings, "Did you do that?" and added, "That's a good kick up the arse for the old guard."' The two went to lunch and Evatt asked Atyeo, 'What should I do about my dress if I truly look 40 years older than I should?'[65]

Atyeo took Evatt to a shop where they bought him a smart new outfit, apparently to Mary Alice's approval. It was the start of a long and productive friendship between the two men. Atyeo was 'a jester who could say to the judge what no-one else could say. He made Evatt laugh at stories that no-one else would have dared tell him.'[66]

The Evatts got to know the Reeds in 1934 and were occasional visitors to both Marne Street and Heide. Evatt was taken by Sunday whom he regarded as beautiful. John recalled it was 'a sort of free for all when we got together – Sam, Bert, Mary Alice, Sam's girl Moya, Cynthia, Sun and myself – perhaps also Allan Henderson [the Reeds' solicitor] and Vivian and Sunny Ebbott – all of us, excited . . . by our discussions, by the feeling of important things about to happen, by the certainty that the future lay where we were looking.'[67]

Stockbroker and arts patron Edward Dyason was the next supporter drawn to Atyeo's show. He provided more tangible support than Evatt by commissioning Atyeo to complete the design and interior decoration of St Filian, his home at Narbethong, and the new facade and interior of Regency House in Flinders Lane. The Reeds did not approve of Atyeo squandering his time and his talent, as they saw it, on such trivial concerns. It constituted 'dangerous risks to Sam's career as an artist' and they believed he should commit himself to painting alone.[68]

Atyeo could not have agreed more but, even with the Reeds' help, he was still broke. Trying to survive as an artist in Australia was a challenge but the country was weathering the Depression and 1932 was its worst year. Atyeo was grateful to Dyason and gave him *A Gentle Admonition* as a gift. Dyason proved important to Sunday, too, introducing her to the Hay diet which assisted her health and which she adopted for the rest of her life.

In 1936, Atyeo was raising money to try his luck abroad. Perhaps it was not only his ambitions but the complications of his affair with Sunday that pressed him to leave. Sunday was devastated when Atyeo announced his departure, even though the affair was bringing turmoil to their lives. It was the same scenario that would unfold a decade later when Nolan, exhausted by the intensity and frustration of his affair with Sunday, would also depart. Atyeo promised, 'I shall work to make a good place abroad and you will come and we will never be separated . . . Sweet Sun sweet thing you did this thing to my heart.'[69]

Atyeo was aware he was a cause for Sunday's unhappiness. When she was at Merthon and he was staying with John at Marne Street, he wrote, 'Don't feel low, you sounded very depressed tonight. Don't get low Sun. When you come back we must be more aware of our relationship and consciously how much we mean to each other, Sun and John and me.'[70] He joked to John, 'Sun and I are going to write a book on relationships, a book of rules.'[71] Atyeo's drawings, *Jester* (c.1934, Heide MoMA) and *Queen* (c.1934, Heide MoMA), are cartoon portraits of him and Sunday: he, the bug-eyed, big-eared clown and she the fine-featured, imperious ruler. They are ironic commentaries on Atyeo's perception of status and power in the *ménage-à-trois*. John's summary of the situation was equanimity itself. 'Ah, it was so hard to cope fully with life poor Samuel, poor me, poor you – at any rate we are all in the same boat and love each other.'[72]

Atyeo was an inveterate womaniser and Moya Dyring, his generous and long-suffering girlfriend, seemed reconciled to the excesses of the man she would marry in 1941. But she did not passively accept the situation. During 1933, when Sunday and Atyeo's affair began, she and John, as Gay Cuthbert suggests, conducted their own affair.[73] The complications did not end there. Cynthia later had a brief affair with Atyeo. Though the connection between Sunday, John, Cynthia, Atyeo and Dyring was creatively productive for all five, equally, it was incestuously intimate and rife with pain and treachery.

Cruelly, Atyeo compared Sunday and Moya. 'Sun looked

marvellous the other night I thought Moya looked humanly comfortable. But my God Christ Pablo and God's son, Sun looked as though she was chiselled out of marble . . . So I thought well I feel like ecstasy.'[74] Though Atyeo was hardly reliable – 'sweet Sun I have been true to you (in my own way)' – Sunday proved herself a passionate, demanding and anxious lover. 'God you are exacting,' Atyeo commented.[75]

John, too, felt Sunday placed unnecessary pressure on Atyeo. 'You must not harass him continually,' he advised her, 'and must give him a bit of rest as too much of that sort of thing all the time is not good for anyone.'[76] He was also concerned about Sunday. 'You *must* have plenty of rest & you must let yourself rest & go to sleep & not lie awake at night & keep doing things all day. Remember that you've got to be good no matter how worried & upset you feel.'[77]

Atyeo, like Nolan, became deeply involved with both John and Sunday. 'I can't find any loopholes in you. Don't get conceited and go about wearing haloes cause when I do make it hot for you oh I'll make it hot for the two of you.'[78] At first Atyeo was critical of John who seemed 'such a timid sensitive fellow'.[79] But his respect for John grew as, gradually, John assumed the role of controller and calm centre of the *ménage-à-trois*.

John interrogated Atyeo about his 'secretive relations with my family Moya etc' which made Atyeo's heart miss a beat. He begged Sunday to have 'absolute faith' in him or he would 'always be frightened of losing you forever and never knowing the reason . . . You are so beautiful and precious and pure like sunlight.'[80] But Atyeo was discomfited by the situation, stating frankly, 'we can't achieve a perfect relationship. I suspect I'm the unfitting cog really.'[81] He confided to John that 'relationships were too difficult

& devastating & that one should become entirely independent' but John disagreed. His answer to Atyeo is the template to Heide's complicated, binding friendships. John explained to Sunday, 'I said that was a lot of rot & that relationships were just as essential as marriage that without them we would be incomplete & that it was only escapism to adopt that attitude when inevitable difficulties cropped up.'[82]

What the Reeds failed to understand or accept was that their artist friends needed the freedom to guide their own lives and destinies. Once an artist had entered the charmed circle of the Reeds' munificence, they were expected to stay – forever. Departure was regarded as the highest form of treachery, an inexplicable act of cruelty and perfidy. '[Sunday] would never end a friendship with anyone. She would not cut you or throw you out of her life.' But Sunday's 'intense loyalty' meant she expected the same in return and if she did not receive it, she felt desolate and angry, and did not hesitate to show it.[83] What motivated such dependence on others and, with it, a yearning for control? It seems that John and Sunday were not enough for each other. The youthful ideal of a communally oriented existence – where friends stayed, lived and worked in their home – became a marriage dependent on friendships as intimate as the marriage itself.

There were several reasons for this. Sunday's inability to have children, and her alienation from her own family, meant the need for a big family had to be met by friendship, not blood ties. Her ache to have a child only increased as the years went by. Secondly, there seemed a lack within the Reeds themselves to be self-sufficient as a couple. Sunday and John did not savour being alone and could not realise their creativity, their hopes and dreams, solely through one another. Their marriage was not an exclusive affair. It was an enterprise that included, and depended upon, the energy of others. Indeed, the story of their marriage is equally the story of other people.

Another issue was John's sexuality. The demise of Sunday's first marriage with its shame and illness had not tempered her sensuality. Sunday was a hunter for love, seductive, courageous, romantic and imaginative. John's lack of ardour created problems for Sunday and she boldly sought out other men. The affair with Atyeo started barely a year after the Reeds were married. While John had an affair, its timing coincided with Sunday's, as if he responded to her infidelity by vying with her and manufacturing his own liaison.

John's ambitions were cultural, communal and co-operative: acting in concert, not alone, was his preferred modus operandi. The group – active, political and artistic – was John's ideal environment, one that he pursued in his associations with the Contemporary Art Society, *Angry Penguins*, *Ern Malley's Journal* and the Museum of Modern Art. John was a very social being, directed by circumstance, at ease with decisive personalities and inclined to be guided by them. Once decided on a course of action promoted by his chosen group, John was steadfast, astute, courageous and loyal. But there was a strain of passivity in John's character, the negative side of his high-minded dedication, that meant that he could, and did, sacrifice himself to what he perceived was the greater good, no matter the personal cost. Above all, he wanted to be useful.

Sunday was prepared to break the rules and go it alone, that is, as long as she had John's support and co-operation. Joy Hester was one friend who both resented and envied Sunday's ability to get what she wanted, even when it meant shamelessly manipulating John. Hester complained to Albert Tucker about Sunday's ruses yet, at the same time, she was impressed by the power Sunday wielded over those she loved, and was unafraid to use. John worshipped Sunday and was prepared to sacrifice himself to make her happy. He was also worried that if he did not, he might lose her. Nor did he comply grimly or miserably, resisting and complaining: he behaved graciously, the warmly welcoming host of his wife's liaisons, the master of ceremonies of the *ménage*.

Perhaps somewhere in John's complex personality, a degree of voyeurism alleviated and even provided a fillip to the agonies of jealousy he must have suffered. In a letter to Nolan, years after the affair with Sunday was over, John observed, 'I have a certain tough resilience that once served you well.'[84] It was one of the rare occasions when John revealed his feelings. The parameters of Sunday and John's characters – and that of their marriage – was charted in its early years through Sunday's affair with Atyeo.

Moya Dyring was many things Sunday was not – easy-going, gregarious, homely and prepared to play second fiddle. With a vividly eccentric clothes' sense and a knack for making friends and throwing parties, Dyring moved easily through the Melbourne art world. She was enthralled by the Reeds and painted a portrait of *Sunday* (c.1934, Heide MoMA) at the height of Sunday's affair with Atyeo. A tender homage to Sunday's feline grace in pastel blues, her eyes are downcast as her delicately elongated fingers stroke a cat.

When Dyring painted *Sam Atyeo* (c.1934, Heide MoMA) his eyes are also downcast: the ebullient, extrovert Atyeo is depicted by his lover as remote, contemplative and self-contained. Dyring also painted a striking, rather debauched portrait of Cynthia in lurid greens and yellows, *Female Figure* (c.1934, Heide MoMA). Dyring makes the most of the sharp angles of Cynthia's face and shows her grasping a quill, symbol of her desire to be a writer. While the portrait of Atyeo is lifeless and closed, the portraits of the two women whom Dyring loved and admired are inspired and vital.

Perhaps hurt feelings about the Atyeo-Sunday affair lead John and Moya to take comfort in one another's arms. John's office was close to Moya's city studio and an obvious place for trysts. Sunday always declared her hand in love but John and Moya managed to keep it quiet, their affair taking backstage to Atyeo and Sunday's.

In 1935, Cynthia suddenly decamped for Sydney. Maybe the intimacies of the first circle were proving too stressful. There she auditioned for films (she had a small part in the Roy Rene film *Strike Me Lucky*) and attended art classes conducted by newly arrived German sculptor Eleonora Lange. Modern Furnishings was managed occasionally by Cynthia, and others, until Edith Macmillan took over the premises for her shop, Primrose Pottery.

Once safely out of Melbourne, Cynthia savaged Sunday in a letter that catalogued both Sunday's faults and Cynthia's insecurities. Cynthia had been accused of gossiping about Atyeo and Sunday. She delared she felt overwhelmed by Sunday's 'terrific personality', making Cynthia feel reduced to a pale imitation of her. Sunday might be 'a genius' but she had the biggest ego Cynthia had ever known. As for John, he should be wary of Sam. Further, John 'would never have married you if he hadn't been crazy about me and you first reminded him of me'.[85] The two women did bear a striking resemblance. It was a hurtful letter, both for Cynthia and Sunday: Cynthia exposed her vulnerabilities and wounded Sunday at the same time. It did not, however, lead to a break.

Dyring was also in Sydney, attending drawing lessons at the studio of Grace Crowley and Rah Fizelle. Crowley had studied under André Lhote but Crowley's form of geometric cubism did not appeal to Dyring who found it 'perfect and unemotional . . . oh so cold'. Dyring was the first artist of a long stream of artists who were keen to hear Sunday's response to their work. 'I am sending you a drawing you might like – anyway send back a criticism and one from John and Sam too.'

Further, Dyring had established a close, protective friendship with Cynthia and told the Reeds, 'Bob and I have had some lovely days together she is very well lost the dark rings under her eyes and enjoying life ever so much.'[86] Shortly afterwards, Cynthia announced she had always wanted to be a nurse and left Australia to seek training, first in New York and then in London. Her departure meant the beginning of the end of the first circle as Atyeo, Dyring and the Evatts followed suit, also quitting Australia in the next few years. Bonds gradually weakened with Fred Ward and the Ebbotts.

But because of their relationship with Atyeo and Dyring, Sunday and John were encouraged to start seriously collecting art. The close friendships, as well as the flame of Atyeo's talent and personality, made them committed modernist collectors. It was Sunday who lead the way. Between 1933 and 1936 they acquired, or were given by Atyeo, nearly a dozen of his paintings and as many drawings, and an almost equal number of Dyring's. Atyeo marks the foundation of the Reeds' collection, and subsequently, that of the Heide Museum of Modern Art.

Modernism had a personal and an aesthetic meaning for Sunday. Read had written that 'everywhere is the same lack of unity, the same absence of authority, the same break with tradition' and that applied to Sunday's new life as well as the art and artists to whom she was attracted. Modernism's bold formal disjunctions were similar to the changes Sunday explored in her own life, where she disassociated herself from her class by befriending raffish, leftwing bohemians and challenged the conventional structure of marriage by conducting an affair with her husband's acquiesence. Modernism's enterprise was deliberately destructive and across art, literature and music there was 'the shock, the violation of expected continuities, the element of de-creation and crisis'.[87] Sunday did not quail to apply such propositions to her life.

Out of her failure to become an artist, a more powerful resolution had arisen: she would position herself as a modernist patron and collector who would offer advice and criticism, love and money, nurture and support to the artists whom she would select as the most gifted and original of their generation. Sunday wanted to discover genius and be the muse that tended it. By failing in her quest to be an artist, she created the role in which she would excel: the inspiring and commanding figure at the centre of her chosen cultural group.

The Reeds were uncomfortable with the title of patrons and dismissed it on every possible occasion. 'Both Sunday and I object very strongly to this notion of patronage,' John told Richard Haese. 'There wasn't any patronage. You know, we were friends of the artists – they were our friends, we were their friends; we had some things, they had other things. We had more money than they did, certainly ... It was *mutual* – we always regarded it as a mutual thing.'[88]

For the Reeds the notion of 'patronage' denied the complex sharing of creative activity that was so precious to them. Equally, such a grandiose term implied an unnerving connection with their patrician backgrounds. But it is silly to deny that Sunday and John were patrons – albeit unusually enlightened and sympathetic ones. They gave money to poor artist friends who became dependent on their support, making, at times, for tricky and unhealthy friendships. The Reeds' courage involved never resiling from their chosen mission: to live as closely as possible to the lives of their friends, no matter how stressful and financially unfortunate were the results for them. 'I have wanted to follow you within experience,' Sunday told Joy Hester, 'to live as closely to you [as] to life itself.'[89]

Sunday, in particular, intended to make a life from art. Though not an artist, she chose the artist's life, which is rarely a happy one, where success is often intangible and failure all too regular and crippling to the spirit, where money is squandered on plans that may come to nothing and an adamant idealism is, by necessity, the first and last refuge. She, too, inherited those burdens. Denying she was a patron was a form of willed naïvété on Sunday's part, where she refused to acknowledge the chasm that separated her from those she loved and attracted. Yet it was intrinsic to her vision of her own life, and of Australian culture, that she could participate democratically at the heart of the creative process, and transform it.

· 6 ·

Heide House

Ah Sun how good it is out here how right you are to make it your life.
MOYA DYRING TO SUNDAY REED, 1937[1]

Sunday was the creator, John was the executor as far as the garden went.
NEIL DOUGLAS[2]

Really the garden just emerged from love.
SUNDAY REED, 20 JULY 1981[3]

I believe one's garden is one's self.
MARION CRAN[4]

WHEN SUNDAY CREATED HEIDE, she categorically rejected a streamlined, functional, modernist environment. Despite her interest in and respect for Ward's, Atyeo's and Cynthia's bold experiments in design and architecture, her home would be eclectic, informal, European and feminine. Sunday marked a zone between the radicalism of modern art and a comfortable, relaxed domestic space. While she pursued, encouraged and collected the former, she did not extend that preference to her home. It was not until the 1960s, when Sunday initiated the design of Heide II, that she chose a clean, white modernist machine for living.

Nor was the Heide garden governed by 'cool' modernism. Sunday's formal French taste for straight lines and box hedging was balanced by a more lavish and romantic sensibility influenced by a triumvirate of English women gardeners, by Monet's Giverny, by Neil Douglas and by Sunday's growing confidence in her own skills.

At Heide, Sunday realised her potential, not only for creating a home and garden that would inspire and attract artists but an environment where her own aesthetic and physical limits would be quickened and tested. At the point where Sunday relinquished her desire to be an artist, she discovered a palette in nature, a place to elaborate the abstract and practical elements of colour, form and structure, and the opportunity to make a beautiful and abundant realm that was wholly her own.

It was Sunday's idea to move to the country. In January 1933, she wrote to John, 'Don't be impatient with me because I talk of living in the country now – I am always thinking about it – & thinking of the days rushing past us & not wanting to waste a second & I get

Above: *Pegg Clarke.* Sunday and family on the terrace at Merthon, 1923. From left: Sunday, Arthur, cousin John, Ethel and younger brother Everard.
Courtesy State Library of Victoria.

Left: *Albert Tucker.*
Sunday Reed milking, 1942.
Courtesy Albert Tucker.

Left: **Sunday the debutante, 1924.** *Courtesy State Library of Victoria.*

Right: *Edwin Adamson.* Sunday and Valerie Fairfax ('Mud') at Sorrento, 1926. *Courtesy State Library of Victoria.*

Arthur Baillieu and Sunday, c. 1920. *Courtesy State Library of Victoria.*

Left: Leonard Quinn, c. 1926.
Courtesy State Library of Victoria.

Above: John Reed with Karel,
1930.
Courtesy State Library of Victoria.

Sunday with Tom Cochrane in Agnes Goodsir's
studio, Paris, 1930.
Courtesy Bruce Lorimer.

Above: Wedding day,
1932.
*Courtesy State Library
of Victoria.*

Left: Sam Atyeo leaving
Australia, 1936.
*Courtesy State Library
of Victoria.*

Left: *Ruth Hollick. Cynthia Reed, c. 1925. Courtesy State Library of Victoria.*

Right: Moya Dyring in her studio, c. 1936. Behind her is *Holly* c. 1934–6, Heide Museum of Modern Art. *Courtesy State Library of Victoria.*

Heide, c. 1936. *Courtesy State Library of Victoria.*

John Sinclair. John mowing the front lawn, c. 1948.
Courtesy Jean Langley/Heide Museum of Modern Art.

Neil Douglas, c. 1970.
*Courtesy Heide Museum of
Modern Art.*

Sunday in the kitchen garden, c. 1946.
Courtesy State Library of Victoria.

Albert Tucker. Christmas at Heide, c. 1946. From left: Sidney Nolan, Sunday, John Reed and John Sinclair. *Courtesy Albert Tucker.*

John Sinclair. John Reed (behind window), Barrett Reid, Sunday Reed and Laurence Hope, Heide, December 1946. *Courtesy Laurence Hope.* Bottles of linseed oil, used by Nolan, are bleaching in the sun.

Nolan, Max Harris, Sunday, John Reed and John Sinclair in the Heide kitchen, c. 1945. *Courtesy State Library of Victoria.*

Danila Vassilieff, c. 1955. *Courtesy State Library of Victoria.*

really paniced [sic] when I think of building town houses & living in them for 5 years.'[5] Both John and Sunday had instilled in them from their childhoods deep feelings for the landscape, and for a rural life. Ethel's long illness had tied them to the suburbs and, with her death, new plans could be implemented.

During 1933, the Reeds contacted architects Meldrum and Pearce to draw up ambitious plans for a country house. The site is unknown. John felt Meldrum's plans looked 'very impressive' and that the projected cost of three thousand seven hundred pounds, including septic tank, water system and electricity, was reasonable.[6] Sunday agreed the plans were good but she was 'losing faith in ever having [the house]'. That was because the Reeds were dependent on Arthur Baillieu's financial assistance and she begged John to 'do something with Dad while I'm away as I tremble at the thought of being present at the first discussion, I know I'll fly into a rage & make things much worse'.[7] The project fell through, perhaps due to Arthur's misgivings.

The Reeds had 'fallen in love with the Yarra Valley where it runs through Heidelberg'.[8] Scouting around the area, looking for properties, they came across a modest, graceful, weatherboard house set back from Templestowe Road, Heidelberg (now Bulleen) on six hectares of paddocks and river flats. It was owned by Mrs Lang, a reclusive widow, whose husband James and his brother William had bought the property in 1893. Sunday and John persuaded Mrs Lang to tell them stories about the place, including her recollection that Aboriginal people used to gather around the magnificent river red gum to the right of the house. The Wurundjeri people are the area's traditional owners. Known as 'the canoe tree', because a canoe or large shield has been cut from its bark, the tree is around five hundred years old.

Since 1860 the land had been cultivated as a market garden by Sidney Ricardo before being bought in the 1870s by Thomas Dowd who built the house and various outhouses including a milking shed and a chicken coop. Market gardeners Venier's and Negri's continued to occupy properties nearby. Subsequently Mrs Lang divided the property, sold the paddocks and river flats, which were used as a dairy farm, and kept two hectares at the front for herself. But the entire property was in a sad state of neglect. John recalled it was 'treeless except for big pines and a few other trees around the house, and some red gums, wattles and willows on the riverbank . . . For the rest, there were only a few broken down hedges and clumps of boxthorn; but the whole landscape with the winding river as its artery gave us a deep sense of pleasure, and even then we saw Heide becoming a little park.'[9]

The attraction of the place, and the possibility of getting a large tract of land for a reasonable price, swayed Sunday whose passion had always been for the coast. Certainly its historical connection with the Heidelberg School offered a vital context to the Reeds' vision of an artistic community. Arthur Streeton had 'discovered' the area in 1898 when he rented Eaglemont, which he described as an 'old weatherboard homestead with eight or ten rooms, standing on the summit of a hill and beautifully surrounded by a little forest of conifers and other fine trees'.[10] Tom Roberts, Fred McCubbin, Walter Withers and later Charles Conder joined him there. Named after the German city of Heidelberg, the suburb was appreciated, by the mid-nineteenth century, for its resemblance to an English village. But the immediate community around Heide was impoverished: it was the height of the Depression and few homes had electricity or a telephone.

On 29 April 1934, the Reeds went to auction to buy the front part of the property. Mrs Lang had died and her estate was selling off the house and grounds. Atyeo and Vivian Ebbott came along to bolster John and Sunday's courage and the bidding was a tense affair with 'two nasty types bumping up the bids'.[11] But the Reeds were successful and 'Heide House', as it was soon dubbed, was theirs. (In German, Heide means 'heath' and 'pagan'.) But they would have to wait until July to buy the remainder of the property, comprising the paddocks and river frontage, which cost fifteen hundred and fourteen pounds, ten shillings.

Heide was an ambitious project and the Reeds threw themselves into it. First, the house had to be extensively remodelled and it would be twelve months before they moved in. Here was the opportunity, if they had the inclination or the funds, to raze the old house and build a new one that would be a testament to modern architecture and the unified aesthetics of modernist design. Instead, they sympathetically renovated the weatherboard house with its simple, elegant proportions. Heide was by no means luxurious. Indeed, the house changed so little over the years that, when the Reeds died there in 1981, it was very much the same house they had bought.

One of Sunday's first ideas was to tear down the verandahs with their iron lacework because she 'wanted it to look like a French farmhouse'.[12] Then she asked Atyeo to design a small, elegant porch, covered with the same slate as the bay windows. Sunday had the front door painted her favourite colour – sky-blue. The kitchen wing was enlarged and the house painted off-white. (Over the years, Heide was also painted pink, then grey.)

While the house was being remodelled, they set to work on the grounds, planting as many trees as possible. But in November there was a record flood and 'most of the trees were either washed completely away or became water-logged and subsequently died'. This was the first of many floods which could come 'at any time of the year and often without warning, and sweep across the flats with astonishing power'.[13] Still, even a natural disaster could be fun for their friends. 'Do you remember the big flood,' John asked Atyeo years later, 'when you and Vivian dived into the water off the hillside?'[14]

One of Sunday's earliest acts as a gardener was to plant English lavender circling the drive. The English variety is hardy and intensely fragrant and it was Sunday's favourite herb: she dried its flowers to make scented bags for clothing drawers and washed her hair in lavender water. Once when Sunday was away, John 'opened all the drawers just for the thrill of seeing something that belonged to you but I was so much overcome by the blasts of lavender that assailed me that half the fun was spoilt'.[15]

The trees John planted were exotics: silver birch, willow, poplar, walnut, golden ash, alder, larch, chestnut, sequoia, linden as well as a rare English hornbeam, the latter Sunday's idea, and a Judas tree by the front gate. In the centre of the backyard John 'blasted holes in the reef just below the house and in one of these I planted a six foot Mexican oak [that] I obtained from the original Nobelius nursery at Emerald'. The tree flourishes to this day and its acorns have seeded the oaks on the flats. John was correct in observing that 'in 1934 very few people, except perhaps the late Edna Walling, had even thought of planting native trees and, in any event, I do not think there was a single nursery which grew them'. He also planted double rows of osage oranges on the 'difficult hillside' – difficult because it bears the brunt of the winds.[16] The inspiration for the Heide grounds was distinctly European and its atmosphere today is akin to a gracious, if slightly scruffy, English park.

In the 1930s, Edna Walling was Melbourne's best-known and most highly regarded landscape designer. Unconventional and dedicated, Walling set herself up in business after graduating from the Burnley Horticultural College in 1917. She attracted clients such as Dame Nellie Melba and revolutionised garden design in Australia. Sunday was acquainted with her work. In 1930, Walling had designed a garden for Ethel, plans that were never carried out probably due to Ethel's illness. The Baillieus sold Balholmen in 1928, so the location of the planned garden is unknown, but it exemplified the kind of splendidly proportioned, formal geometric design Walling unerringly produced for her affluent clients. Formal elements of the pergola and tennis courts are balanced by an avenue of elms and a diamond shaped rose garden which are set against a vast lawn and the flowing curves of colourful, herbaceous borders.[17] Wallings' minutely realised plans are artworks in themselves.

But Sunday and John wanted to design their own garden, rather than call in a professional. Perhaps Walling was too 'Toorak'. So they asked their friends to pitch in. While Dyring proved herself only too pleased, Atyeo was much less willing. John told Sunday that 'Sam wanted to go to sleep when he got out to Heide but Moya made him dig but I don't think he bust himself over it. He was particularly offended that he should have to dig a bed for marrows! Poor Moya could hardly bear to drag herself away from the veg garden.'[18]

It was the start of a ticklish bargain: guests at Heide were expected to pull their weight. Barrett Reid recalled, 'Everybody did their chores. If you stayed at Heide you soon learned you had to do your chores, too. And there was a certain anxiety with people not terribly used to them who were perfectly willing to do the chores and who had to be told what chores to do. I never worked out what I should be doing. But I did separate the milk which was a very boring job.'[19]

But the Reeds were not totally reliant on their friends. There was Mick Riddell, a full-time helper who lived on an adjoining property, and another local, Thomas James Heffernan, a gentle fellow known as Jimmy, who assisted the Reeds and stayed with them for the next decade. Jimmy was also a keen gardener and loved roses. Their neighbours in the small rural community, struggling through the Depression, regarded the Reeds with awe: John was a lawyer while Sunday, wearing slacks and flashing past in a sporty car 'looked like Lauren Bacall'.[20] Mrs Wells, the Reeds' cook and housekeeper, moved with them from South Yarra. Relations between the Reeds and the help were often uneasy. When Mrs Allen, an earlier housekeeper, 'kept interrupting' John at breakfast while he was trying to read a letter of Sunday's, he eventually had to 'speak to her "quite sharply", as the saying is!'[21] The next house-keeper was Pauline who John 'roared up for having the kitchen window so dirty – she looked down her nose as usual!'[22] Sunday, John noted, was not averse to 'roaring up' the help, either.

From the first, Heide's garden was meant to be a communal and sentimental place. Friends were invited to plant trees, so there was Doodie's sycamore and Dyring's bay leaf while Cynthia planted asters. But the real work on the garden would begin in 1936 with the assistance of Neil Douglas.

In 1935, Sunday began decorating the first home that was truly hers. A wide hall with high ceilings and ornate rosettes ran the length of the house. It ended at a curved window which gave a view of the oak tree and the yard like a vivid green picture. Beside the window was Sunday's linen closet. The master bedroom faced the library while the two guest rooms, further down the hall, faced the dining room. The maid's room was at the rear. There were no wall to wall carpets in those days and Sunday scattered plain rugs on the pine boards. At the end of the hall was the kitchen with its one-fire stove and its view of the area that came to be known as the Heart Garden.

Furnishing the house, Sunday chose to surround herself with known and loved family objects, which were also beautifully crafted antiques. There were some concessions to modern taste. When their friend Joan von Bibra travelled to Europe, she loaned the Reeds a cupboard painted by Atyeo, gaily decorated inside and out with flowers and dancing figures. They also bought a long pine dining room table accompanied by French provincial-style, rush-bottomed chairs. In the library, a big new couch and armchairs were covered with cream linen slip covers for easy cleaning.

Since Ethel's death and the break-up of Balholmen, there was a range of furniture for Sunday to choose from, and Heide's high-ceilinged, nineteenth-century rooms were ideally suited to it. It was another reference to the creative power of Sunday's childhood, to the strength of memory and how the bonds of affection could be manifested in a tangible form. In that sense, the Heide interior is a homage to the past but it is a past reconstructed by Sunday.

An important aspect of modernism was its determination to take tradition and subject it to radical, formal reconfiguration, whether in the rhythms of music or the pictorial space of a painting. Sunday's equation of the modernist process meant that when she arranged her new environment, she reconfigured the past by contextualising it with the present, with a modernist art collection and with a fresh, airy, country-style home. Sunday liked stylish simplicity but she also respected quality of materials. Her interior design emphasised retrieval and recycling: nothing of beauty or quality was cast aside for the whims of fashion. The past belonged firmly to the present. Family heirlooms were treasured mementos and she was determined to make them part of her home. Also, no matter how much Sunday wanted to escape Toorak, she belonged to a class whose continuity and stability were represented by property, by objects of great worth and historic significance passed on from one generation to another.

In the master bedroom with its four-poster bed was a floor-length cheval mirror, a cupboard and a mahogany Wellington chest. On the door, Sunday hung a figurine of an angel that Atyeo had given her. It was still hanging on her bedroom door when she died. Sunday also installed her baby Bechstein in the house where she played modernist composers including Debussy and Erik Satie.

One of her favourite pieces of furniture was a late nineteenth-century Louis XIV-style writing desk with a pink velvet top, ebony veneer and brass inlay, where she arranged two exquisite Venetian glass mirrors. Other furniture included a mahogany tallboy, an eighteenth-century rosewood work table and a Gothic Revival oak coffer that was placed in the hall. But Sunday was not averse to violent modifications. She abhorred dark polish so she took the mahogany tallboy and not only stripped its shellac but scrubbed it with an iron brush.[23]

Sunday also inherited a collection of Staffordshire china from Ethel which she displayed in a special cupboard in the hall as well as the mantel in the library. Quaint and quintessentially English, the nineteenth-century mass-produced figures were fashionable in the 1930s. Sunday's collection included whimsical buildings, dogs, a horse, a highwayman and a portrait group of Uncle Tom and Little Eva from Harriet Beecher Stowe's *Uncle Tom's Cabin*. The figures have the feel of childhood and would not look out of place in a nursery, perhaps part of their charm for Sunday. She continued to collect Staffordshire pieces but finally gave up because 'people kept knocking them off'.[24]

Because John had spent so many years on the move, he had not acquired a great deal of furniture. To Heide he brought his books and an oak lawyer's desk, which was installed in the library/study, as well as his personal art collection which included handpainted engravings by Charles Lesueur and Joseph Lycett. Henry Reed gave the newlyweds a complete set of china embossed in gold with a sheaf of wheat, the family emblem.

John and Sunday had a vast amount of fine china including Limoges, Spode and Royal Doulton. They probably needed it. Sunday was not averse to picking up a piece of Spode and smashing it when she was in a bad mood or throwing it at someone who annoyed her. 'Sunday disliked being contradicted,' particularly at breakfast, her most sensitive time of the day.[25] 'Sun was not her best in the morning. She was pretty cranky . . . You had to tread carefully with Sun in the morning. That was her worst time and she'd often have some sort of outburst. There weren't many discussions in the morning. People avoided that.'[26] John 'would be quite firm with her. He'd yell, "Sunday, Sunday, don't be ridiculous. Quite out of hand. Now shut up." He'd say it but she wouldn't take much notice of it.'[27]

Barrett Reid dedicated a poem to Sunday's morning tantrums to which even the Staffordshire was not immune.

The most beautiful woman
is enraged —
brain storm, nerve tornado.
Breakfast cups fly
in the morning sun.

She is a terror,
she turns the teapot
into a question
hanging over our heads.
(Answer me! Answer me!)[28]

On the walls hung the Reeds' art acquisitions from the last five years: Lawlor's *Enjoying Life*, Dyring's portraits of Sunday and Atyeo, plus many works of Atyeo's including *Organised Line to Yellow*, which hung in pride of place over the mantel in the dining room. Agnes Goodsir's *Portrait of Mrs Leonard Quinn*, the study of Sunday the wanderer painted after the miserable break-up of her first marriage, now faced Sunday, happy and content in her own home. But Sunday made the mistake of lending it to Atyeo. He left it with his family when he travelled to Paris and it was subsequently discarded. There was also Streeton's *Nocturne*, his study of Sunday at Merthon, which always hung in her bedroom, and McCubbin's *The Rabbit Burrow*.

The latter, taking as its subject a scene of childhood play in nature, gives clues about the pleasure and inspiration Sunday found in nature as a child (the painting had been in the family since she was nine) and the ways she sought to replicate it at Heide. As Patrick McCaughey observes, 'at the end of his career, McCubbin offers a striking alternative of the bush as a wild garden in whose enclosure the children play with security.' Reaching beyond 'Victorian sentimental genre painting', McCubbin finds a 'rediscovered innocence'. McCubbin's later work, including *The Rabbit Burrow*, suggests 'the *hortus conclusus*, enclosed garden' where 'the safe, secure world is fenced or walled from the wild, unprotected world beyond', reiterating 'one of the oldest images of nature in western painting'.[29] Sunday, who cherished childhood, sought to develop themes of protection, beauty and play when creating her own 'secret garden' at Heide.

The Reeds also wanted to explore their new home's artistic tradition. They bought an excellent early Streeton: *Evening with Bathers* (1888, National Gallery of Victoria) which hung in the hall. From her parents Sunday had also inherited landscapes by Jane Sutherland, Walter and Ethel Withers and watercolours by Emma Minnie Boyd. The Streeton was the most expensive and historically important work in their collection. In 1953 the Reeds bought a second Streeton, *Early Summer — Gorse in Bloom* (1888, Art Gallery of South Australia).

Evening with Bathers was originally known as *Yarra Valley Heidelberg* and was thought to have been painted by Streeton at Eaglemont, the most famous of the artists' camps. It was, however, painted at Box Hill before Streeton set up the Eaglemont camp or painted the Heidelberg district. The Reeds thought it was a painting of their neighbourhood. It was not. Nonetheless, they had bought a superb example of Streeton's vision of the Australian landscape.

1888 was an important year for Streeton. He had suddenly made enough money from the sale of his work to quit his job as an apprentice lithographer and paint full time. Until then he had only been able to paint at the Box Hill camp on weekends.

The camp had been founded by Tom Roberts on his return from England in 1885 and Streeton joined the following year. Started in a spirit of artistic camaraderie to explore the possibilities of plein air painting, the Box Hill camp also included Fred McCubbin, Louis Abraham and Jane Sutherland. Box Hill still provided areas of natural bush quite close to the city, though, unlike Heidelberg, it was not known as a desirable destination for picnics or camping.

It was recalled with great nostalgia by Streeton: 'I close my eyes and see again the . . . black wattles and ti tree down by the creek, the Houstons cabin, the messmate tree and its mistletoe and horehound patch beneath, the run for trains on Sunday night and Prof [McCubbin] far up ahead . . . the flush of the Dandenongs and the quiet and grey valley beyond White Horse Road Macedon.'[30]

Evening with Bathers is a subtle, atmospheric painting that captures the hues and the mood of the landscape at twilight. Under a mauve sky, the pale, vulnerable figures of the bathers are counterpointed by a transparent moon, rising just above the horizon. The broad countryside is registered in soft, misty greens, aside from the luminous curve of the stream. Streeton captures a trembling, melancholic moment as the earth settles down for the night and the bathers, oblivious, are engulfed by the impending dark. As Ann Galbally suggests, Streeton's paintings reveal the poignancy of the passing of time and youth, the same mood constantly evoked in Streeton's letters to Roberts.[31]

Evening with Bathers attests to the Reeds' admiration for the Heidelberg School and claimed a connection between their patch of earth and Australia's best-known art movement. Streeton's letters to Roberts also reveal the bonds of friendship, affection and loyalty that were a fundamental aspect of the group. It is not hard to imagine the Reeds' desire for a similar community of their own, artists who would revolutionise Australian art as the Heidelberg School had. For Sunday, the landscape would become her inspiration, one that she bequeathed to Nolan. In that sense, Sunday inherited the Heideberg School's search for a fresh vision of the Australian landscape and the means to put it into practice.

Though 1935 was a frutiful time, there was a shock, shortly before the move to Heide, when John suddenly resigned from Blake and Riggall's. He had been working contentedly at the firm for nearly a decade and had been made a partner in 1933. The circumstances were scandalous: John was accused of having an affair with his secretary. 'A door swung open that shouldn't have. She was sitting on John's knee.'[32] Henry Reed was horrified but kept a stiff upper lip. 'It was never discussed in the family.'[33] In *Paradise Garden*, Nolan's cruel portrayal of the *ménage-à-trois*, he quipped, 'He kissed his typist/on his knee/it broke his heart/he took up art'.[34]

In such a conservative firm, John's behaviour was regarded as nothing short of outrageous. He was probably given a choice: resign or be sacked. Poor John. While Sunday dealt in a magnificently cavalier and public fashion with her affair, John had tried to be discreet, first with Dyring and then with his secretary. But was it a full-blown affair or merely some foolhardy smooching? Either way, John was punished. Occurring during Sunday's affair with Atyeo, it indicates that John, too, was trying his hand at sexual freedom, with mixed results.

Sunday had not tried to dissuade John from practising law. In fact, she was ambitious for him. Not long after they were engaged she wrote, 'please don't overwork yourself ... but work just hard enough to become a partner within a reasonable length of time'.[35] Sunday needed stability and order in her life, and when John resigned, she felt uneasy, unmoored. A year later she confided to him:

> You know I don't think I have really readjusted myself since you left Blake and Riggall's – curious that you leaving there should affect me so much more than you. Looking back I suspect

that somehow I found it very pleasant to have you rooted there. I believe it balanced happily enough our way together – kept us on an even keel – independence plus the rest & life was crystal clear. There you were & there you stayed & that was that & that was good – that was very good since life to me had been something of a shifting sort of business to say the least of it until we married – on the other hand I'm glad you broke away.[36]

Atyeo's reaction was more robust. 'Think how lucky John must be away from those bloody reptiles he's found them to be my God think! he may have turned into one.'[37] Arthur Baillieu came to the rescue by inviting John to set up an office at Collins House. He also involved John in Baillieu enterprises that included giving him a position on the board of Cliveden, the gracious apartments built by the Baillieus in Wellington Parade, East Melbourne. The Blake and Riggall's fiasco was the start of John's long, slow leavetaking of his profession and it coincided with the move to Heide.

By that time Sunday's affair with Sam had nearly run its course. John advised Sunday, 'if you're going to keep on being disappointed or upset about [Sam] you had better call in the grave-digger right away because you know just as well as I do that his path is not now running a true parallel with ours . . . He cannot be a unity with you because he is not married to you and he cannot be a unity with either of us because our lives (yours and mine) are joined together and necessarily separated from everyone else's. This was not so clear when we were at Marne St though I think that long before we moved the deviation of Sam from us had started. I too doubt whether Sam's life is going ahead in the best possible way but there may be a certain element of selfishness in this feeling.'[38]

With his recititude and calm, managerial manner, John remained the lawyer, even admonishing himself for a moment of 'selfishness'.

The Heide garden's great leap forward was assisted by Neil Douglas. Douglas had been a Gallery School student with Dyring and Atyeo but he'd had to quit during the Depression and survive as best he could. In 1936, when Douglas returned to his property at Bayswater, in Melbourne's outer east, he observed 'the plants which were happy had thrived and spread in the years of neglect and had swarmed over their weaker neighbours . . . I learned how to let plants be themselves, and not to interfere or regiment them too much'.[39]

Douglas looked up his old friends. Atyeo had been 'fairly rough and ready' but when Douglas met him in Collins Street, he noticed the difference immediately. 'Sam's accent had totally changed. No more ocker.' Atyeo offered Douglas 'one of the Lord Mayor's cigars' and explained he was redesigning the decor of the Melbourne Town Hall. He told Douglas, 'I've changed my accent and learned how to behave myself and I go to the best parties.'[40]

Next Douglas contacted Dyring who told him about two friends who had been 'trying to garden and a great hailstorm just came and cut everything to bits'. Moya told Douglas 'the hardy things that you grow in your garden would do well in theirs'. So she took Douglas to Heide where he was impressed by 'the lavender garden behind the white picket fence . . . and a marvellous old mulberry tree that bent right over and touched the ground before growing up again'. Douglas was also astonished by the 'great woolly' English sheepdogs 'bounding around'.[41] The Reeds now had five dogs: the faithful Karel, Rufus, a red setter, and the sheepdogs: Pooh (after Winnie the Pooh), Brother (Pooh's brother, known as Broth) and Tommy. The Reeds referred to them as the Bears.

Sunday responded to Douglas's direct and original interpretation of gardening. Douglas was also an artist with an artist's imagination for plants, colour and space and a poet's way of describing them. The Reeds visited his garden at Bayswater. 'I lived there in a little old mud-brick cottage with an attic all smothered in ivy, a great tumbling garden of two acres, covered with herbs and very old roses. None of us in those days grew Australian things. They were held to be difficult. It wasn't the idea to have an Australian garden . . . Sun took one look at my garden and said, "Come and stay at Heide."'[42]

Douglas had made a garden that needed virtually no water and, like Monet at Giverny, he 'wanted to paint pictures with flowers all year round, so that meant planting different things to bring honey for the bees'.[43] It was 'what I instinctively knew gardening to be and so did Sun . . . to make a heaven on earth all around you'.[44] The garden at Heide was 'founded on a perception of beauty'.[45]

The Reeds paid Douglas a small wage and he lived at Heide from Tuesdays to Fridays, before returning home. It was an arrangement that lasted for over a decade, though it was not always a happy one. 'They thought I was a gifted gardener but they laughed at my paintings', Douglas recalled ruefully.[46] Sunday put it more brutally. 'She told me to stop painting.'[47] But Douglas continued to paint the landscape and, in the 1940s, worked at the Boyds' Murrumbeena pottery works decorating ceramics.

Douglas was soon made aware of Sunday's sensitivities. One day she asked him, 'What flower do I remind you of? . . . I said a petunia and she was very quiet and she was really cross and she went to her bedroom. She'd done her block, you know. She was so cross, she didn't ask me why, so I left in disgrace. I wasn't allowed to talk at tea time, so I shut up.' Shortly afterwards, Sunday came to visit. 'She threw her arms around me . . . and she said, "I'm delighted with you."' At Doodie's for afternoon tea, Sunday had asked, 'What is this lovely seductive scent that pervades the house?' It was petunias. 'Sunday said it smelt like a true angel, like a true person, like all true things. It was just so above the ordinary common perception . . . So I was reinstated.'[48]

With Douglas's knowledge and assistance, the Reeds began a series of ambitious projects but 'Sunday was the creator, John was the executor as far as the garden went. The decisions were always Sunday's. She was the one with the wonderful new vision. She was interested in Gertrude Jekyll and [gardens] that had never been done before in Australia. She used John's [ideas] or used what ideas I might have . . . It was her home and her property.'[49]

In fact, Sunday's interpretation of the garden was rather like the style she displayed in the house: a configuration of old and new, where a respect for the past (a taste for formal French gardening) was enlivened by an awareness of what was fresh and modern (Jekyll's painterly, aesthetic approach). The Heide garden was Heide house writ large.

One of the first tasks was to plant an orchard on the front lawn. It was an idea sympathetic to the area which was 'wholly orchard. It was a rough country road and you couldn't see anywhere for apple trees and peach trees . . . The Reeds who had all the dosh in the world moved these great big trees.' It was hard work. 'We dug a hole around [the tree] and we pulled [it] up. We worked out a way of pulling it up with its soil and trucking it over [to Heide] and putting it in and covering it with hessian.' They not only planted apple and pear but lemon, apricot and plum as well. John was 'mostly interested in the fifteen acres of trees. We got tree catalogues from overseas and garden catalogues from England.'[50]

Not all the tree planting was so successful. Atyeo and Douglas planted over four hundred birch trees at Heide, more than half in just one day. Sam was not an enthusiastic gardener. When he visited Douglas at Bayswater he 'walked on all the seed beds. He just walked in any direction without seeing nature at all.' Planting the birches, Douglas would put the seedling in the ground and Atyeo would secure the stake with a mighty blow from the sledge hammer. 'I said if you miss it, you might hit your toe or your leg . . . [but] Sam was very quick.' Shortly afterwards all the trees died. The soil was 'just unsuitable. It was too dry.' After that disaster, John installed a pump.

The Heide soil was 'fairly deep except on the brow of the hill [where] it was sandstone. Typical Melbourne mudstone'.[51] Simon Dickeson, garden curator at Heide Museum of Modern Art from 1988 until 2000, found the soil 'just absolutely horrible. Leach substrate basically so there are big chunks of rock just below the surface.'[52] When John planted the oak in the backyard, he had to blast a hole in the soil.

Douglas regarded gardening as 'a funny business, very mixed up with painting. A mixture of hard work and aesthetics.' Over lunch he and the Reeds would sit together and pore over 'rare garden books, old English Cottage Lore, Garden poetry, Herb lore, finding the names of plants that had been found in strange places'.[53] John 'took a tremendous interest in even the smallest flowers and their names. He loved their names, some of the marvellous names that plants have. So he saw plants . . . as personalities in their own right.'[54]

Monet's garden at Giverny, not far from Paris, was in Douglas's mind when he created his own garden. At some point in her European travels, Sunday had visited Giverny which provided the example of a beautiful garden that was not only the inspiration for an artist but his prime resource and subject matter. 'I perhaps owe having become a painter to flowers,' Monet remarked.[55] Monet had died in 1926, leaving the property to his family and, in the 1940s, it was not open to the public as it is today.[56] 'My garden is slow work, pursued with love and I do not deny that I am proud of it,' Monet said. 'Forty years ago when I established myself here, there was nothing abut a farmhouse and an orchard ... I dug, planted and weeded myself.'[57]

But as Monet's earnings increased, he was able to employ a team of six gardeners to realise his ambitions. He planned his flowerbeds according to the principles governing his palette, with light colours predominating and monochrome masses in juxtaposition. Monet's had none of the formality of a typical French garden, 'it was a painter's garden where everything followed a certain rhythm'.[58] He also created a dreamlike water garden which inspired his Nymphéas series, surrounded by willows and crossed by a little Japanese bridge hung with wisteria. At Giverny, house and garden merge in one, luxuriant, intoxicating, sweet-scented environment.

There Sunday must have observed how a garden could provide both 'a heaven on earth all around you' and direct the subject matter specific for art. But, without Monet's resources, she did not plan to divert the Yarra to create a water-lily pond, as he diverted his local river Epte, nor did she have a team of gardeners to carry out her wishes. The Heide garden, apart from a series of helpers over the years, was always the work of Sunday's hands.

As Neil Douglas recalled, Gertrude Jekyll, Marion Cran and

Eleanour Sinclair Rohde were an influential triumvirate of gardening writers for Sunday, and the most important was Jekyll.

Gertrude Jekyll is to the twentieth-century garden what Picasso is to painting: no serious gardener can escape her influence. She was a modest but indomitable visionary who wrote ten books in nine years, created her own exquisite garden in Surrey as well as designing many others. Emily Lutyens, wife of Jekyll's architectural partner Edwin Lutyens, described her in old age as 'very fat and stumpy, dresses rather like a man, little tiny eyes, very nearly blind and big spectacles'.[59] Lutyens called her Bumps.

Jekyll had trained at South Kensington School of Art where she studied Chevreul's colour theory, Turner's paintings at the National Gallery and the glowing harmonies of the Impressionist palette. While a student she met William Morris, founder of the Arts and Crafts Movement, who privileged craftsmanship and authenticity of materials. His home, Kelmscott Manor, the laboratory for many of his ideas, was in the Cotswolds, an area Sunday had visited. Morris inspired Jekyll, herself a designer-craftswoman skilled at tapestry, embroidery, metalwork, woodwork, painting and photography, to create a unifying aesthetic for all the arts. She also shared Morris's love of country life.

In 1875, Jekyll met William Robinson, the renegade gardening writer, whose book *The Wild Garden* (1870) was a manifesto opposing both the dull formality of 'trim gardens' and carpet bedding, the 'dreadful practice of tearing up flower beds and leaving them like new graves dug twice a year'. Robinson espoused a new, freer aesthetic where parts of the lawn were left unmown and planted with wildflowers. 'Who would not rather see the waving grass with countless flowers than a close surface without a blossom?' he queried.[60]

Jekyll's gardening career was motivated by personal tragedy. In her late thirties, progressive myopia made her realise she would have to relinquish painting. While she was comfortable working close up, the distance was a hazy blur but it meant that her perception of sweeps of colour, of the habits of light was uncluttered by details and therefore more accurate and impressive.[61] But her aptitude was not only for colour. True to the Arts and Crafts philosophy, Jekyll understood that the whole environment, house and garden, materials and design, created a unity that found comfort and sympathy in their surroundings.

Jekyll did not set out to promote a particular kind of garden and, while her gardening advice was eminently practical, sound and detailed, it was her philosophy that proved enduring and universally appealing. She saw garden design as a fine art, ranking it alongside painting and sculpture, an aesthetic adventure of the highest order. It correlated with Sunday's vision of her creativity that was finding expression at Heide.

This was not to say that Sunday slavishly followed Jekyll's rules. Jekyll was critical, though not as strongly as Robinson, of formal gardens. To Jekyll 'formal gardens always seem to me as if purposely designed to bind upon the shoulders of their owners the ever living burden of the most costly and wasteful kind of effort in the trim keeping of turf and Box edging and gravelled walks'.[62]

After planting the lavender hedge, Sunday planted box in front of the house and made a gravel drive. The front and back lawns were always kept mown. Douglas recalled, 'Sunday had a very formal taste for gardening. She liked a little box hedging and box grew very well there' though, over time, Sunday began to experiment with 'free, rambling effects'.[63] In the early years, before the garden had grown around it, the box hedging made a symmetrical and quite severe entrance to the house. Sunday was influenced by the formality of the past and her garden plans reminded Douglas of 'all the great gardens of France, Italy and Elizabethan England! . . . Look at the gardens of the D'Estes or Marie Antoinette or Capability Brown.'[64] Unfortunately, Sunday's plans have been lost.

Like Jekyll, Sunday loved blue. To Jekyll, 'blue is a colour that is perfect and complete in itself' and blue flowers needed to be 'satisfied' by contrasting them with white or pale yellow.[65] Sunday liked 'Celtic blue and the more romantic colours' while Douglas favoured 'hot orange colours. Sun hated them. So we did fight about that a bit.'[66]

Marion Cran, affectionately dubbed Mum Cran by Sunday, was a gardening writer and journalist who settled in Surrey, not far from Gertrude Jekyll whom Cran credited as doing 'more than any living person to transform the English garden'.[67] The title of Cran's popular 1920s book, *The Garden of Ignorance: The Experiences of a Woman in a Garden*, describes one of its chief attractions for Sunday. Cran was starting her first garden, experimenting, learning, making mistakes and falling in love with nature, just as Sunday was. Cran's 'idea that a garden was a canvas on which to paint, a picture in flowers and trees and winding paths' had never occurred to her until she began her own garden and 'from that moment it never left me'.[68]

Cran was a gardening poet, enumerating the virtues gained from gardening. 'First, foremost, deepest, one learns patience, humility in the constant service of a greater than one's self; unselfishness, gratitude.'[69] She also believed gardens provided a psychological portrait of the gardener, 'an open transcript of the self for all the world to see'.[70] It was the kind of passionate, declarative, lyrical response to nature that appealed to Sunday. Gardening proved an epiphany for both women. Cran learned 'in a dazzling instant that planting was a sacred responsibility. All the flowers I would ever plant in my garden for the rest of my life became my children.'⁷¹

Sunday felt the same. She wrote to Hester, 'Outside the stars twinkle. Come soon again the lavender hour and a thousand bees move through the flowers like a breeze, plums fall and butterflys and everywhere in the garden there is summer-time – sometimes I feel I can hear something as if I can hear the sun shining and the shadows moving their places under the trees, a very faint sound that seems high up in the air like an aeroplane but everywhere a tiny summer engine, sweet sweet oh so precious world how greatly I love you.'⁷²

Eleanour Sinclair Rohde, a gardening scholar, shared precisely this ecstatic, spiritual approach to nature and to the act of gardening itself. *The Scented Garden* (1931) is a sensual social history. Rohde's marvellous description of violets may well have helped inspire Sunday's creation of a violet tunnel, a ditch planted out with violets, behind the oak tree in the yard. 'Violets preserve in their scent the memory of Orpheus, for one day, being weary he sank to sleep on a mossy bank and where his enchanted lute fell, there blossomed the first violet. The magic music of his lute still haunts the secret scent of violets.'⁷³

Susie Brunton recalled that Sunday's 'violet run was about four feet deep . . . and there were black violets and bright and purple and pink and it was absolutely wonderful . . . I don't know how many types of violets were there.'⁷⁴ In her book, Rohde also included recipes from medieval herbals for sweet bags, pot-pourri and cordials.

Sunday was also in the process of making a north-facing kitchen garden to the right of the house where the Reeds planted beans, lettuce, strawberries, raspberries, tomatoes, marrows, parsley, peas, leeks, endives and potatoes. Rohde suggested a herb garden 'conjured up a vision ... of a secluded pleasaunce full of sunlight and delicious scents and radiant with the colours and quiet charm of all the old-fashioned plants one so rarely sees nowadays'.[75] Sunday had seen such kitchen gardens, or potagers, in France and was keen to establish something similar.

By early 1936, John could report proudly that 'the veg garden really looks quite like a veg garden all complete with veges and stakes and strings and everything looks very healthy and doing very well indeed. Some of the beans are over a foot high and the onions about six inches and the lettuces beginning to look like lettuces.'[76] While Sunday told an English wildflower expert, 'I have never collected herbs for medicinal, cooking or other related reasons', it seems unlikely she planted herbs like parsley, tarragon and mint for their aesthetic value alone. 'Really, the garden just emerged from love.'[77]

What did Sunday mean by this? Mary Nolan recalled 'Sunday always used the word "love", love as intensity but it was also love as control.'[78] Gray Smith, Hester's second husband, remembered Sunday insisting that love could have no limitations. When Sunday gave Nolan's Ned Kelly series to the National Gallery of Australia in 1977, the words 'with love from Sunday Reed' were on the label accompanying the donation.

As far as the garden, or indeed any aspect of Sunday's life went, love meant sharing. Love was a compact, a union, requiring a deep connection and commitment. Thus the garden was planted by Sunday with the assistance of John, Douglas, Dyring and Atyeo. Other friends brought plants or helped as best they could. They were expected to. Their involvement was a symbol of affinity, of growth and fruition, the love tokens of friendship, communality, belonging. If Sunday was prepared to share all she had, then her friends were expected to respond in kind, infusing her projects with their labour and enthusiasm. Heide was her garden but it was supposed to belong to everyone, a fact meant to be understood and honoured.

But Sunday's expectations lead to bitter disappointments when her friends did not notice changes to the garden, did not participate as fully as she wanted. She complained to Hester, 'Is [it] that nobody says anything anymore? When we came home from France John and I said we will never again say "Look" in our garden and then we will know. And ever since it has been quite quiet and secret and nobody ever looks now or speaks.'[79]

The garden did emerge from love's inspiring energy and Sunday was its goddess but when she did not receive her due, when those upon whom she bestowed her gifts were not sufficiently grateful or sensitive, she became petulant and sad. 'Nobody ever thanked me,' Sunday told Jean Langley towards the end of her life. That was not true yet Sunday felt betrayed because she believed her benevolence had gone unappreciated. Hers are the words of the unhappy mother who feels she has given everything to her child, even the gift of life itself, and yet the child remains selfish and ungrateful. The Heide garden was a potent symbol of Sunday's creativity. It was meant to enchant and animate, and it did, but it seemed no amount of love received, or returned, could quite balance the equation for Sunday. In the final outcome, she remained hungry.

While Rohde said that 'the herb-garden is never more loveable ... than on a summer day for then it is full of bees and fairies', it was demanding physical work of the kind Sunday had never undertaken before.[80] It pushed her to her limits and she thrived.

Even as a woman in her sixties, Sunday remained 'physically very, very strong'. Peter Hobb, who lived with the Reeds and helped in the garden observed, 'I had seen strong women but not a woman who darted around carrying heavy loads.'[81] Susie Brunton, a close friend of Sunday's who worked alongside her in the garden in the 1960s, recalled, 'She was very strong and very wiry. And she was very tenacious in anything she wanted to do, she would carry it through to the end. But she had a vision and she knew where she was going and she could make things happen in the garden . . . John was very good at doing the hard slog stuff, turning the soil and getting rid of things, weeds and trees and whatever. But Sunday was going to create something out of it and it would just grow, everything she touched would grow.'[82] John observed that 'Sunday cannot work at a normal pace: she gets carried away and goes frantically at whatever she is doing.'[83]

On summer days, Brunton would quail at the rising temperature but Sunday worked on regardless. Hobb recalls, 'Tiny delicate pale blue flowers with dry summer grass and a hot north wind – that was Sunday's heaven. I can see her now, crawling on the ground covered with dirt with a bucketful of weeds in the middle of a heatwave that would knock out women half her age.'[84]

Sunday's 'spirituality' was connected to the earth, manifested in her garden and her home. She was an animist, that is, nature was alive to her and resonating with beauty and feeling. She was also a pantheist who worshipped the natural world as a sacred place. That included animals and lead to her vegetarianism. Sunday even refused to allow venomous snakes to be killed at Heide. Hers was an unfettered, uncodified paganism rooted to the place where she lived, one that suited both her privacy and her individuality.

A photograph of Sunday digging in the kitchen garden in the

1940s is an archetypal image of earthy femininity; of a strong, healthy, determined and creative woman. Sunday sought to share her abundance, to heal and inspire others. Perhaps one of the reasons Sunday poured such energy into the earth was the frustration she felt regarding her own infertility.

Harold Nicolson who, with his wife Vita Sackville-West, created Sissinghurst, one of the most influential twentieth-century gardens, admiringly referred to Vita as Demeter, ancient goddess of the fruitful earth.

But archetypes of pagan mythology always provide counter-balancing shadow sides. Demeter was the ultimate matriarch: powerful but controlling, furious when crossed and liable to mete out punishment to those who disobeyed her. When Persephone, her daughter, was abducted by Hades, Demeter made the earth wither and die until Persephone was restored to her. Sunday shared those characteristics, too. She could be generous and inspiring on the one hand, and engage in acts of anger and retribution on the other.

Jane Brown writes that, 'the secret garden, a hidden place of enchantment and peace, where all our ills can be cured, is one of the most powerful ideas in cultural history'.[85] The Heart Garden, created in 1949, was truly a 'secret garden', in that Sunday told its meaning to no-one except Jean Langley. The area of the Heart Garden has high brick walls surrounding it to the north and west while the house itself provides a third, south wall. The brick walls, built to protect flowers from brutal northerlies, create a sheltered, sunny, peaceful spot. Pergolas were fashionable then (Balhomen had a fine one) but Sunday never had any outside structures built at Heide for entertaining. But the Heart Garden area, close to the kitchen, functioned as the ideal place for summer meals and gatherings.

The garden was also a powerful bond between Sunday and John in their unconventional marriage, rather as it was between Harold Nicolson and Vita Sackville-West. Nicolson and Sackville-West were making Sissinghurst, in Kent, at exactly the same time as the creation of Heide.

Both Nicolson, a politican, and Sackville-West, a writer, were homosexual and allowed one another total freedom to explore affairs. They remained devoted to one another during the course of their marriage, producing two sons, and planning Sissinghurst. Their marriage succeeded because, as their son Nigel wrote, 'each found permanent happiness only in the company of the other'.[86] In the garden, the couple worked in perfect harmony: Vita had the eye for colour while Nicolson was the designer. The Nicolsons moved into Sissinghurst in 1932 and Vita's famous White Garden was finished just after the Second World War but it is unlikely Sunday would have known about Sissinghurst until long after the Heide garden was established.

There was one aspect of the garden about which Edna Walling, Jekyll, Cran and Rohde were all decided: the central importance of roses. Jekyll and Walling never designed a garden without including a separate rose garden and Sunday became a serious rose fancier. She started a rose garden to the south of the house. There she planted some of her favourites: varieties of old roses from France, southern Europe and Asia that included the heavenly scented Damask rose. There were also Gallicas that, as Jekyll pointed out, were associated with 'the history, poetry and literature and lives of civilised nations'. Rose expert David Austin believes Gallicas are the oldest of all garden roses. Sunday also grew *Rosa centifola*, or Cabbage Rose, 'the sweetest scented rose known in English gardens' and *Rosa alba*, the white rose of England.[87]

John was inspired by Douglas's climbing tea rose, Lady Hillingdon, and ordered it for Heide. Lady Hillingdon was an 'aristocratic beauty, breathing high blood in every line of her . . . [with] blooms clear deep apricot, very long and shapely'.[88] Sunday also planted *Rosa mutabilis*, a China rose, near the river bank, which provided the inspiration for Nolan's portrait of her, as well as sweet briars and climbers like *Rosa rugosa*, another Chinese variety. A sentimental addition was to plant her mother's favourite rose in the Heart Garden.

David Austin writes that 'throughout the history of western civilization . . . the rose has been the flower closest to the heart'.[89] It is a distinctly feminine symbol with a rich and romantic history. In Greek mythology, Aphrodite, goddess of love and beauty, was regarded as the creator of the red rose. Hurrying to Adonis, her wounded lover, Aphrodite trod on a bush of white roses and her blood dyed them red. Ancient Romans knew of the rose as the Flower of Venus and as the badge of prostitutes sacred to the goddess. Romans grew roses in their funerary gardens to symbolise resurrection. The rose garden was also the garden of Eros, and the flower a symbol of female genitalia.

The rose's fecund symbolism of beauty and licentiousness made early Christians wary but gradually Mary, the mother of Jesus, became enshrined as the mystical symbol of the rose, a feminine source of divine love. In Gothic cathedrals, often known as Notre Dame (Our Lady), the great stained glass 'rose' windows, modelled on the five-petalled wild rose, face west and were dedicated to Mary. The rose also gave its name to the rosary, a string of beads used for counting prayers. Rosary is another name for a *rosarium*, or rose garden. To Dante, the rose symbolised Paradise. More colloquially, to send roses or offer a single red rose can mean a declaration of love. For centuries, fragrant rose oil and dried rose petals have featured in love charms while rose bud (rosehip) tea is a source of Vitamin C and used to treat colds. Rosewater remains a popular perfume and is used to flavour Middle Eastern dishes.

Sunday, who enthusiastically collected books about the history of flowers, must have been familiar with some of these tales. The rose became a symbol of all that gardens, and Heide, meant to her. Joy Hester understood this. The metaphor of the rose in her poetry was inspired by Sunday and the Heide garden. In the 1950s, when Sunday asked Hester to design glass panels for Heide's front door, Hester drew roses. Sweeney, Hester's son whom Sunday adopted, produced tender, haiku-like poems, many based on emotional connections with nature. In 1960, he wrote, 'I am hiding/in a rose', explaining that 'for me . . . the Rose is the centre of the universe'.[90]

Meanwhile the Reeds and Douglas were also planting a wide variety of flowers including delphiniums, cornflowers, sweet alice, phlox, sweet pea, larkspur, poppies and snapdragons, sourcing plants from locations both conventional and unconventional. Sunday liked humble flowers: cornflowers and primroses were two favourites.

Douglas recalls, 'We used to tour the back streets of suburbs looking for unusual plants hanging over fences, particularly old roses and daisies, no longer obtainable in nurseries. We would take cuttings with us from our garden and would offer them in exchange. We often met lovely people and had some funny experiences, like the time when John and Sun knocked on a door . . . and couldn't raise anybody . . . John couldn't resist and he snipped a cutting, just as the front door opened and a woman yelled, "Ay!" and a man rushed out. John and Sun got such a fright they dived into their car and zoomed off.'[91]

Douglas also introduced the Reeds to Russell Pritchard, an eccentric nurseryman in Bayswater who experimented with cross-breeding plants. The Reeds 'just fell for him. There would be those lovely things that Sun would want and he'd say, "I'm still working on that." Pritchard got to love John and Sun, too. He used to come to Heide.' Pritchard made many other unusual plants available to the Reeds, including a rare miniature primrose. 'How much? "Sixpence will do". That's all he ever charged, no matter how obviously rich you were.'[92]

The Reeds, acknowledging Douglas's immense contribution, offered him his own patch of earth at Heide. Douglas created the wild garden, immediately to the south of the front fence, which takes its title from Robinson's book. It was a deliciously tangled and mysterious place filled with wildflowers, magnolias, bushy shrubs and winding paths. By the 1960s, however, keeping it in some degree of order became the bane of Sunday's life.

The garden dictated the day. Douglas and John rose early and did an hour's inspection of the property and the animals before breakfast. Douglas had encouraged the Reeds to get cows for milk, cream and butter and 'shiny black beetle-backed chooks that laid brown eggs'.[93] Then John set off for Collins House before arriving home for afternoon tea, precisely at four. Sunday spent the day working in the house and garden. The Reeds had 'discipline, absolute discipline, both of them'.[94]

'Arvo tea' was worth coming home for: Sunday's freshly baked scones, home-made jam and plenty of cream. Afternoon tea was an upper-class English tradition, a time for discussion of the day's events, 'tea and sympathy', a soothing break before dinner and day's end. Rituals were important to the Reeds and 'arvo tea' was one they maintained all their lives.

*

In October 1936, Atyeo sailed for France. He painted one of his last, and best, Australian works in the Heide library, and gave it to Sunday. *The Dancer* (1936, Heide MoMA) is inspired by jazz, the music of modernism, with its vitality, its fractured, dissonant, syncopated rhythms. Stylistically, it is similar to *The Thinker* but while that was a study in stillness, *The Dancer* vibrates with energy. Atyeo had Fats Waller blaring as he painted it.

He wrote to Sunday from Paris, 'I knew the dancing girl would not let you down. I too remember every spot, everything we said and did when I was painting her, the changing from red to light blue, the top left hand corner, it was your idea. I like her better than anything I have done. It is so good you have her.'[95]

Atyeo's letter signals the advent of Sunday's role as advisor to the artwork being produced in her home and under her gaze. The smudge of light blue to which Atyeo refers is a subtle abstract passage, emphasising the two-dimensionality of the painting's surface and reinforcing a flattened, modernist pictorial space. It also enhances the rough, textured feeling of the paint. It was a felicitous suggestion.

The time before Atyeo's departure was difficult for Sunday. Even though Atyeo swore his commitment to her was undiminished, Sunday's anguish and sense of loss was very real. Even high-jinks with Atyeo and Douglas in the Heide library after dinner could not compensate.

One evening, Atyeo decided he would write explicit endings to chapters in D.H. Lawrence's *Lady Chatterley's Lover*. The Reeds and Atyeo 'all read D.H. Lawrence', Douglas recalled, 'and believed in free love and thought my moral beliefs were goofy'.[96]

Still banned in Australia, the Reeds had managed to have a copy smuggled in. Lawrence's depiction of the relationship between Lady

Chatterley and Mellors, her gamekeeper, caused an outcry. Not only sexually explicit, it also challenged the prevailing class system by exploring an aristocrat's tutelage in the arts of love by her servant. Published when Lawrence was dying from tuberculosis, and shortly after his London exhibition which Sunday visited, *Lady Chatterley's Lover* is by no means Lawrence's best work but it is certainly his most famous, a manifesto for its time.

Lawrence's intention was to 'put forth this novel as an honest, healthy book, necessary for us all today . . . I want men and women to be able to think sex, fully completely, honestly and cleanly.'[97] Lawrence also recognised that he paid the price for challenging contemporary taboos, it was 'so obviously a book written in defiance of convention'.[98]

The ardent, sensual Mellors arouses Connie Chatterley as her husband Clifford, paralysed by war injuries, cannot. Clifford is a fashionable novelist, adept at gaining the kind of publicity and success Lawrence patently disdains. Mellors represents a free, natural, earthy intensity to which Connie is attracted precisely because it is lacking in her own life. Next to Mellors, the men of Connie's generation seem 'so tight, so scared of life!'[99] Clifford, particularly, was 'never really warm' to her, only 'considerate in a well-bred, cold sort of way!'[100]

Lady Chatterley's Lover examines the proposal that if the marriage partner is sexually unfulfilling, other possibilities must be fearlessly explored. It was the blueprint for Sunday and John's marriage, too. In Lawrence's fiction, relationships are examined through deep, heart-to-heart conversations, expressing an intelligent, articulate intimacy that appealed to Sunday. Lawrence also acknowledges that contemporary relations between men and women are both profoundly necessary and complex. 'For me it's the core of my life,' Mellors reflects, 'if I have the right relation with a woman.'[101]

Lawrence's agonisingly sincere characters find themselves in explosive emotional situations because they are compelled to explore their sexuality, despite the risks. For Lawrence, sex is an undeniable primeval force, 'a dark flood of electric passion', and nature and sexuality are linked in an ecstatic celebration of 'the life-source'.[102]

Lady Chatterley's Lover corresponds with the Reeds' marriage where Sunday's adventurous sexuality is contrasted with John's reserve; where an ardent, working-class lover fulfils Sunday's needs as her upper-class husband cannot. Lawrence also offered support for the unconventional situation the Reeds found themselves in. Remarking on the business with Atyeo, John wrote, 'be a little happy Sun darling even though the world and everyone in it is a bit frightening and even though life is so hard to cope with. Everyone seems to find that, Lawrence and all, so in a sense we are not alone in our struggle.'[103]

Lawrence's emotional honesty and pursuit of love, no matter how disruptive or unorthodox, were crucial influences on Heide's mores, the imprimatur of a distinctively modern, literary sensibility that challenged society's rules. Sunday read Lawrence's other novels and liked his poetry, too.

Lawrence could also provide an erotic parlour game where Atyeo read out his alternative endings to Lawrence's chapters. Douglas was 'very naive at that time, very innocent. This explicit carrying on of the scene after the decent end of the chapter . . . was so liberating and hilarious and electrifying . . . Sun typed them out on her little typewriter and stitched them into the book.'[104]

•

On 15 May 1937, Sunday sailed on the RMS *Niagra* to North America, accompanied by Doodie. Arthur Baillieu accompanied them part of the way. The reason for the voyage was two-fold: first, to seek medical help for a mysterious gastric ailment that was bedevilling her and, second, to visit Everard, her younger brother, who was working at the Wells Fargo bank in San Francisco. Everard had written enticingly of California and encouraged the family to visit.

Sunday had been unwell for some time, assailed by crippling stomach pains. She had consulted several doctors about her condition, including Erskine Sewell, her regular doctor. Early in 1936, Sewell thought Sunday might have an ulcer, then he hypothesised it was an 'excess of acid', and gave Sunday a fresh prescription.[105] There were x-rays and regular examination of Sunday's stools. The whole business put her, she admitted, in 'a messy state of mind' and meant a period of recuperation at the safe nest of Merthon. She wondered if her 'indisposition' found 'a physical manifestation' in her stomach problems. John certainly felt it was a 'nervous illness' and that the stresses and strains of Sunday's 'daily life' were responsible – meaning the pressures and responsibilities of Heide, plus the affair with Atyeo.

But Sunday did not agree about Atyeo. She told John that she had trained herself, when at Merthon, 'to make my daily life into one long dope & I doubt if any small excitement Sam or otherwise have really penetrated these last few weeks.' It made her 'frightened' to return to Heide. At Merthon it was easy 'to dope the days away! At Heide – well you know the answer.' Sunday believed 'rest is what I need to cure my pain' and there was 'every chance' she would be cured at Merthon. But, she wondered, if there 'will always be a sore spot where I run away from things'. She felt 'miserable and selfish . . . I haven't pulled my weight in ages . . . please make me better – I love you more & more yet when you're here I'm lousy and upset you – darling darling John.'[106]

By 1937, with the cause of her illness still undiagnosed, Sunday set off. The long sea voyage would take her first to Sydney, then to Auckland, Suva, Honolulu and Vancouver. There she and Doodie disembarked before catching a train from Seattle to San Franciso.

Sunday kept up her spirits by writing to John. Her first letter included an amusing sketch of her 'funny little cabin', shared with Doodie, 'about 9' × 9' wide along the sides' with 'a fold up basin in between wardrobe' and 'a carpet, a stool, a shelf and a few hooks on the wall'. But the sailor's daughter was 'quite comfortable and warm and beautifully amid ships' and considered her cabin to be 'the steadiest part' of the boat. Arthur was less impressed (so was John) and wanted a better cabin for Sunday, all to no avail. The ship was 'full to overflowing & not another cabin for love or money'. But Sunday was not fussed. The cabins were 'all much of a muchness'. The seas were gentle and Sunday 'hadn't felt at all seasick being very much too busy being homesick and other sicks'.

Before sailing from Sydney, Sunday had a 'terrible day . . . with such a pain I could just drag myself around & I might have been in Timbuctoo for all I knew or cared.' It meant a planned visit to H.V. and Mary Alice Evatt was out of the question. Until the boat sailed, Sunday felt she was walking in her sleep. But John's – and Sam's – letters were there to welcome her, as well as flowers: orchids from her brother Darren, violets from Basil Burdett and a bunch of flowers from Moya Dyring's mother. She was taking 'a dose of . . . new pain medicine' prescribed by Dr Wilson, a specialist, which she felt was 'just as useless as everything else he has given me but fortunately I didn't have awful agonies this time'.[107] Her weight loss worried John and her friends. 'Just be a good girl, Sun,' Dyring advised, 'and eat the rotten ship board food. I know how awful it is but Sun you cannot grow any thinner.'[108]

The night before Sunday left, Dyring had arranged a dinner party for her at Café Petrushka at 144 Little Collins Street. Minka Veal's matchbox-sized café was one of Melbourne's few bohemian restaurants which served good, cheap European cuisine. Adrian Lawlor and Connie Smith were among the guests. Sunday's mood lifted. As Dyring commented, 'Tonight for the first time your bitching witch left you and you had [the] glow of an old self I had not seen for many long days and you seemed happy but a nervous sort of happiness that could not last ... I hate knowing you are not happy about going. I hope in America you get to the bottom of it.'[109]

Sunday did not bother socialising on board. Three days into the voyage from Sydney and nearing Auckland, she wrote to John that 'so far no one has spoken to me & I haven't spoken – & I wouldn't be surprised if I don't speak.' She had 'lost all count of days' on 'this grey sea'. But there were some friends on board.

The Budapest String Quartet had toured Australia in 1937. Brothers Mischa and Sasha Schneider became friendly with the Reeds and visited Heide. Now the 'Budys', as Sunday called them, were on their way to perform in New Zealand, travelling second class. Sunday escaped from dinner at the captain's table to spend time with them. 'You see, it was Coronation night & everything was bedecked with union jacks & crowns & Father couldn't resist making a little speech! I've forgotten what about but something to do with his gracious majesty & the commander – he spoke in a very loud voice.'

But contact with the Schneiders, whom Sunday regarded as 'very sweet and friendly', also had its drawbacks. Over glasses of brandy – 'love brandy' Sunday commented – the Schneiders became anxious about Sunday's 'melancholy state' and encouraged her to 'take your life into your two hands – live from day to day'. Sunday 'just smiled & said I did all those things but I was homesick & did not want to go to America anyway.' They insisted Sunday would meet 'good people' in America, which she doubted.

Perhaps the brandy flowed rather too freely because the Schneiders began making 'some very odd remarks about Sam ... The idea was that Sam got a great kick trying to lead the bohemian life.' The sophisticated Schneiders, mocking Atyeo's pretensions, recalled a lunch at his studio, where they were served on paper plates.

Sunday was furious that her lover and admired artist should be held up to ridicule. 'That you should notice & talk about paper plates. I can't understand,' she admonished the Schneiders. Poor Mischa Schneider 'got deeper & deeper into the water' as he tried to exonerate himself by explaining his own youthful pretensions: pretending to compose music when he could not, trying to smoke a cigar and 'be a big man'. Atyeo, he predicted, would return from Paris 'a changed man'. As far as Sunday was concerned, Sam was 'a big man already'. Mischa was 'genuinely upset that I was so worried – Why do you worry so about everything – he said. What does it matter what I think about Sam.'

But it did matter to Sunday, especially as she admired Mischa. 'I like him,' she told John. 'I more than like him. What do you say then?'[110] She sought connection and balance in her friendships. When it lapsed, she became distressed, seeking to heal what she perceived as misunderstandings. But often her insistence in such delicate matters only made things worse, complicating and confusing what was already problematic. Sunday explained to Jean

Langley, 'I have no alternative to love and the purpose of my heart has never been to protect it from those for whom it beats.'[III]

That night with Mischa Schneider, she felt there had emerged 'a barrier between us, a racial difference or something of the sort that I couldn't quickly penetrate . . . I felt a great difficulty.' A racial difference? The situation seemed to rest on the Schneiders' European savoir faire and their amused perceptions of Atyeo's clumsy attempts to emulate the bohemian lifestyle. Nor did Mischa agree with Sunday's concerns about a barrier. So Sunday brought in the heavy artillery. 'I said I will tell John what you say about Sam & his paper plates: he will understand what I am feeling & tell you.' Mischa politely responded by saying he would enjoy visiting Heide again. 'Is your husband a shy man?' he asked. Sunday 'said no – I don't know why.'

It was not the only misunderstanding Sunday wished to clear up. In her letter to John, she included one of Atyeo's that, she explained, 'is not a happy one as you will see for your self – [Sam] has got some idea . . . that I've been angry with him – or hearing things about him that upset me – poor Sammie – how silly it is.' Atyeo had read 'other things' into her letter where she said 'the world was very frightening & there was no one but John.'

Perhaps Atyeo felt she was rejecting him and choosing John. But, Sunday insisted, 'I have not been happy & the world is frightening.' She had hoped Atyeo would be a bit more sympathetic 'but I can see he is restless and angry'. It gave Sunday the opportunity to observe 'it is a pity that he has cleared off to London – I always felt he might run away from Paris when he got bored & so he has.' John was the one delegated to contact him. 'Please write to [Sam] darling and keep in touch – it is so easy to lose contact & one is so sad when it happens.' But it was John she longed for. 'Darling John you have no idea how lonely I am for you – What big roots we have in each other – it seems my life wherever it takes me – whoever it takes me to – first began with you – do you see? What are you doing with yourself tonight,' she mused, 'sitting in front of the fire with Moya?'[112]

Dyring was staying at Heide while she prepared for her first solo exhibition at Riddell's Gallery. Around the time Atyeo left, Dyring's affair with John also seems to have subsided. John assured Sunday that, during one freezing night at Heide, 'poor old Moya was so cold she had to get up in the middle of the night (not from my bed) and get herself another hotty'. He reflected, 'my relationship with Moya seems to be working out quite all right & we potter about together much the same as usual'.[113] The aside about Dyring rising 'not from my bed' to get herself a hot water bottle indicates Sunday knew of the affair and that he and Dyring were no longer lovers.

Dyring adored Heide and worked hard in the garden. It was her 'only rest and peace and happiness but lonely jeese Sun so different without you there's a blank blankness that is so unbelievable'. Preparations for Dyring's show were stressful. 'I'm feeling life is bloody hell as to no sleep except in Heide bed. I can hear you saying "cut out this neurosis Moya" and wish you were here to say it, it makes a difference.'[114]

Dyring's show was a great success. Not only did she receive an excellent review from George Bell but John bought *Melanctha* (c.1937, Heide MoMA). Bell praised *Melanctha* as the outstanding work in the show, 'a picture tending towards abstraction, well-designed in very expressive colour in which the nuances both of tone and colour are very well handled'.[115] H.V. Evatt bought a portrait of Pat, Dyring's sister.

The opening was dramatic. Evatt was supposed to launch the show but ill-health prevented him and Bell graciously stepped into the breach at the last moment. (A week later Evatt arrived and there was a second opening.) 'We were all packed as full as sardines in a tin,' Dyring told Sunday, 'and the floor wobbled to bursting point till Mr Riddell and his boyfriends downstairs said they had to go out into the street because they were afraid the ceiling would fall in.' For Dyring it was a moment of artistic maturity, where she could congratulate herself on the 'definite break from Sam's influence in my work'.[116]

Rather like Atyeo, Dyring could move easily between different pictorial styles. *Holly* (c.1937, Heide MoMA) has the same vivid expressionist palette as *Female Figure (Cynthia)* but the mood is darker and the female subject seems dissolute and depressed, a modern woman drinking alone in a bar. Bell considered the distortion used in *Holly* 'does not justify itself as inevitable to the design'.[117] In fact, *Holly* shows up Dyring's major weakness, an inability to create a convincing sense of form.

On the basis of *Melanctha*, Dyring was hailed by Bernard Smith as 'perhaps the first artist in Melbourne to experiment with cubism'.[118] 'Cézanne was at that time her guide' recalled John but it is the influence of Picasso's early cubist period that directs the work's shifting planes of colour and brown tonal range.[119] Subject, form and modernist cultural references are intriguingly combined in *Melanctha*.

Dyring takes her title from a novella by Gertrude Stein, a 'word portrait' of an African-American woman, published as the centre-piece to *Three Lives* (1909). Less radically experimental than Stein's later work, it tells the story of Melanctha, 'a graceful, pale yellow, intelligent, attractive negress' whose courageous experiments in love and independence end bitterly when she is rejected by friends and lovers alike.[120]

As a writer, Stein learned much from cubist practice which divorced painting from representation and broke the subject into its component lines and dimensions. Stein knew her experiments with language were similar to Picasso's in painting. Picasso's breakthrough painting *Portrait of Gertrude Stein* (1906), completed during the year she was finishing *Three Lives*, shares something with her literary methods: portraiture is maintained, the subject is recognisable, although slightly distorted to suggest the effects of character.[121]

Dyring was reading Stein and looking at Picasso, and brought both influences to bear in *Melanctha*. The subject, a woman created by Stein's technical experiments in language, is then subjected to Picasso's formal dissolution: a neat double portrait of modernist practice. Though a bold, ambitious work, *Melanctha* does not wholly escape Dyring's problems with form. The figure is unresolved, the brown planes more decorative than assertively structural, as if Dyring herself is unsure of how to break down the figure into its component parts.

During that time, separated from one another and dealing with the departure of their two closest friends, the Reeds suddenly felt daunted about the grand project of Heide.

'We must cope more fully and completely with Heide,' John wrote to Sunday.

I wrote to Sam and said sometimes I thought we had taken on too much and it got us down but I feel at the same time that that should not be so and that we should be able to cope and must cope so that we can feel that we have a stable smooth harmonious base to our habitual life which will give us faith in ourselves and in everything we do.

Yes of course you are right we should have rambley roses along the fence even if they knock the old fence over and we must get the whole place to come together and to come round us closer and be more intimate and we must organise better and plan and work better oh it can all be done all right if we insist and keep on insisting and make it come so. It is so important that we simply must do it.

John ended by saying, 'How I do hope you are well and fit darling and seeing the course of your life more clearly because if one of us sees clearly then I am sure it will help the other too.'[122]

It 'flashed across' John's mind 'very vividly' while he had guests at Heide that 'you not being here alters the whole tone of life . . . suddenly I realised that the essential significance of everything was just about to disappear and that without you there was a terrible danger that I would lose all true sense of values and that all that I was saying would be just trivialities oh darling Sun my world revolves around you and in you.'[123] Heide would be their saving grace, of that John was certain. 'I reckon we just have to work round the core of our lives, build up from the basis of Heide House and ourselves and make it all come good.'[124]

Sunday returned in August, just in time to farewell Dyring whose mother had agreed, after some gentle pressure from George Bell, to pay her fare overseas. Dyring stayed at Heide until she left. 'I packed my bags and walked out of Heide, catching the train to the city, clutching some Heide lavender.'[125] She travelled first to America and then met up with Atyeo in Paris where their relationship was rekindled.

Sunday's long sea voyage generated new energy and confidence. On her return, she also managed to cure her gastric problems.

While Neil Douglas was creating a wildflower garden for Edward Dyason at St Filian, his country home at Narbethong, Dyason invited the Reeds for the weekend. 'Dyason got up the Hay diet for dinner. Sun fell for this and got us all on to [it].'[126] Sunday adhered to the diet for the rest of her life and enthusiastically tried to convert her friends.

Invented by American nutritionist Dr William Hay, the diet was based on food separation: for good digestion, starches and protein should not be combined, so meat is eaten at one meal, potatoes at another. While food separation has been utterly discredited as having any health benefit, Hay's emphasis on natural foods – whole grain cereals, unrefined sugars, nuts and fresh vegetables – provided Sunday with a new attitude towards cuisine and a new sense of responsibility towards health and wellbeing. It also made her feel better. 'Sunday used to say your body is like a car, it is like putting the right petrol in it.'[127] Mrs Wells, their housekeeper, had left and Sunday decided not to replace her. She did the cooking herself and soon became an accomplished cook.

Until Sunday's adoption of the Hay diet, she and John had favoured rich, French-style cuisine that included roast duck, souffles and heavy cream sauces. Sunday told Philip Jones it was 'a real haute bourgeois cuisine'. When they converted to the Hay diet, the Reeds 'threw all that out and had very simple food and we were ill for weeks and then we were perfectly healthy'.[128] The diet remedied

Sunday's nagging digestive problems and gave her, as she told Hester, 'enormous faith in diet'.[129] As soon as they became available, Sunday began buying vitamin supplements, too.

Sunday's new attitude was to get 'the best out of whatever you had. Good cooking is knowing how to get the best out of a basket of very fresh peas, for instance. And how to make your white sauce, how to get the best taste without complicating it. How to make it as smooth as possible.'[130] But Sunday did not slavishly follow the Hay diet, relenting for special occasions like Christmas or birthdays. She also indulged her sweet tooth, making delicious cakes such as rum babas.

Cooking for John and her friends became a pleasurable and inspired task for Sunday, a mixture of hospitality and nurture, where the garden she had created sustained and benefited those she loved. Meals at Heide were memorable events, beautifully prepared and presented, with fresh, seasonal produce from the garden, homemade cream and butter, and choice cuts of meat. To less affluent friends, Heide seemed like an earthly paradise where the senses were sated by a banquet of flavours, scents and tastes.

But Sunday's commitment to diet did mean that mealtime at Heide could be an eccentric experience. Anne Cairns remembered the food was 'heavenly but rather capricious'. Sunday 'could be very strict so there was no question of concessions'. Once, when Anne took her children there, 'we had mashed pumpkin for a meal . . . but we were not allowed salt and pepper. The children wouldn't eat it. They demanded Weetbix and Sunday was very shocked.' Another time the Reeds 'would be eating madly those sausages that are salted'.[131] Occasionally Joy Hester became irritated with Sunday's rules about food. Sunday, censured, responded by saying that 'surely it must be a hundred years since I talked about "starch and protein". I've forgotten what to say. I suppose we have been left with certain prejudices. Mr Hay gave me such a talking to, in the early days, I have never recovered. Perhaps out of all that, and the years, we have learnt a way of eating and thinking about food that seems to fit in somewhere with all our other funny ways but whether it [has] much to do with . . . Mr Hay, I don't know. I only know that nowadays if I ate too much salmon and rice, I should not feel well and so I don't, on the other hand I know some people who would die on orange juice. So there you are. It's a sort of voyage of discovery, isn't it?'[132]

Heide ran like clockwork. The Reeds rose early and breakfast was at seven. Michael Keon savoured the delights of 'fresh orange juice, from Mildura oranges. Thick cream plastered half-inch deep over Weetbix and topped with flaky brown sugar' followed by raisin toast and strong coffee.[133] In summer, they breakfasted outside. Lunch was a simple meal of milk, cheese, bread and fruit. Arvo tea was served punctually at four.

Jean Langley recalled the evening meal would be 'some sort of marvellous meat, beautifully cooked. Sun was a great cook and we'd go and work in the kitchen and get vegies . . . I was very young and stupid but I did my best and Sun would always talk to me while we were doing these things. Then she would go off and have a shower and come back looking absolutely lovely in trousers and a soft shirt. I would go into the library and John would come in drinking a whisky and then Sun would come in and we'd all have a whisky. Then we'd . . . have dinner and it was always just right, never overcooked meat.'[134]

Afterwards, coffee and chocolate would be served in the library where a fire had been lit and Sunday would smoke Sobranies, thin, black, elegant Russian cigarettes. John did the dishes. Barrett Reid recalled that 'it was the first house I knew where the man and the woman did an equal amount of housework. Sunday was terribly good at housework ... They were very fast.'[135]

In 1937, Sunday had settled back at Heide with fresh determination and commitment to her home and garden. Though Atyeo continued to write from Paris, begging for her faith and trust in him, the missives mark the end, not the continuation, of the affair. Heide itself had become the central love of Sunday's life, a place she would never forsake and that would continue to generate new dreams and plans.

Sunday transformed the traditional roles of wife, housekeeper and gardener by integrating them into the larger aesthetic of her modernist enterprise. She had grown more confident about her taste, about the best way to live, to cook, to eat and she also recognised that to assume creative control of Heide was to manage it herself. Housework became an aesthetic exercise, too. 'She took as much pride in keeping her kauri draining board scrubbed as in the rarest flower in the garden. The bleached linen sheets and pillows on the beds were like white camellias.'[136]

Sunday had 'no problem at all with women's lib. She did the washing up, she did the cooking, she did the salad, she grew the vegetables and she had tremendous discipline ... Sun ... had no problems in entering a forum of men, no self-consciousness.'[137] By divesting herself of domestic help, Sunday further removed herself from the past, from a cushioned, Edwardian world where servants automatically undertook the toils and burdens of daily life. By making herself entirely responsible for the maintenance of Heide, she ensured its atmosphere, style and interpretation was also hers. Sunday's version of modernism found a continuing and potent expression in the routines of daily domestic life and seasonal change.

Sunday was in agreement with Lawrence when he pleaded with his generation to 'get back into vivid and nourishing relation [with] the cosmos and the universe. The way is through daily ritual . . . We must once more practise the ritual of dawn and noon and sunset, the ritual of the kindling fire and pouring water . . . This is an affair of the individual and the household, a ritual of the day . . . Vitally, the human race is dying. It is like a great uprooted tree, with its roots in the air. We must plant ourselves in the universe again.'[138]

· 7 ·

Nolan

It was Sunday who had the green fingers. Sunday could spot an artist.
SIDNEY NOLAN[1]

I wonder sometimes that [Nolan] is too gentle a man for a genius but perhaps we have preconceived notions as to what genius should be.
SUNDAY REED TO JOHN REED
JAN/JUNE 1943[2]

From the moment in 1938 when I first met [Nolan] till the day in 1948 when he disappeared from our lives, it seemed to me that the three of us moved together in the most closely integrated way.
JOHN REED[3]

Only Cynthia introduced clarity by telling us that everyone — women, men, dogs — fell in love with Sid.
PATRICK WHITE[4]

Sᴜɴᴅᴀʏ's ᴛᴇɴ-ʏᴇᴀʀ ʀᴇʟᴀᴛɪᴏɴsʜɪᴘ with Sidney Nolan provided a unique partnership and an inspirational direction for them both that also lead to a shift in the interpretation of the Australian landscape. Sunday was Nolan's muse, patron, lover, mentor, artistic collaborator and studio assistant. She believed, as he did, that she was the co-creator of his paintings. Without her, it is hard to imagine the genesis of the Wimmera paintings, let alone the development of the Ned Kelly series. When they met, Nolan was experimenting wildly with painting, poetry and fiction. At Heide, he became an artist.

In 1934, Atyeo made the bold prediction that he and Sunday would be 'sitting on the top rung together'. With Nolan, and in terms of Australian painting, that prediction became a reality. Between 1938 and 1947, Sunday experienced a flowering of her deepest creative desires: she had, in her home, one of Australia's most inventive modernists in whose art she was intimately involved.

The story of Nolan's arrival at Heide has by now taken on the quality of a myth. In 1938, Nolan conned his way into the office of Sir Keith Murdoch, publisher of the Melbourne *Herald*. He was angling for one of the scholarships that Murdoch made available to bright young professionals. But Murdoch was appalled by Nolan's folio, which included a series of abstract figure studies, cranked out by Nolan in a desperate rush. Murdoch packed him off to Basil Burdett who, equally at a loss, advised him to see John Reed.

Nolan found John in his small office at Collins House, his head buried in Wilenski's *The Modern Movement in Art*. Nolan was nervous, 'his speech so mumbled that it was almost impossible to follow him'.[5] Nonetheless, he managed to get his message across, a blatant request for fifty pounds 'and then I can go off to Paris'.[6] After politely but firmly rejecting the proposal, John took Nolan's folio home to be vetted by Sunday and to try and convey to her Nolan's 'wild-cat spirit' and 'the rather inexplicable excitement I felt after our meeting'.[7] Shortly afterwards, Nolan was invited to Heide for dinner. He was twenty-one years old.

The similarities with Atyeo were uncanny and could not have escaped the Reeds. Here was a gifted, ambitious, working-class larrikin eager to drink their whisky, sup at their table and take their money. Nolan was also devilishly good-looking and without Atyeo's fondness for boorish behaviour and the bottle. He was light-hearted, quick-witted, affectionate and prodigiously well-read.

Nolan had grown up in St Kilda where his tram-driver father had run an SP bookmakers to make ends meet during the Depression. Nolan was shrewdly streetwise and bookishly sensitive, equally at home competing in local amateur athletics – he was an excellent sprinter and cyclist – as he was poring over philosophy and poetry at the State Library. He attended night classes at the Gallery School in a desultory fashion, confiding to Albert Tucker that all he learned about in that conservative institution was 'sex and ping pong'.[8]

During the day Nolan worked in the advertising department at Fayrfield Hats in Abbotsford where he designed and built signs and display stands. He even managed to turn that dull employment to his advantage. Vernon Jones, his boss, imported art books and magazines including *The Studio*, and Nolan whiled away his days reading and digesting the latest in European art. He was especially interested in Picasso, Matisse and Van Gogh. He realised that his lack of talent in drawing the human form would preclude him from earning a living as a commercial artist as Tucker, and so many other struggling artists, did.

At Leisham White's commercial art studio, Nolan watched 'the six artists sitting at tilted easels engaged in drawing up newspaper advertisements . . . [F]rom the speed and quality of their work Nolan realised he could never match their technique. It was simply the case that they were good at drawing and he was not.'[9]

In 1938 when Nolan left Fayrfield Hats, the employment alternatives were miserable: he became a cleaner at Essendon Airport, then a short order cook at Hamburger Bill's takeaway in Swanston Street. Arriving at Heide must have felt like being admitted to heaven.

Nolan had already established clear objectives. Firstly it was the intent that mattered not the form, the vision not the medium. Coupled with that was his absolute conviction that 'he had a very special statement to make'.[10] Nolan's delicate abstract and semi-abstract transfers and drawings on blotting and tissue paper were inspired by the linear abstractions of Klee, Chinese calligraphy and Moholoy-Nagy's experiments with collage and photography. They were determinedly modern plus they cleverly avoided Nolan's weakness for tackling the human form in a realist manner.

At the same time, he was flirting with writing a novel as well as fashioning his own poetry. Though Nolan read constantly, he was not so much a reverent student of learning as a bower bird who flitted through Kierkegaard, Gide, Dostoyevsky, Lawrence and Blake, intuitively selecting what inspired or intrigued him. It is interesting to note that one of his earliest extant works is *Illustration for Ulysses* (1936, National Gallery of Australia), James Joyce's grand modernist statement that reconfigured the twentieth-century novel.

Nolan adopted the artist's approach to culture where everything was treated as potential source material for art. It mirrored Picasso and Matisse's response to tribal art where the formal power and spiritual energy of other cultures was brought within, indeed helped to set, the modernist agenda. It was also part of modernism's enterprise to collide differing cultures and media, bringing fresh meaning to both.

A central point of connection between Nolan and Sunday was the word. They were both literary people and shared a passion for French poetry, especially Arthur Rimbaud's hallucinatory masterpiece *Illuminations*. Nolan had been introduced to Rimbaud by fellow Gallery School student Howard Matthews and it 'amounted to a revelation'.[11]

Rimbaud escaped the monotony of nineteenth-century French provincial life by throwing himself on the mercy of Paul Verlaine, one of the most promising poets of the day. Verlaine became his lover in a torrid, two-year affair during which Rimbaud composed both *Illuminations* and *A Season in Hell*. Rimbaud was also a romantic, enigmatic figure, abandoning poetry at twenty to become a trader and gun-runner in Africa.

Rimbaud transformed the possibilities for poetry by self-consciously defying its conventions to present dissonant, opulent, kaleidoscopic images and metaphors, inventing a world of strange and dazzling beauty in free verse. He also re-invented the role of the poet who became an alchemist, a weaver of incantations aimed at changing life itself, at creating what previously did not exist. To achieve this, Rimbaud practised his famous 'long, immense and reasoned deranging of all the senses'[12] and used hashish, opium and alcohol to chart the 'sophistry and the logic of madness'.[13] Unsurprisingly, he was claimed by the surrealists as a precursor.

Nolan was captivated by Rimbaud's art and his myth – the boy genius whose talent for creation was matched only by his destructiveness, his preparedness to live on the edge, to risk everything for art. 'Can one go into ecstasies over destruction, be rejuvenated by cruelty!' Rimbaud demanded.[14] Rimbaud's originality was implicit in his descriptions of the world: a mixture of enchantment and violence, sentimentality and despair, lyricism and suffering, so his poetry has the quality of a very modern and bizarre fairytale.

Rimbaud was the modernist artist par excellence on whom Nolan modelled himself: rebellious and confident, sophisticated yet wilfully naive, open to all forms of experience, making no distinction between high and low culture, a personality whose very contradictions signalled a new kind of art and a new kind of artist. Rimbaud gave Nolan the conviction that, in art, 'the screw has to be turned ever further, that one has to be more violent, more avant-garde, more abstract'.[15]

Sunday understood that, too. She had longed for a brilliant young artist who embodied Rimbaud's orginality and recklessness. It was the promise her own childhood had made to her, that it is primarily from the young that a magical freshness and authenticity can arise. But Sunday's personal project was not to hurl herself into a tortuous abyss of creativity or to risk everything to make art. She had failed at that. Her task was to assist others.

Sunday opened her doors to Nolan and soon he was spending his free time at Heide, mainly reading voraciously in the library. But Sunday became aware that Nolan's excursions into poetry did not match the quality of his art. According to Sunday, 'Nolan had to make up his mind. Without delay', whether he wanted to be a painter or a poet. Clear in her role as guide and instructor, she set out to show Nolan where his true path lay and she used Rimbaud to do it.

Seating herself and Nolan at the dining room table, she arranged painting and writing materials before him and began to read Rimbaud in the original French, instructing Nolan, 'Paint or write down in English what you think or feel when I read to you.' Under these conditions, Nolan wrote 'inspired poetry' and drew 'a phantasmagoria, almost a visual saga, of sheer beauty'. Heide visitor Michael Keon observed that 'by the time Nolan and Sunday had been at [it] a week, I could not doubt that Nolan was painter not poet.'[16] Nolan's poems in the late '30s and early '40s are sweet, light echoes of Rimbaud, carrying none of his power to express savagery or chaos.

But there was more to Heide than Rimbaud and books. The Reeds' art collection was also the subject of inspiration and discussion. Nolan's work, already influenced by the linear abstractions of Klee, meant Atyeo's impact was inevitable.

Organised Line to Yellow, The Thinker and *The Dancer* hung on the walls and gave Nolan the opportunity to see how Atyeo had combined abstracted form, transparent planes, subtle colours and rigorous geometry in a lively, elegant manner. Equally engaging were John and Sunday's tales of Atyeo, a renaissance man who could turn his hand to painting or architecture; an ebullient, memorable character who was their beloved friend and who had done exactly what Nolan desired: set off for Paris to make his fortune. Nolan was eager to hear of Atyeo's adventures. He measured himself against Atyeo's achievements and responded to his art partly in order to best him.

Abstract Painting (1938, Private Collection) shows Nolan's response to Atyeo. Though it is a more radical painting than

Organised Line to Yellow or *The Thinker*, it has the studied, measured, contemplative qualities of those works and a palette that is similar but more heated. *Head of Rimbaud* (1939, Heide Museum of Modern Art), which caused such outrage at the inaugural exhibition of the Contemporary Art Society in June 1939, is a further exploration of linear, geometric abstraction. Painting his hero, Nolan tried to find a bold language of form that matched Rimbaud's confrontational style. Yet curiously, *Head of Rimbaud* conveys the same delicate sensibility Atyeo displayed in his most adventurous abstract, *Organised Line to Yellow*. Nolan also relished experimenting with different media and *Head of Rimbaud* uses pencil, oil and Kiwi boot polish.

Nolan was not alone when he began visiting Heide. His girlfriend was Elizabeth Paterson, a strikingly beautiful Gallery School student and the granddaughter of John Ford Paterson. Scottish-born and trained, Paterson settled permanently in Melbourne in 1884, producing romantic landscapes and taking a distinguished role in the art scene as a president of the Victorian Art School (1892–93) and a trustee of the National Gallery of Victoria (1903–12).

Elizabeth had grown up in Shepparton where her father was a farmer. After studying art at the Bendigo School of Mines, she attended Emily MacPherson College, a domestic science institute, then the Gallery School. The family home was in Park Street, St Kilda. Nolan lived nearby in Smith Street. Elizabeth painted landscapes but they were not modernist. Nolan admired her work, reflecting that his own ambitions lead him to 'ignore the fact that Elizabeth was a good artist as well, attempting to develop her own style'.[17]

Elizabeth's father was unhappy about his daughter's attachment to Nolan whom he regarded as a wastrel. Nor were the Reeds impressed with Elizabeth and, as their friendship with Nolan grew, they sought to exclude her. It may have been a combination of these pressures that lead Elizabeth and Nolan to marry on the spur of the moment in 1938.

After the wedding, the Reeds helped Nolan and Elizabeth find a seaside cottage at Ocean Grove near Geelong where, with the Reeds' encouragement, Nolan intended to devote himself to painting while earning money at a local asparagus farm. The Reeds felt he needed quiet time in order to work productively and he was grateful for their attentions, which also involved regular visits with hampers of food and books from the Heide library.

But, still low on cash, Nolan had to exert pressure on John to buy more of his works. Nolan blithely assured John that his paintings, which he called 'jobs', would be worth a great deal in the coming years. He also believed Australia was going to lead the world as a decisive centre for modern art, exactly the kind of hubris that appealed to Sunday and John.

The Herald Exhibition of French and British Painting, shown at the Melbourne Town Hall in June 1939, was a turning-point for Nolan. It was his first experience of original works by Picasso, Cézanne, Van Gogh and Gauguin and the impact can be assessed, not in any direct way, but in the sheer bravura of *Head of Rimbaud*. Nolan arrived at the exhibition from Ocean Grove wearing gum boots, his only shoes, with Elizabeth who was heavily pregnant. They met the Reeds there who introduced them to Joy Hester, Albert Tucker's girlfriend, whom Nolan remembered from the Gallery School.

The imminent birth of Nolan's child, and his grinding poverty, must have made him realise how far away was the dream of travelling to Paris and making world-class art. Nolan and Elizabeth decided to move back to Melbourne where they set themselves the awful task of running a pie-shop in Lonsdale Street. Tucker and Hester lived a few blocks away in Little Collins Street, also ekeing out an existence. The Nolans' was barely a shop, just a hole in the wall where they fielded orders for sausage rolls.

As Nolan's art developed, Sunday began to assume a central role as muse and patron and Nolan's feelings for her intensified as he became eager to consult her taste, ideas and guidance. Once again John was cast in the role of the helpless observer, his wife's lover's good friend, the able manager of the *ménage-à-trois*. Nor can John have failed to realise, because Sunday kept nothing hidden, how deeply she had fallen in love with Nolan. It must have made John more afraid than ever of losing her.

Nadine Amadio recalled, 'Sunday said that she missed the feel of Nolan. She said that it was a very sensual, sexual relationship . . . John is not a very romantic person . . . Then along came Sid and Sun loved that sort of charm . . . She obviously did feel a little bit guilty [about John]. But not terribly. Once she was actually telling me what a wonderful lover Nolan was. How she loved being with him, how it awoke her physically and mentally. I said, "Was John upset by that?" She said, "No, John loved him too."'[18]

After a few months at the pie-shop, Nolan was saved by the de Basil ballet company who were touring Australia early in 1940. Serge Lifar, the company's principal dancer, spotted a Nolan water-colour in Peter Bellew's Sydney apartment. On the strength of it, Lifar commissioned Nolan to design the sets and costumes for *Icare*, a new, one-act ballet. Nolan's radical set designs explored the same language of geometric abstraction as his paintings. He fled to Sydney to work on the ballet and Elizabeth closed the pie-shop. After the Reeds attended the premiere in February 1940, they fully supported him and the miserable hand-to-mouth existence was over. But it came at a cost.

Elizabeth was irritated and upset by her husband's long stays at Heide and by the obvious attractions Sunday held for him. By the time the Nolans' daughter Amelda was born in 1940, Nolan had become an increasingly errant husband and they were living apart. The marriage had been given little chance of success — there was poverty, the disapproval of Elizabeth's family and, last but not least, the stimulation Nolan derived from the Reeds. John, ever the lawyer, managed the denouement. He called Elizabeth into his office and suggested she and Amelda come to live at Heide. Wisely, she refused. He told her, 'Nolan will come anyway.'[19]

When Nolan moved to Heide in 1941, the pretence which his marriage had become was finished. Whatever Nolan's true feelings about Elizabeth and his baby daughter, his manner, once he was established at Heide, was hard-working and high-spirited. Rimbaud, the great risk-taker, had inspired Nolan in life as well as in art. Neil Douglas remembered Nolan's boundless energy and enthusiasm while painting, Nolan saying 'simply a million times "Look at this!" — blue eyes, pink cheeks but dark hair — sleeves rolled up and Sun's apron on, those quiet pin-point eyes of smiling elation and fun!'[20]

How did Sunday manage the *ménage*? Albert Tucker's photographs, which cast Sunday as Heide's glamorous, glowing centre, indicate it was with aplomb. *Arvo tea* (1945) shows Sunday in the Heide kitchen with Hester on her left and Nolan on her right. As Joy pours the tea and chats, Sunday listens, her handsome features alight with affectionate attention. Nolan, in shadow, holds a teapot made by Arthur Merric Boyd Pottery. Sunday appears natural and relaxed, surrounded by her two favourite artists and closest friends.

But *On the couch* (c.1945) strikes another mood where Nolan, sandwiched between John and Sunday, gazes nervously at the camera, hands held passively in his lap, a smile flickering across his lips. He seems to acknowledge, almost wryly, that he is trapped, a private joke shared with Tucker. John's body language is defensive, his arms are wrapped around his body and his expression is troubled, but Sunday is a study in nonchalance as she reads the paper, apparently oblivious to her husband and her lover. From this photograph, it is not difficult to gauge who was the boss.

By and large the situation was handled so discreetly that occasional visitors to Heide never guessed. Long-term resident Michael Keon was privy to the *ménage*'s day-to-day management. When John announced that, after a short absence, Nolan was returning to Heide, Sunday 'burst into a banshee-like long wail and ran out the back door'. John advised Keon not to follow her. Ten minutes later she returned, kissed John, 'patted' Keon and proceeded to make the evening meal.[21] When Nolan did arrive, John and Keon tactfully left the house to allow the lovers privacy.

There were four bedrooms at Heide, three that ran off the hall, and another that had been the maid's room, at the end of the hall. Presumably, Sunday divided her time between her marriage bed and Nolan's, which no doubt made for some tense evenings and even more uncomfortable breakfasts, a time when Sunday was never at her best.

John coped by returning to his liaison. Moya Dyring was back in Melbourne in 1941 to arrange an exhibition and visit her family, taking over her old studio in the city. Gay Cuthbert suggests that, once again, John found solace with Dyring as the temperature went up at Heide.[22]

In June 1940 Nolan's exhibition in his dilapidated studio at

320 Russell Street had been favourably, if cautiously, reviewed by George Bell and Basil Burdett. Nolan created an idealised environment for the show, a theatrical installation based on his imaginary view of a modernist Parisian studio. The walls were bright pink, fabric hid the bare boards and books were scattered about. On the walls were over two hundred pictures: small abstracts, calligraphic drawings, collages and painted slate tiles. Though Bell congratulated Nolan on striving to explore 'an absolutely pure art', with results that were 'extremely interesting and stimulating', the show was Nolan's farewell to abstraction.[23] The only memorable abstract from this time is the haunting *Boy and the Moon* (1940, NGA).

The event that cohered Nolan's brilliant but erratic talents seemed an unlikely one to inspire an artist. On 15 April 1942, he was drafted into the army and sent to the Wimmera. In December 1941 when the Japanese bombed Pearl Harbor, the Americans entered the war in the Pacific and suddenly Australians felt the war very close to home indeed. Until then, it had seemed a distant European conflict. In the next months, Rabaul in New Guinea was bombed and Singapore fell.

Nolan had no desire to serve in the army and with John's assistance engaged in all sorts of stratagems to avoid conscription that included seeking a position as an official war artist, all to no avail. Suddenly Private Nolan was on a train heading north to an area Richard Haese has evocatively described as 'small town Australia, the black soil plains of the wheatlands, the grey bush and dry scrub of Australia's marginal lands'.[24]

Instead of reacting negatively towards his new circumstances and to the unrelentingly flat landscape, Nolan set to work. But his response was not entirely self-generated.

For some time, Sunday had been discussing with Nolan the proposition that the Australian landscape should be reworked from the modernist perspective, that the radicalism of the Heidelberg School needed to be reconfigured in the contemporary idiom. Nolan was at first adamant that it was impossible, certainly for him. Nonetheless he was intrigued by her suggestion and happy to accept a challenge.[25] He recalled, 'Sunday discussed the possibility of using all this modern experience, and the abstract painting experience, in the service of a revival of Australian landscape.'[26] Nolan acknowledged, 'I did start to change course as a result.'[27] To make her point, Sunday referred to Streeton's *Evening with Bathers*, which hung in the Heide hall, the focus for 'countless discussions' about the interpretation of the landscape.[28]

These discussions were not always comfortable, Nolan realising that once Sunday had her mind set, she expected others, including him, to follow suit. In her domain, she was queen. Now that Nolan was part of the inner circle, he found it could be a daunting and claustrophobic place. Despite his elevated status as Sunday's lover and genius-in-residence – Sunday called him 'Prince' – he was wholly dependent on the Reeds for money, food, painting equipment, even the roof over his head. The personal politics of the situation required all Nolan's considerable skill and charm.

Living at Heide for several years had given Sunday ample time to thoroughly study the local landscape, its features, changing light, seasonal colours and sense of space. She observed that Nolan's version of abstraction, particularly its vivid, lyrical delicacy, could indeed be a good basis from which to build a convincing new approach to landscape. He was also ready to try his hand at anything. Yet it is no wonder that Nolan, with his predilection for abstraction, speed and experimentation, looked at *Evening with*

Bathers and saw no immediate relation to his own practice. But he listened to Sunday, not only because hers was a voice he respected but also he was aware of her knowledge and sensitivity to the natural world, manifest in the Heide garden. Also Nolan had been living at Heide, too, giving him the opportunity to gain a new closeness with nature, and share it with Sunday.

Sunday's was an apposite but disconcerting suggestion. The Heidelberg School, and therefore landscape painting itself, was regarded as reactionary by the modernists, representing jingoistic nationalism, a hostility towards contemporary art and an obsession with conservative values and culture. Streeton's belligerent art reviews and his dismal late paintings were, in particular, anathema. But *Evening with Bathers* belonged to an unsullied early period where Streeton viewed the landscape in a way that was fresh, vital and original, precisely the vision Sunday wanted Nolan to explore.

What did *Evening with Bathers* offer Sunday and Nolan? Streeton's Box Hill landscape is almost featureless: it is devoid of magnificent vistas, dramatic effects of light and shade or anecdotal incidents to attract the eye. Personality, both of the human subjects and the natural environment, is reduced, elusive, potent. The mood is contemplative, the effects understated and subtle. *Evening with Bathers* does not literally describe or illustrate anything except the nuance of light at evening and its effects on the land. It is definitely not heroic. Sunday realised it had an abstract agenda ideally suited to Nolan's skills and pertinent to a new interpretation of the landscape.

Sunday was developing her sense of a specifically Australian modernism. How was it to be realised? What was intrinsic to this country? As the Heidelberg School artists discovered, it was not so much subject matter, though they strived to develop authentically Australian subjects, but light itself. It was their depiction of the peculiarly harsh, bright, drenching Australian light that separated them from the colonial artists whose representation of light was derived, not from what their eyes showed them, but from the softened romantic haze of a European vision. Australian light offered Streeton and company an awakening, a revelation. It was precisely what Sunday saw in *Evening with Bathers*. Light told the story.

Sunday also realised, from her close attachment to her local earth, that the Heidelberg School had, in the late 1880s, focused their attention not on spectacular landscapes in some remote region but on the ordinary and the available. They dealt with a landscape that was familiar and accessible. Nationalism, in its best sense, is the identification and celebration of a country's unique vision of itself and Sunday was aware that Australia's uniqueness needed to be an organic element of its art. Atyeo's modernism was linked irrevocably to Europe and Sunday recognised Australian art could flourish only if it were connected to its roots: the landscape. The Heidelberg School's original interpretation of landscape provided the theatre where the second act of Australian art history could take place; and for her leading man, Sunday chose Nolan.

Aside from small groups of modernists active in capital cities, Australia in the late 1930s was still enslaved to conservative British culture, values and mores. In that sense, Australia, and especially Melbourne, had changed little since Sunday's girlhood. Though influenced by French modernism, she also must have seen it was merely another form of slavery to follow the forms and fashions of another country's art and literature. Australian culture needed to speak with its own voice.

Sunday also chose Nolan to do what she herself could not: paint the landscape from a modernist view. *Landscape*, her drawing, was an attempt to do just that. She had subjected hills, sky and trees to a unified, streamlined, modernist vision. But she had not been able to ambitiously interpret the natural world nor had she achieved the desired level of craftsmanship or originality. Nolan, she knew, was capable of doing that. Nolan also gave Sunday the courage and imaginative breadth to explore her ideas, quickening and expanding them. His generosity and receptiveness meant she gained confidence and began to fashion even bigger plans for Australian culture.

When Nolan reached the Wimmera, it was with Sunday's words ringing in his head. But it was his genius that transformed them into a reality. As Richard Haese has written, Nolan's Wimmera paintings 'ended the tyranny of the picturesque. Henceforth language was what counted and all experience lay open to the Australian artist.'[29]

But for Private Nolan, his first experiences of the Wimmera included the dreary regimentation of army life and the ache of being separated from Sunday. The work was mindless: he guarded stores as well as cut wood and and loaded it onto trains. From 1942 until 1944, wherever Nolan was – Seymour, Horsham, Dimboola, Nhill or the occasional posting to Ballarat – he and Sunday rang each other most evenings but, due to wartime regulations, they could only speak for six minutes, often leading to frustrations and misunderstandings.

After their calls, Nolan would write to Sunday, reviewing their conversation and telling her all that he had felt, seen, done, read or painted that day. The following day, he would often write another letter, revisiting the themes of the letter of the night before whether it was art, literature, politics or his passionate feelings for her. His letters form a precise and illuminating chronicle of an artist's mind at a crucial period of discovery and change, as well as an intimate and deeply moving archive.

Nolan was also writing Rimbaud-esque poems, many dedicated to, and inspired by, Sunday and the Heide garden. Sunday was 'the rose in tears' in the 'humble bright/garden which lives/and grows'. Alternately Nolan addressed her as, 'My love my spangled/dove', declaring he would create for her 'a string/of paintings from here to Seymour'.[30]

Despite the circumstances, Nolan remained good-humoured and optimistic. Often his role was similar to John's: cheering Sunday's flagging spirits, commiserating with her nagging minor health problems, encouraging her to rest and not to work beyond her strength. He contrived a host of nicknames for her: Sock Tops, Tiger Toes, Galaxy, Dearest Duffer, Golden Girl, Lily of the Valley, Blue Rose, Gretchen Gothic, Ribbon, Frou Frou, Lacemaker and, in her role as Nolan's technical assistant, Dearest Craftsman. There seemed nothing the two lovers did not share and Nolan wrote to Sunday as if John did not exist. It was mandatory for a soldier to make a will when he entered the army: Nolan told the Reeds he wished to leave everything to Sunday.

Nolan's letters to John – also written nearly every day – inhabit a parallel reality: they are circumspect, judicious and respectful, dealing with art/political, and rarely personal, matters. They are written in a language between men: comradely but reserved.

Though Sunday later destroyed her replies to Nolan, the diary she kept from 1942–43 thankfully did not suffer the same fate. In its two volumes, she noted Nolan's every phone call, transcribed either the first words of his letters or made a précis of his letters or telegrams, recorded each leave he had and, of course, every lot of painting materials she sent to him and every painting she received back. Sunday's diary not only provides a meticulously accurate record of Nolan's artistic output but it is also the catalogue of a committed and determined curator who has a clear, professional sense of the historical value of such a record.

For example, on Tuesday 2 February 1943 Sunday noted with excitement, 'Telephoned. Painted first Ripolin canvas!' Ripolin, a commercial enamel paint, was Nolan's favoured painting medium because of its speed and brilliant colour. He described it as being like quicksilver. Previously, he had confined using ripolin to masonite boards which Sunday cut to his specifications, primed and sent to him. The same day, Sunday also received a letter where Nolan discussed poetry. The following day she noted 'letter: enclosing poems. Telephoned.' On Friday 5 February 'first Ripolin painting arrived. Telephoned. "Don't be too hard on the painting."'[31]

To read Nolan's letters and Sunday's diary is to be privy to a complete creative partnership, a union of sensibilities so attuned that it is difficult to establish a demarcation line, a separation point, each is so dependent on the other's assistance, opinions and inspiration. To Nolan, their connection seemed as fine as 'needlepoint', making him declare 'we must be becoming painters'.[32]

Nor did John remain all calm equanimity. In nearly every letter, Nolan begged Sunday to visit him wherever he was posted, and she did. But John did not always accept the visits lightly. In February 1943, Sunday told Nolan how John had wept uncontrollably when she told him she was going to Nhill. As a result, she cancelled the trip. Nolan's suggestion – not to discuss impending visits with John – was hardly the kind of advice which was either sensible or which Sunday would follow.

During one leave, Nolan expressed to John his concerns about the pressure the situation placed on Sunday. In John's reply, Nolan was aware that the sadness, hurt and sense of exclusion John experienced in the triangle had reached a profound and worrying level. 'Johnny's middle register', as Nolan and Sunday rather glibly described it, was at breaking point.[33] Nolan continually protested to John that the three of them were a unit, indissolubly entwined, and John could not separate himself from a love shared equally. But finally, Nolan's concerns were not for John. All he wanted was Sunday.

In response to his growing distress, John got involved in a crazy plan during September 1942 to escape the situation and assist in the war effort. He discussed with H.V. Evatt, now Minister for External Affairs in John Curtin's Labor government, the possibility of leading an Australian diplomatic envoy to Russia. If that did not eventuate, he would join the army. The plans, which came to nothing, were greeted with dismay by Sunday and warily by Nolan.

To allay John's anxieties, Sunday tried to keep him fully informed and involved. From Horsham, Sunday 'couldn't resist a quick note' to John, 'picking and brushing my teeth between this' while 'sitting in the sun on the balcony' of her hotel. She was 'enjoying Horsham after all the bad things I thought last time. The hotel is a great improvement & I have been very comfortable & happy', even though she did find 'a flea in bed this morning but he hopped off somewhere quite happily'. She had not enjoyed the journey up. On the same train was Nolan's commanding officer, 'that old bastard Bilby', who always seemed to appear 'on the scene as soon as I do & always with something up his sleeve to do with Nolan'. Bilby was also staying at her hotel.

The lovers had been 'wandering by the river', sitting, reading and talking. She hoped John would be 'pleased with Nolan's paintings' which were 'extremely sensitive I think but more than that vulnerable exposed . . . But all the time there is a deepening in experience and an increasing power to do what he wants to do.' She also wondered whether 'being a girl I do not stretch him enough or air him sufficiently', suggesting that 'it would be good for you both to have a holiday together if his three months leave comes off'.[34]

John's letters to Sunday remain sanguine. He hoped she was not 'too upset by horrible hotels and things' in Dimboola. 'Just remember there's a war on and everything will be all right'[35] but he felt 'lonely in the big bed' without her.[36]

It was the plains themselves, soaked in brutal, effulgent light, that mesmerised Nolan as soon as he reached his first posting at Dimboola on 4 May 1942. That night, Nolan wrote to Sunday, convinced the only way to approach it was to paint 'the land going vertically into the sky'.[37] Like Rimbaud, Nolan could find himself in strange or difficult circumstances and turn them to his advantage, discovering piquant and unusual benefits for his art. It made Nolan, in later life, an inveterate and hardy traveller, the equanimity of his temperament undisturbed by privation or inhospitable climates. It was one of the ways he coped with life at Heide. So it also was in the Wimmera, the great canvas on which he began to create.

As Nolan's letters to Sunday bear out, words were as important to him as painting and his reading list, courtesy of the Heide library, included Rilke, Proust, Kafka, Gide, Malraux, Lawrence, Blake, Marx's *Kapital*, Lenin, Christopher Caudwell, Eliot's 'East Coker' and 'Little Gidding', Dylan Thomas, W.H. Auden, Stephen Spender, Christopher Isherwood and Julien Green. Rimbaud was a constant reference and Nolan felt the Wimmera was the kind of place Rimbaud could have written about.

As Sunday wrote to John, 'Nolan says he is not alongside any painter and is much more at home with writers.'[38] Proust and Kafka made Nolan strive for 'a very simple and lucid language' which he believed few painters apart from Picasso and Cézanne had achieved.[39] On hot days, the Wimmera reminded Nolan of Van Gogh's paintings of the flat, bright Provençale landscape around Arles.

The Wimmera paintings are by no means consistent. They range from confident and magnificent evocations of the land and its people like *Railway Guard, Dimboola* (1943, National Gallery of Victoria) *Farmer's Wife, Dimboola* (1943, Heide MoMA) and *Flour Lumper* (1943, NGV) to smaller, lyrical studies like *Little Desert* (1943, NGV) and *Wimmera River* (1943, NGV). Early works are marred by what Sunday termed 'constructional confusion'.[40]

Going to School (1942, NGV) shows Nolan in transition from geometric abstraction to figurative landscape painting. Its subject is a plane crash observed by a schoolgirl. The vivid yellow earth and intense blue sky that dominate the series provide the background to the plane crash — a collage of wild dark lines and flat planes of colour. Anchoring the composition is the girl's head seen from behind. But the result is an unresolved mass of competing elements, exactly Sunday's point about 'constructional confusion'.

But when Nolan focuses on the strengths he elicits from the landscape — dense, flat, radiant colour; shallow, modernist pictorial space; and the relation of the human form to such an inhospitable land — he produces a masterpiece like *Railway Guard, Dimboola*. Sunday thought of Nolan's paintings as 'transfers' where after-images derived from the landscape resonated in Nolan's mind to emerge later in his art. Nolan agreed and it aptly describes the Wimmera paintings' clarity and vitality.

In his letters to Sunday, Nolan mentions Cézanne more than any other painter, the lightning rod on whose vision he relies. While Cézanne pursued the landscape's form and structure so diligently he opened the way to abstraction, he was also a sublime colourist, capable of limpid, subtle, translucent effects. It was Cézanne's light touch that Nolan sought to emulate.

Railway Guard, Dimboola is a work of beauty, irony and complexity, dominated by the close-up study of a railway guard whose face reads like a map, a part of the country itself. Surrounded by signs pointing in different directions, the guard's expression is of blank bewilderment, as if he has no idea where to go, perhaps an indication of Nolan's feelings about army life and his term of duty in the Wimmera. The composition is tough, clean and sure, balanced by a sharp horizon line where a wheat silo sits. Nolan has thoroughly integrated abstract elements and is in command of an achingly bright palette.

Railway Guard, Dimboola excels at making a highly sophisticated, modernist statement look as easy as child's play. In Horsham in 1943, Sunday recognised the strength in Nolan's new work was because it was 'beginning to root itself in fact', that is, it was addressing the reality of the Wimmera and its people.[41]

Until then, Sunday had not been convinced by Nolan's attempts at portraiture. She was harshly critical of Nolan's abstract 'portrait' *Rimbaud Thinking*, telling him she 'never wanted to see the . . . silly thing again'. Nolan agreed and the painting disappeared into the Heide boiler room. Sunday told Nolan 'quite flatly' that he should look at Albert Tucker's self-portraits and portraits especially *Portrait of Adrian Lawlor* (1939, NGA). Tucker and the people he painted, Sunday believed, were thinkers, conveying a depth Nolan had not mastered.[42]

It was not only Cézanne but another European artist who, as Elwyn Lynn suggests, was influencing Nolan.[43] Danila Vassilieff was a wild, itinerant Russian Cossack who burst onto the Melbourne art scene with his first solo exhibition in September 1937. Younger artists were drawn to him including Tucker, Hester, Arthur Boyd and John Perceval. Vassilieff also caught the eye of George Bell and Basil Burdett, together with the cream of Melbourne's radical intelligentsia – Vance and Nettie Palmer, Adrian Lawlor, Norman Macgeorge and the Reeds.

John opened Vassilieff's exhibition at Riddell's Gallery in stirring terms. 'The work of Mr Vassilieff brings something new and startling to us and for this reason alone the exhibition is the most important which has taken place for some considerable time.'[44] The Riddell's Gallery exhibition proved an unqualified success. Burdett and Bell accorded it brilliant reviews and, for the only time in his life, Vassilieff sold well. For the travel-sore Vassilieff, it was exactly the reception he had been seeking and he decided to make Melbourne his home.

The Reeds bought *Valerie and Betty* (1937, Heide MoMA) from the exhibition. Nolan saw it at Heide and met Vassilieff himself. Not only did Vassilieff handle paint fluidly with a light, draughtsman-like touch but he took as his subjects the streets and lanes of working-class Australia, peopling those streets with children at play, a 'message of irrepressible life in the midst of the Depression'.[45] Vassilieff made no social comment: his message was pure *joie de vivre*. His compositions were apparently gauche and casual, the whole effect raw, immediate and vital. They were not Melbourne's first street scenes – Bell had set similar exercises for his students – but they were startlingly fresh.

As Tucker recalled, Vassilieff would 'set up his easel in the street in Fitzroy, ignore the crowds of kids around him and punch out about half a dozen paintings in an afternoon and they would all be spot on'.[46] Vassilieff's desire was to paint 'living life', unfettered by the practice or, as he saw it, the encumberance of academic tuition. He heaped scorn on conventional art education, dismissing its advantages for the artist.

Sunday and John were deeply influenced by Vassilieff's contempt for art training and the 'finished' artwork. Vassilieff's precepts of spontaneity of method, speed of execution and vigor of brushtroke guided choices the Reeds made as patrons. They were attitudes that influenced Nolan, too.

Vassilieff's other endearing charm was to spin stories, creating a sense of self that was romantic, daring and 'other'. In bland, stolidly English, pre-migration Melbourne, Vassilieff was a rare flower. 'With him,' John recalled, 'no matter how close the relationship, one was always conscious of another world, another civilization.'[47]

Sunday and Nolan were quite a production team. She was at Heide, priming masonite or canvas, buying and mixing paints and making up parcels of books, food and clothes while Nolan was in the Wimmera where he would 'pack up all his work in a sack and send them by train to Heide almost as soon as they were dry' for Sunday's advice and criticism.[48]

By 1943 Nolan was painting flat, either on a table or, preferably, on the floor and he chided Sunday when she baulked at preparing his work this way, telling her 'all good painters work on the floor Sun'.[49] For an exhibition of Nolan's, organised by Sunday at the local Heidelberg newsagent in July 1942, she also made the frames, adding 'framemaker' to Nolan's list of affectionate nicknames. He also shared his doubts with her, wondering if his work in the 1942 Contemporary Art Society exhibition looked 'frail'.[50]

Sunday felt closely connected to Nolan's work. When he first went to the Wimmera and abandoned painting for chalk drawings, she felt Nolan's retreat from painting, he recognised, more keenly than he did himself. Sunday also worried that the chalk drawings were slight and the medium was directing the work too much. Nolan prized Sunday's response to his paintings, a private affair where she would contemplate works, like *Flour Lumper* (1943, NGV) or *Dimboola* (1943, Heide MoMA), that hung over her bed. 'I never think of them being looked at in any way than you do when you lie in your room quietly,' he said.[51] Sunday's visits and her responses to the landscape also enhanced Nolan's visual awareness and afterwards he would write back, commenting on her remarks and all that they had observed together.

Sunday also seems to have worked on at least one of Nolan's finished paintings. It is hard to identify as Nolan does not describe it by title but he does refer to Sunday 'painting out' part of one work.[52] Perhaps it was a natural progression for Sunday, after being involved both in the larger philosophical issues related to the genesis of the Wimmera paintings and in the minute technical details of their preparation, that she would become more directly engaged. On one level, Sunday had never truly relinquished being an artist — creativity was a hunger, an obsession within her — and Nolan gave her the opportunity to make art with him, another aspect of the awakening he offered.

Though it was an extraordinarily productive period for Nolan, by 1944 he was heartily sick and tired of army life. There was also the threat of being sent to the front line in New Guinea, a prospect that had him quaking in his boots. Like Tucker, Nolan tried to pretend he was mentally unstable and consulted Reg Ellery for a suitably neurotic diagnosis. He was dispatched to the Watsonia Army Barracks and then the Heidelberg Repatriation Hospital, neither of them far from Heide, where his condition was assessed. But his superiors were not deceived. Indeed it made them adamant that the recalcitrant Corporal Nolan would do his duty.

John and Sunday were also fretting at Nolan's absence. When it was mooted in February that Nolan would be sent to Brisbane, and from there to New Guinea, John complained to Max Harris, 'it seems fantastic that no place can be found in the machine which would enable him to stay here. We have tried everything we can think of.'[53]

By early July, Nolan had made up his mind 'and he is not going back to the army', John told Harris.[54] Soon after, Nolan went absent without leave. After assuming the name of Robin Murray, John organised false papers for him and Nolan went underground. It was not an entirely dishonourable act. By mid-1944, the Allies had been victorious in Europe and further gains were all but assured as the tide turned relentlessly against the Japanese in the Pacific.

· 8 ·

The Second Circle

I feel you are the stimulus and the decisive sensibility.
MAX HARRIS TO SUNDAY REED[1]

Sunday was the eye, the central force that drew us together.
ALBERT TUCKER[2]

*I was so much older. But it's strange, you know, in those days
we were all the same age.*
SUNDAY REED[3]

THE 1940S WERE HEIDE'S HEY-DAYS when it became the gather-ing place for 'the second circle', a group that included Nolan, Tucker and Hester, Arthur and Yvonne Boyd, John Perceval and Mary

Boyd, Max Harris and John Sinclair. Sunday assumed a more public role as an editor of *Angry Penguins* as well as spearheading the publishing ventures of Reed & Harris and the broadsheet *Tomorrow*. It was a turbulent and momentous era when, surrounded by gifted young artists, Sunday witnessed and participated in a renaissance in Australian art.

Heide was a busy place during the war years. In 1942, for example, Hester had moved in, at Sunday's request, when Tucker was drafted. Nolan would arrive regularly on leave, as would Tucker, and aspiring writer Michael Keon was a guest. Neil Douglas was also in and out. That meant seven people in the house at any one time. Other visitors included Arthur and Yvonne Boyd who 'often went to the Reeds and we always stayed the night. We had beautiful breakfasts in the morning.'4 John Perceval and his bride Mary Boyd, who had both become firm friends, visited regularly, taking dips in the river and staying for 'arvo tea'. The house, with its four bedrooms, was filled to bursting point and guests often camped on the couch for the night.

There was a series of other guests during the war years. At the end of 1940, Cynthia returned. After qualifying as a psychiatric nurse, she had been staying with Dyring and Atyeo at their home in Vence, in the south of France, when war was declared. The war had reduced Atyeo and Dyring to miserable living conditions and, during 1940, Atyeo set off to manage a coffee plantation in Dominica, in the West Indies. Unbeknown to Dyring, Cynthia followed him and they had an affair. In 1941, Dyring and Atyeo married in Barbados, Dyring still none the wiser. It would be years before she discovered the truth of the situation, which devastated her.

Cynthia came back to Australia because she was pregnant. She told the Reeds that she had married a Danish intelligence officer called Jan Knut Hansen, who disappeared behind enemy lines in Romania. The Reeds opened their arms to Cynthia, though John confided years later to Atyeo that they doubted her tale about Hansen. They were at the hospital during Cynthia's labour and saw her daughter Jinx 'five minutes after her birth'. Then Sunday became 'a devoted slave . . . for weeks after. She used to wheel Jinx around the wild garden in her pram for hours and wash innumerable nappies daily while Cynthia was recovering.'[5]

Cynthia did not approve of the *ménage* with Nolan and told him so in no uncertain terms. 'Get the hell out of this situation; it's not healthy and it will kill you!'[6] Soon afterwards, Cynthia left for Sydney where the Evatts found her a house at Wahroonga, near to theirs, and a job as a social worker.

Heide may not have been a comfortable place for Cynthia. Struggling to cope with single motherhood, she canvassed the possibility of having Jinx adopted, then rejected the idea. In a letter to John some time later, Cynthia reflected Jinx could be happier in a 'stable' home but might later require her mother.[7] Jane Grant has suggested that Sunday's longing for a child may have extended to Jinx, making Cynthia uneasy and triggering her departure.[8]

One evening in 1944, Atyeo arrived out of the blue, startling the Heide 'family circle', as John called it – the Reeds, Nolan and John Sinclair, a fellow student of Nolan's at the Gallery School who had abandoned painting to become *Herald* music critic.

John told Max Harris that Atyeo was very drunk, 'loud-voiced and declaiming, shitting, fucking, crapping, cock-sucking, pricking straight from America . . . on a secret mission' for H. V. Evatt. Evatt had plucked Atyeo from the ignominy of the coffee plantation and found him work in Washington where Evatt was involved in planning the new United Nations Organisation. Atyeo was in Melbourne 'incognito and not supposed to show himself to a soul and off back the next day. And we learned all the strange Odyssey of his last nine years . . . He says he will not paint again.' There were 'moments of laughter such as we don't often have and moments of anger and hatred culminating at three o'clock in the morning when he called us all bastards and strode out of the house. Nolan says he lost a half a stone in weight that night.' Nolan rushed after Atyeo and persuaded him to return. 'Finally between love and despair the night ended as Sam fell asleep.'[9]

Another visitor, Anne Cairns, the young wife of Nolan's friend Douglas Cairns, was 'absolutely enthralled' by Heide. Women at that time, Anne felt 'dithered. We were obsequious to men. We were used to being brought up by fathers . . . Sun had this confidence . . . She was organising her life the way she wanted. It was very impressive.' The Cairns moved to Merricks, on Westernport Bay, where they became orchardists and 'in a sort of way tried to reproduce [the Reeds'] lifestyle. They must have worked terribly hard. They made butter, cream. Sun did all the cooking.'

Though 'there was a great air of freedom there', Sunday ruled the roost. 'She made sure she made decisions about who came and how long they stayed', otherwise 'the house would have been full of bots, wretched men pretending to be artists'. Sunday made Anne feel at home and she reflected, 'I had been warned that only people with special talents were welcome at Heide. I didn't find that the case.'

But Sunday had to make some concessions to her big, new, bustling household and 'the house was untidy'.[10] Deliveries of Nolan's Wimmera paintings were hanging on the walls or stacked in the hall, accompanying new purchases from the Boyds, Perceval, Vassilieff, Tucker, Hester, Yosl Bergner, Vic O'Connor and Noel Counihan.

Food was as important as ever. Tucker recalled 'the big legs of pork or ham at Christmas time' and 'spoons standing upright in a bowl of cream'. Sunday also cooked baby carrots in cream, which Tucker 'doted on'.[11] Nolan enjoyed Sunday's roast duck while Neil Douglas's favourite was rum baba. Gordon Thomson, another friend of Nolan's, remembered 'they used to put on these marvellous lunches . . . Sunday had lived in France, she did things the French way. I'd always been used to cut lettuce salads but hers were always torn . . . It was quite a Continental style of life.'[12]

The garden was flourishing, as seen in photographs by John Sinclair and Albert Tucker. From his vantage point in the pine tree, Sinclair's *Heide viewed from the Trees* (c.1948) shows the lush growth of plants around the house, though a neat block of box still edges the drive while *John mowing the front lawn* (c.1948), taken from the Heide roof, indicates how the orchard and the English lavender had thrived. Tucker positioned himself on the wall that protects the Heart Garden for *The view north from Heide* (1943), giving him a commanding perspective of the vegetable garden, milking shed and river flats. In Sinclair's view of *The Vegetable Garden* (c.1945), Sunday is seen hoeing.

Other additions in the war years included the cows, dubbed 'the moos' – Bonnie, Rainbow, Orchid and Orchid's calf, Summer (named by Nolan) – and Min, the first of Sunday's Siamese cats. There were also the dogs Tommy and Hank.

Tucker was appreciative of the Heide garden. Sunday was 'in it all the time, gathering armfulls of roses and putting flowers inside. Sunday always had quite an act of homage to nature which of course set up a very good atmosphere.' Tucker's photographs provide a memorable and evocative record of Heide in the 1940s but Tucker shirked his duties whenever possible. 'They were dealing with the cows, with all these domestic chores that had to be done and which I would try and avoid if I could but I couldn't always.' Tucker would escape to the library where 'I would read my head off'.[13]

Rabbits were a problem, so were birds, and all the fruit trees had to be netted. Nolan and Sunday got together, combining the nets and some of Sunday's cast-offs, to create an amusing scarecrow for the pear trees. Sunday insisted on getting Nolan 'working outside with me', particularly when she had lettuces, peppers and one hundred and fifty onions to plant.[14] Like Tucker, Nolan also observed Sunday's 'homage to nature' and homaged her, in turn, in his portrait *Rosa Mutabilis* (1945, Heide Museum of Modern Art).

Nolan's vision of Sunday shows her enclosed in the heart of the rose bush, the stem from which the flowers grow. She is like a mythic being from Ovid's *Metamorphoses* who is in the process of being transformed, by divine intervention, from the human to the natural realm. As it blooms, *Rosa mutabilis* changes from yellow to pink then crimson. With botanical precision, Nolan employs those hues as a symbol for Sunday's changeability, her varying moods, her blossoming through nature and the Heide earth, and her awakening through her relationship with him. The relationship between figure and landscape was the central motif of the Kelly series, whose originality chiefly lay in the mythic quality Nolan established between Kelly and his environment, a quality first successfully explored in *Rosa Mutabilis*.

Framed by flowers, Sunday's expression is tender, gentle, beatific, the roses like a cloud, a cloak, a halo around her as she hovers above the earth. In the background is the Heide homestead, a clear white shape on the horizon, surrounded by pines. Sunday is a home-grown Madonna, an apparition of beauty and grace, an emanation of the Heide earth. The rose bush still grows where Sunday planted it: near the fence at the end of the paddocks, not far from the river bank.

Planting a rose bush in the midst of a field, and not in the rose garden, was perhaps not wholly an original idea. Parc de la Bagatelle, on the outskirts of Paris, contains one of the world's most famous rose gardens and has been open to the public since 1905. As keen rose fanciers, it is likely the Reeds visited it. In the Parc's open fields, beyond the tended avenues of roses, are found large, solitary, spreading rose bushes exactly like *Rosa mutabilis*.

Nolan was not Heide's only artist-in-residence in the 1940s, nor was he the only one who derived inspiration from it.

Joy Hester was Sunday's closest woman friend. While Hester sometimes found her time at Heide stressful, due to Sunday's moods, it could also be a protective place where Hester felt cherished and nurtured. Sunday implicitly believed in Hester's talent, telling her, 'always I find your response so organic, so completely natural that almost everything you paint is at once both vital and very real for me.' Tucker called Sunday a feminist (hardly a compliment coming from him) and Sunday admitted 'in its fullest sense [that] is true of me'.[15] It made her recognise a young woman artist like Hester needed encouragement from a sympathetic female audience, and Sunday supplied it.

While staying at Heide, Hester did a series of drawings of Sunday's doll Gethsemane, which Sunday had made in the early 1940s. The doll, flaxen-haired, faceless and stuffed with lavender from the garden, was made from cloth and dressed in remnants of Sunday's lace petticoats. Sunday propped the doll proudly on her bed, as a child does with a favourite toy, where 'Gethi' was greeted by visitors. Nolan asked Sunday to send Gethsemane up to the Wimmera to keep him company, which she did. Nolan and Barrett Reid dedicated poems to her, while both Nolan and John regarded Gethsemane as Sunday's symbolic presence when she was away.

Gethsemane was the garden where Christ waited to face Judas's betrayal and his arrest by the Roman guards, where he prayed to be delivered from the suffering ahead.[16] Gethsemane was an enclosed, stony Mediterranean garden, close to the Mount of Olives, planted with olive trees. It is telling that Sunday, a gardener, chose another garden to represent the *via crucis* of her infertility. Gethsemane was a site of lonely vigil, of fear and spiritual isolation where Jesus, 'greatly distressed and troubled', begged his disciples to 'remain here, and watch', telling them, 'My soul is very sorrowful, even to death.' (Mark, xiv, 32.)

In Sunday's fruitful garden at Heide, her refuge, she reflected on her infertility and on the loneliness, pain and fear that had marked its passage in her life. In his poem, Barrett Reid refers to Gethsemane as 'the child unborn'.[17] Sunday recognised that, while the garden of Gethsemane symbolised suffering and treachery, it was also a beautiful place, a sanctuary where strength could be gained. Gethsemane represents that duality. While the doll symbolised grief and loss, Sunday made her from the bounty of the Heide garden, from sweet-smelling English lavender, her favourite herb, suggesting that even the saddest events can be transformed and rejuvenated by the power of nature.

For a little girl, a doll is her plaything, companion and fantasy child. Gethsemane was Sunday's surrogate child and very much alive to her. She wrote to Hester:

Did I tell you that Gethsemane had been very ill this summer?
One very bright morning I decided with a beating heart to bathe
her in the laundry trough . . . She looked so happy, really happy,
and I called the boys . . . to watch her swimming while I washed
her flaxen hair . . . Suddenly I felt she wanted to come out and
I carried her to a sunny spot by the violets and left her sun-
baking . . . Later when I returned I found her, poor little soul,
unconscious and her body was scorched and covered in darkness.
For days she was terribly ill and I thought I would lose her but
I kept her in bed and when she was stronger she had several
serious operations and gradually recovered till one day she
looked quite herself again and as radiant and beautiful as ever.
I took her to Sorrento for a holiday because it was a special
occasion in her life. I am sending you two not very good photographs which I took one day while she sat on the sofa with the
sunlight on her sweet face.[18]

Sunday's is a child's whimsical story, a fairytale, with its images
of play, of imaginary crisis and illness, and magical rejuvenation. It
is another reminder of her vivid and ongoing connection with her
childhood. In Sunday's story, with its happy ending, she is the healer,
the nurse, the doll's good, wise mother, who rewards her patient
with a beach holiday, not dissimilar to the role Sunday played in
real life with her artist friends. Gethsemane's face, however, can
hardly be described as 'sweet'. As Sunday's photograph shows, the
doll's face is large, white, blank and strange.

Hester fastened on that strangeness in Gethsemane in *Gethi in a
Tree* (c.1946, Private Collection). At that time, Hester's drawing style
had been recently liberated by two major influences: newsreel
footage of the concentration camps, which she had seen in 1945,

and Jean Cocteau's *Opium* (1930), a record of the poet's rehabilitation from his drug addiction in word and image. Fantastic, hallucinatory and agonised faces with huge, staring eyes writhe, burn and explode across the pages of Cocteau's book, inspiring Hester to produce the series *From an incredible night dream* (c.1946).

Next came the Gethsemane series. *Gethi in a Tree* is drawn with fierce, rapid brushstrokes. The doll is scarcely recognisable, taking the same organic shape as the tree's fork she sits astride. As Sunday comments in her letter, she was in the habit of taking Gethsemane into the garden. Hester has transformed Gethi from Sunday's beloved toy to a monster, an object to be feared, not played with, propped in the tree like an uncanny idol.

Fairytales do not always have happy endings, like the one Sunday contrived for her doll. They often end in violence and retribution and Hester's utterly unsentimental drawing suggests that is Gethsemane's fate: she is ugly, doomed and unloveable but she has her own demonic, fetishistic energy. If the doll was a substitute or a symbol of Sunday, Hester's image can be read as a portrait of the intense emotions implicit in Heide's intimacies that were governed by Sunday, where 'ugly' scenes of uncontrolled feelings could erupt, frightening or damaging those involved. Hester once declared to Tucker, 'I could cry to be away from it all.'[19] Alternately, perhaps it is Hester herself who is represented by the angry doll, a toy at the mercy of others' whims, indicating the powerlessness and rage she sometimes felt towards her patron. In 1942, Hester dismissively referred to John and Nolan as Sunday's 'toys', with Nolan 'the newer toy'.

Hester, who believed she encountered poltergeists at the St Kilda flat she shared with Tucker, also experienced paranormal phenomena at Heide. When the library door mysteriously opened of its own accord, Hester, her 'eyes as big as saucers', was convinced it was the ghost of Mrs Lang. Hester wasn't interested in the rational explanantion, Neil Douglas recalled.

'At Heide, on the brow of the hill, there is a little convection current and because of the . . . different temperatures, it used to open the back door, this little wind, and it would open the door of the library . . . The door would open and in would come this vague, vague smell of old bones. You see, of course, it was the septic tank.'[20] But Hester was convinced the house was haunted. By identifying as the cause a troubled spirit, Hester referenced the eruption of the deep, inexplicable and unruly feelings she experienced at Heide.

There were many similarities between Nolan and Hester, Sunday's most favoured artists. Both were inspired by literary sources – Hester's chosen poets included Eliot, Cocteau, Ezra Pound and Judith Wright. Both were keen admirers of one another's work, both worked rapidly and effortlessly in public. Hester would sit cross-legged by the fire in the library 'conjuring magical visions with pen and brush'[21] while Tucker recalled that 'Nolan would put newspapers and a board on the [dining room] table and his cans of ripolin and just bash away and be chatting at the same time about Rimbaud, Kierkegaard, D.H. Lawrence and all his various inter-ests. I'd be sitting on the other side of the table talking to him.'[22]

Their practice gave Sunday the opportunity to be involved in the creation of the art work. Hester and Nolan also worked with whatever quick, cheap and ready materials came to hand, choosing spontaneity and speed above the deliberations of craftsmanship.

John Perceval 'loved the Reeds dearly' though he had 'plenty of arguments [with them] about art'. Given Perceval's volatile temper and acerbic wit, they were probably started by him. Perceval didn't register Heide's tensions. 'I went there for holidays and I got well-fed'. Like Nolan and Hester, Perceval made art at Heide. 'I'd sit around and draw at night after a few beers'.[23] One drawing was a study of a dishevelled *Joy Hester* (c.1950, Heide MoMA). But he did not paint there. Together with Nolan, Tucker, Hester and John Sinclair, Perceval was on the Heide payroll, collecting one pound a week from the Reeds.

Survival (1942, National Gallery of Victoria), the first Perceval they bought, was his breakthrough as a major artist. *Survival* is a cry of anguish about the effects of war on the innocent. First exhibited in the controversial Anti-Fascist Exhibition in 1942, *Survival* displays influences from German expressionism to the work of Mexican muralists Orozco and Siqueiros, as well as local social realists Yosl Bergner, Noel Counihan (whom Perceval deeply admired) and Albert Tucker. In the big, bold work, Perceval registers emotional truths and historical realities, locating a critique of contemporary events that was informed, individual and heartfelt, and that became typical of the Heide circle. The Reeds also acquired Perceval's *Boy with Cat 2* (1943, National Gallery of Australia), *Dog Brother*, (c.1942, Heide MoMA), *Performing Dogs 1* (1943, Heide MoMA) and *Suburban Roofs at Night* (1944, Heide MoMA). Perceval regularly visited Heide with Mary Boyd, his young wife. Sunday bought Mary's only remaining painting, *Hands* (1942, Heide MoMA), executed when she was sixteen.

Arthur, Perceval's brother-in-law, sweet-tempered and amiable, avoided arguments like the plague. Despite the Reeds' admiration of him, he was less effusive about Heide. He thought 'it was best to keep a fair distance because you could get eaten up and I didn't like that . . . you could be absorbed into a world in which you would be too inhibited to break out of and I didn't need the stimulation of the emotional involvement.'[24] But Sunday and John were keen supporters of the 'Murrumbeenas', as Sunday dubbed them, after the suburb where they lived.

Between 1943–44, the Reeds bought Arthur's paintings as well as pen and wash drawings, including his first major work *Progression* (1941, Heide MoMA), together with *Butterfly Man* (1943, Heide MoMA), *The Lovers* (c.1944, Heide MoMA), *Crucifixion* [*The Kite*] (1943, Heide MoMA) and *The Cripples* (1943, Heide MoMA). It is no exaggeration to say that, through their patronage of Perceval and Boyd in the mid-1940s, the Reeds helped to support Open Country, the Boyd family home.

Adding Albert Tucker to the group provides an excellent picture of where Melbourne modernism, and Sunday's taste, were heading at the time. It was raw, intense, expressionist, literary, political, urban and sexually charged.

Tucker was the most loudly and determinedly intellectual of the Reeds' new friends, a superb, self-taught craftsman and an ambitious and abrasive individual. During the war, Tucker was embarking on his best work, Images of Modern Evil, a series that charted social change in terms of moral geography, a map of the decline and fall of the human spirit envisaged on Melbourne's streets. The Reeds bought Tucker's *The Futile City* (1940, Heide MoMA), inspired by T.S. Eliot's 'The Waste Land' and by surrealism, together with two Images of Modern Evil, as well as Tucker's more illustrative social realist paintings, *Children of Athens* (1940, Heide MoMA) and *Fisherman's Bend* (1941, Queensland Art Gallery).

Tucker had no wish to work in the public manner of Nolan and Hester. He was also critical of Heide's 'hot house' atmosphere and wished to distance himself from it. Tucker had mixed feelings about Sunday who could be 'a very sensitive woman, very penetrating, full of insight, and quite ruthless and quite manipulative.

And she had a side to her though that was extremely childish. She was the little rich girl who'd go into tantrums if she didn't get her own way.' But, over the years, Tucker was unequivocal on one point. 'Sunday was the eye, the central force that drew us together.'[25]

The Reeds were responding to a new climate in Melbourne painting represented by their chosen artist friends. It was derived from a number of shared sources that included the lively calligraphic style and urban imagery of Danila Vassilieff, together with German expressionism, surrealism and Picasso. Another influence was the young Polish–Jewish artist Yosl Bergner who had arrived from the Warsaw ghetto. Bergner painted what he found in Melbourne's streets: poverty, hunger, despair and alienation, saturating the urban environment with a moving and convincing European vision. The Reeds snapped up works including *The Pumpkin Eaters* (1943, NGA), Bergner's major social realist statement, and *Princes Hill* (c.1939, Heide MoMA), a small, lusciously handled work.

But the tenor of the art, its guts, came directly from the sense of social upheaval brought about by the war, to which the group fully responded. Even Nolan, who eschewed what was obvious or literal, produced *Portrait of a Soldier* (1942, NGA), an addled mask of fear, confusion and pain. The city was, for Boyd, Perceval and Tucker, a prime site of exploration. For Hester, it was the human face.

Influencing them all was a profound commitment to a better world, a socialist utopia, a new world order that would come into being after the war. Internationally it was the honeymoon period for leftwing intellectuals as they looked to Russia, and Stalin, as ideal representatives of the future good. Hester, Perceval and Arthur Boyd were Communist Party fellow travellers. Yvonne Boyd was a member of the CPA for a time and painted social realist pictures.

Nolan deliberated long and hard about joining the Party (and finally didn't) while Tucker joined the Artists' Branch of the CPA.

Politics was a core feature of contemporary culture and to be modern was to be on the left. How did the girl from Toorak mesh with her radical friends? Politically, Sunday regarded herself as a communist. Barrett Reid recalled, 'She used to say with some seriousness, though it was always a poetic statement [rather] than a statement of reality, she was a communist. She always said that until the day she died.'[26]

Sunday was no theoretician. Wading through D.S. Mirsky's *Russia: A Social History* (1931), she complained to John that she was only up to page forty-five and 'floundering in the heavy sea of politics, good Lord does this go on for much longer? Capitalistic, socialistic, communist, imperialist, radicals, fabians, proletarians, conservative, nationalistic, individualistic, laborists, democrats, fascists, bourgeois, intellectuals, bureaucrats, progressives, suffragettes, dictatorships & heaven knows what else.'[27] Sunday's politics were personally honed and she was uncomfortable with categorisation, perhaps because she had been categorised, and criticised, on the basis of class.

Sunday explained to Hester, 'For many years, ever since I came to live at Heide and perhaps before, I have wanted to share whatever I have that others are without.'[28] Jean Langley was aware that 'Sunday was ashamed of the Baillieu money to some extent and therefore she wanted to put it into the world and share it'.[29] Sunday told Langley, 'I am often miserable for being luckier than you, for having money when you haven't. I have done nothing in my life to deserve it. After all it is just luck'[30] and insisted 'darling, you must think of dollars as apples from my kitchen garden and in fact that is what they are.'[31]

Sunday and John showed their commitment to communism through financial aid. When Malcolm Good, a founding member of the Contemporary Art Society and a friend of Tucker's, stood as the CPA candidate at the federal and state elections in 1943 and 1945 respectively, the Reeds financed his election campaigns. But it did not earn them respect. Langley recalled, 'when they tried to support Malcolm Good as communist candidate, the communists wouldn't have a bar of them, landed gentry from Tasmania'.[32] John's background meant he could never join the Party, something he desired to do, though he would later admit he had never read Marx.

Nor did the Reeds' generosity eradicate misunderstandings about money at Heide. Sunday felt it was 'very lonely and strange to be different to those you love and to be told so many times [that] my cheeks are always hot'.[33] The Reeds bought art regularly but they did not splurge and often bargained for a better price, a trait which did not endear them to their artist friends. After buying a Perceval for five pounds, Hester remarked to Yvonne Boyd, 'You know Sun and John. If they know the artist, they think they can get it cheap.'[34]

A case in point about money was a theft that occurred during Yosl Bergner's one and only visit to Heide. Over dinner, Bergner regaled his hosts with his 'complete disregard for truthfulness and honesty . . . in his dealing with others and, to cap his argument, he said, "I would not hesitate to steal from my mother."'[35] Bergner was no doubt having a fine old time pulling the Reeds' legs. But when John found some money missing from his dressing-table, he made the mistake of rushing off to Noel Counihan, Bergner's friend and leader of the social realist group, and accusing Bergner. Counihan went berserk, to put it mildly.[36]

Sunday recalled, 'Counihan said when the money box was

stolen, "Well, you deserve it, you shouldn't have so much money anyhow" – or some such thing – but I have never forgotten, nor have I forgotten for that matter so much that has been said and done in and out of Heide and now I have come to believe it is true, and I should not have what others haven't and over and over I try to think how I can pass it on to you all and run for my life.'[37]

Sunday did not belong anywhere. Her class, and members of her own family, regarded her with horror because she had flung open her doors to a bunch of red artist ratbags, while those with whom she had thrown in her lot could never quite forget the differences between herself and them. It was a situation that was never solved and remained a jagged and recurring theme in many of Sunday's friendships.

The radical treatment of the body, with its references to sexuality, is a confrontational element in the work of the second circle. All the artists represented the body as the subject of violence, fore-grounding it as the vehicle for desire, madness, black humour and despair. It is impossible to look at works like Boyd's *Butterfly Man*, Hester's *Gethi in a Tree*, Nolan's *Giggle Palace* (1944, Art Gallery of South Australia), Tucker's *Images of Modern Evil* and Perceval's *Survival* (1942, National Gallery of Victoria) without reflecting on the prevailing wartime climate and the torrent of images, available through newsreels and newspapers, of mutilation, destruction and death. Also implied in these works were the fears of the artists them-selves that they would be sent to the front line of battle, where their bodies could suffer the same terrible fate. (Excluding Perceval who had suffered from polio as a child and was not fit for combat, and Hester.) The pressures on Boyd, Nolan and Tucker were nearly unbearable: Nolan fled the army, Tucker became progressively ill before being granted an honourable discharge and Boyd teetered on the edge of a nervous breakdown.

Experiments with, and responses to, a changing moral climate may also have influenced the representation of the body. Hester and Perceval were unfaithful to their partners while Nolan conducted an affair with a young married woman, a committed Marxist, who was a close friend of Hester's. Tucker, the avowed puritan, was galvanised by the sexually charged atmosphere in Melbourne's wartime streets and affronted by the new freedoms offered women. Boyd was anguished by the sheer awfulness of army life. In the hands of these artists, the body is grossly distorted, not beautiful, sensual or alluring but hectic, reckless, crudely powerful and enormously energetic.

Nolan contorts the human form into bizarre shapes in *Bather and Sandcastle* (1945, Private Collection), Boyd's *Butterfly Man* is a crazy creature running riot in the streets, in Tucker's Images of Modern Evil gremlins with grotesquely truncated torsos prowl the darkness, Perceval's *Floating Mask 2* (1943, Private Collection) shows a nightmare world of disembodied heads while in Hester's Faces series, the face is transformed into a frightening mask, a shriek of agony, a mirror of wartime horrors. The artists offer exuberantly uncensored and unfettered explorations of the flesh and all, apart from Nolan, find darkness in the hearts of the insatiable beings they depict.

As a patron, Sunday never encouraged artistic experimentation for its own sake. It had to have a larger purpose – such as her suggestion to Nolan that he rework the landscape from the modernist view. Otherwise it had to be integral to, and grow naturally from, an artist's vision. What Sunday sought in art was a vital, individual, authentic statement and, arising from that, an intimate friendship with the artists themselves. It is interesting that for one who favoured light over dark, lyricism over the direct statement and sentimentality over harshness, Sunday could so wholeheartedly respond to the tough, new painting of the 1940s.

What convinced her was the passionate humanity throbbing at the heart of the works produced by the second circle. Just as the Heide garden had grown and changed, as Sunday's formal taste in garden design for geometry and straight lines was overtaken by a more lavish, romantic, informal sensibility, so her taste in art expanded to accept the brilliant, brutal, uncompromising work produced by the group.

While Sunday assumed an inspirational role with Nolan and provided a stimulating climate in which Hester's work developed, all the artists in the circle sought and respected her opinion.

Nadine Amadio felt Sunday 'understood art like nobody'. Amadio, a writer and music critic, believed 'Sunday taught me how to look at art . . . She always asked me what I thought. She'd say, "Why don't you look into it and tell me yourself what you see. Does it have humanity?"'[38] Hester lauded Sunday who responded on 'aesthetic grounds with a high degree of intelligence'. Though at times, Hester felt Sunday's reponses could be 'uneven', at her best she was 'unbeatable for insight and sensitivity'.[39]

Sunday took her time, quietly observing an artwork until she had absorbed its impact, as Nolan had noted about *Railway Guard* and *Farmer's Wife, Dimboola* which hung in her bedroom. It was a process that took place at Heide, Sunday's ideal environment in which to appreciate art. Nor was she afraid of expressing her opinions as they formed: it was part of the slow, personal, 'organic' response she prized.

When Tucker gave her a portrait of Nolan (now lost), Sunday

agreed with Tucker that the painting had 'all the good paint qualities you spoke of, amongst other things a piece of background so
personal to yourself which I enjoy a great deal and later a hand
which seems both very sensitive and real'. But she had reservations
about Tucker's interpretation of Nolan which meant, due to 'my
preconceived notions . . . I am unable yet to adjust myself to
yours! . . . Minor points such as the illusion of blonde hair, the
knotty paint and the rather unexpected treatment of the eyes
confuse me into thinking there is no likeness at all. On the other
hand when I walk past quickly I sense a sudden reality though
once again when I stop to search I find no explanation. But I am
slow about these things and I will watch it and see what happens.'[40]
Patience, respect and careful observation were hallmarks of
Sunday's response to art.

Sunday was also adept at titling paintings. Tucker named his
claustrophobic portrait of terror depicting his fears of army life and,
potentially, of death, *No Way Out*. But that was too literal for
Sunday. Reading Dostoyevsky at the time, she retitled the work
The Possessed, a more apposite and evocative choice (1942, NGA).

But she could also be harshly dismissive – telling Neil Douglas
to quit painting because she regarded his work as inferior. When
Boyd and Perceval began to paint religious themes in the mid-'40s,
both the Reeds were critical of the step, of which Perceval was well
aware. Nor did Yvonne Boyd win Sunday's attention. An ambitious painter, she was an intelligent and attractive young woman
who engaged in long, serious discussions about her work with
Hester. Sunday, who liked Yvonne personally, ignored her work.
Sunday's generosity was selective and the temperature outside the
warm zone of her interest could be decidedly chilly.

In those years, Sunday also continued to explore her sexual

choices. She set her cap at the dynamic and capable Peter Bellew who was editing *Art and Australia*, declaring that if he didn't agree to have an affair with her, she would throw herself out the window.[41] Nor was she averse to Tucker. Standing beside him in Templestowe Road outside Heide, Sunday moved closer and rubbed her thigh against his. Tucker, ever the puritan, insisted, 'I didn't understand it' and stepped away.[42] John Yule, an associate of the Boyds, was astounded by Sunday's intense physicality. She 'just threw herself into your arms'.[43]

Given the body's radical treatment by the Heide circle, it is worth examining how Tucker depicted Sunday in his many photographs of her. During the war years, Tucker was the Heide circle's photographer — and played that role for some of Melbourne's bohemia, including members of the Montsalvat colony and the Boyds, becoming an 'accidental historian', as he later called himself. Taken as a group, his photographs of Heide are his best — vivid, intimate and spontaneous. Though frankly critical of Sunday, and of Heide's 'hot house' atmosphere, Tucker's photographs represent Sunday with an admiration approaching awe.

Christmas at Heide (c.1946) is Tucker's iconic image of the Heide 'family'. It is Christmas morning, the dining room table has been cleared of the Kellys and is cluttered with gifts (books as well as bottles of whisky and brandy), discarded wrapping paper, jars of Sunday's homemade jam, teapots, plates, cups and saucers. A Chinese paper lantern swings in the summer breeze. Like *In the Library*, Tucker shows Sunday as the focus, the centre of the group. Calm, smiling and beautiful, she is a chastely attired domestic goddess surrounded by a bevy of half-naked men — Nolan, John and John Sinclair. Though Hester was present, she is excluded, marginalised, like *In the Library*. Sunday's gaze is not directed at Tucker, or Nolan,

John Sinclair. Nolan, Sunday and John holding Min the Siamese cat, Point Lonsdale, c. 1945. *Courtesy State Library of Victoria.*

Sunday Reed. Gethsemane, 1952. *Courtesy Peregrine Smith.*

Ivor Kershaw. Sweeney in the Heide library, 1950. *Courtesy State Library of Victoria.*

The hall at Heide I,
c. 1950.
*Courtesy State Library
of Victoria.*

John and Sunday's bedroom showing Louis XIV-style table, baby Bechstein and
rose-patterned wallpaper, c. 1955. *Courtesy State Library of Victoria.*

Above: Nadine Amadio. Self Portrait, c. 1955.
Courtesy Nadine Amadio.

Left: Georges and Mirka Mora in their wedding clothes, Paris, 1947.
Courtesy State Library of Victoria.

Nigel Buesst. Sweeney at Strine's, c. 1965. Courtesy State Library of Victoria.

Summer at Aspendale. From left: John Perceval, Georges Mora (from rear), Mary Boyd, John Reed, Mirka Mora (from rear), Sunday Reed, c. 1966.
Courtesy State Library of Victoria.

Susie Brunton and her son, Paris, Aspendale, 1971.
Courtesy State Library of Victoria.

Museum of Modern Art of Australia, Tavistock Place, Melbourne. Exhibition of
Australian domestic architecture, October–November 1960.
Courtesy State Library of Victoria.

Nadine Amadio. Sunday with Heide II under construction, c. 1964.
Courtesy Nadine Amadio / State Library of Victoria.

Wolfgang Sievers. West Aspect, Heide II, 1968. *Courtesy State Library of Victoria.*

Wolfgang Sievers. Heide II interior, 1968. From left: David Aspden, Les Kossatz (above), Syd Ball (below), Ron Upton (sculpture). All sculptures on bench, Danila Vassilieff, Col Jordan (wall), Arthur Boyd, foreground right.
Courtesy State Library of Victoria.

Nigel Buesst. Hal Porter and Sunday at Heide, c. 1964.
Courtesy State Library of Victoria.

Nadine Amadio. Sunday feeding cats in the Heart Garden, c. 1964.
Courtesy Nadine Amadio / Heide Museum of Modern Art.

John Reed. Wildflower hunting: Jean Langley and Sunday. The Pinnacles, Flinders Ranges, 1974. *Courtesy Jean Langley.*

Left: Peter Hobb at Heide, 1970. *Courtesy Peter Hobb.*

Right: Sunday and John, 1979. *Courtesy Herald-Sun / State Library of Victoria.*

but at her husband. It is a tender and trusting look, acknowledging, amid the bohemian chaos, a complex union that invited others to sup at the banquet of their marriage.

In *Pick Up* (1941, NGA) and *Victory Girls* (1943, NGA) Tucker judges women (and men) harshly for their libidinous desires: sexuality is the path to the underworld, the realm of the damned. In Images of Modern Evil, Tucker eviscerates the human body for moral meaning. The result are tortured and tormented figures, their warped forms transformed into creatures part human, part monster. But, faced with photographing Heide's emotional complexities, Tucker finds judgement less easy to sustain. The feminine dominates, not darkly as in his paintings, but as a force that was assured, whole, radiant and empowered.

While Nolan, Hester and Perceval were inspired by Heide and produced art there, Sunday did not encourage her artist friends to decorate the house, apart from Nolan. One day, he and Sunday got the idea to paint the library walls deep ochre, to John's astonishment when he returned home.

There was also Nolan's ambitious project, while on leave from the army, to paint a large scale version of *Boy and the Moon* on the Heide roof (which Sunday used for nude sunbathing). Nolan told his biographer Brian Adams he was inspired by the scale of the Mexican muralists and, on a more practical note, the corrugated iron roof needed a coat of rust protection. But the white, moon-like head resembled the Japanese rising sun on the enemy's national flag. Soon it was spotted by pilots of local aircraft. Two intelligence officers from the RAAF promptly arrived at Heide and ordered the image to be erased.

As a site for creativity, as a garden salon with liberal sexual mores, Heide draws comparisons with Charleston and with Farley's Farm, both in Sussex and contemporary with Heide.

Virginia Woolf found Charleston for her sister Vanessa. In 1916, Virginia wrote to Vanessa, 'it's the most delightful house . . . It has a charming garden, with a pond, and fruit trees and vegetables, all now rather run wild, but you could make it lovely. The house is very nice, with large rooms, and one room with big windows fit for a studio . . . The house wants doing up – and the wallpapers are awful. But it sounds a most attractive place – and 4 miles from us, so you wouldn't be badgered by us.'[44] Charleston has been restored and now operates as a house museum.

Vanessa wanted an escape from London, not only for herself and her two sons, but because her lover, artist Duncan Grant, was a conscientious objector during the First World War. Under wartime law, he had to find gainful employment on a farm and Vanessa organised it. Pacifists were eyed askance. So was Vanessa's *ménage* which included Duncan's lover, writer David Garnett. Vanessa's marriage to critic Clive Bell existed in name only, though he often stayed at Charleston. In 1918, Vanessa gave birth to Duncan's daughter, Angelica, and while it spelled the end of Vanessa's sexual relationship with the artist, their creative partnership flowered until her death.

Vanessa and Duncan festooned Charleston with rich, colourful designs influenced by Cézanne, Matisse and Bonnard. Their philosophy, inherited from William Morris, united art and craft in a modernist environment and their paintings utilised the same bold, simplified patterns that distinguished their work as designers for the Omega Workshop, founded by Roger Fry. Charleston, where Vanessa and Duncan spent both wars, was used largely as a summer holiday house for the rest of the time. But, because of its exquisite and unique decoration, it feels like a much-loved and lived-in home.

Curator Wendy Hitchmough describes it as a house that was 'always full of people and people were encouraged to be creative there.' Including Fry who built a much-needed fireplace in the study. Hitchmough observes, 'Vanessa was very much at the hub at the house. She was nurturing.'[45] Vanessa was also a woman of immense calm and fortitude who disdained convention.

Like Sunday, she ran the house smoothly keeping her lover, his lover and her husband within her orbit and not at each other's throats. Regular guests included Lytton Strachey, economist Maynard Keynes and, of course, Virginia and Leonard Woolf. Vanessa's studio, where she spent her mornings uninterrupted, is the largest and airiest room in the house, full of her paintings, easel and brushes and a clutter of treasured mementos. The garden is romantic and lush with a thriving vegetable patch.

Vanessa may have been a household goddess but she did not bear her domestic burdens alone. Unlike Sunday she had three servants. The Bloomsbury set was not wealthy (Maynard Keynes helped support Charleston by paying rent even when he wasn't staying there) but they expected a life commensurate with their class and that meant someone to cook the dinner. When the summer was over, Duncan and Vanessa packed up the house and returned to the comforts of London. Winter is bleak on the Sussex downs and Charleston is closed to the public in those months. It is also remote. When Vanessa first went to see it, she caught the train down from London and cycled from Lewes, the nearest town. Even today, it is quite a hike.

A short distance from Charleston, Farley's Farm was a weekender for critic and surrealist painter Roland Penrose and his wife, photographer Lee Miller, and provided a base in England for the surrealist circle.

Miller had been a frontline photographer during the Second World War and accompanied the American troops when they entered Berlin. She visited Hitler's apartment and had a bath there, washing off the filth of Dachau, which she had visited with the Allied army of liberation. But after the hectic and traumatic pressures of the war years, Miller spiralled into depression and began to drink heavily.

Despite the tensions, Penrose and Miller, like the Reeds, were excellent hosts. Miller liked to cook – cookery became her outlet after she abandoned photography – and guests included Man Ray, Max Ernst, Dorothea Tanning, Paul Eluard, Joan Miró and Picasso, together with Penrose's lovers.

Through his connections with the surrealist circle, Penrose amassed a fine collection and surrounded himself with works by Ernst, Miró, Paul Delvaux, Wolfgang Paalen, Eileen Agar, Dora Maar and Eduardo Paolozzi. A ceramic tile by Picasso is set into the kitchen wall above the stove. Penrose's own paintings – he relinquished art to become a critic and to found, with Herbert Read, the Institute of Contemporary Art – bear testament to his considerable gifts. The garden has sculptures by Henry Moore and Kenneth Armitage. But Farley's was not a site to make art, the artist guests using their time to relax and take advantage of Penrose and Miller's hospitality.

While Penrose knew the Bloomsbury group through Maynard Keynes, his own commitment to the radical tenets of surrealism meant that, after the 1930s, they were not in sympathy. Surrealism's charter was to transform art and society by using provocative, often sexually charged imagery. Nor were the surrealists averse to publicity. Grandstanding was the last thing the austere Vanessa would choose to do. Privately, Penrose considered the Bloomsbury group were artsy-craftsy fuddy-duddies, set in their ways. Vanessa refused to be over-awed by the stylish, cosmopolitan crowd at Farley's Farm. When Picasso came to visit, Penrose called Vanessa and asked her to drop by. Vanessa considered it, then declined. She was simply too busy.[46]

Sunday's modernism was cooler and cleaner than Vanessa Bell's: there are no patterned walls and painted mantels at Heide. Nor did the Reeds have a retreat from what country life offered – though Charleston and Farley's distance from London, and Sussex's harsh winters, make them more a problematic exercise on that score than Heide. The Reeds dug in at Heide, and apart from a few periods when they felt daunted by its demands, they did not consider living anywhere else. Nor did they return to the city for light relief. They turned their backs on Toorak and did not resile, no matter how badly the great enterprise of Heide sometimes fared.

There was another reason Heide became a centre for the modernist cause during the war years.

John had relinquished his dismal attempts at practising law and was now a power-broker of the first order. His involvement with the Contemporary Art Society – he had been asked by George Bell to draft the CAS constitution and was elected to its first commit-tee – had catapulted him into the stimulating and treacherous arena of Melbourne art politics. In 1942, he was approached by the intrepid Adelaide poet Max Harris to become an editor of his journal *Angry Penguins*.

Initially, John was diffident, telling Harris, 'I do not fancy myself as an editor, even of a limited section of a magazine'.[47] But Harris's infectious enthusiasm did the trick and shortly afterwards John was proposing, 'I should be the Collaborating Editor of the Art Section'. While he still had doubts about his capacities as an editor, he was 'so deeply involved in the contemporary art movement that it would be a mistake for me not to participate in this new direction'.[48]

Sunday must have breathed a sigh of relief. John's new commitments cancelled his plans either for departing for Russia or joining the army. It also meant he had work that was engaging and demanding. Harris was delighted: John had agreed to finance the journal.

Sunday insisted those around her live up to their capacities and was keen to assign them roles. In John's case, it was as an instrument of greater forces. She felt 'John's life is what it is because he has accepted the inward flow of life and given to it – that he has been used – to me is most beautiful.'[49]

It was not, however, John's money that bankrolled *Angry Penguins*, or the ambitious publishing project of Reed & Harris, or, for that matter, Heide itself. It was Sunday's. If she was determined to give her money away, then the years 1941–46 would put her to the test, as she poured Baillieu money into a series of cultural projects that nearly sent her and John broke. Alister Kershaw, whose satiric poem 'Denunciad' was published in *Angry Penguins*, knew Sunday was 'reputed to be [John] Reed's mentor in artistic matters, which may have been true, as well as his major source of financing, which was certainly true.'[50]

After winding up his practice in 1943, John had only a small income and no capital. Henry Reed was not a generous man. He expected his children to make their own money and there were no hand-outs, as Cynthia discovered as she wandered the world trying to make a living. But Arthur Baillieu had seen to it that Sunday, and his other children, were well provided for.

Arthur died late in 1943, an inheritance increasing Sunday's financial security and making possible the new projects. Sunday nursed her father as he gradually grew weaker, sharing her distress with Nolan and John who consoled and sympathised with her. But Arthur's death did not bring Sunday closer to Darren and Everard.

Sunday 'claimed she was expelled from Merthon by her two brothers, and she longed for it'. (Everard, not Darren or Sunday, inherited Merthon.) As far as Darren and Everard were concerned, Sunday was 'bringing communists into the house and when challenged with this, she was very indignant. The upshot was she never went to Merthon again.'[51] It was a bitter blow to lose her precious childhood holiday home and spiritual retreat. From then on, holidays were spent in a rented cottage at Point Lonsdale, on the other side of the bay.

With her flair for ideas and organisation, Sunday quickly became involved in all aspects of *Angry Penguins*. She wondered whether the magazine should change its name. Whimsically, Nolan suggested 'Sunday Best' and promptly began addressing her as 'Miss Editor'.

Reading and editing the contributions to the magazine gave Sunday a firsthand opportunity to assess how much good local writing was available. It must have seemed that the renaissance in Australian painting was being matched by a similar rebirth in Australian letters. In a matter of time, John announced to Harris that Sunday had had 'a brain wave' and 'we have decided to start a publishing house in order to give a real local outlet for local material and would be happy if you would come in with us, the three of us being on an equal footing'.[52] Soon, John had asked Nolan to come in as a fourth partner and had established an office at 360 Queen Street.

Sunday's work on *Angry Penguins*, and Reed & Harris, would be based at Heide, her dedicated sphere of activity, and she rarely visited the city office. It was similar with the CAS. Though she kept herself informed of CAS business, and John consulted her on the hurly-burly of its politics, she did not attend meetings. Sunday's bad hearing – she had an ear trumpet but it was of little use – meant large meetings were frustrating experiences for her. The small scale of Heide, where she could be heard and listened to in the way she desired, made it, once again, her chosen domain.

The Reeds saw *Angry Penguins* as a vehicle to promote the second circle and did so unflaggingly in the journal's short but intense life. John wrote about Tucker, Perceval and Boyd, Tucker reviewed Vassilieff and Nolan, Hester's work was reproduced, as was other members' of the group. It was not entirely a club for Heide afficiados: Noel Counihan, Vic O'Connor, Sydney surrealist James Gleeson and Adelaide surrealist James Cant also made the grade with recent paintings.

Harris was determined to publish 'the rare and chance good things that come our way – two or three a year and largely within a fairly narrow circle'.[53] It was an unfortunately blinkered attitude, shared, it would seem, by all the editors. Harris did seek to establish international contacts and credentials, publishing Herbert Read and his follower, the anarchist writer and poet George Woodcock; the poetry of Dylan Thomas; George Seferis; Henry Treece and Robert Penn Warren together with local poetry by Alister Kershaw, James Gleeson and Harris himself plus fiction by Peter Cowan, Alan Marshall, Greville Texidor and Hal Porter.

But the standard of the writing was not uniformly high. It meant *Angry Penguins'* literary qualities were not its most memorable feature and it was the work of painters, not writers and poets, that mark *Angry Penguins'* best efforts. At the time, Sunday's taste in Australian letters included Katharine Susannah Pritchard, Eleanor Dark and Judith Wright – though none of them appeared in *Angry Penguins*. Other writers whose work she admired included Katherine Mansfield and Gertrude Stein. Sunday told Michael Keon she admired Mansfield's 'beautiful obstinacies', the way her short stories managed to keep alive 'honest-to-goodness lyricism' in a context of 'bitter realism and personal constraint'.[54]

Sunday was interested in relating painting to poetry by connecting the work of Nolan and Harris. She canvassed the possibility with John of seeing 'some real overlapping in Max and Nolan's work. Their work is in no way similar and yet it is of course in the sense of an awareness of each other and a quickening on both sides – Nolan says he is not alongside any painter and is much more at home with writers – and Max – which I think unusual and an exciting and rich prospect. Max too may have tentative feelings in that direction.'[55]

In her project to translate three of Rimbaud's poems for publication, Sunday sought Nolan's assistance. Nolan's short essay on Rimbaud, 'Faithful Words', appeared in the same 1943 issue, together with *Bathers* (1943, NGV). Nolan hailed Rimbaud as bearing the 'birth-marks of an angel naked and possessed'.[56] Arguably *Angry Penguins'* best issue, it also included Tucker's controversial essay 'Art, Myth and Society' and John's review of the Anti-Fascist exhibition.

Sunday worked closely on the poems with Nolan. She sent him a French dictionary, so he could appreciate Rimbaud in the original, and posted him her translations at various stages, eager for his comments. She was also keen for Nolan to complete a series of paintings to illustrate her translations which he did not do, a bone of contention between them.[57]

Curiously, Sunday did not select the wild, free form verse of
Illuminations or *A Season in Hell* but earlier, more conservative works.
Graham Robb has described these 'affecting sonnets' as 'the acceptable face' of Rimbaud.[58] 'Poem' (titled 'Sensation' by Rimbaud) could
be a description of Sunday's favourite things: nature, summer,
freedom, love and bohemia.

> On the fine nights of summer, I will go on paths
> Pricked by the wheat, to tread on the slender grass;
> Dreamer, I will feel the freshness on my feet,
> And let the wind bathe my bare head.
>
> I will not speak, I will not think,
> But love will fill my heart,
> And I will go far, far away, bohemian
> By nature – happy as with a woman.[59]

'Dream for Winter' was equally lyrical and, unusually for
Rimbaud, both tender and sentimental. Two lovers travel in 'a little
pink carriage / With blue cushions' where 'a nest of kisses rests / In
each soft corner'. The lovers draw close against the 'evening shadows
making faces through the windows'. They embrace and 'a little kiss,
like a mad spider' runs 'on your neck' and the lovers search for 'that
little beast – who travels so much'.[60] The third poem, 'Dreamer',
nudges nearer to the fractured imagery of Rimbaud's best work.

Harris would write that Sunday's translations reproduced the
poems with 'an almost absolute literalness'.[61] Perhaps Harris did
not know his French but Sunday's translations were by no means
literal, she took liberties with the poet's words and intention,
making them very much her own.

In 'Dreamer' – titled 'My Bohemia' by Rimbaud – Sunday
subverts the poem's irony with a lyrical romanticism. In the first

verse, and in the poem's title, Rimbaud mocks himself, the ambitious young poet roaming the countryside in search of passion and inspiration. 'Oh la la! que d'amours splendides j'ai revées!' Rimbaud jests. 'Oh dear me! what splendid loves I dreamed!' But Sunday's translation, 'Oh what I love I dreamed', is a murmur of longing, not a self-deprecating aside.[62] Sunday resists Rimbaud's wicked humour, which was part of his assault on the conventions of poetry and, indeed, on convention itself, and she allows the lyrical mood created by the nature imagery of the poem's later verses to saturate its entire effect.

But she creates exquisite passages, too. When Rimbaud writes, 'Mes étoiles au ciel avaient un doux frou-frou', Sunday's translation is lovely. 'My stars in heaven softly rustled their silk'[63] and much more evocative than Graham Robb's, 'My stars made a soft swishing in the sky'.[64]

Why did Sunday not hurl some of Rimbaud's thunderbolts at the Australian audience? 'O the ashen face, the shield of hair, the arms of crystal! the cannon on which I must swoop down through the clash of trees and the buoyant air!' Rimbaud sang in *Illuminations*.[65] Was that why Nolan did not choose to illustrate Sunday's translations, because they were not as radical as the poems he liked? Perhaps Sunday viewed her translations as an introduction to Rimbaud. First the audience would receive a palatable taste of Rimbaud's genius and then graduate to the more sophisticated fare of *Illuminations*.

Sunday's selections and translations indicate the strengths and weaknesses of her taste that emerged both in her patronage, and in *Angry Penguins* itself. She responded to what was fresh, bold and youthful but her sentimentality that privileged the personal and intimate statement, that connected her vitally to her childhood and gave such importance to loyalty and friendship could also make her err on sentimentality's worst side, manifesting in a self-indulgent, sickly sweet romanticism. At times, Sunday lacked objective critical distance and the ability to discern major from minor art.

The translation episode ended as an unhappy and humiliating one for Sunday, one that revealed the volatile relations between Harris and the Reeds. Harris irreverently introduced the poems, enumerating their 'deceptive simplicity' and 'surface sentimentalism'. He also invoked his editorial powers, substituting 'faery shadows' for 'fantastical shadows' in 'Dreamer'.[66] Blithely unaware of his gaffe, Harris asked John's opinion about his comments.

John, quietly furious, regarded 'the whole thing as a bad mistake', believing that Harris had been 'intellectually patronising'. He refused to 'say anything about Sunday's feelings' leaving Max to speculate just how upset and angry she was. John continued, 'As the acknowledged leader of the progressive writers of the country haven't you rather let other writers down at this particular moment when an attempt was being made to begin the establishment of a real appreciation and understanding of Rimbaud.'[67]

Harris was furious at being censured. As far as he was concerned, his remarks indicated 'perfect intuition' and identified 'the very heart of Rimbaud'. He was not at all remorseful and 'indeed rather proud of that little piece of prose'.[68] Pressure was brought to bear, however, and, in the following issue, Harris wrote rather ungraciously that 'the Editors had been asked by Sunday Reed to publish her revised translation' of 'Poem'. He also mentioned Sunday was grateful to writer Erik Schwimmer who had pointed out 'a mistake'. Where Sunday had translated 'bohemien' as exactly that, 'bohemian', its more common translation is 'gipsy'.[69] She seemed to have also misunderstood that when Rimbaud writes 'la Nature' he means the natural world, not one's individual nature. That, too, was amended in the new version. Translation is a matter of such fine and subtle emphases, as Sunday now sorely realised.

It was left to Nolan and John to commiserate with her. The Reeds fought with all their friends and the closer the friends, the worse was the battle, the grief and the aftermath. The Reeds expected, and did not always receive, the reconciliations they sought. After an argument with Tucker, Sunday wrote to Hester telling her that 'John and I are very sad. We are sorry for whatever mistakes we have made. In fact we hope it is a real way of learning to be better, learning to be more than we are, not to cause hurt.'[70] At Heide, Harris reflected, the pressures were 'mighty'. The Reeds may have had 'very pure and beautiful intentions', giving 'so freely to the creative spirit wherever you find it', but he also chided them for their unrealistic expectations that lead them to 'perpetually feel let down'.[71] Fights and misunderstandings erupted, creating the feuds and the wounds that play an intrinsic part of the Heide story.

No wonder Sunday published nothing more in *Angry Penguins*. But her involvement (and money) remained integral to the project, Harris declaring, 'I feel you are the stimulus and the decisive sensibility . . . You are a symbol Sun and that symbol means a great deal. Believe that.'[72] Books, as well as the journal, were busily being produced under the Reed & Harris imprint, including Reg Ellery's *Schizophrenia: The Cinderella of Psychiatry*, Max Harris's novel *The Vegetative Eye* (both covers illustrated by Nolan), and Cynthia's first novel *Lucky Alphonse!*

The most testing time for *Angry Penguins* came in 1944 during the Ern Malley hoax when the editors were held up to public and international ridicule for accepting poems concocted by Harold

Stewart and James McAuley as the work of an undiscovered genius. The untutored, original, gifted artist was the rare creature Sunday constantly sought and, falling for the ruse, she and her fellow editors were hoist by the petard of their own sensibility.

The event had a slow, shattering effect on the spirits of the Reed & Harris team, especially on Harris himself who was virtually destroyed as a poet, not only due to the hoax but by the added stress of a court case for obscenity which followed. Sections of the literary world were gleeful at the downfall of the 'pretentious Penguins', as Noel Counihan called them, and Sunday was dismayed by 'the personal animosity which one finds almost everywhere in references to us or our activities'.[73]

Reed & Harris staggered on gamely for another three years but the heart was gone from the enterprise. In 1945, Albert Tucker was appointed sociological editor, in charge of a section of the magazine that explored 'aspects of the social scene which are particularly related to culture and the role of the artist in society'.[74] It seemed tailormade for Tucker but that, too, became fraught with problems. Tucker believed he was excluded from contributing to editorial policy and from the powerful circle formed by the Reeds, Nolan and Harris. Perhaps if Tucker had been inside it, he would have realised what a thorny place it was. He bargained hard with John about money and status, and won, but it meant more hurt feelings all around.

Sunday came up with one final idea, a news and political broadsheet called *Tomorrow* edited by Jack Bellew, Peter's brother, a neighbour at Point Lonsdale and an ex-chief of staff at the Sydney *Daily Telegraph*. Bellew's co-editor was John Sinclair, *Herald* music critic and the Reeds' close friend, who threw his considerable organisational and journalistic skills into the project.

But the whole adventure was a financial disaster for the Reeds.

'In simple terms we are broke,' John advised Harris, 'and are closing down. In less than three years Reed & Harris has absorbed £7000 or more and *Tomorrow* another £2500 and the end has now come . . . Neither Sun nor I have much to say just now: we are faced with the end of our work and are thrown back on ourselves with nothing else left.'[75]

Accompanied by another acrimonious dispute with Harris, the Reeds could not help but experience the collapse of Reed & Harris on a debilitatingly personal level. 'Its failure has left us both bereft of all but the very deepest threads of living . . . Sun and I are at Heide living our days and comforting each other as best we can. We have not read a book in many months.'[76] For John, in particular, it was the wreck of his hopes of a communally oriented, avant-garde group of people who would stand shoulder to shoulder to change the culture. Sunday and John shared their friendships but if Nolan was Sunday's special animating force, then Harris had been John's.

When Malcolm Good took John to task for his friendship with Harris, John replied it was 'not through any wild impulse to be associated with a brilliant young man but because of the very deep conviction of his unique qualities'. Nor did John choose to strike back at his enemies about the Ern Malley hoax, telling Good, 'You have said in effect that this is my opportunity and you have called on me for bold action. Now, I am not a person who essentially deals in terms of bold action.'[77]

The Reeds spent most of the winter and spring of 1946 in Queensland, licking their wounds. They visited the young Brisbane poet Barrett Reid, who became a close friend, and they travelled to Green Island in the Great Barrier Reef. Nolan stayed at Heide, managing the property in their absence. He reacted with quiet disbelief when John wrote telling him that they had hatched a plan to stay in Brisbane and run a bookshop. It was Sunday's idea, and it came to nothing, but it indicates how desperately the Reeds wanted to escape the site of the vanquished hopes and dreams that Heide now represented.

In a state of despair and confusion, John also announced he would make the ultimate sacrifice, leave the *ménage* and allow Sunday and Nolan to pursue their life together. Gently but firmly, Nolan dissuaded John explaining, 'I do not expect or want you to write that your life has to find a new orientation. I do not think it fair on yourself.'[78]

In November, the Reeds returned to Heide to complete the final chapter of their shared life with Nolan.

· 9 ·

Ned

Nobody knows anything about my case but myself.
NED KELLY[1]

We have dreamed all these things in our deepest lives. It is our self we are making out there.
DAVID MALOUF, AN IMAGINARY LIFE[2]

People used to say to Sun . . . 'You shouldn't have taken those paintings. You shouldn't have kept them.' She'd say 'Yes, they're mine. I helped make them.'
NADINE AMADIO[3]

DESPITE THE ERN MALLEY DEBACLE and the slow collapse of Reed & Harris, Heide's moment as a centre of modernist endeavour and a nurturing environment for first-rate Australian art had, in fact, arrived. Between March 1946 and July 1947, Nolan completed the Ned Kelly series on the dining room table. The best paintings of Nolan's career were completed with Sunday by his side.

Nolan had done his homework about Kelly before setting off, late in 1945 with Max Harris, for a brief visit to Glenrowan in northern Victoria, the site of Kelly's capture and the death of his gang in 1880. Nolan told his biographer Brian Adams that he and Harris had first canvassed ideas about Kelly while preparing *Angry Penguins* for publication.

Nolan's reading list included J.J. Keneally's *Inner History of the Kelly Gang* and Tucker loaned him the 1881 Royal Commission report.[4] While Elwyn Lynn commented that the detailed and voluminous report had daunted most researchers,[5] Nolan did not plough through the entire thing: he read one of the volumes Tucker picked up in a secondhand shop. Henceforth, Tucker dubbed Nolan 'Ned', a sobriquet that tickled Nolan and he later used it to sign his letters to Tucker. Nolan's other influences, named in his famous declaration about the series, were Kelly's words, Rousseau and sunlight.

It is impossible to imagine the evolution of the Kellys without Nolan's years in the Wimmera where he mastered a new approach to the landscape and, equally importantly, fell in love with the landscape itself. The Wimmera is not easy to love: flat and almost featureless, it is not conventionally alluring. But it offered Nolan a challenge he met exceptionally well, where he grasped its particular Australian qualities of light and space and interpreted those qualities in the modernist idiom. Its flatness also presented the abstract qualities crucial to modernism's enterprise and to which Nolan's sensibility was finely attuned. Despite the pressures of army life, Nolan had responded well to his time in the bush, producing new work and becoming keenly appreciative, not only of the landscape, but of the characters and folk tales of country life.

Hester regarded Nolan as the 'Cézanne' of Australian painting. She wrote to him at Dimboola, praising *Bathers* (1943, Heide Museum of Modern Art) as his best work to date. Nolan replied that if Australians committed themselves to 'what is before their noses' real progress might be made, despite 'the famous colonial cultural disadvantages'.[6] Now Nolan was preparing to build on those insights.

After absconding from the army, Nolan lead a strange, secretive existence, living at Heide but also staying at a loft in Parkville, which Sunday furnished for him, even including her baby Bechstein. The Reeds referred to him, even in letters to one another, as Robin in order to make his new identity foolproof. They were hardly conditions conducive to producing art and it took until 1945 for Nolan to begin sketches on the Kelly theme and until 1946 to start the major paintings.

The authenticity of the Kelly myth, into which Nolan tapped, has been proved by its continuity and renewal – books, films and plays appear with each decade, examining further evidence and opinions on Australia's most enduring and popular legend. Self-reflexively, the texts and images feed off previous interpretations. For example, Peter Carey has said his novel *True History of the Kelly Gang* was inspired by Nolan's paintings while at the 2000 Sydney Olympics, the Kelly mask, as interpreted by Nolan, was a feature of the opening event.

There are many interpretations of the Kelly series. Andrew Sayers has suggested, 'almost all of the writing which has been produced on the Kelly series has revolved around an examination of "the Kelly myth" but what did Nolan understand by "myth" when he painted the series?'[7] As Ned Kelly was the embodiment, the carrier of the myth, it is probably more useful to ask, what did Nolan understand about Kelly when he painted the series?

The series' first impact is its startling modernity: the Kellys look as fresh and vital today as they did when they were painted decades ago. Nolan delivers the landscapes drenched in brilliant light and colour, and in two differing modes – either lyrically, like *The Burning Tree* (1947, National Gallery of Australia) and *Morning Camp* (1947, NGA), or with intense clarity and with passages approaching abstraction, like *The Chase* (1946, NGA) or *The Encounter* (1946, NGA). Nolan had developed these alternating styles in the Wimmera paintings. But it is the Kellys' laconic Australian humour that makes the series both memorable and modernist.

Though Kelly dominates the landscape in *Ned Kelly* (1946, NGA) he looks neither comfortable nor at home, but absurd. The mask is fixed to his head, dominating his body and removing all trace of personality, relegating him to the role of a mythic being moving through the land. Kelly is a tragi-comic figure, alien and bizarre. He is a man no longer but an embodiment of a particular kind of Australian tragedy that takes place in the landscape, under pitiless blue skies.

Australian bush heroes tend to be anti-heroes. Their hubris and hardiness is admirable but there remains, enmeshed in their acts of bravery, an embarrassing and undeniable smell of failure, the foolishness and pig-headedness that leads them to their doom. Burke and Wills' heroic trek from Melbourne to the Gulf of Carpentaria ended with their deaths in 1861. The explorer Ludwig Leichhardt and his entire party vanished somewhere in central Queensland. In 1931, Harry Lasseter, determined to find a fabulously rich gold reef in the Northern Territory's MacDonnell Ranges, perished and was never found. Kelly's quixotic and implausible revolt against Queen, government and the Victoria police made him one of their number.

Modernism's taste for parody meant it refused to romanticise or glorify the heroes of history, even the popular ones. It was modernism's task to subvert and displace traditional historical narratives, providing the perspective for the questions Nolan posed in the Kelly series. What made a hero? How can his tale be told truthfully and in a modern manner? Nolan's adaptation of the Kelly narrative was sophisticated and witty, and though he took Kelly seriously, he could not help poking fun at him. Nolan mocks Kelly, making him poignantly human, touchingly fallible and utterly mythic.

The Australian sense of humour takes snide delight in deflating self-importance, bringing what is pompous or pretentious down to earth with a thud. Bleakly and cruelly accurate, it can also be a cover for hostile philistinism, exactly as Nolan and his fellow editors had experienced over the Ern Malley hoax. The hoax provided a context for the Kellys, and a subtext, where brave modernist ventures could be subjected to the sneers of the cognoscenti and the sling-shots of the crowd.

In *The Trial* (1947, NGA) the grand, final work in the series, Kelly dominates the courtroom through sheer size. Arms crossed belligerently, he confronts a nervous Judge Redmond Barry who has sentenced him to be hanged, and he towers over the ineffectual, martinet-like police officers. Kelly had the last word. 'I will meet you there!' he told Barry. Though it is a scene of deadly earnestness, Nolan has constructed the composition with the playfulness of a fairytale. Kelly, the storybook giant, overwhelms his assailants. Though captured, he gains the moral victory: death will make him a martyr and a folk hero, a potent symbol of Australian anti-authoritarianism.

Kelly was not a man who legitimately earned society's respect or rose to a valued position. He is a subversive trickster figure with the honour of a thief. Foxy and reckless, he metes out rough justice on his own terms and in his own territory. His death at twenty-five makes him an eternal youth and the feelings he evokes — of spirited rebellion against authority — are the emotions of youth, the urge to challenge tradition and depose the father.

Nolan remarked that the Kellys could be read as an autobiography, revealing the 'emotional and complicated events in my own life. It's an inner history of my own life.'[8] Robin Murray was Nolan's chosen name, his alter ego, and, from such a literary man as Nolan, it offers clues about his identification with Kelly.

Nolan could have chosen Robin for Robin Hood, a mythic figure of the English landscape, the 'good' bandit with his band of merry men, a champion of the common people who robbed from the rich and gave to the less fortunate. But, unlike Kelly, Robin Hood is not an historic figure but a folk tale hero, a symbol of the forces of nature who offered an alternative to 'normal', civilised life and who was derived from the Green Man, the nature god of Celtic pagan tradition. Perhaps Nolan chose Murray for Victoria's most important river that marks the state's northern border, another identification with landscape.

Robin Murray was Nolan's outlaw self, a self he relished, despite the dangers, a Rimbaud-like character who lived beyond moral boundaries and who created art from urgency and rebellion. To avoid detection, Nolan and Kelly constructed 'masks' of alternate personae: Nolan's was Robin Murray while Kelly's was a suit of armour that disguised and protected him. Nolan had relinquished social convention by abandoning his wife and child and moving into Heide. Kelly flouted the law by evading the police and committing bank robberies.

The Kelly series gave Nolan the chance to examine, concealed beneath the narrative, some of his own actions. Mary Nolan told T.G. Rosenthal that Nolan had said the central figure in *Mrs Reardon at Glenrowan* (1946, NGA) was his first wife, Elizabeth, holding Amelda.[9] He repeated the image in both *Glenrowan* (1946, NGA) and *Siege at Glenrowan* (1946, NGA). Though in these works the figures are much smaller, it indicates how important the image was to him.

Mrs Reardon was trapped in the Glenrowan Hotel as it began to burn: as she rushed outside, she was shot at by the police but escaped unharmed. In the painting, Mrs Reardon and her baby are suffused by golden light, a reflection from the flames so, at first glance, they seem to be on fire. Nolan, like Rimbaud, had a rare gift for combining beauty with violence and achieving a lyrical result. 'She thought she was trapped' begin Nolan's accompanying comments to *Mrs Reardon at Glenrowan*.[10] So, perhaps, did Elizabeth, caught between Nolan and the Reeds.

In *Mrs Reardon at Glenrowan*, Nolan allows himself to 'save' his wife and daughter from potential catastrophe, first from the burning hotel and then from the police fusillade. He invents a happy ending for a story that did not have one. During this time, Elizabeth and Nolan were divorced, and Elizabeth remarried. Perhaps Nolan felt he had indeed 'saved' Elizabeth from a disastrous situation, and that she was better off without him. Mrs Reardon is a touching image of the archetypal Madonna, a woman who risks death to protect her child.

It is interesting that Nolan painted *Mrs Reardon at Glenrowan* in October 1946 while Sunday was absent from Heide and holidaying in Queensland. Perhaps it was an image he did not wish to explore in her presence.

Nolan painted all but one of the Kellys on the Heide dining room table. Barrett Reid remembers his first visit to Heide, late in 1946, when 'the dining room was a studio with tins of ripolin, bottles of oil, a scrubbed long table and on the walls many charcoal drawings of bearded heads. I saw real painting, free and authentic, for the first time. I had arrived just as the Kellys were nearing completion; the large hardboard panels, the cardboard studies, the many drawings captured and controlled my eyes'.[11]

Tucker was astonished by Nolan's 'terrific capacity and inner strength to be able to operate in that kind of circumstance. I certainly couldn't. Not a hope.' Tucker also observed that 'the bulk of the time that Nolan [worked] at Heide, Sunday was virtually in his pocket'.[12]

Nolan and Sunday had developed a close working relationship with the Wimmera paintings, but it was hampered by distance. Now they could work side by side. Literally. Sunday stood next to him, watching as he painted. She recalled, 'sometimes he would pick up a brush with his arm around me'.[13] It seemed their creative partnership was complete. Sunday confided to Nadine Amadio that 'she felt that they conceived his art when he was inside of her,' an image of consummate creative union.[14] When Nolan quit Heide, he wrote to John, 'I do not ever feel that the Kellys belong to anyone other than Sun.'[15]

Later, when the Reeds' relationship with Nolan was reduced

to nothing more than a nasty squabble, John tried to put the record straight. 'Your paintings were part of your contribution [to Heide], even though you said Sunday painted them as much as you did . . . you said all your paintings were for Sunday, and I am quite sure you did not think of them otherwise. They were created with her in a sense which is almost literal, and it is certain without her, without your life at Heide, a great many would never have been painted.'[16]

If the Wimmera paintings represented the landscape in a new way, the Kellys told its story with a similar originality. Nolan had culled a myth from the land that was breathing vigour into his work as he surpassed Sunday's wildest hopes as the modernist par excellence of Australian art. Indeed, Nolan would surpass, and discard, Sunday's creative input as he matured to take full control of his own art and life. The Kellys are Sunday and Nolan's swansong; the last, brilliant burst of their creative duet.

What appealed to Sunday about Kelly and made her such a close collaborator in the paintings' production?

If Sunday had made a wish-list of the things that would most thoroughly shock and offend her family and her class, she could not have done better than her actions in the 1940s. She flirted with communism; took as her lover an artist who was the son of a St Kilda tram-driver, and advertised the situation by moving him into her home; she financially supported a group of rowdy leftwing intellectuals and poured Baillieu money down the drain in a series of radical cultural enterprises. She even helped fund Malcolm Good's Communist Party campaigns for state and federal parliament, which was reported in the press.

Sunday could not be blamed for feeling she was an outlaw and a renegade, loathed by the society that had borne her. And she paid for it, earning the wrath of her brothers and being denied access to her childhood home. Though Sunday had an affectionate relationship with her father, it was not without its storms. Michael Keon remembers that when Sunday arrived home after her regular Monday evening dinners with Arthur, Heide resonated with slammed doors and bad tempers.

Given Sunday's slow simmering discontent about the Baillieu clan's strictures and its oppressive masculinity, her program of rebellion cannot have been entirely accidental. She flouted every rule and every convention under whose aegis she had been raised. She seemed determined to confront and infuriate, by every means possible, the people who gave to her, and who made her, what she was. If Sunday's artist friends regularly bit the hand that fed them by berating her for her privileged upbringing, then she was prepared to act in precisely the same manner towards her family. Sunday was defiantly and relentlessly self-willed in creating a scandalous bohemian existence and tossing it in her family's face. Worse still, she effectively sacked her family and replaced them with her artist friends, her elected relatives and chosen intimates.

Ned Kelly was no stranger to Sunday. More than Nolan she had observed at close hand the powerful elites, had witnessed the operation of society at its highest, most clandestine and clannish level. She knew it was an old boys' club. The men in her family were some of its key members. No-one was more aware than Sunday what a character like Kelly was up against, not only in terms of a last-ditch rebellion, but also in terms of the disgust and disfavour emanating from an establishment that wanted to destroy him, both as a man and a symbol.

If Nolan chose Kelly because he saw similiarities in their Irish larrikin temperaments and, symbolically, in their predicaments, Sunday chose Nolan for the same reasons. She cherished her wild

Irish lad because he helped her to challenge the prohibitions she chose to flout, in art and in life. Kelly was, for both Sunday and Nolan, another Rimbaud figure, a youthful martyr, an agent provocateur whose inflammatory actions provided a focus for cultural iconography and change.

As lovers, Nolan and Sunday were also outsiders, 'on the run' from convention. It is a theme that emerges in their correspondence: a sense of desperation, a recognition of the fragility and danger of their situation, a belief that their love and their potential happiness as a couple was constantly under threat and that any future security might be cruelly denied to them. It heightened the affair's romance and passion, adding piquancy, sexual electricity and yearning. 'Everything hurts,' Nolan declared at one point. 'Everything does which ever way we turn now.'[17]

But it was not only the symbolic and personal aspects of the Kelly legend that appealed to Nolan and Sunday. Both were interested in childhood, popular culture and film, all of which inform the Kellys. Orson Welles was a favourite director/actor of Sunday's and she endorsed Reed & Harris's publication of the memoirs of popular comedian Roy Rene, known as Mo. Stationed in the Wimmera, Nolan was impressed by Walt Disney's animated feature film *Dumbo*. He told Sunday how the film's fantasy and humour reconnected him to childhood memories of Luna Park, particularly the carousel with its 'flying' horses.

For Sunday, childhood was a vital link both to her own, and others', creativity. She found the fairytales of the Grimm brothers and Hans Christian Andersen 'wonderful'. But fairytales should not be thought of as 'magic apples picked off the tree of life. They had to rise from human experience; specifically . . . from childhood experience – waking experience, to some extent, perhaps, but much more from nightmares and bad dreams.' Sunday felt that filmmakers, together with other creative artists, could gain access to childhood's 'wonder and magic'.[18]

The Kelly series has a fairytale atmosphere. There is Nolan's lyrical touch that leavened scenes of violence or tragedy with humour and playfulness. In *Death of Constable Scanlon* (1946, NGA) Kelly looks comically dolorous as Scanlon, whom he has just shot, flies through the air with his horse. There is the way Nolan used scale to tell the story – making Kelly enormous and the police puny. Also, when the twenty-seven Kelly paintings are hung together they have a cinematic quality, like scenes on a strip of film.

Sunday's contribution to the series was profound, and profoundly practical. As usual, she assisted Nolan by priming the masonite and mixing the paint.[19] Now she went one step further and began to paint some sections of the paintings. Given Sunday and Nolan's symbiotic working relationship, it was not such a big step to take, and probably one encouraged by Nolan who fully respected his 'dear craftsman'. While it is not known how often she and Nolan worked together in this way, Barrett Reid believed Sunday painted the red squares on the courtroom floor in *The Trial* (1947, NGA) which was painted in January, 1947.[20]

It is also possible she worked on the patchwork quilt in *The defence of Aaron Sherritt* (1946, NGA), after she returned to Heide from her holiday in Queensland in November. The quilt, on Nolan's bed at Heide, was given to him by Douglas Cairns while in the army. (Sunday had a crotcheted patchwork quilt on her bed.) The painting refers to an incident when the Kelly gang shot Aaron Sherritt, former friend turned police informer. Inside the house, Sherritt's wife is forcibly restrained by the police who are too cowardly to venture out and discover Sherritt's fate.

Nolan dedicated an exquisite watercolour to Sunday, titled *For the one who paints such beautiful squares* (c.1946–47, Heide MoMA). On the reverse is written 'Sydney Nolan [sic] "For the one who paints such beautiful squares" (Sunday: Re Kelly Paintings)' in an unknown hand. In a surreal landscape, the figure of Sunday/Mrs Sherritt is wrapped like a mummy in the same red striped outfit she wears in the painting. Red is also the colour of the squares in *The Trial*. She floats above what could be a blue sea (a ship sails away on the horizon) or the earth – objects that could be fruit or flowers lie at her feet. It is a homage, more elliptical than *Rosa Mutabilis*, to Sunday's connection with the swell and the fruits of creativity.

The red squares in the foreground of *The Trial* have been painted with a stencil: they are of the same size, even and regular, sharply geometric with precise edges, unlike the squares in the background (hallway) area which are painted in more cursory manner. The figures of Kelly and the seated policeman have been painted over the tiles, which means the tiles were painted first. Nolan completed Judge Redmond Barry, the jury and attendant police before Sunday set to work.

In Nolan's notes to the series, he wrote 'the tiled floor in red and white was in a house I was in once'. Nolan discussed his ideas with Sunday and that would include the best way to execute the tiles. His own touch was light, swift and painterly, perhaps why his 'dear craftsman' was better suited to the methodical process of reproducting the tiles. It is the perfect job for a studio assistant: not the main task of painting the famous helmet or giving expression to Kelly's strange eyes, swimming like fish in an aquarium, but the meticulous details, the fine tuning, the expert addition to the whole.

Nolan's brushstroke, like Kelly's bravado, could be charmingly reckless. Painting perfect squares was not the job for him, and he knew it. Sunday's 'beautiful squares' make a bold contribution to *The Trial*, creating a vivid ground that intensifies a dramatic moment. In a brilliant series, *The Trial* is arguably the best work, the finale (though not the final work painted). It must have been gratifying for Sunday to participate so thoroughly and it makes comprehensible her statement about why she refused to return the Kellys to Nolan. 'They're mine. I helped make them.'

The patchwork quilt in *The defence of Aaron Sherritt* is more problematic. Unlike *The Trial*, these squares have been painted freehand, though, like *The Trial*, they have been painted prior to the figure of the policeman who lies on top. They have Nolan's casual boldness of touch but many have been painted over, creating a shadow effect, so a deep red becomes murky brown after a coat of blue. Did one hand determine the square's initial colour and another create the final decision about tone and effect? Nolan and Sunday may have worked on the quilt together.

Nolan described the Kellys as a kind of autobiography. Mrs Sherritt is held against her will, in her own bedroom. Despite her best efforts, she cannot escape, placing her in a difficult, humilating and uncomfortable situation. The two men who restrain her are cowards, fearful for their safety and dependent on her for their protection. The scene may not only refer to the bonds that kept Sunday trapped in her marital bed but also to John's and Nolan's dependence on Sunday, their mutual unwillingness to let her go. Indeed, one policeman holds Mrs Sherritt by the throat. The quilt had special meaning for Nolan and Sunday: it symbolised their bed, their refuge, the place where they made love and where, Sunday felt, Nolan's paintings were conceived. But by November 1946, Nolan had realised Sunday would never willingly leave John for him, despite John's momentary loss of nerve in Queensland, and

Nolan's fatigue and frustration about the nearly decade-long affair was growing more acute. In a sense, all the characters in *The defence of Aaron Sherritt* are trapped: the police by cowardice, Mrs Sherritt by force.

Women play a subtle but crucial role in the Kelly series. There are the three images of Elizabeth/Mrs Reardon, together with one of Sunday/Mrs Sherritt.

In *Quilting the armour* (1947, NGA) Kelly's sister Margaret is shown at evening, lovingly sewing soft blue fabric into the head-piece of the armour. Though Nolan does not create a specific portrait of Sunday – her hair was fair and her eyes blue while Margaret Kelly's are brown – the long, strong face with its large, deeply lidded eyes echo Sunday's features. Sunday reminisced about her ancestors, the Belgian lacemakers of Liège, and Nolan dreamed up nicknames for Sunday the needleworker – the 'lacemaker', the 'Belgian girl'. They also had a fantasy about going to Belgium together and exploring Sunday's family background.

Sunday was an excellent seamstress, mending the clothes of the Heide household, and she enjoyed the skills and craft of needle-work. Nolan would have been familiar with seeing Sunday at Heide, repairing his clothes or John's. *Quilting the armour* is an image of womanly protection and care, a role Sunday dutifully fufilled in relation to Nolan, Sunday declaring at one point, 'You make me feel like Florence Nightingale.'[21]

Margaret Kelly tenderly holds the mask, Kelly's symbol, in her arms, as if the violence it represents can be softened and beautified, healed and repaired by a woman's touch, by sympathy and support – the things Sunday offered Nolan. Sunday/Margaret's sewing is also a creative act: she assists Nolan/Kelly by her skills, she enables him to fully function, to move comfortably and she participates with her talents in his project, just as Sunday did in Nolan's paintings.

Nolan did not omit Heide from the series. *Constable Fitzpatrick and Kate Kelly* (1946, NGA) shows the smirking policeman in the Kelly kitchen, making an unwelcome pass at Ned's young sister. Nolan notes 'that is what the fireplace looked like' but it is also what the Heide kitchen looked like, with its woodfire stove, kept burning by Sunday, an image of nuture and contentment, where the kettle boiled for 'arvo tea', a ceremony commemorated in Albert Tucker's intimate 1945 photograph of Sunday, Nolan and Joy Hester.

Aside from the tiles in *The Trial*, there are many patterned effects in the Kellys that contribute to the series' lyrical charm: the floral fabric of Margaret Kelly's dress in *Quilting the armour* makes her appear like a flower of the evening, blooming in the landscape, while the exuberantly 'feminine' floral wallpaper in *The defence of Aaron Sherritt* and *Constable Fitzpatrick and Kate Kelly* acts as a counterpoint to examples of ungallant male behaviour towards women. Flowers were Sunday's quintessential symbol, as Nolan so aptly registered in *Rosa Mutabilis*. In three paintings that physically, symbolically and psychologically refer to Sunday and Heide, Nolan chose the imagery of flowers, of beauty, growth and resilience, to produce an ambience of vitality and grace, symbolising the creative, healing feminine in a narrative of male violence and tragedy.

In July 1947, Nolan finished the series and almost immediately departed for Queensland. Barrett Reid, who made a lightning visit to Melbourne at Christmas 1946, had suggested Nolan see the north, staying first with him in Brisbane, then the two of them could go travelling together. Nolan was about to follow the Reeds' path through Brisbane to the tropical beauty of the Great Barrier Reef and Green Island.

After producing the best work of his career, after a decade of passion and tension with the Reeds, a failed marriage and divorce, a stint in the army and an underground existence as a deserter, Nolan desperately needed a break. But Sunday was anxious she was about to lose him and was disconsolate as he packed. The Reeds drove Nolan to Essendon Airport where they reluctantly bid him farewell. When the plane briefly refuelled in Sydney, Joy Hester was at Mascot airport to greet him.

* IO *

Motherhood

*Have you met Picasso, unpacked the Nolans or generally got anywhere
with the life of Paris?*
JOHN SINCLAIR TO JOHN REED, 29 DECEMBER 1948[1]

For myself Australia is the only romantic place in the world.
SUNDAY REED TO JEAN LANGLEY, 24 DECEMBER 1948[2]

Love with Sun is final.
SIDNEY NOLAN TO JOHN REED, 25 SEPTEMBER 1947[3]

THE LATE 1940S WAS A PERIOD of stark contrasts for Sunday. She
lost Nolan to her sister-in-law Cynthia, generating issues about
possession and betrayal that lasted, not only for the remainder of

Sunday's life, but of Nolan's, Cynthia's and John's, as well. To escape from the sadness of the break-up, and in the hope of winning Nolan back, she and John travelled to Europe, on an ambitious project as curators of an international exhibition of the Kellys.

At the same time, Sunday experienced the pleasures and the pressures of motherhood, a role she had yearned for and thought could never be hers. When Hester and Tucker's marriage broke up in 1947, they agreed on one matter: both wanted Sunday to care for Sweeney. By the following year, Sunday's relationship with the little boy had deepened and she sought to adopt him. The trip to Europe was also to secure permanency for that role. It was a time, less of creative expansion, than of reflection and readjustment. Sunday's most significant creative act, apart from the energy she poured into her adopted son, was to make the Heart Garden, the memorial of her love for Nolan.

During 1947, the second circle slowly shattered. A fateful journey by Albert Tucker to Japan in February 1947 began a diaspora that affected the core members of the group. Within the year, Tucker, Hester, Nolan and Harris all occupied differing roles in relation to the Reeds. Sunday's friendship with John Perceval and Mary Boyd remained as strong as ever but Yvonne and Arthur had left Open Country to live at Martin Boyd's home at Harkaway, near Berwick, and saw less of the Reeds.

But it was not only a period of attrition. John Sinclair's girlfriend, Jean Langley, was welcomed to Heide, becoming Sunday's close friend. Langley, an ebullient, charming and kind-hearted young woman, was a budding artist, an associate of the Boyds and a good friend of Neil Douglas. By letter from Brisbane, Barrett Reid became a trusted confidante. The animal family grew, too, and Sunday began breeding Siamese cats, not professionally but for her own pleasure.

*

Tucker had jumped at the chance of a free trip to Japan, engineered by the freewheeling American writer Harry Roskolenko and, despite Hester's misgivings, he set off on the three-month adventure. In his absence, Hester had an affair with artist and picture-framer Gray Smith, also married with a young child, with whom she fell in love. When Tucker returned in April, she confronted him with the affair and, in a fit of confusion and guilt, fled their Elwood flat. Tucker was stunned, not only at Hester's news, but because John had informed him of a diagnosis Joy did not know: she had Hodgkin's disease and was given only a short time to live. The doctor, recommended by the Reeds, had told them, not Hester. Once John apprised Hester of this, she and Gray left for Sydney. Tucker, unable to care for Sweeney alone, took him to Heide.[4]

Sunday may have longed for a child but these were not exactly ideal circumstances. Tucker insisted on a number of conditions regarding his son's care: Hester's access to Sweeney had to be carefully monitored and she was forbidden from taking him back. After making the rules and requesting the Reeds abide by them, John and Sunday then discovered, via Nolan, that Tucker was planning to leave the country. John was outraged, asking Tucker when had he planned to tell them? Tucker was adamant that only by seeking his destiny overseas could he cope with the failure of his marriage. After telling the Reeds he needed a year to sort out his thoughts on Sweeney's future, he sailed for England in September 1947.

Hester, undergoing treatment for her illness in Sydney, was slowly regaining her health. Despite the circumstances, she created the Faces series, an impressive body of new work. She was also writing poetry and maintaining an intense correspondence with Sunday. But Tucker need not have worried: she had no plans to retrieve her son.

In a blunt, pragmatic letter, Hester told Tucker the Reeds offered Sweeney more than she or he ever could. She advised him to use his head and remember that he was first and foremost a painter.

Sunday was stunned by the turn of events. Firstly the idea that a break could be permanent (precisely the situation that was evolving with Nolan) was antithetical to the way Sunday conducted her relationships. She fought with her friends, often and fiercely, but she forgave them and expected forgiveness in return. But Hester was just as fixed in her position as Tucker. She was not coming back, either to Tucker or to Sweeney. As she told Sunday, when she met Gray someone 'shut the door' on the rest of her life.

Hester symbolised the leavetaking of her son in her art. Late in 1946, Hester began a new Gethsemane series. No longer wildly spontaneous, like *Gethi in a Tree*, the doll now had a face and that face, in *Gethsemane* V (c.1946, Heide Museum of Modern Art), was Sweeney's. In an eerie coincidence, only a few months before she left Sweeney, Hester transformed him into Sunday's precious doll, the symbol of her lost and grieving motherhood. Sweeney's still, calm face with its upward gazing eyes and hallucinatory expression is a visionary and ecstatic image, one that implies transcendent knowledge. Sweeney had now become the symbol of Hester's lost motherhood: the child she gave to Sunday to make her own. *Gethsemane* V is a complex image of the powerful creative and emotional bonds between the women. More darkly, it essays the notion that Sweeney was a toy to be exchanged, to be offered as a gift from one to the other.

Sunday was devoted to Hester, declaring, 'I have wanted to follow you within experience, to live as closely to you [as] life itself.' That included the 'sudden placing of Sweeney' into her life and the 'responsibilities, readjustments and involvements' it entailed.[5] For

Sunday, Sweeney was part of Joy and to be treasured for that alone. But she was at a loss when she realised Hester would not return to claim her son and resume her life with Tucker. Sunday was aware that 'you and Bert alone can make these decisions' but she hoped Tucker and Hester would 'sense the human necessity that may still be between you both'.[6]

Hester's response was categorical. She did not wish to see Sweeney and she was not coming back — 'he is yours till the gods say different'.[7] Perhaps part of Hester's ambivalence towards her son came from her conviction that he was not Tucker's child but the son of a musician, Billy Hyde, with whom she'd had an affair. Though it was not a story she canvassed with the Reeds at the time, she later convinced them, and Gray Smith, of its truth.[8]

The situation turned Heide upside down. Suddenly Sunday had an anxious and confused little boy to care for, a child who had lost both his parents in a matter of months. At two and a half, Sweeney was blond-haired, blue-eyed and angelically beautiful, and like most children his age, active, inquisitive, noisy and robust. Sunday was his unofficial godmother. In several of Tucker's 1945 photographs of the Reeds, Sweeney, Hester and Nolan on holidays at Point Lonsdale, Sunday clutches Sweeney tightly. Heide seemed the perfect environment for a child. If Sunday was Hester's 'mother', then Sweeney was now in the care of two doting grandparents, both in their forties.

Sunday simply adored him. At Christmas she

. . . put a big Father Christmas in Sweeney's window while he was asleep made out of his red dressing gown and a stuffed head with a long beard of cotton wool and cherries for his eyes, then, in the morning in the middle of all the unwrappings, we gave him a canvas swimming pool (about the size of a double bed) to put in the orchard. It seemed a great success and Swene promptly jumped into it with all his clothes on! I made a tree for the dinner table and filled it with small candles and tinsely [sic] things and we had crackers which were full of little Jap toys which Swene liked almost best of all . . .

. . . Swene has been the most beautiful of Christmas boys. I don't need poetry in books anymore and sometimes I think how perhaps the young poets are only searching back to their childhood to say again the same things that nobody noticed when they were little. Swene tells me everything about the world that I want to know.[9]

Whether it was John's choice to have Sweeney, or whether he wanted a child as keenly as Sunday, is unknown. But if he'd had doubts or objections, it is likely they would have been swamped both by the force of Sunday's needs and the imperatives of the situation itself.

Christmas 1947 was a tense period, despite the sense of wonder and fun that Sunday conjured for Sweeney and the resolute cheerfulness she presented in her letters to Hester. She was anxious about Nolan who was on his way to Sydney, after travelling through Queensland with Barrett Reid.

Sunday had handled Nolan's absence badly. She stopped writing to him for a while, and he responded in kind. It was left to John to act as the go-between. But, as Sunday withdrew into frustration and unhappiness, Nolan found he had a taste for travel. He expanded outwards to the world, discovering new horizons, friends and contacts and gaining a sharper perspective on his career. Travel and new locations stimulated him, just as they had in the Wimmera and Kelly country. Nolan began painting the landscapes of the north, several depicting the story of Eliza Fraser, the woman who lived with Aboriginal tribes and after whom Fraser Island is named.

Mrs Fraser's story began with misfortune and ended in betrayal: she survived the wreck of the ship on which her husband was captain only to be abducted by a local Aboriginal tribe. After being assisted by the convict Bracefell, and promising she would recommend his behaviour and so gain him a pardon, Fraser denounced him as soon as help appeared. Patrick White gives a gruesome account of her adventures in *Fringe of Leaves* (1976), a tale to which he was alerted by Nolan. *Mrs Fraser* (1947, Queensland Art Gallery) is an image of woman as beast, reduced to an abject and vulnerable creature crawling through an endless swamp. It is akin to Nolan's image of Sunday in his *Paradise Garden* poems where she is presented as deceitful and coldly inhuman, the seductress Eve who tempted and betrayed Adam.

On the basis of these paintings, Nolan arranged an exhibition at Brisbane's Moreton Galleries. Meanwhile he and John discussed the possibility of showing the Kellys in Melbourne.

Nolan had arrived at Heide a boy and left as a man. He was now master of the situation, recognising the Reeds had become pathetically dependent on him and he had the upper hand. From July 1947 until January 1948, Nolan wrote elliptically to John of his feelings, playing cat and mouse about his plans for the future as the trajectory of his journey drew him further and further away from Heide in spirit. The mood of Nolan's letters is sombre and distant. Passion has been replaced by weariness, love by the wary measurement of Sunday's emotional barometer and the *ménage* itself reduced to a series of embarrassed and embarrassing negotiations. But one thing was certain. Even if Nolan did return to Melbourne, the liaison was over. He was aware 'how desperately you are both living at Heide'[10] but it was clear that the three of them had 'reached our human limits'.[11] For Nolan, the completion of a circle, and a time, had been reached.

What, finally, could Sunday offer Nolan? She was not prepared to leave John, or Heide. Nolan was an immensely ambitious man. He was when he arrived in John's office in 1938, and remained so. Nolan wanted to conquer the world and he needed an astute, intelligent woman by his side. Sunday had already created her world at Heide and even if, at times, she felt daunted by its challenges and wanted to run away, she always returned home. It was the safe place and designated realm of her creativity. But it wasn't Nolan's home. He had to share it, and Sunday, with John. Significantly, Nolan had turned 30 in 1947, time to begin life as a mature, independent man.

Barrett Reid, travelling with Nolan, and besotted with him, a condition that seemed to afflict most people who spent any length of time in his company, observed the depth of his frustrations. One evening at a Brisbane café, Nolan, who rarely drank much, began 'hitting the whisky rather hard'. Reid suspected he had received a letter from Sunday. 'The woman who ran the place said, "You'd better go out and help your friend."' Reid found Nolan out the back near the lavatory 'hitting his head against the wall, against the brick wall violently . . . I went out and I stopped him.'

When Nolan decided to set off for Sydney, he suggested Reid accompany him, advising, 'if I was going to be a real poet this is what I had to do. Give up all my friends because I invested too much of my time in [them]. I said, "I can't come to Sydney. What would I do for a start? And what about all the obligations I had to my friends?" [Nolan] was furious about that and for about two days we talked about it.'[12] Nolan left for Sydney alone.

At New Year, Nolan stayed briefly with Hester and Smith at Point Piper, sharing with them, and complaining of, the stresses and strains of life at Heide. The Reeds were already alarmed when Nolan signalled he may remain in Sydney. But his most disconcerting move was to visit Cynthia.

In 1947, Cynthia had wreaked vengeance on her family by publishing her autobiographical novel *Daddy Sowed a Wind!* No-one was spared, not even her kindly, forgiving, older sister Margaret whom Cynthia cast as Elizabeth who was 'tall; stooped and looked bilious'.[13] John was Luke, 'so sophisticated, handsome and superior', who ignores his youngest sister Hyacinth (Cynthia), then, as an adult, tries to seduce her.[14] Hyacinth flees in horror.

Luke's fiancée Ariel is, of course, Sunday who talked 'so fast and so softly it was impossible to understand her' and had a 'remarkable resemblance to a sheep — perhaps it was in the eyes, pallid, protruding and curiously unseeing'.[15] Hyacinth has an unhappy affair with Claus, actually conductor Bernard Heinze with whom Cynthia perhaps had an affair. In the novel, Claus abandons Hyacinth and marries Ariel, cataloguing Heide's claustrophobic intimacies and betrayals from Cynthia's perspective.

Unsurprisingly, Cynthia did not submit the manuscript to Reed & Harris. When Henry Reed caught wind of his daughter's book, he tried to buy every copy he could and burn them. In retaliation, when he died in 1956, Cynthia received nothing in his will.

What had turned Cynthia so viciously against Sunday and John? They had cared for her after Jinx's birth and invited her to make her home at Heide. In 1945 Cynthia wrote congratulating John on becoming a publisher. She recognised that despite 'the bitterness' that sometimes arose between them there was a core that was 'deep and loving'. She confided the sad details of yet another disastrous affair to him, insisting her dreams had always 'centered around one man, a man I suppose who does not exist'. At the end of the letter, she mused bleakly, 'not yet not yet', as she counted her morphia tablets 'over and over'.[16] It was not the first time Cynthia alluded to suicide in her letters to John.

Reed & Harris published *Lucky Alphonse!* in 1944 but Cynthia was anxious about John's reaction, recalling that, when she was a teenager, John said the best place for her writing 'would be the fire'. She felt her writing would not 'rock the world' and that her novel showed 'no genius' but she wanted to write 'nakedly and brutally of reality'.[17] John was not overly impressed with *Lucky Alphonse!*, originally titled *Lulu*. He told Max Harris that 'your response to *Lulu* seems a very valid one and I have passed it on to Cynthia more or less intact and have told her we would publish the book though we did not necessarily accept it in the full sense of the word'.[18] It was hardly wild enthusiasm. Cynthia's problem tended to be over-statement, a failing she would address by taking up the more objective form of travel writing.

Perhaps the very successes of the Reeds' life – their enduring marriage, productive friendships with artists, diverse cultural projects as well as the stability and beauty of Heide – made Cynthia resent Sunday. She was alone, anguished and insecure, a single mother who slaved away at a job she disliked. From the distance of Sydney, the Reeds seemed to have it all while Cynthia struggled to make ends meet.

After the publication of *Daddy Sowed a Wind!*, the Reeds were understandably anxious about Nolan visiting Cynthia. It is tempt-ing to speculate that Nolan began his relationship with Cynthia merely to wound Sunday. Yet, in fact, Cynthia and Sunday were very alike: the same thin, elegant, stylish looks, the same patrician upbringing, the same vivid intelligence, sensitive response to art and design, strong, frank character and opinions, passion for literature and worldly, well-travelled background. They were both older than Nolan, Cynthia by nine and Sunday by twelve years. Cynthia was a manager, like Sunday, good at inspiring and directing the creative energies of others, as she had shown at Modern Furnishings. Nolan had become dependent on Sunday as his collaborator and muse, and he needed another, similarly powerful, mature, feminine force.

Like Sunday, Cynthia was fragile, highly strung and tempestuous, as well as witty, seductive and loyal. But, unlike Sunday, she could be provocatively rude and terrifyingly sharp-tongued, often alienating people at first meeting and making them remember her with dread. Even Patrick White had to admit she was 'difficult'. But Nolan captivated Cynthia, charming his way beyond her reserve; her suspicion was that he was perhaps on a mission from the Reeds.

Until Nolan arrived on her doorstep at Wahroonga in January 1948, Cynthia and Nolan had had no direct contact since 1941 when she sternly advised him to quit Heide. Despite the fact that Nolan must have found Cynthia attractive in her own right, it remains curious that he abandoned the bed of John's wife and, almost immediately, entered that of his sister. If Nolan wanted to put Heide behind him and sever his connections with the Reeds, it was hardly the cleanest way to do so.

After a short time in Cynthia's company, the tone in Nolan's letters to John changed. It was no longer defensive, cajoling and indecisive but peremptory, almost hectoring. Nolan knew 'perfectly well', and so did John, that Sunday was depressed and unhappy. As far as the complexities of the situation went, Nolan believed he had 'misunderstood nothing' and was irritated that John assumed he had.[19] At the same time, Nolan expected John to organise an exhibition of the Kellys in Melbourne.

When Barrett Reid discovered that Nolan was living with Cynthia, he telegrammed him, '"You bloody bastard" and [Nolan] wrote back, "Thanks for your short and melodious greeting."' Next Cynthia invited Barrett to stay, saying, 'Sid's best friend had to be her best friend.' The visit was not harmonious, Barrett feeling 'it was nearly a whole week of her getting at me and trying to destroy my friendship with Nolan . . . Cynthia was attacking Sunday and John all the time I was at Wahroonga.'[20]

On 23 March, Nolan and Cynthia married and travelled down to Heide the following day to see the Reeds. The visit was a disaster, as Nolan explained to Brian Adams, his biographer.

Sunday had retreated to bed, her preferred place when she felt miserable. Joy and Gray were staying at Heide after returning from Sydney, to the confusion, no doubt, of Sweeney who had not seen his mother for nearly a year. Though often critical of Sunday, Hester told Tucker in 1945 that, despite Sunday's failings, she would 'always stick by her'. Hester was no longer Nolan's ally. In fact, she was more dependent than ever on the Reeds. Gray had become Sunday's devoted companion, sitting on her bed for hours, holding her hand, tending her and buoying her spirits.

The Nolans' visit was played out like a French farce with Sunday in hysterics, Gray threatening violence and John trying to restore order. The couple fled back to Sydney. As far as the Reeds were concerned, Nolan had committed a 'brutal and unnatural act in which he cut the joined hearts which once held us all'.[21] For the Reeds, the relationship with Nolan had never and would never end.

With Jinx, Nolan had a ready-made family which delighted him. In letters to Heide, while he was travelling, he mentioned Sweeney often and affectionately. Straightaway he adopted Jinx.

Cynthia did not want to stay in Australia, nor did Nolan. Short of funds to travel overseas, they began making plans to travel through Australia. It seemed Nolan was the very man Cynthia had been waiting for. Soon they would depart for the world and their gypsy existence would inspire Cynthia's travel writing. A new and more successful creative direction for her, it glowingly chronicled Nolan's activities, a marketing tool surely not lost on a canny entrepreneur such as he. He was also prepared to be the father of her little girl and to offer Cynthia the big, exciting life she had always dreamed was her destiny. Nolan was also capable of managing Cynthia's sharp, erratic personality that had acted to the detriment of other relationships.

But while Nolan's life entered a happy and satisfying phase, Sunday was in despair. She had not only lost her lover but her creative partner, a role she had explored with Atyeo but fulfilled with Nolan. Adding to her gloom were the failures of *Angry Penguins*, Reed & Harris and *Tomorrow*. Everywhere she looked was disaster.

Just prior to Nolan's marriage, John had written to Barrett Reid canvassing, once again, the idea of a bookshop in Brisbane. 'The feeling we had in Queensland,' John told Reid, was 'that the Australian idiom was a much more lived and real thing up there than in the south.'[22] Reid knew at firsthand how impractical such an idea would be. With his partner Charles Osborne, Reid was already running the Ballad Bookshop. Reid was a librarian at the Public Library and funded the bookshop from his own pocket which paid the rent and went towards defraying Osborne's wages. He also worked there during his free time. There was simply no money in it. Max Harris offered the Reeds the same advice.

Aside from an escape from Heide, John was also searching for creative projects to arouse Sunday's depleted energies. The prospect of running a small business like a bookshop, surrounded by bright young friends like Reid and Osborne, combined with Brisbane's balmy climate, probably appeared restorative. But they took their friends' advice and abandoned the plan.

It was the Reeds' new task, managing the exhibition of the Kellys at Tye's Gallery, that lead to their next project: organising an international tour that would help Nolan to establish the larger reputation he desired and affirm the Reeds' faith in his genius. Perhaps then Nolan would return, satisfied Sunday could offer him all he wanted. Sunday was obsessed with Nolan, telling Jean Langley, 'There is just Nolan. You must believe me that I would give you tickets, money, everything, tomorrow if you could bring Nolan to Heide to see me for even five minutes. Every day I think it will be today. He will come today.'[23]

The trip also offered a holiday not only to France, Sunday's favourite country, but journeys to England, Italy, Belgium and Holland together with the possibility of resolving the matter of Sweeney's adoption with Tucker, who was living in Paris. They put together what cash they could and arranged with Jack and Molly Bellew to take care of Heide. In August 1948, they sailed for France.

The journey began with a disaster. Sunday wrote to Hester that

> about an hour after we sailed, Sweeney got the top right hand middle finger squashed in the hinge side of our cabin door. John shut it hard and it is unbearable to think of . . . Swene managed to come through it all without fainting away although I think I have been fainting away ever since and Weeney has been

wailing at night like a migrant bird but it was a great shock I think and he was very sick for two days, not able to eat or drink anything and I expect we were seasick although it is hard to say what we were, we were so upset.[24]

When they reached Fremantle, the Reeds took Sweeney to see a children's specialist at a private hospital. It was 'a horrible day in one way but we were so cheered that the X ray showed no bones broken ... Swene had an anaesthetic and a needle stuck in his arm and all the usual awful things that happen to us on these occasions but he behaved like an angel.'[25]

In Sunday's first letter from Paris, she told Hester, 'God knows how homesick I am. How lovely is Aussie.' The Reeds were staying at the Grand Hotel Haussmann in Rue du Helder which was hardly grand but centrally located near Galeries Lafayette, the big department store, and the Opéra, on the classy right bank. They were trying to find an apartment and settle in Paris for a year but 'we are still here in this little hotel quite unable to find anywhere to live ... Sometimes I wonder just how long we can go on looking and what is the alternative? How long will we survive in this world of ours in one room. And the budget always exceeded just eating one's food in restaurants.'

Nolan was also on Sunday's mind. 'I have been feeling very strained and forgive me that I cannot write enough or bring you healing, if only I could. I can only say how much your love means and how since Nolan left me, when in the buses and the trains and walking down the streets I often think I am dying and the blood drains from my face and pours out of me and then your love and Gray's comes into me and so with John I try to go on my way, on your way. May I learn the way.'

Sweeney looked the part and had 'a beret and looks just like a French boy'. But he was already tired of Paris, and it sounded as if Sunday was, too. 'Why did we come to Paris, Sun?' he asked her. 'Why don't we go back to Heide?' But Sunday hoped to find a kindergarten 'a French one. I daresay I could find him a place with the American children but I don't want to as I'm anxious he should get to grips with the language.' Sweeney was getting 'to grips with the language', as Sunday wanted. 'Already he is able to ring up in the morning for our breakfast . . . even if his accent is like John's!'

Though Sunday admitted that she, John and Sweeney were not exactly talking 'ten to the dozen' at least 'we are absorbed in the language as one has to be if one lives here. We read nothing but French which improves as the days go on.' Sunday enjoyed Julien Green's *Mont-Cinere* and Sartre's *Les main sales* because 'I read in French fairly easily.'[26]

Sunday was concerned about the quality of food in postwar Paris – they were issued with coupons for Sweeney's milk, and for butter and cheese for themselves. Sunday needed her creature comforts and was desperate for a good cup of tea. She was 'just indifferent to the tea here and have ceased now to worry whether it's good or bad'. (The Reeds asked John Sinclair to send them over two pounds of tea.) Their daily menu, Sunday told Hester, consisted of Russian bread with honey for breakfast. Lunch was 'tomatoes and apples and milk and cheese and [we] eat it on the bed and dinner we go out. Swene, as often as not, asks to have his dinner in bed and has raw egg and orange juice and tomatoes and mayonnaise and apples and glucose'. They also bought 'figs and raisins and a cake for arvo [tea]. Two cakes to be exact. They are madly expensive, and chocolate, too.'[27]

The whole family was 'a bit the worse for wear I think through lack of butter and fats which I get a mad lust for, rather like wanting a cigarette and not being able to have one. Jonny has got a cold, the first for years and years and Weeno got his usual bronchitis and I just tottered around like [a] scarecrow.'[28]

The Reeds had brought dry and tinned food with them but it was stuck in customs with the Kellys. It was a stressful period. As Christmas neared, the Reeds were still staying at the hotel. 'I need not tell you what living in a room is like. Paris or no Paris,' Sunday wrote to Hester. 'We are still exceeding our budget too and live in a constant state of frustration and cannot buy anything other than necessities. And we see so many things we would like to send you or to take back to Heide and as we walk down the streets we get window-looking cramps in our heads turning from side to side! Imagine being in Paris without even a bottle of scent.'[29]

But there were benefits: Bach, Palestrina and Mozart concerts in the evenings plus the pleasures of Paris itself. 'So often we walk in the Tuileries,' Sunday told Langley, 'where I especially love the garden and the statues . . . rising out of the fog, their hearts beat and they seem to turn their heads gently as you pass and I wonder when everyone is sleeping at night what they do. The fogs are lovely, the sun like a rose coloured balloon in the sky and if you look down you will see it again just the same lying quite flat in the fog of the river.'[30]

The business with the Kellys dragged on. 'The French are quite mad on the question of bringing paintings in and we have got quite a guilt complex with all the goings on and backwards and forwards to place after place.'[31]

Apparently, the Reeds had not investigated the intricacies of French customs' regulations before their arrival. It placed them in a quandary, firstly about how to retrieve the paintings and secondly, where to exhibit them. Their journey had been optimistic but ill-conceived: they had made no plans for locating appropriate venues for the Kellys prior to their departure. The desire to leave Heide, and Australia, far behind was the pressing need, not the nuts and bolts of organising an international tour. It was also a situation that symbolised Sunday's unwillingness, and inability, to deal with Europe on any other than her own terms.

As a young woman, Sunday had been a keen observer but never a participant in European cultural life. Even now, in a ground-breaking role as an Australian freelance curator trying to impress upon Paris, the centre of modernism, the importance of an Australian modernist, her attitude was detached, polite and prag-matic. She had come to give the Kellys a European airing, but that was all. She did not seek to position herself as an informed collector of modernist art by haunting the galleries, seeking introductions, socialising with the right crowd or buying art.

It seemed Sunday had been at the centre of her own world for too long to ingratiate herself within that of Paris. 'Is Paris romantic? . . . For myself Australia is the only romantic place in the world, something I have known since I was little and more and more with the years and more again since I left it this time and I am indeed a homing pigeon.'[32] Despite her command of the language, she remained a tourist and beyond the safe harbour of Heide, she could not muster the courage to navigate new waters. The litany of complaints in her letters to Hester is the tourist's classic diatribe, miserable minutae about bad food, inclement weather, high prices and minor illnesses.

Thank goodness we have had a beautiful rain today to clean the Paris streets which are always so dirty you dare not look and yet you must and I'm afraid we are always thinking what a dirty old place Paris is. I can never keep my clothes clean and even sitting in the metros the dust and fog seem to penetrate even my coat so that my panties are black at night and unless you know the right soap (which I didn't know for weeks) you can't possibly wash them because the water is so madly hard that ordinary soap just makes mud.

. . . Oh to be beside your little stove in the lamplight with the big moon coming up behind the gums, or to be at home with Min [Sunday's Siamese cat] in my arms beside a summer fire with the marzipan cake and you all on the sofa.[33]

These are not the observations of a sanguine and sophisticated traveller comfortable in a European milieu, responsive to nuance, delighted by change, alert, curious and adventurous. Sunday grumbled. Her letters to Hester form a lifeline, linking her back to Australia, the bush, Heide and Hester's love, emphasising what was central to her existence. Further, the city itself had become an alien experience: Sunday had been living in the country since 1935 and the grime and noise of a metropolis like Paris took some acclimatisation. It was only when the Reeds started travelling that Sunday's spirits lifted.

Sunday felt excluded by Paris and by its complex cultural history. 'Everything is so much a miracle of scene in time and distance that as you walk one's entry into the world leaves no displacement so fixed and permanent is the scene – a perfection of relationship that takes one's breath.'[34]

It was an attitude that did not encourage the Reeds to network, to use current parlance. They did not initiate contacts with European gallery dealers, museum curators, critics and editors who could advance their cause but waited for others to act as the go-between. Nor did they seek out artists. When Atyeo first went to Paris he met Osip Zadkine, Albert Gleizes, Brancusi and Henry Miller within a short time while Tucker was manfully attempting to stake his claim on European soil.

While in Paris, John wrote to Picasso, telling him that 'my wife and I, in Australia, have watched your work with love and wonder and now that we are at last in Paris and have seen it spread out in all its great richness, we have been moved even more profoundly than we had imagined possible.' John invited Picasso to see the Kellys which carried within them 'some vision, some experience which cannot be found or does not spring from the old world but only from a country which is new in the sense that Australia is new.'

John explained he and Sunday had brought the Kellys to Paris because 'we love the work itself and we love the man that created it'. Surely the master of modernism would have 'some real and active desire to see what has come from our lovely country?'[35] Picasso did not reply. Though dignified and well-intentioned, the letter is a study in idealism and inadequacy: John did not have the connections or the *savoir-faire* to foment such an alliance. Nor did Sunday.

Julien Green, one of Sunday's favourite authors, lived in Paris. Sunday wished 'he were in the telephone book so that we could go and stand outside his house and wave to him and Weeno might say, 'Bonjour Monsieur, ca va?'' as he does now with everyone.'[36] (Green lived in Rue Cortambert on the right bank.) Tellingly, Sunday does not consider ringing or writing to Green herself, merely standing outside his house and waving. It is an image of timid and respectful distance where Sweeney, in the fanciful scenario, is designated as the bold one who speaks.

Sunday's deep, original and productive exploration of Australian modernism had, in effect, alienated her from modernism's source. Unlike Tucker, Nolan, Cynthia, Atyeo and Dyring who made Europe their home for many years, Sunday had established her home, and her homegrown modernism, firmly in the Heide earth. Europe was foreign and its modernism a parallel but separate endeavour from the ideas Sunday had developed at Heide and that had borne fruit in the artists of her circle in general, and in Nolan's work in particular. After all, Sunday was not in Europe to renew or challenge her modernist vision or to seek out the latest developments in contemporary art: she was there to promote and showcase Nolan's work in the hope of winning him back. Nolan, needless to say, wanted nothing to do with her plans.

While the Reeds waited for the Kellys to be cleared from customs, they entered into painful and delicate negotiations with Tucker regarding Sweeney's adoption. Sunday tried to balance her desire to have Sweeney 'forever if finally that is what you want of me', as she told Hester, with Tucker's concerns – he was hesitant about the finality of adoption and unwilling to relinquish his role as a father.[37] Whether the Reeds knew that, according to Hester, Sweeney was perhaps not Tucker's son goes unmentioned by them both in their correspondence with Hester and their talks with Tucker. Sunday and John realised the situation was already distressing and humiliating enough for Tucker without questioning his paternity.

Though in the ensuing decades Tucker would insist that Sunday had duped him into agreeing to relinquish Sweeney and had stolen his child, there is no evidence to suggest it. Even after the adoption process had begun, John told Tucker that he and Sunday would 'even now willingly change it if that seemed right, so do not hesitate to say if your thoughts have changed'.[38]

Equally, Sunday's letters to Joy are a model of balance, generosity and openness. 'There is just one thing that we must ask you to tell us,' Sunday wrote to Hester, 'if perhaps you have been feeling that you would like Wene beside you again . . . If this is true of you darling then you must indeed say so now and we ask you to tell us so that together we can seek only the deepest springs in each other to bring Sweeney permanence and peace.'[39]

For her part, Hester's position was unequivocal, and had been since 1947. She did not want her son back. She told Sunday, 'there is nothing that would make me feel more at ease than for you to adopt Sweeney.'[40] Hester recognised that 'I have forced [Bert] into this position . . . and his fight is really (in regards to Weeno) not with his own renouncings, or feelings, and not with or over Weeno, but with me.'[41]

Tucker, separated from Sweeney for just over a year, was thrilled to see him again, and Sweeney, now two and a half, was delighted to spend time with him. Tucker took Sweeney on day trips to Versailles and around Paris. Their prolonged contact made the need for a decision harder for Tucker: he did not want to lose his son. In fact, he found the matter too upsetting to discuss.

There was one traumatic occasion when Sweeney refused to return to John and Sunday at the end of a day with Tucker who was to deliver the little boy to the Reeds. But Sweeney jumped out of the taxi, crying, 'I want to stay with Bert!'

After nearly two months in Paris, the Reeds grew frustrated and finally decided they 'would have to lead the way' with Tucker. Sunday told Hester 'we talked for a long time. It was not at all a happy talk and ultimately I felt too tired in myself to continue it, so that nothing was resolved ... And so the matter was left.'

Tucker felt the Reeds should continue to care for Sweeney but no formal arrangements should be made. 'Bert ... feels that Sweeney's position is so to speak sufficient unto the day and that it is unnecessary to force anything further on himself.' While Tucker knew that, unless he was willing to return to Australia, he could not look after Sweeney himself, he also wished to 'maintain the concept of parenthood'. Sunday was aware Tucker felt 'it would be best for Sweeney to live with him if it were practical'. But Sunday desperately wanted a child and did not want to lose Sweeney. While she knew Tucker would not 'willingly take Sweeney away from us', there remained the possiblity he could and the situation could become 'a battleground at any given moment'. If the adoption were to 'become real', Sunday wrote to Hester, 'then we must be free to see it as real'.[42] Sunday begged Hester to keep her informed of her thoughts on the matter.

In January, the situation reached a climax. 'Since we came to Paris,' Sunday told Hester, 'it has been a period of tension and continual anxiety so far as Sweeney and Bert were concerned and I have worried terribly trying to resolve some way that would bring peace for everyone.' Following a day with Sweeney 'that seemed to bring about some sort of crisis in Bert', he put forward three proposals to the Reeds.

In order, they were: firstly, that Tucker should take Sweeney; secondly, that the Reeds should continue their life with Sweeney, providing his 'background and environment'; and last that the Reeds 'should adopt Sweeney subject to some arrangement being made whereby [Tucker] would receive sufficient income to allow him to continue his life as an artist — that only by continuity of creative activity could he survive Sweeney's adoption.'

Sunday explained to Hester that 'we have told Bert quite finally that we will not be involved in any matter of money related to the joining of Sweeney's life with ours'.[43] Hester agreed. She wanted to have 'nothing to do' with the third proposal, saying, 'I will not have Sweeney bartered to save Bert.'[44]

Tucker believed he had been misunderstood. Of the Reeds and Hester, he was the only one in disagreement with the adoption, making him feel trapped. Aside from Tucker, all three were secure in their own lives. Hester had settled with Gray Smith at a small property at Hurstbridge, bought for them by Smith's aunt. Joy was in remission, producing drawings and poetry, and feeling 'top hole'.[45] Sunday's income, though battered by *Angry Penguins'* losses, allowed her and John to lead a life of enviable leisure. Tucker, alone in Paris and facing a host of financial, artistic and emotional problems, felt it reasonable to ask for a sum of money.

He was furious that the Reeds had misconstrued his request. It meant all his explanations were to no avail. The Reeds had completely misunderstood him and he felt alienated from them. He told Sunday and John that there was now a chasm between them and he could see no hope of reconciliation.

Though his words sounded final, they were not, though it took until June for Tucker to finally reconcile himself to relinquishing Sweeney. It was a traumatic decision for Tucker and his later criticism of Sunday had more to do with his own guilt and pain about the adoption than it did with the facts of the matter. Tucker also had to explain the situation to Sweeney.

> We were standing in Rue de Rivoli . . . and so I thought, you know, this is a hard one to handle, and so we walked up Boulevard des Capucines . . . and I was talking to Sweeney. I said, 'Well, look, Sweeney, you know I'd like you to live with John

and Sun now because they've got a lot of money and they can educate you and feed you and keep you well and secure, whereas I'm very poor. I haven't got any money and I can't look after you' . . . [Sweeney] said, 'Well, why don't you go to the bank and get some. That's what John and Sun do.' And so then I explained, 'Well, Sweeney, the problem there is that you have to put the money in the bank first and I haven't got any money and so I couldn't put any in the bank so there's none that I can take out.'[46]

Tucker had reservations about the Reeds' abilities as parents. Not long after he left Australia, Tucker wrote saying he was concerned that Sweeney had invented an imaginary companion called Lely and it made him wonder if Sweeney was spending too much time alone. John replied soothingly that Tucker was 'wrong to think of Sweeney as lonely or missing other children . . . Sun has thought a lot about him in relation to other children . . . and is not unduly stressed with the idea of the absolute necessity of throwing Sweeney into the common melting pot, so to speak.'

The Reeds felt Sweeney's 'potential richness and strength' might be lost or 'injured' with other children. They were prepared to wait until Sweeney's 'own inner direction' was 'so well established that he could go out and meet [other children] and retain his "priority".' As far as the Reeds were concerned, 'it is all too easy for a child's powers to become disorientated'.[47]

Sunday's idealisation of childhood made Sweeney the inheritor and symbol of Sunday's central aesthetic. But, under her aegis, childhood could be a rarefied realm. Such ideas are implicit in John's reply to Tucker. Sweeney was not about to be cast into the 'common melting pot' where his special gifts, his 'richness and strength', might be sullied and 'injured' by other children. He must develop his personal vision, his 'priority', which might be erased or diluted if he had to mingle with the herd. It was an idiosyncratic attitude towards childrearing and Tucker had every right to feel concerned.

Sweeney attended pre-school in Paris and, Sunday told Hester, he 'seems very happy about it though I don't know why ... You know what I feel about schools but I feel over and above all that Swene needs to see children and that as a temporary arrangement it is good.'[48] Sunday, who had loathed school and found home education with her mother and sympathetic governesses the most conducive learning environment, was making plans to tutor Sweeney herself.

It would be difficult to imagine a more adoring, playful and generous mother than Sunday. Yet her friends had reservations about Sunday's parenting. Nadine Amadio felt she was 'too indulgent probably and I don't think it was good for Sweeney ... [The Reeds] did impose huge high expectations on Sweeney which was hard on him. He said, "I don't know what they want of me but I just can't do it" ... John's sternness, which became almost double with Sweeney, was not going to help him at all because Sweeney didn't have the ability to jolly him out of it. Sun's total indulgence was probably not good either.'[49]

Gordon Thomson put it rather more bleakly. 'Taking over of Sweeney by the Reeds was disastrous. Anybody who knew less about children than John Reed, I don't think you could imagine. He was good with dogs, you see, and Sweeney was brought up like a shaggy dog. Poor old Sweeney had a hell of a time.'[50] Neil Douglas believed 'Sunday knew nothing about raising children. It was a pitiful situation.'[51]

Jean Langley, who often minded Sweeney, observed there was

'domestic discipline but no self-discipline [at Heide] . . . I don't think Sunday believed in it.' Sweeney was 'most impressive . . . and he liked an audience and he liked communication and he was a very beautiful child'. But he was 'a nervous little boy, he was frightened to swim in the river, he was frightened of lots of things . . . I found him a little tyrant on one hand and very sweet on the other . . . Everything about Sweeney was put down to the fact that Joy deserted him.' Sweeney was 'absolutely' indulged because of that.[52]

After the traumatic discussions with Tucker, and with Sweeney's future still unresolved, the Reeds left Paris to go travelling. First there was Sweeney's third birthday party celebrated with Sam Atyeo and H.V. Evatt. (Atyeo and Dyring had just separated, and Dyring had returned to Australia.) Then the Reeds bought a Peugeot, Sunday reckoning, 'we think if we can't have an apartment we might as well have a car so that we can move off if we want to.'[53] The Reeds then made the odd decision to board Sweeney with a French family in Tours. Meanwhile, they drove to Venice and to the south of France.

Traditionally, the upper classes paid others to take care of their children, often for years on end. The most notable example is the wet nurse, where a wealthy woman's newborn infant was given to a local woman to breastfeed and care for. The child often spent its early years with the wet nurse and her family. Such notions were obviously not foreign to Sunday, who perhaps had decided she needed a holiday from stress, and that included Sweeney. It must have been confusing for Sweeney, who, in his short life, had lost one set of parents, gained another, travelled overseas and then spent time in Paris with Tucker. Unsurprisingly, he did not settle with the Mosser family in Tours.

Madame Mosser wrote encouraging letters to Sunday about

Sweeney's health and wellbeing, assuring her that 'he is entirely used to our life – it took him about two weeks to adapt himself entirely – especially as he was not well, poor darling.'[54] Once again, Sweeney had come down with bronchitis.

When the Reeds collected Sweeney in June, his tales about Madame Mosser and family were not cheerful. Sunday told Gray Smith that Sweeney 'will not go back to Tours and [he] says French people never open their windows and that Papa used to bang the table with all the food on it and break the plates and Maman had to go to bed and I suspect that all these things are true but not as true as the real reason. Anyway I would not like him to go away from us again, it is too soon.'

The Reeds took Sweeney to the Ile de Porquerolle, a beach resort on the Côte d'Azur, near St Tropez. 'You cannot imagine such bliss,' Sunday told Gray, 'and we have never loved the water more – one floats infinitely in pale crystal. Sweeney, too, goes with us to the deep, unafraid, kicking legs, beating arms, laughing yet sinking much to his great disappointment and ours ... he is gloriously brown and fair and such a Joy boy since he came back to us.'[55] Sunday documented Sweeney's lively presence on their travels by taking many photographs of him.

At long last, the Kellys had been released from customs and deposited at the Australian Embassy at 14 rue Las Cases. The Reeds got on with the task of showing them. At the Embassy, Gardiner Davies proved extremely helpful in all matters relating to the exhibition's organisation and tour. The Reeds also relied on and lobbied an old friend, Peter Bellew, a former editor of *Art in Australia* and Sunday's one-time lover, who was now head of the visual arts section at UNESCO in Paris.

Ronald Walker, the Australian ambassador, had arranged for

the Reeds to meet Jean Cassou, chief curator at the Musée d'Art Moderne. Cassou was impressed with the Kellys but could only offer the peculiar possibility of a forty-eight-hour showing. Davies advised against it and Bellew came up with the idea of showing them at the Maison de l'UNESCO where they were exhibited in December 1949. It was a coup for the Reeds and the first time an exhibition of Australian modernist paintings had been brought to Paris. Cassou agreed to write the catalogue introduction.

Tired of waiting and running low on funds, the Reeds had returned to Australia in July and so did not see the exhibition but Tucker did, writing that the impression of Australian light and colour was exhilarating in the grey Parisian winter. Gino Nibbi offered to show the Kellys at his Galleria ai Quattro Venti in Rome, a combination bookshop and art gallery. Gardiner Davies took on the responsibility of organising the last leg of the Kellys' tour. Nibbi's son, Tristano, remembered that, disappointingly, the Kellys created barely a ripple in the Roman art world.

While the practicalities nearly defeated the Reeds, it is a tribute to their persistence that the Kellys were shown at all. The trip was founded, like everything on which the Reeds set their hearts and minds, not on commercial or even practical realities but on idealism and a willingness to sacrifice themselves, their money and their time for projects they believed were worth supporting.

Early in 1950, John wrote to Nolan telling him that 'apparently there were about 300 people at the Opening including Jean Cassou and Torres Bodet (Director General of UNESCO and himself a poet) and both were very enthusiastic'.[56]

If John expected Nolan to be grateful and respond, he was mistaken. In that sense, the trip was a failure. Nolan was not coming back. It must have been a frustrating experience for such an enterprising man to ignore his first international showing. Ambition, it seemed, was nothing compared to the rancour he harboured for the Reeds.

Back at Heide, reflecting on the journey that had taken place, not only to Europe to show the Kellys, but since 1938 when Nolan had arrived at Heide, Sunday began making the Heart Garden. On the north side of the house not far from the old mulberry tree, she dug a heart shape about three feet wide and four feet long and planted it out with 'chamomile and little herbs and things'.

Jean Langley recalled 'it had a sentimental beginning, it was like a private love letter'. It was also a secret garden, its meaning communicated only to Langley. 'I was there when Sunday was making it. Whenever John wasn't there, we'd have a little talk about love and the past and Sid would creep into it but it was what Sunday called girls' talk. She never talked about him in public as far as I knew.' From John Sinclair, Langley had learned that 'after Sid left everyone sobered up quite a lot in terms of drinking and partying ... We were all aware that there was a melancholy period in [the Reeds'] lives.'

Langley was a budding artist who became a skilled and sensitive draughtswoman and a wildflower painter. At the time, she was studying tonal painting under Justus Jorgensen and 'trying very hard to be a [Max] Meldrum student'. Langley had previously worked at Arthur Merric Boyd Pottery decorating pots alongside Neil Douglas and had minded the Kelly exhibition at Tye's Gallery, prior to meeting the Reeds.

With Langley, Sunday 'exchanged some sort of intensity – without words – a sort of femininity ... I don't know whether she told anyone else about the making of the Heart Garden. She knew

I liked things to be sacred, as she did.' As Sunday worked on the Heart Garden, her friendship with Langley flowered. 'She called me sister – I was twenty years younger than her, just a kid. She needed someone she could have talks about her emotional intensity with. I was a pretty intense girl.'[57]

Sunday needed to manage her friends' competing affections. Hester was possessive about Sunday and newcomers to the Heide circle, like Langley, were made to feel they were encroaching on her territory. 'Joy didn't want to share Sun with anybody,' Langley recalled. 'Joy would bitch me, make sort of funny remarks . . . and Sun would come to my defence . . . and Joy would actually lose because Sun would stand up and support me.'[58] Perhaps Hester was anxious that a younger woman artist could usurp her position and Sunday's attentions would be directed towards Langley instead of her. Joy was as dependent on Sunday as ever. So was Gray.

When the Reeds returned from Europe, Smith suggested he and Joy come to live at Heide. Gently, the Reeds put them off, Sunday telling Joy that 'I have always felt that you and Gray should have your own world around you and perhaps I feel you are still in someone else's and have not yet found together the nature of the responsibilities that truly belong to you.' Sunday hoped Gray and Joy would 'discover the simplicity in your living that will solve practical and working issues more easily. I do [not] know at all that Heide is an answer.'[59]

Sunday liked Langley's drawings and thought she was wasting her time learning to paint. She encouraged Langley to 'free up' her drawings. But Sunday's hands-on approach could be daunting. 'She'd say, "Why don't you let me sit behind you and watch you?" And I'd say, "No, I can't! No way I could do even the botanical things with you sitting behind me!" But she loved to see people's hands doing it. She loved the whole business of it.'⁶⁰ It made Langley wonder why Sunday did not draw or paint but Sunday, who prized honesty, never discussed her time at art school or her attempts to be an artist.

The Heart Garden is the template of Sunday's aesthetic. Sunday had to be occupied with the process of creation. Working in the Heide earth and relating to the cycles of nature were manifestations of grand dreams and small mementos. Heide was the soil of her Australian modernism and the place where she buried her sorrows, then watched them flower.

Nature is relentlessly optimistic and transformative: what dies can live again. A cutting strikes, a fallow garden bed finds renewal in another season, an inclement position for one plant is ideal for another, stronger, hungrier one. Growth never ceases but flows forward, wild, insistent and tenacious. Mourning her lover and her creative partner, Sunday returned to the soil to represent, and to heal, her grief.

It is a cycle symbolised by Demeter, the goddess of growth, Sunday's perfect archetype, who was portrayed in classical art as a beautiful, maternal, fair-haired woman dressed in blue. When Persephone was taken to the underworld, Demeter mourned, and when the gods of Olympus refused to help, she turned the land to winter and famine threatened to destroy the human race. Finally, the gods relented and, reunited with her daughter, Demeter commanded the earth to flower, and fertility and abundance were restored.

Sunday was the nurturing, generous mother, like Demeter, a bountiful harvest goddess, not only to Sweeney but to all her friends. Langley recalled that 'everybody used Sun and John as if they were a second lot of parents . . . a new set of parents who were rich, who would pay for them everywhere they went, [who] would provide them with beautiful Christmas presents, every year. How many people they sent hams to at Christmas, I can't imagine . . . This was a gift from the gods, so to speak, but then on the other hand [the artists] didn't think much about them.'[61]

It made Anne Cairns wonder if Nolan was too well-loved. 'I wasn't surprised when Nolan left because it was fairly oppressive in a way to have so much affection, so much interest. It's a bit like a child growing up. You can have too much love from your parents.'[62]

Sunday was aware her love could be demanding and possessive, even destructive in its imperiousness, and she fostered dependency: Nolan was supposed to need her forever. She mused, 'When will I leave my loves alone I wonder? Go quietly into the earth and be as dead as a doornail.'[63] It is a telling metaphor. Persephone 'died' in the underworld and was restored to life by her mother's agency. Sunday, too, was restored. The powerful, fecund aspect of Demeter, plunging her hands into the earth to make the Heart Garden and bringing new life from it, was also an aspect of Sunday's and it would not allow her to remain 'dead as a doornail', despite her melancholy. Spring, in fact, was just around the corner.

The Third Circle

Melbourne seemed the place to be.

BARRETT REID[1]

THE 1950S WERE A TIME OF OPTIMISM and regeneration for Sunday as she and John embraced a new circle of friends and new cultural projects.

The agent of change was Barrett Reid who moved to Melbourne in 1951. He encouraged the Reeds to re-establish the Contemporary Art Society and introduced them to a younger generation of artists, poets and intellectuals including Charles Blackman and his first wife Barbara, Robert Dickerson, Nadine Amadio, Laurence Hope, Peter Burns, Charles Osborne, Philip Jones and Judith Wright. With the arrival of French émigrés, Georges and Mirka Mora, the

Reeds found themselves once again at the vibrant centre of Melbourne's cultural life.

Together with John, Sunday became a director of the Gallery of Contemporary Art, an activity that, for the first time, drew her away from Heide and into a public role in the art world. With Reid and Max Harris, the Reeds also launched another literary magazine, with the ironic title *Ern Malley's Journal*. Mary Boyd, John Perceval, Joy Hester, Gray Smith, John Sinclair and Jean Langley all remained close friends and visitors to Heide throughout the 1950s. The house itself underwent long-needed renovations.

But the sensibility of Melbourne figurative art — introspective, poetic, dreamy and apolitical, symbolised by the Child — was quite different to the 1940s. Though it was closer to Sunday's own taste, Heide did not assume the pivotal importance of the previous decade. There were no more artists in residence. The boldness that had marked Sunday's amorous conquests also went quiet, and for the first time since she and John married, she was faithful.

Modernism itself was no longer a grand, groundbreaking adventure. Having won its battles across the art forms, its most visible manifestation internationally was abstraction. Sunday remained as responsive as ever to fresh developments — 'always in search of the newborn' — and she responded to local abstract painters. For the first time since Atyeo's and Nolan's early experiments, non-figurative art made its way into the Heide collection.

Barrett Reid was sixteen when he first made contact with the Reeds. A precocious schoolboy poet, he was co-editing *Barjai*, an arts magazine, when he contacted John to protest the inclusion of Hester's stark, minimalist drawing, *The time-lag* (1942, Heide

Museum of Modern Art), in *Angry Penguins*. Aside from that, *Angry Penguins* impressed him with its translations of Rimbaud, Lorca and Rilke, plus new poems by Dylan Thomas, Kenneth Rexroth and Robert Penn Warren.[2] Reid's poetry was published in the Ern Malley issue.

When the Reeds visited Queensland in 1946, Barrett met them for the first time. He recalled that 'in romantic excitement I imagined the editors and the artists [of *Angry Penguins*] in all the wild and woolly colours of Bohemia', so when he went to collect John and Sunday from their hotel for dinner, he 'waited in the lobby anxiously glancing at the lift for the wild ones of my imagination'. Then 'my gaze turned to the staircase and there, arm in arm, walking quietly down were two very beautiful people. Good heavens, I thought, they're respectable. I could have taken them home to my (almost) nineteenth-century father.'[3]

There was only one reservation on the Reeds' part about their new friend. He was homosexual. Nolan was irritated when John questioned him about Reid, insisting Barrett and his partner Charles Osborne were boyhood friends and that their association could not be categorised as 'transitory or strange'. Whether or not it was homosexual, Nolan refused to speculate.[4]

Sunday, despite her own freewheeling moral code and sophisticated tolerance for all manner of extremes in art and life, was blinkered about homosexuality. 'Girls and boys are made for each other,' she insisted. To Philip Jones, Barrett's companion from the mid-'50s, her comment was embarrassing to say the least. Nadine Amadio reflected that it was 'hard to believe that this enormously intelligent woman did have that side to her'. Sunday encouraged Amadio to have an affair with her close friend, musician Jamie Murdoch, who was gay. Sunday 'couldn't seem to understand' it was impossible.[5] Yet such reservations did not impede the growth of friendships with gay friends including Reid, Osborne, Jones and Hal Porter.

Late in 1946, Reid hitchhiked down to Melbourne with painter Laurence Hope, on their way to visit Max Harris in Adelaide. Reid had met Hope, a disaffected Sydney art student, the year before, soon after he arrived in Brisbane. He was 'sleeping in a tramway shelter, wrapped in a pink feltex blanket, very holey'. So Reid 'shook his shoulder and said, "Look, you can't sleep here, mate. The cops will pick you up."'[6] Reid escorted Hope home where he lived with his '(almost) ninteenth-century' father and his sisters. Hope's melancholic, intimist paintings were not only collected by the Reeds, who remained lifelong friends, but also proved influential to Blackman.

When Reid and Hope arrived in Melbourne, they went straight to the office of Reed & Harris. The first people they saw were Albert Tucker and Harry Roskolenko. Reid recalled that 'with one glance Bert summed up the situation: "You're too late," he said, "it's all over."'[7] Undeterred, the two made their way to Heide where they stayed for a few days, before Nolan put them up at his Parkville loft.

Hope was impressed by the Kelly series and Nolan's procedure for working flat with ripolin. It was not as easy as it looked. 'I tried out one. Made it too steep. [Paint] running all over the place. Meanwhile [Nolan] was painting a portrait of Barrie.'[8] (*Portrait of Barrett Reid*, 1947, Queensland Art Gallery). Nolan also did *Portrait of Laurence Hope* (1947, Art Gallery of South Australia). Reid and Hope were also introduced to Hester and Vassilieff, Reid buying Hester's *Gethsemane V* (c.1946, Heide MoMA).

Hester was impressed with Reid and his poetry, telling Sunday she was amazed that 'such a young boy' could be 'so wise' and make 'such deep observations'.[9] She was referring to Reid's 'Fraser Island

Looking West', inspired by Reid's journey there with Nolan, a poem
he brought with him to Heide.

Out west in childhood
there grows a flower
in the wet years;
sometimes it is red
sometimes it is blue
sometimes it is white with tears

And in this sandy forest
a ganger takes a part
of a sprig with a flower
and wears it in his hat,
wears it all day,
a wave to memory setting him apart.[10]

Like most guests, Reid was lured into the garden to work during
his visit. Sunday had a new idea: she wanted to create a holly hedge
that would act as a bird hide, so the birds could stay clear of Heide's
growing army of cats. Min had had five kittens while the Reeds
were in Europe. The Reeds built a cattery at the rear of Heide I
that, as Mirka Mora recalled, contained 'almost forty cats. They all
cried loudly, they were Burmese and Siamese and pissed on all the
paintings standing in the corridor'.[11] In fact, Heide had become a
drop-off centre for the unwanted cats of the neighbourhood and,
with their usual kindness and sense of responsibility, the Reeds had
taken on the task of caring for them.

Reid and John were co-opted into helping Sunday to plant the
holly hedge down in the paddock where it still grows. Former
Heide MoMA garden curator, Simon Dickeson, considered it

'looked good' but was 'hideously hard to maintain'.[12] Sunday herself finally had to admit it was a failure: the birds did not use it.

When Barrett returned to Brisbane, his friendship with the Reeds intensified and he confided to them that 'in my times of despair I look to that part of myself which is Sun and yourself for hope'.[13] Reid also keenly felt, and judiciously assessed, the collapse of *Angry Penguins*. 'The failure of *Angry Penguins* won't immediately affect the creative artist,' he wrote to John, 'but it is certainly a death blow to the creative critic, and after him the audience for creative work.' He also felt it was important to continue 'the *Angry Penguins*' tradition with a magazine whose main function would be to endure, to conserve what ground has been gained'.[14]

Sunday was in total agreement. John told Barrett that 'Sunday has always urged that *Angry Penguins* should be left alive – that it is one thing which forms a focal point in this country'.[15] Sunday hoped to raise the ghost of *Angry Penguins* with Barrett's help. While Reid felt he hadn't 'the quick sort of brain that is required for directing any such journal', he was, he continued modestly, 'very good at answering correspondence and getting work and alliances from people . . . So here I am if I can ever be of any use.'[16] Five years later, these discussions bore fruit in the publication of *Ern Malley's Journal*.

Getting alliances from people was certainly one of Reid's great strengths. He was a charming man with a light, quick, humorous manner; a good listener who was also sure of his opinions and not afraid to canvas them. He was socially adept and inquisitive, as interested in painting as he was in poetry and literature. Already he was building around himself a network of bright young things, some of whom would make Melbourne their home.

Reid got to know the brilliant young poet Judith Wright and

her husband, Jack McKinney, who were living at Mt Tamborine. Wright's first collection, *The Moving Image*, was published in 1946 and was much admired by Sunday and Hester. Reid introduced Wright to Nolan, the Reeds, Laurence Hope (who lived near Wright and McKinney for a time) and Barbara Patterson. Afflicted by a slow but inexorable blindness, Patterson met Hope's friend, Charles Blackman, another escapee from the Sydney art scene, when he arrived in Brisbane in 1948, and they later married.

Blackman was about to blow into the Reeds' life like another Nolan, another Rimbaud-worshipping, sensitive, talented, rambunctiously confident, working-class lad who had produced virtually nothing but who had every intention of being Australia's top artist. As Felicity Moore noted, Blackman was an omnivorous reader and an enthusiast of Verlaine, Baudelaire, Ezra Pound and T.S. Eliot.[17] His training had been piecemeal and uninspiring: evening classes at East Sydney Technical School, a short stint with Meldrumite painter Hayward Veal and life-drawing classes at the Studio of Realist Art. Perhaps his first non-literary revelation was Nolan's exhibition of Fraser Island paintings at Brisbane's Moreton Galleries in February 1948. Nolan's lyrical touch, and Hope's melancholic renderings of lovers, would provide the form and mood for Blackman's early essays in paint.

His first visit to Heide was a disaster. The Reeds believed, wrongly as it turned out, that he had stolen slides of the Kelly series. Barrett, who had arranged the meeting, was outraged. He told John and Sunday that Blackman had written to Barbara, 'a frightful revolting letter, saying that everything he did in Melbourne was consciously done and to a plan so as to destroy any chance of his being caught in webs of friendships he doesn't need'.[18] It's more likely that the working-class boy was overwhelmed by Heide's glamour and decided, as Yosl Bergner had a decade before, to act up. As late as 1951, Barrett was still complaining to the Reeds about Blackman. 'Everything he has done – paintings included – so far fail to convince me of anything central to his being but he seems desperately struggling to achieve some kind of identity.'[19]

Despite the inauspicious start, Blackman's visit to Heide was, in fact, the beginning of a beautiful friendship with Sunday that developed more fully after he settled in Melbourne. Heide was important for Blackman's development and Sunday proved an intuitive, nurturing spirit. Soon Blackman and Sunday were swapping literary heroes, with Sunday introducing Blackman to Colette's novels.

At Heide he saw Nolan's Kelly and Wimmera series, plus his St Kilda paintings, which had an immediate impact: Blackman set off for St Kilda and began to paint it, too. *Eager Bather* (1951, National Gallery of Victoria) and *Sunset, St Kilda* (1951, NGV) show Blackman swallowing Nolan whole, producing gawky figures lost in space, themes he would later develop more effectively. From Nolan, he learned how to deal with the figure and pictorial space in an imaginative, modernist manner. Vassilieff and Tucker as well as Boyd, Perceval and Hester also impressed him.

Nolan had arrived at Heide and tested himself against Atyeo, seducing the Reeds into the bargain. Blackman knew he had to measure himself against Nolan. But there would be no love affair.

Barbara Blackman was wary of Sunday and resisted the lure of Heide. She recalled her first meeting with Sunday in her memoir, *Glass After Glass*. '[Sunday] was in her soft blue shirt and trousers and spoke with a soft blue voice . . . "Hello. I'm deaf and you're blind. I wonder how ever shall we get on?" Actually, I don't think we ever did.'[20] Barbara felt Sunday was 'hard on artists' wives' and believed that 'artists shouldn't have wives'.[21] Perhaps she was fearful

Sunday might try and take Charles away from her. But she was impressed by Heide, despite the tensions.

> [The Reeds] ruled over a kingdom of the aesthetic such as most of us had never known before, a kind of Heaven, where we felt awed and chosen to be guests, whose esoteric rules we were always in danger of trespassing upon. Simplicitas, dignitas, pietas were in modern demonstration in that scrubbed farm house rich with books, paintings, music and an air of intimacy with them. The Reeds were imperious, courting and cancelling, promising and denying.[22]

Charles was free of such anxieties. He admired the way the Reeds 'didn't worry about money'. Like Perceval, he found Heide a 'happy household' for an artist to work in and Sunday 'a gifted and sensitive human being'.[23] Soon Sunday was advising Blackman on his paintings with Charles agreeing that 'the things you said about the pictures so far [are] essentially pretty true. Things being forced too quickly, not enough digestion as it were.'[24] John, too, wanted to help Blackman as he struggled with his painting but he felt Blackman needed 'more than encouragement, more than I can give him'.[25]

Melbourne offered Blackman a great deal: as well as the Reeds, he befriended a group of crucial, senior artists that included Vassilieff, Hester, Perceval and Boyd, all of whom provided excellent examples both of the poetic, inner world Blackman was drawn to investigate and the expressive form with which to articulate it. As Blackman saw it, the '*Angry Penguins* group had disbanded and I brought something new to this group . . . Nolan and Tucker were very much in the foreground, they were not the heroes of the past.' As far as the ambitious Blackman was concerned, it was 'good they weren't around'.[26]

Late in 1951, Reid and Charles Osborne closed the Ballad Bookshop and headed for Melbourne. Reid had fallen foul of the authorities at the Public Library and had secured himself a position at the State Library of Victoria, where he would have a long and distinguished career. Despite his own poetry and commitment to the arts, Reid never gave up his day job.

Reid once admitted that the Ern Malley debacle had put him off publishing his work because of the damaging manner in which a hostile philistinism had attacked and demoralised modernism's project. No doubt he was also aware of the personal cost: Max Harris had produced little poetry of value since, while the Reeds had been impugned and humiliated. Instead, Reid chose the intimate realm of Heide as his ideal audience. 'How can I write poems for the world if I write them only for you?' he asked Sunday.[27]

Barrett was good for the Reeds and, equally, they were good for him. He became a healing force after the loss of Nolan and the disappointments of *Angry Penguins* and Reed & Harris. Here was a talented, perceptive young man, brimming with plans to revive the very things the Reeds felt they had lost. Plus he seemed on the cusp of fulfilling his destiny as a poet. He seemed not Nolan reborn, but Harris.

The next arrivals were from Paris. Georges and Mirka Mora were Jewish immigrants, part of the wave who fled Europe, dark with the shadows of a recent war and looming with the awful possibility of another. Georges (Gunter Moravksi) had served in the French Foreign Legion and the Resistance while Mirka had been briefly incarcerated in a French concentration camp. After the war, Mirka studied at École d'Education Par le Jeu et l'Art Dramatique, a theatre school.

Georges, poised, cultured and with a flair for business, and

Mirka, attractive and vivacious, became energetic contributors to the Melbourne art world. By mid-1952, they had settled at 9 Collins Street, the historic artists' studios where Tom Roberts, Arthur Streeton and Jane Sutherland had painted. John felt they 'introduced quite a new atmosphere of hospitality, gaiety and warmth' to Melbourne.[28] Mirka worked as a dressmaker, making shirt fronts for a department store, while Georges ran a noodle factory.

The morning after Mirka met John Sinclair at a party, Sunday rang. Mirka recalled 'a little voice with an unforgettable tone – soft, persistent, rare'. Sunday asked Mirka to make her a dress. 'I chose some very fine white linen, batiste, and the dress was so lovely that Sunday hung it on her bedroom wall. She never wore it, choosing to look at it instead.'

Soon the Reeds and the Moras were spending their weekends together, Mirka finding 'the [Heide] library was a haven, full of French books'.[29] She also enjoyed speaking French with Sunday. 'I thought I was back in France.' Sunday made 'fresh raspberry jam *à la minute* for arvo tea'. At Heide, 'everything was an event. Sunday prepared everything beautifully. It was stylish, simple and comfortable.' The Reeds were '*agréable*'.[30] During the week, the Reeds visited 9 Collins Street bringing 'rare roses, eggs, cream, asparagus, fruit and books'.[31]

The Reeds had a profound effect on Georges. While Mirka developed as an artist in the Melbourne milieu, Georges had no specific direction. The Reeds helped shape his career as one of Australia's most respected art dealers. In 1970, with two decades in the art world behind him, Georges declared that 'never in my life has anybody or anything had such a decisive effect as you (and Sunday)'. He was 'in a way what you made me' and 'proud' of it.[32]

The Reeds fought with all their friends, there were always hurt feelings, misunderstandings and issues about loyalty and possession, and the Moras were no exception. Mirka could feel wary of Sunday whom she recalled saying, 'I can't have power over you.'[33] But the loyalty the Reeds inspired in their friends remained constant. Georges, a reserved man about personal matters, developed a particularly close friendship with Sunday. When his marriage to Mirka ended in 1970, Georges unloaded his grief to Sunday. 'To whom, I ask you, could I write such confessions?'[34]

1953, the year Blackman had his first solo exhibition at Peter Bray Gallery, proved a turning-point in the Melbourne art world.

Sunday had started buying Blackman's work the year before when he held a show at his Hawthorn studio, and in the next six years, acquired twenty-nine works – drawings, gouaches, ceramic tiles and oils, a testament to Sunday's faith in his emerging talent. Blackman's Schoolgirl paintings were tender and bold, formed by a host of essentially Melbourne pictorial influences, an immersion in poetry and literature and an identification with the wounded feminine, the latter instigated by his wife's battle with impending blindness and by Blackman's own identification with a world of lost innocence and private sensation, symbolised by young girls. It was Sunday's sensibility par excellence. No wonder she bought up big.

The Schoolgirls are pivotal because they focus on a crucial image that defined Melbourne figurative painting, positioning it for attack by abstract painters and leading, in 1959, to a group that included Blackman, Boyd and Perceval banding together under the banner of the Antipodean Manifesto.

The Child was the symbol of 1950s Melbourne art, an image

shared by Blackman, Hester, Boyd, Perceval, Hope, John Brack and Mirka Mora as well as Sydney artist Robert Dickerson. It was not new. Boyd's *Progression* (1941), Perceval's *Boy with Cat 2* (1943, National Gallery of Australia), Tucker's *Children of Athens* (1942) and *Fisherman's Bend* (1943), Hester's *Gethsemane V* (c.1946) and *Child of the High Seas* (c.1948) – all in the Reeds' collection in the 1950s – indicate how the suffering of the innocent haunted Melbourne's wartime artists. It also shows Sunday's receptivity to an image that connected her to the sensitivity and imagination of childhood, her sacred domain.

Interestingly, in 1953 the Reeds bought *Early Summer – Gorse in Bloom* (1888, AGSA), a work they had first admired in 1944 when it was shown in Streeton's memorial exhibition at the National Gallery of Victoria. In the foreground is a little girl wearing a white frock and a red bonnet, holding a sprig of gorse, an image of the Child in the landscape. *Early Summer – Gorse in Bloom* was reproduced in *Angry Penguins* where John extolled its virtues. 'For sheer delicacy and feeling for its subject, it would hold its own in any country.'[35] The painting, a key early Streeton, not only celebrated the classic dazzling blue and gold landscape of the Heidelberg School but employed the motif of the Child, the imaginative source for many Melbourne-based figurative artists. It hung in pride of place at Heide where Blackman, Hester, Boyd and Perceval could admire it.

Why did some of Australia's best painters, and Sunday's favourite artists, turn inward? The anger of the 'masculinist' 1940s was gone. The '50s was a decade of prodigious growth and stability in Australia yet, as Bernard Smith observed, 'younger artists turned steadily away from all forms of realism; and contemporary life, if portrayed at all, was usually accompanied by an air of wistfulness' while Manning Clark believed intellectuals were confronted with 'a new world', a time of cultural breakthrough.[36]

But Australia was a conservative place. The Menzies government ushered in the decade with the introduction of an Act designed to stamp out the Communist Party, an idea soundly defeated by a referendum. The Korean War, the Petrov affair and the formation of the Democratic Labor Party all assisted in whipping up a virulent, rightwing reaction to progressive thought. Worldwide, it was the era of the Cold War, of communist witch-hunts and unbridled paranoia. *The Day the Earth Stood Still* (1951), a popular Hollywood movie, was the first of a number of science fiction films showing the earth under threat from an alien invader.

Melbourne artists seemed in mourning for a vanished world. Anguish, nostalgia and loss arise in their art, represented by mostly under-nourished children — large-eyed little girls who represent a fragile, feminine realm; lonely figures who roam dismal environments suffused with sadness and a sense of alienation. Blackman's Schoolgirls, Hope's Lovers, Boyd's Bride series, Hester's large drawings of children holding birds, Dickerson's frightened waifs and Perceval's rather more cheerful ceramic angels and paintings of his children, all catalogue the same image.

Furthermore, Sunday, Hester, Blackman and Reid shared literary interests that counterpoint the image of the Child. As well as treasuring Rimbaud's luminous evocations of childhood, Sunday quoted the touching, romantic poetry of John Shaw Neilson to Blackman and he used Shaw Neilson's 'Schoolgirls Hastening' in the catalogue to his 1953 show.

> Fear it had faded and the night
> The bells all peal the hour of nine

Arthur Streeton. *Point King, Sorrento,* Sunday's beloved holiday home, Merthon, 1920. Oil on canvas. 39.5 x 48.0 cm. *Private Collection.*

Sunday Reed. *Landscape.* c. 1933. Charcoal, pastel and coloured pencil on paper. 20 x 24.5 cm. *Private Collection.*

Arthur Streeton. *Evening with Bathers*. 1888. Oil on canvas. 40.5 x 76 cm.
National Gallery of Victoria.

Left: Sam Atyeo. *Organised Line to Yellow*. c. 1933. Oil on canvas. 68 x 48 cm.
National Gallery of Australia.

Right: Sam Atyeo. *Wyperfeld National Park*. c. 1933. Oil on plywood. 66 x 50.6 cm.
Heide Museum of Modern Art.

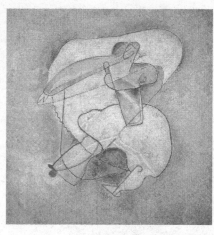

Left: Sam Atyeo. *The Dancer*. 1936.
Oil on canvas. 59 x 54.5 cm.
Heide Museum of Modern Art.

Below: Moya Dyring. *Sunday.*
c. 1934. Oil on composition board.
36 x 26.7 cm.
Heide Museum of Modern Art.

Above: Moya Dyring. *Melanctha*.
c. 1934. Oil on canvas on plywood.
31.3 x 22.9 cm.
Heide Museum of Modern Art.

Left: Adrian Lawlor. *Self Portrait*.
1938.
Oil on cardboard.
61.5 x 48 cm.
Heide Museum of Modern Art.

Danila Vassilieff. *Valerie and Betty.* 1937. Oil on plywood. 45 x 53.5 cm.
Heide Museum of Modern Art.

Arthur Boyd. *Butterfly Man.* 1943. Oil on muslin on cardboard. 55.5 x 75.5 cm.
Heide Museum of Modern Art.

John Perceval. *Boy with Cat 2.*
1943. Oil on composition board.
59 x 43.8 cm.
National Gallery of Australia.

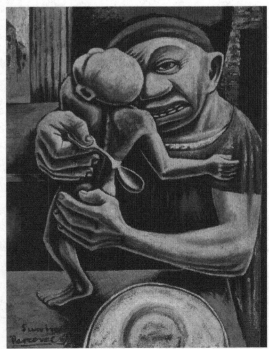

John Perceval. *Survival.*
1942. Oil on
composition board.
122 x 93.5 cm.
National Gallery of
Victoria.

Joy Hester. *Gethi in a Tree (Gethsemane I)*.
c. 1946. Brush and ink on paper.
35.6 x 24.1 cm.
Private Collection.

Joy Hester. *Gethsemane V.* c. 1946. Brush and ink, gouache on paper. 25.2 x 31.2 cm.
Heide Museum of Modern Art.

Joy Hester. *Face VI.* c. 1947–8. Brush and ink on paper. 31.2 x 24.8 cm. *Heide Museum of Modern Art.*

Sidney Nolan. *Rosa Mutabilis.* 1945. Ripolin enamel on composition board. 91.5 x 122.0 cm. *Heide Museum of Modern Art.*

Schoolgirls hastening through the light
Touch the unknowable Divine.[37]

Reid's poem 'Moonlight', published in 1953, also traces intimate zones of love and tenderness.

So that air is
so that kisses are
so that lovers make wounds with their kisses
at that time
when moonlight
ah at that time

As flowers at midnight
lovers in flame
birds inside houses
inside moonlight, moving
without doors
yes at that time.[38]

Hester had been writing poetry since the early 1940s and she privileged their importance by exhibiting them alongside the Sleep, Love and Faces series at her first solo show in 1951. After she moved to rural Hurstbridge in 1948, the natural world became a fecund metaphor for love, sensuality, bliss and union. Her most accomplished poem 'Awake' begins, 'there's one awake in the fern world/in the forest of my heart'. In another poem, the lover is asked to 'try me again, repeat the hour/make the wattle bough come heavy'. Hester found herself in 'the love garden/... at the very heart's core', and revelled in the inspiration she found there.[39] Hester believed Gray Smith's love had assisted her recovery from cancer and her poems bear witness to love as a creative force and a healing gift.

Sunday and Hester both admired Alain-Fournier's haunting novel of lost youth, *Le Grand Meaulnes*, the writer declaring 'my credo in Art and Literature is childhood. I want to recapture childhood without being childish.'[40] Both were also 'deeply affected' by Jules Supervielle's short story 'Child of the High Seas' which inspired Hester's drawing of the same name.[41] A ship's captain, dreaming of his dead daughter, conjures up her presence in a sad fairytale of loss and yearning. He imagines that she lives all alone on the ocean, going about her tasks in perpetual solitude, fated to sink beneath the waves at the approach of a ship. Hester described the story to Barrett Reid as 'a strange and lovely thing' which presented itself to her 'as a series of pictures'.[42]

Rimbaud, Shaw Neilson, Alain-Fournier and Supervielle created a plaintive poetics of loss that resonated with Sunday's sensibility and that of Melbourne art.

The '40s were riven with fierce political disputes and loyalties that bled into the art world. But Blackman and Dickerson were adamantly apolitical. Boyd, Hester and Perceval, while leftwing, kept their opinions to themselves. There were no more great debates about the social relevance of art, no forum, it seemed, for opposing the conservatism of the times.

The hopes of the 1940s – that the postwar world would deliver a socialist utopia, dreams that the Reeds also shared – had been dashed by the grim reality of the Cold War and the horrible truth that the Soviet Union, glorified for its heroic efforts during the war, offered not liberation but savage imperialism and a new and pernicious tyranny. In 1956, Russian tanks rolled into Hungary, crushing both its revolution and international hopes for a benign form of communism.

In the brutal, post-Holocaust, post-Hiroshima world, the Child also stands for a loss of faith, finding herself in a place leached of the fervent political idealism that aroused the artists of the '40s. Paradise had not arrived. The Child, born of the dreams of the past, is perplexed and forsaken by the present, a limbo where she wanders fruitlessly, searching for home, shelter and rest; for family, nourishment and protection – things she so patently lacks. Though the Melbourne art world was dominated by male artists in the '50s, the sensibility is emphatically feminine.

The figure of the Child operates on a personal level, too. On the surface, the lives of Perceval, Blackman, Hester and Boyd were happy, family-oriented, settled and productive. Often their own children were the subjects for their art. There was a contentment and pleasure to life that the older artists had not known during the war years. Due to the success of Arthur Merric Boyd Pottery, Perceval and the Boyds were making a comfortable living.

Yet a shadow side was emerging. During that time, Perceval and Blackman were developing a destructive dependence on alcohol. Blackman was also facing his wife's impending blindness, placing pressures on him to tend her and his family. Hester, after an eight-year remission, was once again assailed by symptoms of cancer while Arthur Boyd nursed Yvonne through a serious illness.

At the heart of their lives, there was trouble, worry and unease. Images surfaced of vulnerable children, victims of an unjust, unfeeling, unpredictable world. The Child could represent their own children and loved ones, whom they were powerless to protect against life's vicissitudes, as well as the hurt, bewildered children whom the artists, at their core, felt themselves to be. Blackman, small and thin with enormous eyes, pictured himself as the Child in his *Self Portrait* (1956, Heide MoMA).

The world, the Child conveys, is a fearful place – a dark wood, a deserted street, a Mad Hatter's Tea Party. What she must do is keep vigil, and wait patiently for these times to pass.

Sex had raged through the art of the '40s and violent, orgiastic sexual fantasies inflamed the art of Tucker, Boyd, Perceval and Hester. Of the Heide circle, only Nolan's determined lyricism seemed immune. But the Child, on the cusp of sexual awakening, remains pure and hers is the skinny, unwomanly body of a virgin. Formally, too, a new conservatism is registered. The body is not torn asunder, as it was in Hester's Faces series, Boyd's *The Orchard* or Perceval's *Negroes at Night*; it is made whole. The great staring eyes that gazed from the wartime work of Hester, Boyd and Perceval remain a key motif. But they are no longer mirrors of madness, horror, desire and despair. They are poignant, attentive and appealing.

During the '50s, Sunday experienced her own confrontation with childhood's promise and pain while rearing Sweeney. Significantly, her doll Gethsemane, symbol of infertility, disappears from Heide around this time and no further mention of her is made. Sunday was now coping with motherhood and she had some harsh lessons to learn.

Having decided Sweeney would not attend kindergarten or school, Sunday was tutoring him at home. In 1950, when Sweeney was five years old, John told Tucker that Sunday 'is now teaching Sweeney to read and write and that is going very smoothly and happily. Goodness knows what system it is but Sweeney seems to enjoy it all and is learning quickly and easily.' Further, Sunday was 'much opposed to kindergarten methods of encouraging "art" activity . . . and she is extremely strict about [Sweeney's] creative life which arises within our own living spontaneously and is directed always by his personal relations and moods.' In short, Sweeney could do what he liked.

As far as friends went, while it would be 'ideal, of course' if Sweeney had 'a little brother or sister', there were 'numbers of children next door and round about with whom he is quite free to play'. But, the Reeds felt, these children were 'quite ineffectual and ordinary little creatures such as he would indeed find at school, they do not provide him with the companionship that is necessary'. John was of the opinion that 'Sweeney would agree if he knew how'. The little boy was 'gay, red cheeked, particularly well and altogether very beautiful and pleased with himself. His ego is terrific!'[43]

A year later, Sunday's teaching experiment had fizzled, John reporting to Tucker that '"school" seems to be going through a difficult period, a kind of mutual staleness, the teacher disinclined to teach and the pupil disinclined to learn and the hours of attendance on both sides somewhat haphazard'.[44]

Sunday had no training as a teacher, no expertise in conducting a sustained program of education and, while a student, subversively followed her own instincts. While it proved for her a productive, though patchy, method of education, it did not suit Sweeney, as she began to discover. Sweeney was a problem child. He was intelligent but wilful and he refused to knuckle down to the routine of study. He stubbornly followed his own path but it was not the one the Reeds deemed appropriate.

By 1954, Sunday and John were at a loss as to how to manage Sweeney and resorted to desperate measures. Finally, they conceded he needed to go to school and he attended Preshill, an experimental school, whose standards did not satisfy John. Then they decided to place him at Geelong Grammar, John's old school, as a boarder. He was nine. They hoped its discipline and arts-oriented curriculum would help Sweeney in a way Preshill had not. It was 'the very reverse of anything we had ever intended', John admitted to Tucker, adding 'it would also be a good thing for him to be independent of Heide for a while'. Such an admission, that Sweeney was to be banished from Heide, indicates just how arduous the task of controlling him had become.

With disappointment, John recognised that 'Sweeney seems unlikely to be a great scholar, though his headmaster said he was among the six most intelligent boys in his class ... he appears to have no particular urge to acquire knowledge' and was 'not the sort of boy you are likely to find curled up in a chair reading a book'.[45]

The following year Sweeney went back to Preshill but returned to Geelong as a boarder in 1957 and remained there until he finished school. As far as John was concerned, Sweeney was 'a bloody awful scholar and goodness knows what his particular bent is going to be'.[46]

But, much as the Reeds knew Sweeney needed discipline, they were horrified when they found he had been caned, even though John was aware that Sweeney's 'nature and personality' was different to that of 'timid and retiring boys'. They were also concerned that the school diet, with its paucity of fresh fruit, was 'not only useless but actually harmful' and believed Sweeney should not be 'compelled to eat anything'.[47]

Having a child is a fundamental creative act and one of the reasons Sunday longed for it. Equally, motherhood is life's most demanding job and Sunday had taken it on board at forty-two. When Sweeney turned ten, she was fifty. Raising him was not like having wild, gifted artists to stay, folk who knew their own minds and who would follow their own course come what may. Parenting is about love and discipline in equal measure. Sunday hoped Sweeney would instinctively create his own program of study, art and play. But that was impossible. He was a child who needed a firm hand.

He was also a troubled little boy with two sets of parents. In addition, he had two new half-siblings: Joy had Peregrine, a son, in 1951 and Fern, a daughter, in 1954. John confidently told Tucker that Sweeney 'knows that Joy is his Mummy' and it presented him with 'no confusion and in dealing with the world about him, his clarity and intuition are quite extraordinary'. As the years went by, the Reeds would discover that their optimism about Sweeney's ability to cope with the changes and reversals of his childhood was sadly ill-founded.

As a tidal wave of emotion flooded through Melbourne painting, the art world was galvanised by young Turks who wanted change. The art may have looked shy and retiring but the personalities certainly were not. Barrett Reid, together with Charles Blackman and Laurence Hope, were keen to revive the Contemporary Art Society, and they wanted John Reed to take charge as he had in the heady days of the 1940s.

The Reeds represented tradition to their younger friends, and it was exactly the kind of tradition the Reeds wanted to establish. Essentially, it comprised Sunday's vision of Australian modernism plus John's ideals of comradely cultural activity. The younger generation was inspired by the example of the CAS, of *Angry Penguins* and Reed & Harris – and, by extension, of the Reeds themselves, the patrons par excellence. It was a heartening moment where John was seen as the modern artist's staunch and commanding supporter and Sunday as the power behind the throne, the creative force that made Heide tick. Together, they were a couple with an awesome reputation; 'the Reeds', admired by some, criticised by others, a controversial and significant team.

On the walls at Heide, the younger group saw major art by the Heide circle, work that was highly esteemed and remained influential. The Reeds also relentlessly promoted those artists, especially Tucker and Nolan who were no longer there to promote themselves. Perceval, Boyd, Hester and Vassilieff were also present to indicate that the artistic excellence of the '40s was not a passing phase but a vital part of the contemporary scene.

In 1957, John reminded Tucker that 'to whatever extent your name and work are known in Melbourne, they are known almost exclusively because of the unceasing insistence of Sun and myself. Time and time again in conversation, and where ever possible in print, we have brought you forward and spoken of you in no uncertain terms.'[48]

But when John was asked by Barrett Reid and Blackman to re-activate the CAS, he wisely told them 'he wouldn't be part of it, unless there was a real demand among the artists'.[49] The first meeting, in November 1953, with everyone packed into the basement at 9 Collins Street, must have convinced him there was. Sunday accompanied him. Even her deafness would not prevent her attendance.

John told potential CAS members that, as far he was concerned, 'creative activity' had been at 'a low ebb' since 1947 and that 'public interest in art was completely lacking'. There had been 'no question of winding up' the CAS. Instead, 'the intention was always that it should remain available for the moment when, once again, there was a real part for it to play'.[50] In the hurly-burly of the first meeting, John was elected president with Danila Vassilieff as artist vice-president, Barrett Reid as lay vice-president and Peter Burns as secretary. Barbara Blackman was treasurer.

Sunday piped up and nominated Jean Langley for the council. 'Why?' a voice challenged. 'Because she's intelligent,' Sunday coolly replied.[51] Langley was elected, together with Arthur Boyd, Erica McGilchrist, Ian Sime, Charles Blackman, Clifford Last and Georges Mora. It was this group, together with Sunday, who were responsible for organising the CAS's first annual exhibition in seven years, opening in April 1954 at Tye's Gallery, a furniture shop in Bourke Street. Peter Burns designed a stylish catalogue: indeed, the clean modern lines of many CAS, Gallery of Contemporary Art and Museum of Modern Art publications were the result of Burns' good taste.

All the artists on the council exhibited, along with Hester, Gray Smith, Mirka Mora, Clifton Pugh and Laurence Hope, as well as Sydney artists including Jean Bellette, John Coburn and Frank Hinder.

John was back on the hustings, announcing that 'the insistent demand of a new generation of artists and of those who live alongside them has made the revival of the [CAS] an urgent necessity'. It heralded 'a new phase of artistic activity'.[52] John's optimism indicated the CAS's infectious energy and enthusiasm and, in the next few years, the activity and discussion it generated revitalised the Melbourne art world. Exhibitions became the CAS's raison d'être. 'It must always be remembered that the CAS is essentially the society of the young creative artist.'[53] Until the end of the decade when the commercial galleries took over, the CAS was one of the most important venues in town for new or established talent.

Peter Burns had been persuaded to take the position of CAS secretary by Barrett Reid. (He was later its vice-president.) A freshly graduated architect, Burns had co-founded a journal called *Architecture and Arts* in his final year. The position of CAS secretary was honorary but, as Burns soon found, John expected nothing less than wholesale commitment. He would regularly ring Burns at midnight. '[John] never wrote me letters. He was on the phone all the time. He told me the nights were his time and he didn't go to bed until the early hours. He was fairly demanding.' Burns believed 'Sunday was the muse to John Reed. I always got the impression that when he was saying something, it was really Sunday speaking.' When Burns saw Sunday, her presence was 'austere, spare, gaunt . . . she was a listener'.

More than that. The Reeds bought works from each of Burns' three solo exhibitions between 1957 and 1959. 'I'm sure it was Sun, picking them,' Burns reflected. *Seen by Ulysses 4* from Burns' 1959 Argus Gallery show met with a very Heide-style disaster. 'It was standing in the hallway and one of the cats pissed on it. Sunday tried to remove the urine stain with Jex. John brought it back to me and I tried to fix it and I ruined it. John said, "It's all right, don't worry. Keep the money and keep the painting."' Luckily, Burns' *Fossil* (1958, Heide MoMA), an elegant, minimal abstract, survived.

There was a small band of artists determined to make abstract art in Melbourne in the mid-1950s including Roger Kemp, Leonard French, Clifford Last and Julius Kane. But it was the heat and noise generated by Ian Sime that made abstraction difficult to ignore. 'He was a brilliant propagandist for non-objective art. He was so articulate. He was the man, the main man,' recalled Burns. At CAS meetings, Sime 'got right into it. The meetings could get wild. You could cut the air with a knife.'[54]

Sime's contact with American art took place during the Second World War in Tokyo when he worked in the United States Information Library. After returning to Australia, he continued to have material sent over. Almost alone, he raised Melbourne awareness about postwar American abstraction. With his wife Dawn Sime, Erica McGilchrist and John Howley, he lead a small but committed band of abstract painters. John Olsen, who was teaching in Melbourne in 1955, admired Sime as 'the most aware and verbal protagonist of Abstraction'.[55] Sime influenced younger painters like Don Laycock and Howley[56] and John Reed admitted Sime 'opened up a whole new field for us'.[57]

Sime might have been keen on the luscious, dramatic, painterly excursions of Jackson Pollock or Mark Rothko but *Painting I* (1955, Heide MoMA) is closer to the decorative work of School of Paris artist Alfred Manessier that Sime had seen in the 1953 French Painting Today exhibition in Melbourne, than the ambitions of the New York School. Sime was an excellent colourist but his real vigour and nerve lay in his intense and voluble declamations about abstraction, rather than the act of painting itself.

Sime was impatient with the Child's dominance in Melbourne art. He sneered at Arthur Boyd's subjects, 'these pathetic people, too human to be true are still children and they satisfy with their archaic squalor, that part of us which wants to return to the security of dependence. They say in their cracked voices, "We are terrible and lovable, we are warm flesh and soft emotions, we are stupid and ungainly, and irresistible." '[58]

Sunday never had a problem with wordy, opinionated artists, or with profound disagreements between the artists she knew and respected. Her even-handedness was one of her strongest assets. She refused to take sides when new developments in art were emerging, preferring to watch and wait, then to snap up whatever she thought was the best and most representative. It meant she was capable of buying Sime's *Painting I* and listening to him fulminate in favour of abstraction while following Charles Blackman's every step with bated breath. Sime was never part of the inner Heide circle but the Reeds respected him, and bought two works. Sunday was not dismissive of abstraction, not in 1935 and certainly not in 1955. Abstract paintings by Dawn Sime, Peter Burns and Len Crawford were also bought for the Heide collection.

The spirit of the CAS had been revived but Sunday was having less success with the resurrection of *Angry Penguins*. Together with John, Barrett Reid and a rather unwilling Max Harris, she was collaborating on *Ern Malley's Journal*, its very title commemorating the modernist battles of bygone years.

In 1952, L.H. Davison had started a literary journal called *Direction* and edited the first issue with Barrett, with the Reeds helping to solicit essays and poems. But when Barrett and Davison parted company, Sunday decided that she and John would use the material that they had 'harvested', as Sunday put it, for their own magazine. The Reeds decided it would promote, as did *Angry Penguins*, the artists, poets and writers they admired and, between 1952 and its demise in 1955, it canvassed the talents of Arthur Boyd, Charles Blackman, Robert Dickerson, Ian Sime, Jean Langley, Peter Cowan, Barrett Reid, Greville Texidor, Joy Hester and Jules Supervielle.

In July 1952, Sunday wrote to Hester, telling her about the new magazine and that Barrett and Harris would be involved. She wondered 'if you and Gray would each give a poem ... We would like to come and tell you about [the journal] and talk about poems and which one of yours and which one of Gray's you would like best – that is of course if you are pleased about it all.' But she asked Hester to 'please keep the Journal confidential for the moment'.[59]

Sunday cherished Hester's poems. 'I look forward to publishing all your poems before it is too late for me,' she declared. 'It hasn't anything to do with the Journal but is only to do with me and with you and John and I hope you will help me to start putting them together.'[60] Unfortunately, the book of Hester's poems did not eventuate.

In the first issue of *Ern Malley's Journal*, Barrett's essay, 'New Time, New Place' foregrounded *Angry Penguins*, making it the journal's benchmark and context. Reid also made 'the war years' sound a world away (and a rather more exciting one) than 'the present conditions in which we work and write'. He also defended Hester's poems which were 'under much fire from Adelaide', meaning Harris.[61]

The debate, and the misunderstandings, sparked by Hester's poetry provides an indication of *Ern Malley's* strengths and weaknesses. Sunday told Hester that 'Awake' and 'Micetto' were Max's choices. In fact, Max 'fell in love with your "Micetto" poem . . . and wants to publish [it].'[62] But Harris, as Reid noted, was critical of Hester's poems which he regarded as flowery and romantic. Perhaps he changed his mind. Perhaps he sought controversy. Perhaps Sunday was caught in the middle.

'Micetto', a poem about one of Sunday's Siamese cats, is Hester's poetry at its worst, lame and sentimental, but 'Awake' is an accomplished work, redolent with nature imagery, both sensual and moving. In a subsequent issue, Elizabeth Vassilieff tore into Hester's poems as 'sterile subjectivism'.[63] Sunday had warned Hester that Harris wanted 'to work in this way . . . to subject [poems] to open criticism' and 'expose, as it were, various sensibilities and positions' but it made Sunday uncomfortable since 'John and I do not really work this way at all'. The business of collaborating with Max was 'complex' and Sunday had been feeling 'rather strained'.[64] It must have been a painful episode for Hester and she never published her poetry again.

Similar problems had dogged *Angry Penguins*: an uneven quality in the literary contributions plus clashes between Harris and the Reeds. As usual, Sunday was funding the journal and, as usual, no-one got paid. But this time, the larger culture failed to provide an adequate springboard and the journal suffered the fate of some small magazines: the people involved just seemed to be talking to themselves. The '40s had been animated by international debates about the social role of art, by the presence of war, by the utopia of socialism. Unfortunately, the early '50s had no such bigger picture on which to draw.

But, as a vehicle for promoting the Reeds' favoured artists, *Ern Malley* did a good job. John wrote articles on Boyd and Blackman, together with the first major article on Robert Dickerson, an artist with whom he developed a strong bond. John had met the former boxer and factory worker through Barrett. When Dickerson arrived at Heide, Barrett warned him not to sit on a particular chair 'because Nolan sat there'.[65] But Dickerson got on well with John and they shared an ample correspondence. He and Sunday were not close.

Dickerson was soon introduced to Blackman and they developed a friendship marked by rivalry. Blackman showed him how to mix powdered paints but soon Dickerson was 'fed up with Blackman and his paintings. He ... tries to talk down to you all the time.'[66] In fact, there were similarities in their art, as well as their egos.

Big-eyed, waif-like loners inhabit Dickerson's starkly constructed, subtly hued paintings. The spotlit stage, where he places his subjects, accentuating their vulnerability, was derived from the boxing ring where he felt he was 'living in a nightmare, isolated in this white square space'.[67] Another impact was the island of Morotai, near New Guinea. Stationed there while waiting to be demobbed from the army, Dickerson began to draw and paint the local children who were 'so undernourished and thin, and with that intensity children have'.[68] The Reeds bought *Prone Figure on a beach* (1955, Heide MoMA), inspired by one of the Morotai children.

Poor *Ern Malley's Journal* received a drubbing from all and sundry. Sunday told Hester 'we hear [the second issue] is "a flop" and that Neil Douglas threw his copy out of the train and that Martin [Smith] says "someone should tell us". So you and Gray are not the only ones.' She was prepared to admit that Peter Cowan's short story was perhaps not his best and that John Yule's critical essay about Australian culture, 'Cloaca Maxima', was 'rather a muddle of sorts' though she was 'shocked' when Hester described Greville Texidor's translation of Lorca as 'pretty'. Sunday was 'sorry all the young ones are turning up their noses. It would be nice to have their warmth and sympathy.'

It was more than that. The opprobrium left Sunday wounded and made her reflect that 'the years have been heavily laden and lately I do not seem to have met them in the same way, and I have failed more than is good for one's face and I wonder if my mother or my father would know me if I passed by.'[69]

The toughest report card came from Albert Tucker who was living at Grottaferrata, in the Alban Hills outside Rome. He had been away for six years. Critical of the journal's narrow range, he queried why poets of the standard of Judith Wright, A.D. Hope and Kenneth Slessor were not included? He also disliked Harris's recent poetry and Hester's first published verse. He demanded to know why Hester was messing around with poetry. On a broader level, Tucker felt the journal lacked artistic impartiality. It read like the product of a band of like-minded friends with this barely known figure of Malley raised to the level of a deity.

Tucker did have some salient points but he put them so forcefully that John was stunned. It took him nearly four months to reply. 'I am conscious of some underlying sense of bitterness in yourself . . . I have the feeling that, for you, all the world is one side of the fence and you are on the other, and that you are determined to throw as many rocks over the fence as you possibly can – and it does not matter much who gets hit.'

John agreed with Tucker that the quality of Harris's poetry had 'failed to develop as it normally should' and had 'lost much of its validity' but he was surprised Tucker criticised Hester who, John believed, was 'able to distill some essence of herself in all that she does, and that quality persists in her poems'. John also defended his selection of contributors. 'Is it so unlikely we would draw on those we know, particularly in the first issues?' A variety of poets and authors were lobbied for contributions: many did not respond. John finished tiredly, 'we do not pretend to be a record of contemporary masterpieces, but hope to be part of the living organism of creative activity . . . No apologies on that score!'[70]

In the next letter, Tucker's allowance was suspended. John explained that 'the demands on Sun over a long period have greatly increased and now far exceed our income, both spiritually and financially, so to speak, involving all sorts of personal issues and conflicts to which there does not seem to be any answer, other than to try to live the best way we know how'.[71] The Reeds paid Tucker his annual instalment of 144 pounds for that year but it would be the last.

It was another difficult transition in Tucker's long and complicated relationship with the Reeds. Once again, despite the hurt feelings all round, the situation was handled with dignity and tact, and, once again, the friendship was preserved. When Tucker wrote, gallantly accepting the end of his stipend just before Christmas, Nolan and Cynthia were staying with him at Grottaferrata, no doubt an interested audience to Tucker's uncensored thoughts about the Reeds.

But there was more for Sunday to do than feel disheartened about *Ern Malley's Journal* or cavilling artists.

Renovations had begun at Heide in the summer of 1952, marking a long and disruptive period. By the end of the following year, John explained to Tucker that Heide was 'in a very dilapidated condition and really needs quite a lot doing to it' but 'we now hope we are getting somewhere'. The rear of the house was being completely remodelled by Freeman's architectural firm who were 'turning the present kitchen pantry and porch into a big livingroom with French doors', plus adding 'a very modern and compact new kitchen'.[72] There were terracotta Belgian tiles for the kitchen floor and sun room, as well as new shelves for the library that extended to the ceiling.

Sunday also decided to knock out the wall between the second and third bedrooms and turn it into one large bedroom for John and herself. She created a beautiful and very feminine room. French doors, hung with white lace curtains, opened into the garden, suffusing the room with light. The skirting boards were painted silvery grey, and the ceiling a soft green. A final romantic touch was rose-festooned wallpaper. The baby Bechstein remained and the angel Atyeo had given Sunday in 1935 was still on the bedroom door. *Rosa Mutabilis* was on the wall.

All did not go smoothly. The architects, Barrett Reid recalled, were 'famous for being the experts on colonial and Victorian architecture. They were pre-eminent' but they were 'very snobby'.[73]

There were the usual problems associated with renovations. To cope with the worst of the noise and mess, the Reeds bought 'a little two-roomed fibro-cement cottage' and 'had it moved holus-bolus onto the Heide hillside, and here we have lived ever since, while workmen picnic in the old house under the pretence of doing various renovations'.[74]

'We go on every day,' Sunday told Hester, 'clearing one muddle and making another and from the fire to the frying pan all day and I am becoming more and more unbearable every moment.' Paintings were moved from the dining room's 'ugly shelves' and stored in the doll's house, the old milking shed that had now been waterproofed. Unfortunately, the waterproofing was not of good standard and some of Tucker's paintings were slightly damaged, much to Sunday's dismay.[75] Nolan's Kellys were stored there, too.

The changes certainly made Heide more comfortable but, just as in 1935, Sunday decided against cool, contemporary decor. Her taste remained French and feminine, in keeping with the spirit of a Victorian home. 'There was nothing modern in that house.'[76] Except for the television. In 1956, the Reeds were the first among their group to own a set. They put it in the library and invited their friends over, and the Blackmans and Peter Burns crowded onto the couch and watched in fascination.

Sunday might have complained about the renovations' long, slow haul but she relished their benefits because it meant involving her friends in her plans.

Sunday asked Hester to design glass panels for either side of the front door. Hester chose a rose, Sunday's particular favourite, and a theme running through the new-look Heide. Hester was an interesting choice: her free drawing style meant she was not a designer in a conventional sense but that is probably why Sunday chose her. It was also a sentimental decision. Who had shared more thoroughly in Sunday's life at Heide than Hester? Who better understood the emotional symbolism of the rose/heart, with its resonances of love, fruition and change?

But the project was not without its minor dramas. Hester wrote to Sunday in a bother, believing she had lost the first set of drawings, which had been 'all parcelled up' and ready to post, so she sent Sunday another set.[77] (In fact, the first lot eventually arrived.) It meant Sunday had half a dozen designs to choose from.

Essentially, Hester drew the same rose each time – a handsomely realised, lush flower in full bloom, its petals, leaves, thorns and stem simplified and stylised. Hester accompanied the first drawings with an untitled poem where she selects 'this one rose', offering 'this gentle thing' and asking of Sunday 'only your observance'. The rose is a gift from artist to patron, a symbol of the creative self, as well as the deep bond between the two women. Hester herself is the rose, her veins exposed, 'flattened and green', before the trusted audience of her friend.[78] It is an image both of performance and submission, where Hester is aware she represents a precious source of creative energy beloved by Sunday but, at the same time, she must surrender and expose herself, making herself vulnerable to Sunday's sometimes exhausting needs. It is a tender and fearful poem, freighted with the implications of Hester and Sunday's complex friendship.

Hester's rose design was a success and Sunday had it cut into multiple images on the blue-white glass panels next to the front door.

Hester was not the only artist involved in the renovations. Mary Boyd designed tiles of delicate wildflowers and playful cats that Sunday placed above the old stove in the kitchen. In this way, Sunday integrated into her environment the work of two women artist friends. For Hester, it was at the front door, the place of entry and welcome. For Boyd, it was in the warm, nourishing environment of the kitchen. Both sites indicate Sunday's commitments: the first symbolising the openness with which she embraced new art and ideas while the second referring to the sustenance, both physical and aesthetic, she offered. Both are images of connection and sharing.

The garden was as huge a task as ever. In the house, Sunday now had help one day a week. Barrett 'never liked Mrs McPherson [because] she was always taking vegetables from the garden. But Sun had told her she could do that. I was annoyed that she'd taken so much. That was all the help they had.'[79]

When Sunday fell behind with the garden she felt frustrated because it meant the Reeds would be 'living off the greengrocer for months'. Sunday wished she had 'four hands and four legs', then she 'might catch up with the seasons and travel round the garden in time'. Sometimes she felt it was all too much and 'one day we will get back to the beginning when old Mrs Lang knew best and had Heide with nothing but a pepper tree'.[80]

When the Reeds returned from Europe in 1949, they had created red gravel paths around the house which were now driving them mad because keeping them smoothly raked was an arduous business. Sunday 'used to go along on her hands and knees and she would make it all level and it was absolutely beautiful.'[81] More reason to be annoyed that the paths were ignored by friends.

That was not their only problem. With spring rains and long grasses came the snakes. The cats were at risk because they attacked the snakes. Sunday was 'fluttering around the house thinking of snakes . . . and pussies and I know I could not take it again. We have made grass on the old rose garden so there will be no more snakes there.'[82]

Though Sunday did not breed Siamese professionally, she applied the same passion to cats as she did to everything else. There were trips to Sydney to find pedigreed felines and she imported choice specimens from England. She had two catteries built: one at the back of the house for the Siamese, who were not allowed into the garden, and one near the garage for the other cats. Maxine, a former matron at the Austin Hospital, often visited to discuss cats. In London, Alannah Coleman was dispatched to examine Sunday's selections from breeder Brian Stirling Webb. Coleman, a friend from the 1930s, had been at the Gallery School with Hester. A stylish and charming woman, she was doing her best to promote Australian art in London. She was also a cat lover.

At Stirling Webb's home, Coleman inspected 'your two little boys the older one is perfection and I can't see that he can fail to grow up to be a wonderful cat . . . Your other little puss is still such a tiny baby it was a little hard to tell . . . I thought (the older one) was Webb's best cat. His eyes were deep blue cornflowers . . . and with the most splendid paws . . . I think you will be pleased with them.'[83] When new heaters were placed in the house, Sunday covered them with blankets, making cosy beds for the cats. 'It was like a furlined room.'[84]

When Zindabad, a favourite cat, died, Sunday mourned that he had left her 'to join all my other little immortals'. Death seemed 'a terrible price to pay for comfort' and Sunday found 'the whole concept of illness, then death, quite unnatural and horrible. At first I am furiously angry and later defeated and overwhelmingly crushed – this "forever" thing is unbearable'. She 'tenderly planted' Zindabad in his 'eucalypt grave' and half expected him to 'grow in the spring – what joy to see his beloved face shooting up with the violets. I wonder why cats should not do this but they don't.'[85]

When Sunday dreamed she 'couldn't see an inch of my bedroom carpet, there were so many cats milling around, John said it was no dream'.[86] Among the twenty-four cats were Micetto, Midnight, Lavender, Squirrel, Snowdrop and Geoffrey. The latter was 'a huge grey tabby. He used to be like the Cheshire cat in a tree, he would land on people and sort of flatten them he was so big.' At times it seemed 'the whole house was a cattery'.[87] Often smelling of cat's piss, it could be an overwhelming experience for visitors.

Sunday's gardening ambitions were not diminished by time. In fact, her commitment to nature was growing more radical and profound. When Gray Smith cut down trees on his property, Sunday was distressed. She asked Smith and Hester to forgive her for 'involving you in my anguish about your trees . . . but under-standing does not stop me crying out against it and more and more as I grow older and the days seem shorter I suffer for my own part in all the muddle and you will find me in my garden, the tears falling while I turn under the earth all the growing things I love and name – the tiny blue speedwells and so many beloved little friends – just to exist in the chosen way.'[88]

Edna Walling's *The Australian Roadside*, published in 1952, alerted the Reeds to the importance of planting native trees and shrubs to help preserve and maintain the Australian environment. Up until then John felt 'very few people . . . had even thought of planting native trees and . . . I do not think there was a single nursery that grew them. Most people, including myself, took it for granted that native plants belonged only to the bush.' Walling privileged the aesthetic value of natives, like eucalypts, that bordered road-sides, and whose beauty was ignored by gardeners.

Sunday's growing guilt about her own 'part in all the muddle' was because the Heide garden had been planted with exotics. But, as John pointed out, 'it was not till well into the '50s that native plants became slowly available and Sunday and I realised that there were serious limitations to the artificial growing of plants which were not truly adapted . . . to the Australian landscape.'[89] One of the native's prime benefits is the small amount of water it needs compared to an exotic. However, Sunday was not averse to blaming John. She told Jean Langley, 'Oh, Jeannie, John brought all these ridiculous English trees into the garden and why did he do that? Why did John bring all these silly English trees in there?'[90]

By the early '60s, Sunday and John were planting natives. For Sunday, there was a deeper level. The planet was alive and inter-connected to her, each part was meant to be treasured and respected. Nature sought harmony – 'just to exist in the chosen way'. John and Sunday were energised by their beliefs, making them fervent conservationists.

But there was also the sorrow and anxiety, registered in Sunday's concerns about Gray Smith's trees, that the natural world was suffer-ing and she was not doing enough to remedy it. Sunday, as earth mother, identified with the wounded, fragile planet and took responsibility for its wellbeing. She made the Heide earth a place of protection and healing for her 'beloved little friends', that were not merely shrubs and flowers, but vital beings with whom she shared her life.

Now We've Got Our Gallery

I think you realise as well as we do how much can be achieved by being wholeheartedly behind a thing, by supporting it practically whenever possible and by supporting it psychologically at all times.

JOHN AND SUNDAY REED, GALLERY REPORT, CONTEMPORARY ART SOCIETY MINUTES, 1957[1]

IN 1956, THE CONTEMPORARY ART SOCIETY took the plunge and went professional as the Gallery of Contemporary Art. On the one hand, it was a bold move that would lead to the foundation of the Museum of Modern Art of Australia. On the other, it was the beginning of a grand and ill-fated scheme that would sap the Reeds financially and emotionally. Typically, they not only entered into the new plans with determination and commitment, but Sunday helped to engineer them.

The Reeds' confidence in the new venture was partly founded on their changed fortunes. In 1956, Henry Reed died and John inherited Wesley Dale, the vast sheep and cattle station near Deloraine, where the Reeds had summered when John was a child. John sold it and, for the first time since he had relinquished the law, his income flowed into Heide. Sunday no longer carried the entire financial burden. It meant they could dream even bigger dreams and squander Reed money with the same aplomb as they had squandered Baillieu money.

In June 1956, the Gallery of Contemporary Art was launched by H.V. Evatt, the Reeds' old friend and champion of modern art, at Tavistock Place, Melbourne. John and Sunday had offered to become honorary directors and it was an offer too good to refuse, even though there was disquiet within CAS ranks about the Reeds' growing power.

The year before John had withdrawn his nomination as CAS president, offended because 'the Society apparently wants a change'.[2] He was referring to criticism of him, some of it coming from young, outspoken painter Clifton Pugh. But when the ballot was cast, John was re-elected with a decisive margin. John told the CAS he would not stand for president again. He had grander plans.

Early in 1956, a disused bluestone building was found in Tavistock Place, off Flinders Street, for the rent of ten guineas a week. Erica McGilchrist remembered it was an 'old factory full of machinery with grease everywhere. Even the bluestone had been plastered'.[3] When Peter Burns visited the site with the Reeds, John enthused, 'Now we've got our gallery, Sun.'

For the long upstairs room, Burns devised plans to plaster the walls, paint the ceiling and polish the floors. It was Burns' first commercial job as an architect and his innovative sense of design enhanced Tavistock Place. Artists got together, painting and cleaning it up.

Differences of opinion soon arose between Sunday and Burns. As the renovations progressed, the Reeds invited Burns to lunch at the Florentino, a classy Italian restaurant in Bourke Street. Burns was suitably impressed. But 'slowly the reason for the lunch was revealed'. Sunday insisted Burns change his plan to break up the gallery space with perspex and wood partitions. Burns felt 'the interior looked barren. Sunday thought otherwise.' Later, when Sunday visited the site, she was furious that Burns had not made the changes. 'But we took you to the Florentino!' Sunday cried, before rushing downstairs. John went after her, assuring Burns, 'Don't worry.' Burns quietly persisted, and kept his partitions. But he did paint the gallery's ceiling midnight blue, at Sunday's suggestion, recognising it 'set off the white walls and the lighting beautifully'.[4]

The CAS had been remarkably successful in the scope and appeal of its large-scale shows. In 1954 the Royal Tour exhibition included major modernist statements from the Reeds' collection such as Atyeo's *Organised Line to Yellow*, Boyd's *Butterfly Man*, Nolan's *Stringybark Creek* and Tucker's *Vaudevillian*, contextualised by current works from Sime, Dickerson, Blackman, John Brack and Norma Redpath. It cleverly situated new CAS work within a tradition of Australian vanguard art, with the Reeds as bearers of the flame. Its annual exhibition in 1955, amid the mirrored background of Preston Motors, was a 'dazzling spectacle' and the 'most successful [show] ever organised' by the CAS.[5] There was even a celebrity opening, courtesy of Sir Ralph Richardson. The CAS blew its own trumpet and declared that it 'completely' dominated the scene.[6]

The Royal Tour exhibition indicates the Reeds' awareness of their role, and that of their collection, in the story of Australian modernism. Encouraged by Blackman, Reid and Georges Mora, the Reeds decided to take on the lease of Tavistock Place. They also underwrote the entire financial enterprise. (One thousand pounds was contributed to the Gallery Fund but it barely covered the renovations.)

But not all of the CAS council was thrilled. There were rumblings about the Reeds' motives and their increasing power. John was furious at the 'hostile and suspicious attitude of other members' which was 'distressing' both for Sunday and himself. He demanded acquiescence, and got it, Barrett Reid offering lavish thanks on behalf of a suitably chastened council. Even then John was not quite mollified and reminded the CAS of the 'magnitude of the undertaking for Sunday and himself and how it would mean a total re-orientation of the way they live'.[7]

From then on, Sunday attended CAS council meetings. At one rowdy meeting, just three months before the Gallery of Contemporary Art opened, John and Sunday suddenly withdrew their offer. They felt the CAS was not allowing them the freedom they needed to run the gallery their way. Once again, Barrett was the peacemaker, begging them to reconsider. Sunday had already told the CAS she had no intention of being a gallery manager: she was most definitely a director and she could not continue if she were expected 'merely to perform menial tasks associated with the gallery'. The CAS was 'a human thing' to her, she was involved with its 'spiritual significance' but the council was behaving like 'an employment bureau' and she 'refused to go in such an atmosphere'.[8]

It is interesting to view Sunday in a public role, at public meetings, for the first time. Previously, it was a task she had abhorred, preferring her private domain at Heide, and where her hearing problems could be better dealt with. She had a succession of hearing aids which never worked properly. Peter Hobb remembered Sunday throwing one into the fire in frustration.

But the chance to promote Australian art, and the artists she admired, made her accept the challenge and step from behind the scenes. By the '50s, the strengths of the Heide collection and the validity of Sunday's own taste, now being affirmed by a younger generation, gave her both a long view of Australian art and fresh courage in herself. She suppressed her nervy sensitivity and, in meetings, proved herself stubborn, strategic and forthright. She had a clear picture of the gallery's future and her role as director and was quite prepared to browbeat the opposition into accepting it. After all, she and John had learned their tactics in the school of hard knocks of the 1940s when Melbourne's art politics were played as a blood sport.

In the Gallery of Contemporary Art's first six months, Sunday and John devised a program that showed artists who were central to the CAS (Blackman, Ian and Dawn Sime, Erica McGilchrist), those who were currently associated with the Heide circle (Laurence Hope and Robert Dickerson), two big CAS exhibitions and, of course, Nolan's Kelly series. What was the point of having your own gallery if you couldn't show Nolan? It was a sound and clever program that answered competing needs: the CAS regarded it as their gallery and council members expected to show there, the abstractionists were determined to have equal space with the figurative painters while Sunday had her own agenda about selecting the best recent art. It was a 'very exciting and happy period' for her and the gallery was soon booked up for the next year.[9]

Sunday was now a curator: choosing the art, hanging the shows, proofreading catalogues, dealing with visitors, making phone calls and organising openings. Willing helpers like Barrett Reid, Philip Jones, Leslie Stack and Len Crawford relieved the Reeds on Wednesdays and Saturdays. It was hard work and Sunday revealed herself as quite the professional.

In December, 1956 Danila Vassilieff had an exhibition of water-colours. He and John hung the show but Sunday did not approve, so she decided to completely rehang it which meant they were in the gallery 'until nearly midnight'. Because of the reflections, 'all the glass and frame', Sunday's idea was to place 'two or three meshes out from the wall', breaking the works into groups and creating more visual interest. She was pleased with the result and with Vassilieff's new work which was 'so exciting'.[10] John was less impressed, confiding to Tucker that he found much of Vassilieff's recent work 'pretty ghastly'. Even Vassilieff's bold new sculptures, cut from Lilydale limestone, left John cold.[11]

By the end of 1957, the Reeds had to acknowledge the grim reality. The gallery was running 'at a steady but substantial loss' which the Reeds were carrying. Unfortunately, there was 'inade-quate public interest and an insufficient number of sales . . . we cannot hope to make the Gallery a paying concern'. Part of the problem, the Reeds admitted, was themselves. 'We are not salesmen and it is equally clear that sales are of vital importance.'[12] Partly the fault was with the Reeds: they were intractable idealists. They couldn't make money if their lives depended on it.

But the issue was larger than personalities. The art scene was changing rapidly and the modern art world was coming into being. It meant that the very energy the Gallery of Contemporary

Art tapped was emerging elsewhere. The boom in Australian art that would transform the lives of several of the Reeds' friends, including Boyd, Perceval, Tucker and Blackman, was about to happen.

In the same week the GCA opened, so did Australian Galleries with a successful show by John Perceval. Run by Tam and Anne Purves in Derby Street, Collingwood, it became one of the country's most prestigious commercial galleries, attracting major artists and helping some to make their fortunes. Alan McCulloch praised the Purves's objective of 'introducing the artists of Australia to the many potential buyers who never ordinarily visit a gallery'.[13]

McCulloch was not only Melbourne's most important critic, he was an artist and close friend of the Boyd family. As well as that, he was his own man, fearless about his opinions and independent of cliques and factions. When Perceval showed at Australian Galleries, McCulloch not only commended the art, he described the gallery as a 'public relations office to relate the world of art to that of big business'. It was fulfilling a 'very valuable function'.[14]

McCulloch had earned the Reeds' ire by sounding a warning about 'the atmosphere of introspection' in CAS shows and he listed Blackman, Hester and Hope as some of the chief offenders. By 1957, he was at war with the CAS (and, by extension, the Gallery of Contemporary Art), accusing it of 'inbreeding'. He went on to say that 'the figure isolated in space with perhaps disproportionate eyes and hands has now become the gimmick of CAS exhibitions'.[15] The Reeds were furious and wanted to ban McCulloch from the Gallery of Contemporary Art.

The Reeds were used to battles and relished a cultural stoush. But once they had hurled their projectiles from the safe bunker of Heide where they could retire and lick their wounds if things went badly. Now they were out in the open as gallery directors, part of

the art world and dealing with the public – including critics, collectors and artists – on a daily basis. In one sense, both Sunday and
John had the makings of fine directors – they were visionary, determined and committed – but their refusal to compromise, to woo
clients and negotiate with their enemies weakened their ability to
fulfil their dreams.

Despite the GCA's parlous financial situation, the Reeds decided
to take the next, enormous step. 'Already with Georges Mora, we
have talked endlessly of plans for the future – plans for the establishment of an Australian Museum of Modern Art.'[16] The ideal, of
course, was New York's Museum of Modern Art, sponsored by the
Rockefellers. But it was not only an ideal that prompted the step.
The Reeds and their friends were responding to change. The art
world's vitality meant Australian art had actually begun to sell and
new galleries were springing up in Melbourne and Sydney. Also,
the Gallery of Contemporary Art was effectively operating as a
museum: it made no profit and did not act as an agent for artists.
Finally, the Reed faction wanted to disentangle itself from what it
perceived to be the demands and the amateurism of the CAS, and
cease to be its showcase.

In June 1958, the Gallery of Contemporary Art re-opened as the
Museum of Modern Art of Australia (MoMAA).[17] Sunday gave a
substantial part of the Reeds' collection as the basis for a permanent
collection. This was topped up by the inaugural show, a gift exhibition where artists donated their works to the collection. The Reeds
did not make any spectacular claims for their collection, saying 'it
has never been suggested that [it is] in itself adequate for the require-
ments of a fully equipped' museum and it was 'quite obvious to all
concerned that it must be used as a nucleus'. Its 'great strength . . . lies
in its representation of the young Melbourne painters of the '40s'.[18]

Included were major works by members of the first, second and third Heide circles, plus recent paintings donated by John Brack, Roger Kemp and Clifton Pugh. The Reed collection offered an excellent survey of Melbourne painting through the prism of Sunday's taste but two years in the spotlight as a gallery director had been enough for her. She relinquished her directorial ambitions and went home to Heide. John became the sole director of MoMAA, an unpaid position as usual.[19]

But Sunday continued as an adviser and helper, not only assisting in the planning of shows but pitching in when necessary. At William Dobell's opening, she 'served hundreds of drinks almost from the inside of a cupboard' and then washed '500 glasses in two pink and blue plastic buckets . . . It is really hard work because as you know we just have no space at all and no facilities.'

The exhibition was a great success – 'just millions of people turned up from everywhere, people who have never been in the Museum before or even looked at a painting and believe it or not we took a thousand pounds on the door!' But it did not alter Sunday's attitude towards Dobell. 'I hate his work.' The only reason the crowds came was because 'the world is so corrupt'.[20]

Sydney art, and Sydney itself, offered Sunday a challenge she had never been able to meet. Cynthia Reed showed the prints of influential modernists Thea Proctor and Margaret Preston at Fred Ward's in 1932 but Sunday did not buy any. In 1947, Brisbane had sufficient charms to lure her into considering settling there and starting a bookshop. But Sydney did not offer the same sense of hospitality or potential. When Nolan decided to stay in Sydney at the end of 1947, John and Sunday were outraged. The Reeds ignored major work by Sydney artists such as Dobell, Russell Drysdale, Donald Friend and Jean Bellette and, until the 1960s, there were no Sydney painters in the Heide collection. Even then Sunday chose the cool abstracts of David Aspden and Syd Ball, not the sensuous celebrations of John Olsen or Brett Whiteley.

What did Dobell, and Sydney art, represent that Sunday so 'hated'? Dobell was not only a skilled portraitist but a notorious one. In 1944, when Dobell won the Archibald Prize for *Portrait of an Artist*, (1943, Private Collection) a portrait of his friend Joshua Smith, he became the subject of a nasty courtroom drama. Mary Edwards, a failed contender for the prize, moved that the NSW Supreme Court set aside the award on the grounds that the painting was not a portrait but a caricature. In the heated debate that followed, the Reeds, tellingly, did not publicly defend Dobell. The case against Dobell was dismissed but it exhausted him, and wounded him as an artist.

Dobell was no modernist. A superb, traditional draughtsman and craftsman, his influences number Titian and Rubens, not Cézanne and Picasso. He also earned his keep as a portraitist to the ruling class, not exactly a vocation Sunday respected. The decorative qualities of some postwar Sydney art, cruelly dubbed 'the Charm School' by Robert Hughes, may have been another reason Sunday resisted Sydney art.

A long-established rivalry between Melbourne and Sydney, based on differences of character, of space, light, topography and climate, resonated with her. Sunday was quintessentially Melbourne: formal, intense and serious. Art, as far as she was concerned, was no laughing matter and Sydney's hedonism did not seduce her. The issues were also personal. Sydney was a dangerous place. She had lost Nolan there, and Hester, for a time. Nadine Amadio was Sunday's only close friend in Sydney but Amadio lived outside the city, along the coast. For Sunday, connections needed to be personal to be significant: somehow Sydney had not included her or paid her sufficient due.

MoMAA was confronted with two major problems that it never solved: it was broke and homeless.[21] Sunday told Jean Langley 'we will all be so thankful when, and if ever, we move into a beautiful new building of our own ... John is almost off his head sometimes with all the various tensions' which left Sunday 'a bit wobbly'.[22]

From 1958, until MoMAA's demise in 1965, these tensions only grew worse. Kurt Geiger, who ran a successful chain of women's shoe stores, chaired the museum's board and invited other prominent businessmen, including racing driver Lex Davison, surgeon Alan Wynn, solicitor William Shmith and lawyer and academic Zelman Cowen, together with Barrett Reid and Georges Mora, onto the board. There was also a women's council, chaired by Elizabeth Summons, to organise fundraising social events.

But there were, unfortunately, no Rockefellers in Melbourne in 1958. Soon John realised 'the businessmen on the council knew nothing about art'. Worse still, they 'didn't understand the role we expected them to play'.[23] That role was to bankroll the museum, which they refused to do. Barrett also felt there was a reluctance regarding modern art because it was 'disruptive, revolutionary, not acceptable' and local businessmen 'weren't committed enough to an area that could become socially unpopular'.[24] John was disappointed to find that 'eighty percent of our time was spent in discussing money matters'. He also felt the financial side of MoMAA was conducted 'very unprofessionally. We had no money but incurred expenses and hoped for the best.'[25]

The museum also had a formidable foe. Eric Westbrook, director of the National Gallery of Victoria, was planning a splendid new cultural centre in St Kilda Road, with architect Roy Grounds. MoMAA went begging, asking to be included and given their own space within the complex. But Westbrook, reasonably enough, wanted to create his own arena for Australian art, and after twelve months, MoMAA's council had to admit the response from the NGV was 'clearly unsympathetic'.[26]

John was furious, both with Westbrook and with the state government who was pouring funds into the cultural centre and ignoring MoMAA. Secretly, John had Peter Burns draw up plans for the construction of the new MoMAA, to be built in the gardens directly opposite the NGV in St Kilda Road. Though the plans came to nothing, it reveals how badly John wanted to punch the NGV in the eye.

Despite the financial turmoil, MoMAA presented an adventurous and consistent program. Retrospectives of Boyd, Hester and Vassilieff were combined with sculpture, photography, architecture and design shows.[27] In the early '60s, the 'Young Minds', 'Survey' and 'New Generation' exhibitions fulfilled the museum's charter of showing youthful and experimental art. Fred Williams, Jan Senbergs, Robert Jacks, Paul Partos, Les Kossatz, George Baldessin, Ron Upton and Gareth Sansom were some of the artists included. On the advice of Elwyn Lynn, John showed the work of Mike Brown, Ross Crothall and Colin Lanceley, collectively known as the Annandale Imitation Realists. They plundered the styles of pop art, collage and assemblage to create a junk-filled environment that lampooned the vulgarity and materialism of contemporary society.

Sometimes the museum even made money, particularly with popular exhibitions like ceramics from Picasso's studio and Dobell's retrospective. In 1961, the treasurer could report that MoMAA was 'financially stable', even if it was only for a few months.[28]

John had help in running the museum. Philip Jones was assistant director. Ruth McNicoll managed a second gallery and ran her own program. McNicoll and John were at loggerheads almost immediately but the relationship with Jones proved more fruitful.[29]

Jones, Barrett Reid's partner, was a lively, good-looking young actor who had been living in London before returning to Australia to perform in radio dramas. He met Barrett in 1954 and the Reeds shortly afterwards. Jones 'didn't think Melbourne was a dull city and I'd lived in London. People like Barry Humphries have written ... how awful Melbourne was and how wonderful London was. I never thought that ... I was looking for a suitable culture to surround myself with and found Barrie [Reid] and Heide. I just felt at home.' When he first met the Reeds, he thought they were 'upper-class English, with that slight eccentricity of dress'.[30] Diplomatic and loyal, Jones became John's righthand man at the museum and a close friend for the rest of the Reeds' lives.

Georges Mora often called in to assist John, recalled Asher Bilu, who was also a regular visitor. John had a 'tiny office', just a 'desk and a chair and two or three Vassilieff sculptures on the floor'. Bilu was privy to the extent of the problems the museum was facing. 'It wasn't just paying the rent, it was the Melbourne establishment.'

Bilu had arrived from Tel Aviv in 1957. Though untrained as a painter, Bilu was confident. 'My heart was big. I knew I was going to be an artist.' Two years later, he showed cosmically inspired abstracts at Alan David Gallery in Dalgetty St, St Kilda. The Reeds arrived one afternoon with Georges Mora, introduced themselves and Sunday promptly bought *Abstract* (1957, Heide Museum of Modern Art) a white-toned, delicately handled gouache. David's gallery was a centre for abstract art showing Thomas Gleghorn, John Coburn, Dawn Sime and Erica McGilchrist.

John 'followed Sunday's instinct' and in 1961, offered Bilu the first of two shows at MoMAA. Spending time with John in his office, where he was regaled by John with stories about Nolan, Tucker and Vassilieff, Bilu felt 'John wasn't basically a visual man. He really didn't have the vision. The vision was Sunday's. She was his eyes. He was Mr Loyalty. He was as solid as a rock.'[31]

In 1962, John invited Pamela Warrender to chair the board. Tall, commanding and energetic, Warrender was a member of the Myer family. 'I knew nothing about the politics [of the art world] but I knew everybody.' Warrender set about trying to raise both the revenue and the status of the museum. It was a difficult task.

She soon found that John had a bad reputation in high society. 'Everywhere I went nobody liked him ... He was a communist.' Sunday came in for criticism, too. It was felt 'she was a bit of a ratbag for having left the nest and married this communist'. As far as the museum's aims went, in the wider world 'modern art didn't exist'. Warrender was mindful that Sunday and John 'worked together. There were no decisions made without Sunday.'

The elite of Melbourne had not forgotten John and Sunday's misdemeanours, or forgiven Sunday for abandoning and insulting them. They were certainly not going to finance her latest escapade. It was another cruel and subtle strand in the web of the museum's failure. As far as the establishment went, it was time for revenge on those renegade Reeds. Sunday, in particular, would have hardly missed the point.

Warrender and John decided on a bold plan: they would exhibit the Kellys in London. The international success of the show would convince local businessmen to rally around the museum. 'The idea was to get a lot of publicity to make the Australian corporate world wake up and realise the value of those paintings.'[32] Of course, there was a subtext for the Reeds. Perhaps this time Nolan would respond with the old warmth and he would return to the fold. The Reeds had not achieved their goal with the earlier Kelly exhibitions in Paris and Rome but perhaps, fourteen years on, they would.

There had been contact with Nolan but it proved painful and frustrating. In 1957, Bryan Robertson, director of London's Whitechapel Gallery, was organising a Nolan retrospective and wrote to Sunday asking that the Kellys, and many other Nolan paintings, be dispatched immediately. 'Nolan tells me that he left on loan with you the entire output of his work until 1948.'[33] The Kellys, he recognised, were Sunday's.

John wrote to Nolan explaining it was impossible to send the paintings so quickly. Furthermore, he reminded Nolan, 'you once wrote and said for Sun to take what she wanted, and though she has never "taken" anything it is impossible now to speak of "loans".' John ended his letter, 'I know it may be difficult because of some change in yourself to accept the fact that for Sun there is no change, and that your paintings are just the same in relation to herself as they ever were.'[34]

The Reeds sent none of their Nolans to the Whitechapel retrospective, but Nolan persisted. (In 1955, he had painted a second Kelly series for an exhibition at London's Redfern Gallery.) He entered into a correspondence with Sunday (via the British Council) that bore fruit the following year, and Sunday agreed to return two hundred and eighty paintings and drawings – but not the Kellys. They were destined for MoMAA's permanent collection. Anyway Sunday would never have relinquished them. On Nolan's cable, which gave Sunday the address to send his work, she wrote 'my beloved paintings returning to you. Sailed yesterday.'[35]

The process of packing up Nolan's works and sending them back was traumatic. Barrett recalled the amount of time involved and the 'high drama' because Sunday 'couldn't bear the thought' of renouncing the works. 'John would get me to talk to her because John could see that Nolan must have the paintings because they were his. The only thing stopping [it] was Sunday getting so upset and I remember John getting me to speak to Sunday to say, "Look, Sun, the paintings have to go back."'

The works were removed from the doll's house, where they had been stored, then carefully wrapped. 'Sunday, more than halfway through the exercise, became hysterical with grief. No-one could cope with her. Running into the rose bushes and God knows what she did. I had to grab her. John was hopeless and I had to just grab her and hold her and stop her damaging herself and torturing herself until she calmed down which was some hours. She couldn't have let those paintings go without such a scene because they were part of her, they were really part of her.'[36]

Prior to the 1964 London show, the Reeds asked Fred Williams to conserve the Kellys. The Reeds were keen admirers of Williams' art. An exhibition of his etchings, produced during a stay in London, were shown at the Gallery of Contemporary Art in 1957. The Reeds bought several: the best is the witty and rhythmic *The Boyfriend* (1956, Heide MoMA). Later they bought *Trees in a Landscape* (1963, Heide MoMA) an elegant, minimalist evocation of the Australian bush. But Williams retreated from a close involvement with the Reeds, feeling an artist could be 'absorbed' by Heide.[37]

Williams set about the work at Hawthorn Galleries, a framer's where he worked part-time. It was a touchy job, due not only to the delicate task of restoration, but because Sunday was anxious about her beloved Kellys. She didn't want them kept at a framer's. The Kellys were damaged, mainly from cat's urine, and Williams had to remove the acid. The Reeds tended to be casual about conservation. Broad shelves, built in the Heide I dining room in the '40s, meant paintings were piled one on top of the other – a bad storage method, as Tucker pointed out at the time, and that also lead to restoration problems. The Reeds were pleased with Williams' careful work but they were taking no more chances: after that, the Kellys were placed in a bank vault.

In June 1964, when Pamela Warrender set off for London to show the Kellys at the Qantas Gallery, she had some idea of the minefield she was entering. Nolan had insisted that neither John, Barrett nor Georges Mora should accompany the exhibition. To John's humiliation, 'this was done openly through Qantas'.[38] There was worse to come. Warrender received a message that 'Cynthia Nolan was ready to pirate the paintings that were hers. She was going to come in and take the paintings.' Warrender had security tightened around the exhibition, but Cynthia did not appear.

But Nolan's relations with Warrender were cordial and the two set off for Paris to view the Qantas Gallery there, where the Kellys were also shown. On the way to Paris, Nolan told Warrender, 'it was Sunday who had the green fingers. Sunday could spot an artist.'[39] That was not all Nolan told Warrender. He was very 'bitter' that the Reeds held some of his paintings.[40]

John responded by writing Nolan a long letter, a joint effort with Sunday, Barrett and Philip Jones. 'Your attitude approaches an implication that we have stolen your paintings.' John reminded Nolan of their life together with its 'pattern of complete mutuality and intimacy', where 'each made his own contribution . . . and your paintings were part of your contribution, even though you said Sunday painted them as much as you did.' In fact, had not Sunday's 'loving self-sacrificing heart' overruled John, 'you would not have got a single one of your paintings on the basis of the cold inhuman attitude you adopted.'

Despite that, John had to admit his feelings for Nolan were 'the same as ever, just as is my feeling for your painting.' He mused, 'perhaps you came into my life too late for me to be able to change: perhaps the experiences I have shared with you have been too deep to eradicate.' There was also John's 'profound consciousness of my own inadequacies and of the suffering, both Sunday's and yours, for which they were in part responsible.' Once again, John was the honourable knight, taking the blame because his 'inadequacies', his inability to let Sunday go, had acted as an obstruction to Sunday and Nolan's love. 'We want to live in peace with you – and Cynthia', he pleaded.[41] Nolan did not reply.

Warrender felt that the Kelly exhibition was not a roaring success. 'The English audience was there for the party, not the paintings.'[42] Nor did it have the desired effect on Melbourne's business community. There was no brake, however, on Nolan's growing reputation. In 1963, he had been made a commander of the British Empire for services to art in Britain and showed works based on a recent visit to Africa at Marlborough Fine Art, a top London gallery. His exhibitions and visits to Australia were regular, well-documented and well-received.

Warrender returned to Melbourne and found that her relations with John were increasingly strained. Both were frustrated by the museum's lack of progress: it had gained no major sponsorship, continued to operate at a loss and had no permanent home. Each found the other autocratic while communications between them seemed always on the verge of breakdown. Warrender decided that the museum should add 'design' to its name, to appeal to a wider audience. John was not pleased with the decision and felt he had not been consulted sufficiently. When the museum quit Tavistock Place and moved to the fourth floor of Ball and Welch's department store, it seemed to signal a new era of stability and prominence but, in fact, the museum was in its final phase.

The late 1950s were a watershed in Melbourne art. First, there was Charles Blackman's exhibition of his best paintings, the Alice in Wonderland series, and next there was the Antipodean show.

Not only had Blackman been instrumental in the revival of the CAS, he was a faithful member of its council, religiously attending meetings, which often occurred on a weekly basis, between 1953–59. When he showed the Alice paintings in February 1957, he chose the Gallery of Contemporary Art.

Blackman's life was hectic, yet artistically the pressures paid off. He worked as a cook at the Balzac, Georges Mora's restaurant in East Melbourne, cared for his family and painted intensively. Always there was the struggle for cash. Sunday worried about 'the constant strain [for Charles] of coping all alone with poor Barbara's sad blind eyes'.[43] If the Schoolgirls marked Blackman's maturity as an artist, then the Alice series is the highpoint of his career. It has the authority of original work.

During 1956, when Barbara was pregnant with their first child, she and Charles listened to a recorded reading of Lewis Carroll's *Alice's Adventures in Wonderland*. Soon Blackman was conjuring Alice's fantastic journey through an unpredictable and sometimes hostile underworld, where she proves herself wiser and more resilient than the array of perverse creatures she meets. 'I don't want to go among mad people,' Alice tells the Cheshire Cat. 'Oh, you can't help that,' said the Cat. 'We're all mad here.'[44]

Not only are the Alices arresting images, they are large paintings for the time. *Alice* (1956, Heide MoMA), also known as *Golden Alice*, measures 189 by 133 cm. Perhaps Blackman was encouraged to paint big by the arguments of abstractionists such as Ian Sime who insisted that modern painting must have an ambitious scale.

Tender, strong and moving, Blackman's *Alice* has the enchantment of a fairytale without any cloying charms. Originally, fairytales were not designed for children; part of a sophisticated oral folk tradition using ancient stories and archetypal symbols, their relevance depended on deep cultural and spiritual connections. As moral fables, they became, by the nineteenth century, educational material for children.

Blackman grasps the potency of myth, its truth and complexity. Alice's loss of innocence begins when she tumbles down the rabbit hole and into the underworld. It is a rite of passage reminiscent of Greek mythology where Persephone's abduction into the underworld by the god of hell symbolises a personal transformation from innocence to knowledge, implying the rude shocks that can take place in the transition between a carefree, childlike existence and the responsibilities of adulthood. In such circumstances, character is tested, strengths and weaknesses are revealed. Alice's trials on her journey of self-discovery may have been especially relevant for Blackman as he prepared to take on new duties as a father. There must have been anxieties about how he, and his near-blind wife, would cope with the tasks ahead.

Sunday's *Golden Alice* is the best of the series. At the Mad Hatter's Tea Party, Alice's big, untrusting blue eyes brim with fear and determination. In a world turned upside down, the tea party is nothing more than a banquet of bad behaviour by the Hatter, the Dormouse and the March Hare with Alice an increasingly bemused, and hungry, guest. Blackman shows Alice isolated at the end of the table, her tea cup flying away. A posy of flowers, symbol of purity and regeneration, is clasped to her breast. She is depicted as a child–woman, on the verge of change, and her pressed lips indicate the troubling nature of the voyage. *The Shoe* (c.1957, Heide MoMA), another choice of Sunday's, succinctly evokes the moment Alice is transformed into a giant after drinking a potion.

Alice is Melbourne's Child image par excellence. As an iconic figure, she does not tell a specifically Australian story like Ned Kelly: she belongs to a more diffuse realm of international literary symbolism. But, despite her girlish fragility, Alice has capacities Kelly does not. Alice triumphs, outwitting those who challenge her, returning to the real world whole, and wiser. Kelly is the quintessential anti-hero, his success lies in failure. Both Kelly and Alice undergo the 'hero journey' – they leave home and tackle obstacles that make them resilient and self-aware.

Alice is the honest fool who innocently wanders into peril, who endures and succeeds. Alice grows up. Kelly does not. Kelly's reckless journey, that ends in death, means he remains forever the young rebel, his short life frozen into a series of tragic gestures. But it is Kelly, tellingly, who piques the national imagination, who remains problematic and fecund, whose story we need to tell and retell. Kelly's very lack of resolution offers scope for the mythos of a country whose identity is also youthful and in the process of being charted and whose role, on the world stage, is determined by larger forces. Kelly is a tragic figure while Alice, for all her adventures, is the bearer of good tidings, the archetype of the happy ending.

Barbara Blackman played a key role in the series' inspiration. So, perhaps, did Sunday. Fair-haired and blue-eyed, Sunday looks similar to Alice with her distinctive, long, strong-jawed, serious face. Alice is shown with flowers, Sunday's special symbol, quoted by other artist friends like Dyring, Nolan and Hester in their portraits of her. The tea party could stand for 'arvo tea' at Heide. Perhaps Blackman had observed how Sunday, in the midst of company, could suddenly become sensitive to her surroundings, appearing withdrawn and watchful, like Alice.

Sunday and Blackman's friendship was based on a shared sensibility and literary interests. She was, at that time, his most consistent and generous patron. He relied on her judgement about his work and she was closely involved in its production. For example, the formula for the tempera underpainting in the Alice series was devised from a book given to Blackman by Sunday.[45] The Child was Sunday's special symbol, too, and childhood her sacred realm.

Blackman's *Alice in the Garden* (c.1951–52, Heide MoMA) is probably a portrait of Sunday in the Heide garden. Blackman did not know of Carroll's novel until 1956 but the work's incorrect title is felicitous because it identifies Sunday as Alice. If Sunday can be read as Alice, then it is fitting that such an iconic image is associated with a woman who did so much to inspire the interpreters of Australian culture.

In the late '50s, Blackman met another sensitive, inspiring woman. Nadine Amadio, a gifted photographer and writer from a family of musicians, became Sunday's close friend and, later, Blackman's chronicler and muse. Amadio was introduced to the Reeds by Barrett.

When Amadio arrived at Heide, 'I walked in the front door and there at the end of the hall was Charlie's *Golden Alice*. For me, for ever more, *Golden Alice* was the spirit of Heide.' Sunday was in the garden and she 'just seemed the epitome of everything growing in the garden: fragile, beautiful'. Amadio believed Sunday 'showed me a side of her that perhaps she hadn't shown other people, a slightly childish girly giggly [side]'. Amadio, thirty years younger than Sunday, experienced no age difference. 'I never thought of her as a mother.'

The Reeds introduced Amadio to Blackman and Perceval, among other artists, while she interested Sunday in modern composers like Bartok.

In 1958, Amadio published a children's book, *The Magic Shell*, comprising her photographs and text, which she dedicated to Sunday and to Jamie Murdoch. A young boy, wandering along a beach, meets a mysterious young girl. Dressed in a seaweed skirt, she is a spirit of the sea. They spend a day having adventures, then the girl disappears. When the boy finds a conch shell and holds it to his ear, it sings of the sea, an emblem of the girl. Amadio's book shares the Child theme that haunted Blackman's art and was so important to Sunday.

John and Sunday often visited Amadio in Sydney, sometimes together, sometimes separately. John regularly went to Sydney on MoMAA business, Sunday in pursuit of Siamese cats. Once Amadio photographed the Reeds gazing rapturously into one another's eyes. The photographs were meant to be fun, a light-hearted parody of romantic love, but the Reeds' profound affection for one another make them moving portraits of a marriage.

On another occasion the Reeds and Amadio met for an uncomfortable dinner at Robert Dickerson's. His wife had prepared the meal. Amadio recalled, 'Sunday said, "Oh, I couldn't eat that."' Amadio concurred. 'I couldn't eat it, either. John gritted his teeth and said, "Look, these people don't have much money and they've gone to a lot of trouble. You and Sun will sit there and eat it."' They did.[46]

The Antipodean Manifesto has been the subject of controversy since it appeared in August, 1959. Announcing itself as a report on the battle between figurative and abstract art, it dismayed the Melbourne art world. Abstract painters, the manifesto declared, with their 'bland and pretentious mysteries' were not producing an art 'for living men'. Instead, they 'reveal, to us, the death of the human spirit'. The image, on the other hand, was 'the recognizable shape, the meaningful symbol' and 'the basic unit' of the artist's language.[47]

The Antipodean group comprised Blackman, Boyd and Perceval, together with John Brack, David Boyd, Clifton Pugh, Robert Dickerson and historian Bernard Smith. No girls allowed. Informal meetings and discussions soon developed into the idea of an exhibition with a manifesto, a show of strength by Melbourne's vanguard of figurative painters against the perceived threat of a tidal wave of abstraction. It seemed that Ian Sime had done his work all too well in promoting the abstract cause.

The group's most controversial member was Smith. Was he a silver-tongued Svengali luring unsuspecting artists into his net? A power-broker cunningly orchestrating a cultural coup? At the time, Smith, a senior lecturer in art history at the University of Melbourne, was friendly with some of the best and most articulate painters in town. Brack, austere and intellectual, was engaged in satiric paintings of the human condition, and enjoyed crossing swords with Smith. Other artists in the group, particularly Pugh, Perceval, Blackman and David Boyd were hardly docile, or innocent. They were passionate and informed, and could be practically pugilistic when it came to defending their artistic beliefs. At the time, Smith was writing *Australian Painting* (1961), the first major scholarly account of Australian art.

Smith was an old adversary of the Reeds. How well they remembered his alliance with Noel Counihan and the Social Realists during the war. How bitterly they recollected the way he had excluded Nolan and criticised Tucker in *Place, Taste and Tradition*. To them, he was a Marxist ideologue who had returned, like a vampire from the '40s, to suck the blood from their intimate circle. In the Reeds' reaction to the episode, they epitomised the Melbourne art world's sense of personal affront.

As far as John was concerned, the whole idea of the Antipodean Manifesto was 'nonsense'. It was 'Bernard Smith's brainwave' and an 'extravagant and unnecessary' episode.[48] From today's vantage point, it is hard to see abstraction as a serious threat to Melbourne. Some local abstract painters, including Leonard French, Roger Kemp, Len Crawford, Don Laycock, the Simes and Erica McGilchrist, may have been vocal in defending their own interests but they did not receive anywhere near the amount of praise or attention as their figurative comrades, unlike Sydney where abstraction was triumphant.

Some artists chose to belong to neither camp. Mirka Mora explored both figuration and abstraction. *City* (1957, Heide MoMA) is a delicately constructed, rhythmically patterned work of interlocking streets and buildings, based on the urban environment which, living in the centre of town, Mirka knew so well. *The sky is full with stars* (1958, Heide MoMA), shows Mirka's future direction. Cleanly drawn, decorative and vibrantly coloured, a poetic and sentimental figure of a girl holds a flower to her breast. The Reeds did not quibble: they bought examples of both Mirka's styles.

Mirka took the manifesto personally. She was 'disgusted at the Antipodeans who betray all the painters of the world'. She felt 'nausea for their paintings, because the men who painted them are dishonest deep, deep in their heart'. It was all Smith's fault. 'Their Chairman' had lead them into a 'well organised farce', she wrote.[49]

The Antipodean Manifesto shares in the atmosphere of the Cold War with its sense of menace, of dangerous international alliances and the possibility of being suddenly overwhelmed by hostile forces.

As a modernist, Sunday was an internationalist and the manifesto must have seemed parochial to her. But there were other reasons the situation made the Reeds uneasy. Smith had created strong bonds with their circle. His influence indicates that the Reeds were not as central to the lives of those artists, or to the changing art world, as they had been. The artists had found a champion in Smith. No doubt the fact that he was writing a book on Australian painting gave him an added lustre.

But what was Sunday and John's real commitment to Boyd and Perceval during the 1950s? The Reeds had ceased buying their paintings in the mid-'40s, disapproving of the religious themes both artists explored. In the early '50s, Boyd and Perceval were involved in making ceramics, which the Reeds admired, buying Boyd's glazed ceramic tiles and one of Perceval's cheeky, endearing ceramic angels, as well as his commercial ware: goblets, plates and beakers. John regarded Boyd's 1954 ceramic sculpture exhibition as 'miraculous' and he was furious that it was ignored 'in the same way as the Kelly exhibition was'.[50]

But, as the '50s drew on, Boyd and Perceval made major strides as painters. Perceval's luscious, vivid studies of the Williamstown docks, with their tug boats and wheeling gulls, were his signature paintings and deservedly famous. None were acquired by the Reeds. Nor were any of Boyd's Bride series (1956–58) which examine racial and cultural tensions on a grand scale. It not only indicates a lack of engagement with Perceval and Boyd's art but reveals deeper issues to do with the Reeds' particular style of patronage.

By the late '50s, Boyd and Perceval had begun to achieve a modicum of success. Was that why Sunday was now loath to buy their work? If she was 'always in search of the newborn', did it mean that when her friends gained acceptance, her financial support was removed, her commitment discharged? Tellingly, Sunday continued to collect Hester and Vassilieff, two artists still struggling to gain acceptance.

The Antipodean exhibition marked the end of a highly productive decade in Melbourne and a diaspora, similar to the one that occurred in Melbourne in 1947, took place. In 1960, Blackman went abroad on a Helena Rubenstein Travelling Scholarship. Arthur Boyd and his family had left for London some months earlier and his brother David Boyd soon returned there. In 1962, Ian Sime departed for Darwin.

For Sunday, there were leave takings of a sadder, and more final, nature.

In March 1958, Vassilieff died of a heart attack in John's arms at Heide. He was fifty-nine. The wild Cossack who'd had such an impact on the Reeds as collectors and had inspired two generations of young Melbourne painters, had lead an increasingly isolated and restless existence. Separated from his wife Elizabeth, he taught art at various schools and travelled to the Murray and Darling Rivers for regular painting trips. He also produced an impressive body of sculpture, animated figures carved from Lilydale limestone. But, John told Tucker, Vassilieff had been 'pretty depressed, feeling that he was alone in Australia, ill, and with his work unappreciated, and he often talked of going back to Russia'.

That evening Vassilieff had arrived at Heide and, after having tea with the Reeds, had a rest on the library sofa while they completed some chores. 'An hour later,' John wrote to Tucker, 'he was dead, having had two coronary occlusions in rapid succession.' Gently, knowing Tucker's deep feelings for Vassilieff, John wrote, 'You were one of the people most often in his thoughts.'[51]

When Hester wrote an appreciation of Vassilieff for his 1959 memorial exhibition at MoMAA, she was dying. She described Vassilieff as 'a seer ... Painting to him was a life force ... His life and work were continuous explosions.'[52] After a long period of remission from Hodgkin's disease, Hester had fatally succumbed to the illness. From the mid-'50s, Sunday battled alongside Hester, supporting her in every possible way, including purchasing a home for her in Box Hill.

When Hester died in December 1960, Sunday wrote to Jean Langley:

I want to tell someone that I love that I have lost someone I love. Joy died last Sunday. For Joy I can't think of anything more dreadful and terrifying than her last week in hospital. It is easy to say her suffering has ended too but this does not comfort her. I saw her the night before sweating and dying and she said goodbye darl. In the last few years her struggle just to survive and be with her children and Gray almost completely isolated her from the world, a world in which I found she could no longer cope with other relationships or loving. But I did see her in a very ordinary way, not I suppose often, but fairly regularly, particularly the last bad year when she was in and out of hospital so often. We never really talked about anything anymore. We would look at each other and our eyes would reveal some kind of a certain knowledge – as if together we had made something and that it had been completed. I understood this. The deep river flows on locked in my life with Sweeney. I loved her very much.[53]

In 1963, the Reeds organised Hester's retrospective at the museum. For the first time, her work received good reviews.

· I3 ·

Heide II

There's a whole generation
With a new explanation.

Scott McKenzie, 'When you come to San Francisco'

Sunday celebrated her sixty-second birthday in a new environment. Heide II, down the hill from the old house, is a spectacular home-as-art gallery, the triumphant, final expression of Sunday's thirty-year commitment to modernism. David McGlashan was the architect, though John remarked the house was 'perenially inspired by Sunday'.[1]

On its completion, Sunday abandoned Heide I and everything in it – from the baby Bechstein to the rose-patterned wallpaper to Atyeo's angel on her bedroom door. Even the bulk of the library, the Reeds' pride and joy, was left behind. Sunday helped create a house that, by rights, should have been conceived when she moved to Heide in 1935, in the hey-days of modernism – a dazzling, stark, airy, white cube.

For an old radical like Sunday, the '60s was a dream come true. It was a decade that was determinedly youthful, optimistic, libertarian, communally oriented, internationalist and political. Not since the '20s and '30s had such a feast of hedonism been combined with a climate of leftwing idealism.

Sexual freedoms were explored within the radical context of the women's movement and the gay rights movement, challenging marriage, monogamy and heterosexuality. Opposition to the Vietnam War had galvanised the left internationally and a new generation took to the streets in mass protests. The civil rights movement in America gained momentum as the Australian land rights movement began. Many experimented with nature-based, anti-materialistic, communal lifestyles, as well as plenty of drugs. There was also a fascination with non-Western, third-world cultures, particularly India, influencing music, fashion, tourism and spiritual choices. Money was dirty, world peace was possible and youth was victorious. All you need is love, sang The Beatles. Love, Sunday's raison d'être, was the word of the decade.

Sunday's connection to the dynamism of the '60s transformed her surroundings and her taste. She was involved in architectural projects that included Heide II and a beach house. She favoured hard-edge abstract painting and sculpture, together with the bold colours and shapes of '60s design. She revelled in contemporary music from Stockhausen and John Cage to The Beatles and Ravi Shankar. She also threw herself into the massive task of creating a new kitchen garden alongside Heide II. A long-held wish was realised and she started her own bookshop.

When Sweeney, following in the family tradition, opened his first gallery and began a publishing company, he brought to Heide a new generation of painters, sculptors and poets. There were other young friends, too. Susie Brunton, a keen gardener, and Peter Hobb, an artist, pitched in and helped to run the property. Hobb became a fixture at Heide, the Reeds' friend and companion until their deaths. But not everyone was under thirty. Hal Porter was also a friend, dedicating *The Paper Chase* to Sunday who 'is younger than I'll ever be'.

In November 1960, Sunday announced excitedly to Jean Langley that 'the land at Aspendale . . . is now a reality and ours at last!' The Reeds had bought 'a small block but really on the beach'. It was next door to the Moras' beach house. 'At the moment [it] has a condemned house on it which we will pull down after the New Year and then build a light house or a rocket . . . Just to think I will walk out my door and into the sparkling sea. Oh boy oh boy.'[2]

The Reeds had been considering the idea of a beach house for some time. Sunday loved the sea and it had been years since she'd had regular summer holidays at Point Lonsdale or Merthon. After buying land at Balnarring, on Westernport Bay, the Reeds asked Peter Burns to design a house for them. But, on reflection, they decided Balnarring was too remote. They settled on Aspendale, an inexpensive bayside suburb, made attractive by the Moras' presence. By chance, 6 Gladstone Avenue, the block next door to the Moras, had come up for sale.

Burns had designed the Moras' house, too. On a narrow strip of land, it was a difficult project and Burns' solution was to 'build a house like a tube'.[3] The Reeds' block was double the size. Though

Burns completed three designs for the Reeds, they were not satisfied and cancelled his contract, though he did not allow his chagrin
to show. The Reeds then approached architect David McGlashan
who designed a simple, elegant, light-filled pavilion that gave the
appearance of 'resting gently on the dunes'. The living space faced
the beach and took full advantage of the view with floor-length
windows and a deck. Behind the living room was a courtyard, filled
with sand, and connecting bedrooms and bathrooms. As Eve
McGlashan recalled, the Reeds 'let David do what he wanted to
do' and they were very pleased with the result.⁴ It was the beginning of a splendid creative partnership between Sunday and
McGlashan that would see her commissioning three more projects
from him. Aspendale became the site of communal summer holidays
for the Reeds, the Moras, their families and friends.

Sunday enjoyed the new sensations of space and light in the
beach house, the clean lines, the whiteness, the large, open rooms,
so different to Heide I. By 1962, the Reeds were hatching plans for
a new home 'to be built under the big gum tree'.⁵ (In fact, the final
site for the house was further down the hill from the canoe tree.)
They were also thinking about Heide I's future. They asked trusted
friends, including Neil Douglas and his wife Abigail Heathcote, as
well as sculptor Ron Upton and his wife Libby, to consider living
at Heide I and taking care of the property. Though Douglas stayed
at Heide in the late '60s, neither he nor the Uptons were able to
commit themselves to Heide I.

To design the new house, the Reeds rehired McGlashan. An
early plan was to raze Heide I and build on that site. McGlashan,
concerned about the noise from an increasingly busy Templestowe
Road, designed a house with a series of courtyards. But Sunday came
up with a new idea.

Inspired by memories of the Mediterranean and antiquity, Sunday wanted a house 'that didn't look brand new', telling McGlashan, 'I want mystery, I want something that could be a ruin but was actually a house.' McGlashan was excited by the proposal. 'He certainly picked up and ran with that and understood exactly what she was saying,' Eve McGlashan recalled. Sunday 'pulled the building out of him. She was the very best client. She wouldn't take no for an answer.'⁶ John described Sunday's idea to a friend. 'You know, you see pictures of old ruins, and other pictures of some remote Greek village all white walls and flat roofs which you don't see and no visible doors or windows.' The house would be built of 'Mt Gambier limestone ... except in front, where there are big windows [and] you cannot see anything but walls.'⁷ It was meant to be 'a romantic building, ageless with a sense of mystery ... a gallery to be lived in'.⁸ Created by McGlashan as 'a work of art', it was always meant to be a gallery, the open nature of the construction lending itself to the possibility of extension.⁹ As Neil Clerehan remarked, 'John Reed did get his Museum of Modern Art — out of Melbourne and on his own terms.'¹⁰ It remains McGlashan's most impressive and best-known work.

Construction began in 1964, John's inheritance underwriting the expensive enterprise. The limestone had to be brought from South Australia, the interior floors and all the benchtops were travertine. The design's 'very simplicity — there are no internal doors, no woodwork except the ceiling and no paint anywhere, and everything is based on a 12 inch module' — created 'unprecedented problems'.¹¹

Heide II's construction began in the same year as the humiliating episode with Nolan's London exhibition and at a time when John's relations with Pamela Warrender were deteriorating. Galled by the lack of commitment on the part of corporate Melbourne, Warrender had suggested that the Reeds play Rockefeller and fund the museum themselves. John dismissed the idea, telling Warrender that he got 'impatient with the talk of Sunday's and my wealth. In fact we cannot afford to do what we are now doing and it is a continual financial worry to us.'[12]

The Reeds had been supporting the Gallery of Contemporary Art and the Museum of Modern Art for nearly a decade. Perhaps they were afraid of throwing good money after bad. In 1962, there was a moment of hope when Warrender approached lord mayor Maurice Nathan and asked him for land to build a new museum. After much discussion, Melbourne City Council agreed to offer part of Lincoln Square in Lygon Street, Carlton. Architect Guildford Bell drew up the plans and once again Warrender did the rounds of corporate Melbourne to ask for assistance. The only person who responded was Ken Myer of Myer department store. 'So we failed,' Warrender reflected.

In May 1965, John resigned as director. Warrender recalled, 'We had a godalmighty horrible board meeting and he resigned. He was fed up with Melbourne anyway. Tired and cynical. He said "Pamela does not have confidence in me." '[13] But John did not altogether cut his ties. He was prepared to be involved with the museum but not while Warrender was the chair. 'My participation at this stage introduces a disturbing element,' he wrote to her. 'As you know I have definite ideas about the Museum but it seems that it is best for me to maintain for the time being a relatively passive role,' adding, 'I will of course be available if there is any point you and Georges [Mora] wish to refer to me.'[14]

Shortly after John's resignation, the museum closed, though there followed a brief, valiant effort by a New Project Committee, including Warrender and Georges Mora, to revive it. John was deeply disappointed, and it marked the end of his professional life. The years of struggle had made him melancholic. 'My opinion of myself tends to get poorer and poorer,' he wrote to Peter Cowan, 'and my ego gets little to build on. If it was not for Sunday I think I would have disappeared long ago.'[15]

While John had been trying to stabilise MoMAA, Sunday was at Heide, overseeing the new development. 'It was her baby, it was her creation. She was much more involved than John.'[16] Heide II was a more realistic and promising project than MoMAA had ever been: hard on the heels of failure, the Reeds were establishing their own museum, built on their land, to their specifications, to represent their taste and house their collection. Not only was it an antidote to MoMAA's sad decline, and John's sense of defeat, but history would prove it was the most practical, forward-looking step. Their long cherished plan to create a park now incorporated an art gallery.

At the time, their friends, watching Heide II's painstakingly slow birth, were astonished. To Jean Langley it seemed 'absolutely amazing that they should start again. I couldn't believe it.' She was surprised at 'the modern shapes and the structure of the place ... at the big stark white walls which in those days looked extremely white as they were going up.'[17]

Sunday had not only abandoned the delicate, French, sentimental touches that had impressed visitors to Heide for thirty years but a cosy, contained, nineteenth-century interior. Heide I was like Balholmen, Sunday's Toorak home, writ small, with its antique furniture, fine china and clutter of treasured keepsakes. Its most modern element was the art on the walls. Sunday had always maintained a balance between the art she collected and the environment she created.

But McGlashan's beach house had offered Sunday a fresh experience of space, unconfined by conventionally sized rooms, one that allowed the natural world to flood the interior with light, colour and beauty. Nor was the beach house a private place: its interior was completely on display due to its large windows. McGlashan had sought to dissolve the barriers between inside and out with the transparency of glass. His inspiration was undoubtedly Mies van der Rohe's Farnsworth House, a radically minimalist glass and steel construction in the countryside near Chicago. 'We'll let the outside in,' Mies explained to his client Edith Farnsworth.[18]

After returning from the effulgent splendour of Aspendale, Heide I could have been a gloomy experience. With its huge north-facing windows, Heide II allowed the Reeds to incorporate the natural world they loved much more thoroughly into their lives: the living room offers a panoramic view of Heide park, a landscape that was changing due to the regular planting of native trees.

Art, too, was changing. The program at MoMAA had showed abstract artists like David Aspden, Syd Ball and Col Jordan who heralded the big, bright, sharp '60s look; works best featured against an expanse of white walls. Sunday was keen to collect the new art. But such works could look odd in Heide I. They needed room to breathe, generous spaces and high ceilings. In Heide II, conservative divisions between domesticity and aesthetics were dissolved, as McGlashan created for the Reeds a total environment that was dramatic, severe and beautiful, and where art and nature, the Reeds' twin passions and inspirations, dominated. In 1968, the house was awarded the Victorian Architecture Medal by the Royal Australian Institute of Architects.

There was one touch at Heide II reminiscent of Sunday's past. Merthon was built of pale sandstone, the colour intensifying the effect of sunlight and giving the house, and the entire township of Sorrento, a brilliant, summery appearance. Sunday had always favoured pale colours and Merthon was her cherished childhood retreat. But Sorrento limestone was no longer available, quarries on the Mornington Peninsula having closed. Mt Gambier limestone had advantages, other than its availability: it could be used both inside and out, plus it weathered quickly.

Neil Clerehan described Heide II as 'a shining paradigm of Victorian Modern. In plan it is Mondrian. In space it is antipodean John Johannsen [sic]. It is International Style set down amongst the melaleucas.'[19]

The house took three long years to complete and the Reeds had 'an absolute hell of a time getting it finished'.[20] R.Q. Evans, the builder, had to deal with complex plans and a difficult site halfway down a hill. A year after work had started, John wondered 'if it will ever be finished . . . Poor Evans has aged about ten years Sun says, and now all the men have been stricken with Hay Fever which has been particularly bad this year, and are all feeling miserable.'

It was a nervewracking period for all concerned. 'Sun panics every time she goes down to inspect the latest development,' John noted and while he had to admit 'David [McGlashan] is generally right . . . there is no doubt the house will owe much of its inspiration to Sunday.'[21] Sunday and McGlashan had 'terrible clashes'. Sunday insisted McGlashan modify some ideas, telling him, 'It's not a museum, it's a house and I have to have things on the walls.'[22]

McGlashan confided to Philip Jones that Sunday's decisions to change aspects of the design, and her need to control it, nearly gave him a nervous breakdown. Sunday insisted, for example, that the west wall be pulled down because the proportions were wrong. It had to be re-erected six feet further out. It was just one of the dramas that lead to an 'impressive number of rumours' about the house and its construction.[23]

John felt 'one very good thing is that it fits so perfectly into the hillside and adds to the whole quality of the landscape'.[24] Clerehan, too, commented on Heide II's 'self-effacement'. Yet, when it was first built, before the surrounding trees had grown and when the limestone was new and achingly bright, Heide II stuck out like a sore thumb. Neither 'romantic' nor 'ageless with a sense of mystery', it looked provocatively modern, harsh and geometric, commanding attention with sharp lines that rebut the soft, green, undulating landscape. It seemed a big, white bunker had appeared on the Heide earth.

The transition from Heide I was not easy and aspects of the new house proved challenging. In fact, John told Mary Boyd, moving was 'a terrible upheaval' and he felt it would be 'a long time before we settle'.[25] 'The sheer beauty' of Heide II would have to 'compensate for everything'.[26] Susie Brunton, who stayed regularly at Heide II, felt 'it worked beautifully. The whole space worked on a human level.'[27]

But there were problems. The furniture, for example, was purpose-built. Sunday had agreed to let McGlashan design all the furniture. As Clerehan pointed out 'there are no floor coverings, curtains or soft furnishings'.[28] Soon after they moved in, John told McGlashan that 'the actual living use of the furniture . . . has not been the success we had anticipated'. That was because the furniture was 'primarily "architectural": and looks right for the house, but in daily use it presents quite serious problems.' The white terrazzo tables looked 'very beautiful but are quite unrealisitically heavy'. Their surfaces were 'far too porous for something in continuous use, and, unavoidably, getting stains on it'. The living room chairs, with their thick wooden arms, were proving 'unwieldy' and did not offer 'domestic flexibility' while the beige ottomans were 'unfunctional'.[29]

Despite the discomforts, the Reeds made few modifications. Upstairs was a 'conversation pit', the cosiest nook in the house: a room where two couches, covered with untreated wool, were set against the walls and faced an enormous fireplace. The wool, from Tasmanian black sheep, was another idea of Sunday's. The carpet, also meant to be sat on, was covered with the same material. Dubbed the railway-carriage, it was the place where, Philip Jones recalled, 'we huddled every night. We retreated. We didn't use the expanse like old Heide.' It was also the TV room: the Reeds ate their dinner on their laps and Sunday never missed an episode of the police drama 'Homicide'.

But even the carriage was rather uncomfortable: the couches were set into the wall some distance from the fireplace and could not be moved, so Sunday insisted on having her favourite '50s butterfly chair near the fire. Above the larger couch were bookshelves, not head-rests. Luckily, the house was centrally heated so the Reeds did not have to rely on the fire for warmth. Anyway, there were no doors to contain heat. The fireplace was really for decoration.

Sunday 'missed a lot of her books. She missed a lot of the homeliness of Heide I. The carriage was a refuge in that way. The shelves were not neat and tidy. There were letters and photos and blocks of chocolate and little treasures.' For the Reeds 'life was outside. Night time was the carriage time.'[30]

Each week the marble floors had to be specially cleaned and the Reeds employed Ard ver Ness for that purpose. When the Reeds found they did not use their new dishwasher, preferring to do the dishes in the sink, they gave the dishwasher to him. Philip Jones considered Heide II 'a beautiful object that didn't work'.[31]

As a visitor to Heide II in the 1970s, my experience was of vast shiny white surfaces, and silence. It did not seem like a home, at least not one that I had ever been in. I felt I had entered an awe-inspiring gallery. I imagine the Reeds must have grown used to their guests' astonishment. The hallway ended in a sheer drop to the living room floor below. A wooden handrail was placed, not on the right where it could provide balance and protection, but flush against the wall. The first time there, I crept down the stairs in terror, expecting to trip and break my neck, wondering why two older people would subject themselves to such peril. (Sunday did once fall down the stairs but did not injure herself badly.) Entertaining children at Heide II must have been a nightmare.

Modernist architecture has shown considerable antagonism towards the home. Le Corbusier, arguably the twentieth century's most influential architect, railed against the 'sentimental hysteria' surrounding the 'cult of the house' and proclaimed his determination to create 'a machine for living in', a white, geometric cube.[32] As one writer has suggested, perhaps because most architects' careers begin with domestic commissions, modernist architects have been more vehement in their antipathy to the home than modernist painters – and more able to display that antipathy.[33]

Ornamentation came in for special scorn, Viennese architect Adolf Loos famously equating it with crime and degeneration, inappropriate to a forward-looking modernism. The clutter of daily life must be swept away, presumably by women, and surfaces kept immaculate. All that was decorative and sentimental, and therefore traditionally feminine, was banished from the modernist domestic interior.

Heide II bears the marks of such attitudes, for good and ill. It is a magnificent setting for art. As a home, it unequivocally states

modernism's ideal, which Sunday followed: no matter how difficult, the new formalism must be embraced. It was why she would
not get rid of the ottomans or the unwieldy chairs. They were part
of the challenge. Heide II was also Sunday's pet project. Perhaps she
refused to admit defeat.

Information about modernist architecture was available to
Sunday in the '30s. Her circle, including Sam Atyeo, Cynthia Reed
and Fred Ward, were espousing modern design. Ward and Atyeo
were aware of the Bauhaus and Atyeo himself could have designed
a stylish machine for living at Heide. Adrian Lawlor built his own
at Warrandyte in 1939. Why didn't Sunday create Heide II then?

It may have been a matter of economics. In 1933, the Reeds had
architects draw up plans for a new house but they had fallen
through. Subsequently, there had never been enough ready cash.
More pressingly, there were needy artists, publishing ventures and
art galleries to support. The Reeds kept their lifestyle simple, not
only from personal taste, but from good manners. Building a
mansion could alienate their poverty-stricken friends. When they
asked Peter Burns to design a beach house, they made it clear they
did not want anything grand.

But by the '60s, many of those same friends, including Boyd,
Tucker, Blackman and Perceval, were successful, buying their own
homes in Australia and in England. Sunday could give herself the
freedom to plan her dream house. Heide II indicates how grand
that dream was. She recognised that the language in which
modernism spoke was now irrevocably abstract and she was determined to live in a house built on those principles.

Heide II also has a grandeur in keeping with the great homes in
which John and Sunday had grown up. Their large, lush property
is viewed from the windows, exactly the type of vista the landed

gentry desired, and one that the Reeds had encountered from child-hood as their birthright. Though John and Sunday deliberately eschewed their past, Heide II gave them the opportunity to connect with their visionary, empire-building forebears to whom a commanding view implied ownership and power.

The new site had practical advantages. Heide I faced noisy Templestowe Road and the area itself was no longer a quaint neigh-bourhood full of orchards: it was part of the suburban sprawl. The Reeds did not require Robin Boyd's provocative treatise, *The Australian Ugliness* (1960), to alert them to the 'visual squalor' that resulted from unchecked urban development. 'New rules are needed now,' Boyd insisted.[34]

Heide II was built for the future, to take its place as a public gallery that would last for generations. Over time, as its walls have weathered and eucalypts and other surrounding natives have grown to full height, Heide II assumes a sympathetic and serene place in the landscape.

In the '60s, Sunday pursued popular culture with conviction. There were few aspects of the youth culture of the swinging '60s she did not explore. The exception was drugs. In that regard, the Reeds were old-fashioned and abstemious. Aside from a whisky in the evening and an occasional glass of wine, Sunday's only other vice was cigarettes – she had been smoking since the 1920s – but even then, it was an after-dinner luxury.

Sunday was excited by the 'new aesthetic, new surfaces and colours' of the '60s. Peter Hobb recalled that 'suddenly the house was full of brightly coloured plastic bowls from Finland ... That would not have worked in the old house ... At Christmas everyone was given brightly coloured T-shirts and skivvies. Red, yellow and green. There were also plastic buckets to carry out the chores, all bright reds and yellows. This was Sunday's doing.' Many of the objects came from Merlin Cunliffe's store, Thesaurus, in Glenferrie Road, Malvern. Cunliffe, who was also Sunday's cousin, imported bold Marimekko fabrics from Finland, together with a range of modern Scandinavian furniture and design.

On the walls at Heide, hung hard-edge, colour field paintings by Col Jordan, Syd Ball and David Aspden. Hobb reflected, 'I'm sure she saw [the buckets etc.,] as an extension of the flat areas of colour on the colour field paintings.'

Hobb, a young neighbour of Barrett Reid's and Philip Jones' from St Andrews, had arrived at Heide, already interested in art and a fan of Mike Brown's, when he was twelve. 'The first thing that Sunday did was very proudly take me into the library [at the old house] and hand me a copy of John Lennon's book.' *In His Own Write* (1964) was a collection of Lennon's witty, surreal drawings and prose. Sunday 'was mad on The Beatles. I think she suffered from Beatlemania.'[35] The Reeds attended The Beatles' Melbourne concert. They were probably the oldest people there. Despite 7000 fans 'screaming at the tops of their voices', John enjoyed it and found the group 'extraordinarily likeable, enthusiastic and witty'. They also flew to Sydney to see *Hair*, the defining musical of the '60s, and had 'the happiest possible evening'.[36]

Hobb became a regular visitor, spending the weekend and sleeping in the carriage. (There were no guest rooms at Heide II.) Sunday was concerned about his health and insisted on dosing him with fresh orange juice and nourishing food. When he was older, the Reeds paid for his tuition at the Gallery School.

Soon Hobb was accompanying Sunday to a variety of concerts

including Little Richard, Ravi Shankar, Ali Akbar Khan and Stockhausen. She also dispatched him to Discurio, Melbourne's best record store, to buy John Cage albums. Stockhausen composed electronic music, surrounding himself on stage with banks of equipment, while Cage created performances, often in collaboration with dance, where silence, random sound and noise expressed music's new possibilities.

But Sunday 'wasn't always serious when it came to music. She liked youthful energy.' Little Richard was 'very wild' and she 'loved every moment of seeing him jump all over the piano, playing with hands, elbows, boots and screaming high notes that happened to be in tune'. Sunday did not allow her hearing problems to impede. The sense of display, of performance was equally important. Hobb felt 'Stockhausen's sounds actually meant little to Sunday. It was the excitement at the thought of it.'[37]

Sunday's fashion sense did not undergo a change despite the op, pop and psychedelic taste of the '60s. She continued to don the same colours – white, cream and pastels – and style – straight-leg trousers, tailored shirts and loose jumpers. Seeing Sunday for the first time, dressed in white with silver hair, standing at the top of Heide II's terrifying stairs, she seemed to me a spectral presence, an emanation of that white, bright environment, a spirit of place. She remained slim and fit, as did John. A careful diet, natural vigour and not a small degree of vanity meant neither succumbed to the soft spread of middle-age.

The Heide II kitchen garden was underway. Peter Hobb helped but Sunday's chief assistant was Susie Brunton.

Sunday and Brunton's first team effort was a scheme to sell herbs from the Heide I garden. It was Sunday's idea to help Brunton raise money to buy a car. 'We could pot up herbs . . . and . . . have a nice barrel out the front [of Heide I]. Sunday said, "Now we have to have nice pots, we can't have just ordinary pots."' So she designed white plastic pots with mauve labels.

Brunton did the research while Sunday edited the mass of information and wrote out the labels. 'The stories of the herbs, their families, were important to her. She was incredibly knowledgeable.' For parsley (*Petroselinum sativum*), Sunday wrote, 'The seed is so slow to germinate it is said it goes seven times to the devil before it comes up.' For chives (*Allium schoenoprasum*), she advised 'finely chopped are delicious in salads and omelettes' while feverfew (*Chrysanthemum Parthenium*) was an 'old fashioned medicinal herb for curing fevers and melancholy'. For a time, Heide Herbs were sold from Thesaurus.

But establishing the new garden was Sunday and Brunton's major task. Transforming the cow paddock was 'a massive job'. Sunday planned to have the garden contained 'and the rest would be natives'. One problem was that it flooded every year. Sunday 'worked so hard it was just amazing. Every day after lunch we would be back in the garden until afternoon tea time.' Sunday would out-pace Brunton, forty years her junior. 'She would always say, go and sit down and have a lemonade and I would say, you go and sit down, and she would say, no, I will do some more.' It made Brunton feel 'so guilty'.

The area was rife with tiger snakes but Sunday would not allow them to be killed. 'They all had to be put in these big hessian bags and taken away and let loose. Big hessian bags full of snakes. John used to say, "They'll all come back, they're heading back for Heide."'[38]

Sunday did not create a modern garden – or an Australian one – to complement her ultra-modern home. There were no minimalist plantings, open spaces or natives: the effect was luxuriant, sentimental and European, the paths tumbling with roses and sweet-scented jasmine climbing over the gate. Once again, Sunday formed a dialogue between the modern (Heide II) and the traditional (the garden), between the European and the indigenous, creating a context for one by contrasting it with the other, as she had done in the '30s by placing contemporary Australian art in a Victorian home. The siting of the kitchen garden emphasises the point: Heide II's best view is gained from there.

'I love my kitchen garden so much,' Sunday told Langley. 'It is a pity one cannot have an aussie kitchen garden yet it is true that all these flowers and herbs are my closest friends! Have you any suggestions for making it prettier. Tell me what you do not like? I asked Neil [Douglas] this question and he said, just standing there on one of the little paths, "There are tears in my eyes. I'm crying."'[39]

Meant to be of a 'very personal nature, embracing specie and other old roses, herbs and allied plants together with all her vegetables', Sunday hoped it would be remembered 'just as a kitchen garden I made and not as a "herb" garden.'[40] Old roses included gallicas like *Officianalis*, *Duchesse de Montebello* and *Cardinal de Richelieu*, as well as beautiful bourbon roses such as *Madame Pierre Oger* and *Souvenir de la Malmaison* (the latter planted in the hawthorn hedge). Sunday also favoured some modern hybrids like the exquisite pink rose, *Constance Spry*, developed by David Austin in 1961.[41] Sunday made a list of herbs in the kitchen garden and saved the list by placing it in her copy of Gertrude Jekyll's *Home and Garden* (1900). It includes lavender, chives, oregano, thyme, garlic, tarragon, sage, catnip (for the cats to enjoy, no doubt) and chamomile. She also planted an abundance of flowers – marguerite daisies, sweet alice, belladonna lilies, violets, foxgloves, nasturtiums, columbines, marigolds and several varieties of pelargoniums and chrysanthemums – plus a healthy selection of vegetables. Sunday also included plants commonly regarded either as weeds (Patterson's curse and morning glory) or dangerous (opium poppy and hemlock).[42]

Peter Hobb had 'never seen anything like it before. It looked like something from a picture book. John was getting old saplings and putting them together in a tepee form and growing beans up them.'[43] John was 'very good at doing the hard slog stuff, turning the soil and getting rid of things, weeds and trees and whatever. But Sunday was going to create something out of it and it would just grow. Everything she touched would grow.' Hobb built two sturdy wooden benches in the garden's centre.

Sunday was not averse to culling plants wherever she could. 'We would pinch things out of the [Royal] Botanical Gardens,' Brunton recalled, 'and you would have "Botanical Gardens" written on it when you got home. We saw another wretched couple wandering around the herb garden and they were doing the same thing, we realised. So there was a lot of stuff at Heide from the Botanical Gardens.'[44] It took nearly a decade before the kitchen garden was 'fully developed and self-contained', with its own 'shingle roofed potting shed and a 4-foot high picket fence round it'.[45]

Sunday was strictly vegetarian but cooked meat for John and their guests, usually chicken, sometimes steak. It was no longer an eccentric choice: the '60s ecology movement espoused a reverential, holistic attitude towards the earth and vegetarianism was widely practised.

Lunch was always at 1 pm, usually 'a big bowl of salad ... with grated carrot, sultanas, lettuce and tomatoes and anything fresh from the garden with mayonnaise, lots of nice interesting breads and some cheese'.[46] The Hay diet forbade cheese and bread together but Peter Hobb made Sunday reconsider. 'I was outside working pretty hard on the garden and I was hungry.'[47] Dinner was often 'brown rice and vegies', followed by yoghurt with stewed fruit – 'and chocolate. John loved his chocolate.'[48] But the food was not dull. Asher Bilu was in awe of Sunday's culinary skillls. She was 'amazing ... the way she cooked, the way she used herbs – zucchini and vegetables and herbs – it was another realm.'[49]

During the upheaval of the move, the cats 'lived where they wanted to. Some moved down the hill with Sun and John and some preferred to stay where they were. Every night at cat-feeding time, Sunday would prepare all the cat food down at new Heide and then walk up the hill with bowls of cat food.'[50] A new cattery had been built in one of the Heide II courtyards.

Each week Sunday cooked half a dozen rabbits for the cats. It was done 'in a big enamel pot, you would have all this rabbit everywhere. So feeding time was quite mad ... It was bedlam.'[51] Not content with twenty-four cats, the Reeds also acquired an English sheepdog called Go-Go and Pumpkin, known as Pumpie, a crossbreed. There were two cows, steers not milking cows, named Cappuccino and Espresso, whom Sunday had saved from being destroyed and who kept the grass down. The Reeds also had chickens.

Sunday's black and white cat, Cigale, nearly crippled her. He 'dive-bombed my legs when both of us were running in opposite directions and I tripped with my arms full of saucepans, and fell bang on my knee. It was an awful agony and my knee dangled like a puppet and I had to be taken off in an ambulance for an x-ray. I have never been in one before.' Sunday's left knee was broken in two places and the surgeon, Dr John Starr, announced an operation to remove the knee cap. But Sunday resisted.

'I said I would like to see if my knee would heal naturally . . . I would not budge . . . In two or three days my knee started to respond like a house on fire and John Starr beamed at me and said he was sure it would get completely well without anymore trouble and he added, I'm astonished. I wish there were more like you!' Sunday adding, 'Oh what a victory!'[52]

But the inactivity chafed and a week later Sunday told Langley, 'Now that spring is here in the garden there is so much to do and it makes me angry that I can't yet wheel the barrow up the hill and still find it difficult to run.'[53] Sunday's speedy recovery boosted her belief in natural healing and her own resilience. If she got a cold 'all hell would break loose because she would say, I never get sick. Bloody cold, I haven't had a cold in years, and she would say that every year. Filthy cold, filthy things.'[54]

Barrett Reid and Philip Jones were dividing their time between Heide I, which they were looking after, and their own home at St Andrews, which had been bought for them by the Reeds. Jones had new duties. In 1966, Sunday came into an unexpected dividend from her investments, worth ten thousand dollars. She immediately knew how to put it to use. She summoned Jones to Heide for dinner, pointedly without Barrett, and announced she wanted to start a bookshop with Jones as manager.

Since the 1940s, Sunday had longed to have her own bookshop. Jones was delighted. He had a less than satisfying job as a sales representative for Longman, the educational publisher, for whom he had also worked in England. The plan was to stock avant-garde poetry, fiction and art books. 'Australian publishing was starting to go ahead,' Jones remembered, 'and we wanted to be predominantly Australian.'

Jones found a small shop for lease at 181 Exhibition Street, with a storeroom and an upstairs flat, and Sweeney named it Eastend. With her usual enthusiasm, Sunday decided the shop must be completely renovated and employed McGlashan to do it in '60s style. He created a red plastic floor, painted the walls white, built blond timber shelves and erected a big plate glass window. The flat was renovated so Jones could stay there. Yevgeny Yevtushenko, the celebrated Russian poet then touring Australia, opened the shop in April 1966.

But Sunday had spent most of the money on the renovations, so there was little cash to run the shop. Jones was unable to fund it and struggled to make a living. Sunday also became dispirited when visiting warehouses with Jones to select books for the shop. 'We would finish up with only half a dozen titles. Sunday would get furious because she expected a cornucopia of delight. "Where are the American books?" she would ask.'

Nor did Sunday want Barrett connected with Eastend. Reid had managed the Ballad Bookshop in Brisbane, knew the pitfalls involved and had advised the Reeds against starting a bookshop back then. Naturally Jones turned to his partner, now a senior librarian at the State Library of Victoria and responsible for establishing libraries throughout the state. 'Sunday was difficult. She was always finding fault and complaining. She wanted it to be hers, not involve Barrie.'

Jones felt himself caught between two stools. The very avant-garde identity of the shop meant certain titles did not sell. 'Nobody bought the art books.'[55] Or the Australian range. Jones employed

Suzie Baldwin as an assistant. Sweeney also worked there for a time. Sunday terminated her connection, leading to a period of estrangement between her, Jones and Barrett. Sunday complained to Langley, 'It looks as if my bookshop has come to an end as far as I'm concerned and I am full of tears and disappointment.'[56]

In 1965, Sweeney returned from London where he was working at the Institute of Contemporary Art. He had also made contact with poets as well as with old friends in the Australian art community, including the Boyds and Percevals. London had transformed Sweeney who 'left a rocker thug and came back a cultivated young man'.[57] In January 1966, he opened Strines Gallery – funded by the Reeds and designed by McGlashan. Peregrine Smith recalled the gallery 'had a lot of style, it was much more advanced in style than other galleries. It was a monument to white, it was bathed in light. Sweeney was very excited about it.'[58]

At twenty-one, Sweeney was ambitious, confident and impeccably hip. The unhappy, chaotic years of his adolescence seemed behind him as he assumed a prominent role in the Melbourne art world and surrounded himself with a group of young artists and poets. It must have been a heartening moment for the Reeds, so close to MoMAA's failure, to see Sweeney carry forward their aspirations and emerge as a gallery director. Until it closed in August 1969, Strines' stable included Mike Brown, Syd Ball, Trevor Vickers, Col Jordan, Les Kossatz and John Kryzywokulski. Nor did Sweeney ignore the Heide heroes – he had exhibitions of Hester, Vassilieff and Nolan.

As well as Strines, Sweeney had started a poetry press called Still Earth that, in its short life, published Russell Deeble, Shelton Lea, Michael Dugan and Bruce Dawe. Sweeney also wrote, and published, his own poetry.

Ron Upton opened Strines with a notorious exhibition. The vice squad arrived and, on the basis of one drawing, charged Sweeney and Upton with obscenity. The case was dismissed and, though it provided unequalled publicity for the gallery, it was an anxious time. Support was rallied by the Reeds and an impressive list of witnesses, including Joseph Burke, Herald professor of fine arts at the University of Melbourne, agreed to be called for Sweeney and Upton's defence.

Upton already knew Sunday and John: they had bought *Three forms* (1964, Heide Museum of Modern Art) a large, ciment fondu sculpture from his first solo show at the Argus Gallery. Upton had to return to Heide several times to repair the work. Not only did cows from a neighbouring property break in and cause damage while Heide II was under construction, they also used the sculpture as a rubbing post.

Sunday felt relaxed with Upton, arriving unannounced at his home to select works on paper for the Heide collection. Upton made etchings and monoprints, as well as sculpture, all employing the same organic forms. One evening after dinner, Sunday showed Upton and his wife a 'very special box in which she kept all those small things that were dear to her heart' including 'a number of very small Nolan paintings on canvases prepared by her'.

When the Uptons were building their home at Yarrambat, the Reeds were ready to help, appearing 'on a day [when] they knew we were going to fit the guttering . . . they were not too proud to act as labourers and comply with my instructions.'[59]

Despite having the grounds around Heide II to place sculpture, Sunday collected few works and seemed blinkered in regard to three-dimensional art. During the 1950s, there had been a surge in Melbourne sculpture, courtesy of Clifford Last, Julius Kane, Inge

King, Vincas Jomantas, Lenton Parr and Norma Redpath. In that period, Sunday only bought Vassilieff.

Once committed to an artist, however, she was prepared to follow his or her direction. Les Kossatz, introduced to John and Sunday by Barrett, made the transition from printmaking to three-dimensional figurative work in the mid-'60s. *Love kite* (1967, Heide MoMA), a brilliantly colourful work partway between painting and sculpture, decorated the Heide II living room.

Kossatz found Sunday 'much easier to communicate with than John. John was fairly aloof.'[60] Upton, too, felt, 'I had a closer spiritual "tie" with Sun than I had with John.'[61] Though Sunday 'never cast an opinion as such', Kossatz was 'impressed by her encouragement. She didn't make a stand as a tastemaker. There was no form of judgement' but 'there would be enthusiasm in her encouragement. She was open-minded.' Soon Kossatz was adopted into the Heide family. The Reeds 'wanted a relationship with an artist, they wanted your company'.

But Heide was not Kossatz's only artistic milieu. He was also involved with a group that included Fred Williams, Roger Kemp, Jan Senbergs, George Baldessin and Leonard French. It was 'another camp' that 'never became part of Heide'. French had loathed the Reeds in the CAS days while Williams had decided to distance himself. Kossatz introduced the Reeds to Baldessin, a prodigiously gifted young printmaker and sculptor, who in 1966 dedicated an etching to Sunday. It was a contact, however, that did not flower. When John approached Baldessin, asking if he could include Baldessin in an article he was writing, the artist refused. Though the Reeds were still seen as 'the people to have on side', for some younger artists their patronage was not considered necessary.[62]

Even if they were impressed by Heide and 'all the beautiful

things, the paintings everywhere', some of the younger generation did not readily connect with Sweeney's parents who could seem 'ethereal, a bit strange. [They] never quite looked you in the eye, especially Sunday.'[63] Heide 'wasn't the centre of anything'. Asher Bilu thought Sunday was 'very delicate, very quiet, very soft, very tender and benign'. She wore 'soft pale wonderful jumpers' and 'because of the lack of hearing, she had to draw you closer to her . . . there was a magnetism because of this closeness and you had to touch her.' She seemed 'something of an enigma, Garboesque'.[64]

Such comments indicate the remove between Sunday and the contemporary art scene she admired. She may have followed its developments and installed its examples on her walls but she was no longer an influential figure, no longer the patron vigorously creating her circle. In fact, there was no circle.

Charles Blackman was living in Sydney and had little contact with the Reeds. In 1967, John Perceval and Mary Boyd had separated. From London, where Mary was living with her children, she wrote 'my very dear Sun' a torrent of letters, detailing her feelings. Sunday had sustained Mary through her life's 'most terrible and traumatic times . . . You alone have let me lean on you completely.'[65] Once, Mary arrived from England and walked into the Reeds' bedroom in the middle of the night, surprising them. While Sunday had great affection for Mary, she also felt 'Mary is not able to understand anyone else's tiredness. I do not say this unkindly but I feel when I am exhausted she is disappointed in me.'[66]

Sometimes Perceval, who was also miserable about the break, stayed at Heide consuming a bottle of whisky a day. 'He answered questions – just a word or two no more,' Sunday told Langley, 'but he could not make any real contact with us . . . I cannot describe his appearance, particularly his face or what was once his face, it upsets me too much today to think of him but nevertheless I cannot stop myself from thinking.'[67]

Tucker was living at nearby Hurstbridge but did not visit Heide: he brooded over Sweeney's adoption and was ready to denounce Sunday, and Hester, to anyone who cared to listen. He believed the women had conspired against him. Langley and John Sinclair were still visitors – but separately as they, too, had parted for a time. The Moras had also separated and rarely visited. It could make Heide 'very, very quiet'.[68]

Hal Porter was one of the few older friends Sunday made during that period. Introduced by Barrett, he met Sunday at Aspendale and immediately struck up a friendship. In 1963, Porter had published *Watcher on the Cast Iron Balcony*, the first volume of his autobiography, to acclaim. The second volume, *The Paper Chase* (1967), he dedicated to Sunday.

Porter had studied at the Gallery School in the 1930s and, in 1937, exhibited alongside Tucker and several students of George Bell's at the Athenaeum Gallery. As a denizen of Melbourne's cafés, galleries, dives and student parties, Porter was intimately acquainted with bohemia, which he documented in *The Paper Chase*. He was a difficult man, a flamboyant homosexual, given to alcoholic excess, rightwing views and vituperative wit, who lived in the remote country town of Bairnsdale, where he had grown up.

Porter was impressed with the Heide garden. As Mary Lord, his biographer, writes, 'almost at once Hal and Sunday were exchanging plants and cuttings', including red gallica roses and violets.[69] When they met at Aspendale, Porter told Sunday, 'I knew I had met someone not only special to me but also special to the world – special to flowers & herbs & houses & cats, special even to dying leaves & brazen weeds.'[70]

Soon Porter was arriving unannounced at Heide, extremely drunk, with friends, or even a bemused taxi driver, in tow. Later, he would apologise profusely, distressed that Sunday thought he was 'evil'.[71] Porter dedicated *The Paper Chase* to Sunday, not only because 'my heart orders it so', but because he wanted to atone for his bad behaviour.[72] He had intended to write a novella for Sunday but chose his memoir instead.

Sunday, watching Perceval's marriage collapse from the weight of his alcoholism, was concerned about Porter's fate, too. 'I never use the word "evil". I never do,' she wrote. 'I must have said finally, when we were leaning over the little rose hedge, Oh Hal, you are wicked, which is different and only meant that I was worrying about you drinking too much whisky.'[73]

There were also a string of cancelled dinner arrangements. Philip Jones would be sent to collect Porter from his city hotel and bring him to Heide, only to find he was roaring drunk and committed to a previous engagement. It placed strains on Sunday's affections for Porter, as it did with most of his friends.

Sunday was impressed by another writer at this time. When she read Russell Deeble's first volume of poetry, *War Babies*, she invited him to Eastend. Deeble met Sweeney there and the two young men, both theatrical, enterprising and irreverent, became friends immediately. Sweeney published and promoted Deeble's poetry while Deeble assisted Sweeney in organising literary events at Strines. Invited to Heide, Deeble, an eighteen-year-old cadet journalist from Dandenong, felt he had 'stepped into a Scott Fitzgerald novel'. Sunday offered him the patronage to write full-time. But, Deeble felt, there was a price to be paid.

'They made sure I was as unmarried as possible. Sweeney was the agent of the poison and Sunday was the maker of the potion.

They told my wife I was having affairs. Being silly and determined to get ahead in the arts, I turned a blind eye to it. It caused a tremendous amount of upheaval and subsequently Wendy and I separated.'74 But Deeble remained a close friend of Sweeney's and, after he returned from India, the Reeds offered him the use of Aspendale. Sunday continued to assist him financially during that time.

After being approached by Geoffrey Dutton at Sun Books, John commenced writing his memoirs. Both flattered and daunted by the task, John told his brother Dick that Dutton, a poet and writer who had published in *Angry Penguins*, suggested he should write about 'my life in the art world, so I am giving it a try . . . I will perhaps call it "Artobiography".' Though John did not write 'at all easily' and wondered whether it would be 'worth publishing anyway' he was 'quite enjoying' himself.75 But within months, the project had stalled. Writing about the 1940s proved especially difficult and John began using a tape-recorder to overcome his block.

Sunday did not help matters. She and John 'both had different opinions about things and Sunday kept saying, "You can't say that because so-and-so is still alive." There was a lot [he] couldn't say because people were still alive and it was controversial of course.' The arguments went 'backwards and forwards through the house . . . Finally John said it was impossible, he couldn't do it with Sunday putting her tongue's work in.'76

John did produce a short, handwritten manuscript but it was not long enough, nor did John believe it merited publication.77

Excerpting his youth, John began his narrative in 1926 when

he met Clarice Zander who 'lead me to art'. He tried to do exactly as Dutton asked: emphasise his contact with the art world and modernism. The manuscript ends with an account of MoMAA and John's impressions of the contemporary art world.

Though John found writing about the war years a challenge, it is by far the most engaging section. John's sober, factual style changes to a moving account of its personalities – Nolan, Perceval, Boyd and Tucker come alive through anecdote and impression while their work is assessed with admiration and perception. The mood is nostalgic. Unsurprisingly, Nolan is captured with evocative tenderness. Until the early 1970s Dutton persisted in trying to extract a manuscript from John, all to no avail. John later admitted to Dick, 'I find I can write a good short article if pushed but I do not seem to have the ability to sustain or develop a theme over any substantial length, as became apparent when I tried to write my "Artobiography".'[78]

When the new National Gallery of Victoria opened in 1968, the Reeds were quick with reproach. 'How ugly and unsympathetic the National Gallery is,' Sunday commented to Langley. 'Do we ever relax there?' But she gained 'great pleasure' from seeing Jack Manton's collection of the Heidelberg School. The paintings 'always move me and make me feel at home'. Not that all the works were of a high standard but she was 'easily endeared to unimportant little streams and I think "mistakes" and "failures" if you can use those words teach me and inform, and because of this become my friends. In this way I experience more fully and learn more about my own kind of seeing and loving.'[79]

Sunday may have identified with grazier Jack Manton. He commenced collecting with a passion in 1961, after falling in love with the Heidelberg School, and built a varied collection that included gems such as Charles Conder's *Coogee* (1888) and Julian Ashton's *The Milkmaid* (1888). The collection was exhibited at the National Gallery of Victoria in 1973, where Sunday saw it, and acquired by the state government in 1978. One of Manton's early acquisitions was Fred McCubbin's *Winter's Morning* (1914), a painting similar to Sunday's McCubbin, *The Rabbit Burrow* (c.1910, Private Collection), bought by her parents. In *Winter's Morning*, as Patrick McCaughey notes, 'McCubbin offers a striking alternative of the bush as a wild garden in whose enclosure the children play with security.'[80]

When John rebuked the NGV, he chose a public forum. He told a journalist from the *Herald* that aesthetically, the Cultural Centre was 'not a happy choice'.[81] Elsewhere, John would refer to the NGV as 'an architectural abortion', telling Alannah Coleman, 'if you tried for a lifetime you could not think of a worse way to give paintings a chance to be seen for what they really are. This applies particularly to the modern ones.'[82]

Furthermore, John told the *Herald*, the NGV collection was 'a lot of junk. Their buying, by and large, has been pretty deplorable, particularly in the contemporary field. Very often the wrong artist, or else the wrong work of the right artist has been bought. It needs a highly specialised person to recognise and buy the right thing.' John was, of course, attacking Westbrook, along with Brian Finemore, who had been curator of Australian art since 1959, both of whom he loathed.

The Reeds' views were not uncommon. There was strenuous public criticism of Grounds' austere, grey, vault-like building and also of its brown, wooden, interior walls, so unflattering to the display of art. John was also concerned that the NGV's acquisitions policy had serious flaws: major wartime works by the Heide circle, the core collection of MoMAA, had not been purchased nor were the 'right' works by artists from Sweeney's gallery being considered. The NGV's ascendance also cruelly reminded John of MoMAA's collapse. He blamed Melbourne. 'It was this gutless community that wouldn't support the Museum of Modern Art,' he declared.

Sunday no longer enjoyed consistent and direct contact with artists but John saw it differently. 'Sunday gets little or no recognition . . . She probably has the most sensibility of anyone in the community, an immediate understanding of the creative process when she sees it.'[83] Increasingly isolated from the contemporary art world, and ignored by the powerful new cultural groups represented by the NGV, John felt resentful and excluded – both for himself and Sunday.

From letters written to Langley during the '60s, Sunday seemed better able to handle the reversals of time and history than John. Her tone, despite registering sadness at loss and change, remains buoyant and optimistic. She makes plans for a new garden, a beach house, a trip to discover wild flowers.

The seasons were a fully lived and refreshing experience. She loved 'the winters at Heide and looking through the bare trees almost to the river where it is all so dreamy and pale blue in the mist . . . the garden [is] full of wet sweet jonquils and winter cherry and in the veg garden there are fine winter salads – lambs' lettuce, rocket and endive.' There was the fun of a new cat to go 'walkies' with in the wild garden. 'We throw the little cumquats down the path and chase them to keep warm.' The 'days fly past and there is just so much to do I can't keep up in my old age'.[84]

A true modernist, Sunday focused on a future where her plans would be realised. 'I'm not very good at looking back because I find my relationships are always very present and in the future and I look at paintings that way.'[85] She also believed in the saving grace of forgiveness, 'the measurement of love and understanding that so greatly outweighs all else'.[86] No wonder John felt that without her he would have 'disappeared long ago'. Les Kossatz observed the Reeds were 'a very loving couple, they were one person. But Sunday was the life of the relationship.'[87]

In 1969, Sweeney married Pamela James. It was the second marriage for both. At eighteen, Sweeney had made an unhappy marriage to Gail, a local girl, and they'd had a daughter, Cherie. The Reeds were anxious about Sweeney's prospects with Pamela, too.[88]

Sweeney did not feel at home in Heide II, or in the special self-contained flat designed for him. He and Pamela moved into Heide I, which Sweeney loved. 'He has very deep feelings for it,' John observed, 'in spite of the fact that in most ways he is such a modern sort of boy, and is obviously happy to be back there again.'[89] Sweeney set about making Heide his own with the flash taste of the moment including flock wallpaper, brown shag pile carpets and lights in the shape of chrome, mobile balls.

The dining room table, where Nolan had painted the Kellys, was removed, though the main bedroom was left the same. Mike Brown lived in the dining room, smoking dope and painting a sinuously shaped, brilliantly coloured mural which he adorned with empty cigarette packets. He also painted over Mary Boyd's tiles in the kitchen. Sweeney tore up the orchard and replaced it with natives and put down crazy paving in the Heart Garden. Sunday loathed Brown's mural and was shocked by the alterations. But the Reeds behaved with impeccable parental composure and said nothing.

Sweeney's career was up in the air. Strines and Still Earth had both closed and Sweeney was at a loose end. The demands of managing a gallery proved 'more than [Sweeney] could carry, in spite of a quite considerable degree of success'.[90] But, at that point, Sweeney's indeterminate status caused Sunday no great concern.

Reversals had been an integral part of her cultural projects, too, and her past was littered with schemes gone wrong from *Angry Penguins* to *Ern Malley's Journal* to MoMAA. Sunday was also no stranger to losing large amounts of money on such ventures. She was keen for Sweeney to start another gallery, not only for his own sake, but because she experienced the contemporary art world, in whose development she had ceased to play a part, vicariously through him.

Sunday's relationship with Sweeney was much stronger than his relationship with John. Sweeney 'preferred to deal with Sunday, he always spoke fondly of her. It was Sunday he addressed rather than John.'[91] Ron Upton's 'first glimpse of Sweeney was when Sun and Sweeney, arms around each other's waists, were virtually dancing down the hill towards Heide II'. Sweeney had recently returned from London and 'it was clear that they were very pleased to be reunited . . . and not afraid to express their pleasure'.[92]

Sunday was forgiving of a creative individual's wild ways, and if Sweeney's ambitions foundered, then she would insist he try again, and give him the money he needed. John, not so impetuous, attempted to control Sweeney's plans and his spending, making for tension between them. John's role with Sunday was similar. Impulsive and idealistic, she was always ready to splurge on creative people and projects. John stayed her hand and managed the details.

Sweeney had a penchant for grand plans, too, though he found their momentum difficult to sustain. He and Sunday were similar — constantly dreaming, scheming and planning. In that sense, they were truly mother and son. But, unlike Sunday, Sweeney was bedevilled with a fiercely erratic temperament and an inability to accept reversals. Sunday grounded herself in the Heide earth and found balance there, together with John's calming strength. Sweeney seemed unable to locate his energies in the same positive patterns. In the late '60s, his chief virtue was optimism, the belief he could achieve any goal he desired – with Sunday's help.

* 14 *

Full Circle

Love's intention and the reverse of love's intention slowly mark my life . . .
and on the banks of these dark rivers we become — become what we
are to each other and become what we are to ourselves.

SUNDAY REED[1]

THE FINAL DECADE OF SUNDAY'S LIFE was tragic and bewildering, as a series of catastrophes demoralised and finally overwhelmed her.

In 1971, Nolan published *Paradise Garden*, his savage portrait in verse of the *ménage à trois*. Five years later, Cynthia committed suicide. Mary Boyd married Nolan in 1978 and her thirty-year friendship with Sunday was ruptured. By then, John Perceval was in a psychiatric hospital. In 1979 Sweeney committed suicide. Subsequently Pamela moved to the country, taking Sunday's grandsons, Mishka and Danila, with her. John was diagnosed with bowel cancer and, despite a first successful operation, developed the illness fatally. Barrett Reid contracted Hodgkin's disease. Sunday herself had influenza, shingles, a fractured hip and sciatica, progressively weakening her health. Following long negotiations, Heide II and the Reeds' collection were sold to the Victorian State Government to become a public gallery and park. In 1980, Sunday and John moved back to Heide I.

There were good times. With Langley, the Reeds went wild-flower-hunting all over Victoria and into South Australia which proved inspiring for Langley's work and great fun for the Reeds. An old friendship was revived with Atyeo, triggering a lively corre-spondence, while Reid and Philip Jones came back into the Reeds' lives. There was also more contact with Everard and Darren, Sunday's brothers. A book, an exhibition and several major galleries recognised the Reeds' contribution and their circle.

In 1964, John had accused Nolan of behaving like 'an executioner' towards him and Sunday.[2] With *Paradise Garden*, the axe fell. The Reeds were aware, if Nolan's refusal to allow John to accompany the Kellys to London had not made it plain enough, that Nolan was angry with them, and wanted the world to know it.

If *Paradise Garden* had not been published, Nolan's dispute with the Reeds, symbolised by Sunday's refusal to return the Kellys, would amount to little more than an art world feud between a painter and his former patrons, a complicated situation involving property and hurt feelings. After all, it had been nearly twenty-five years since Nolan left Heide. He was at the pinnacle of his career, surrounded by friends who included some of the chief power-brokers in the English scene – Kenneth Clark, Stephen Spender and Benjamin Britten. But *Paradise Garden*'s subject – Nolan's cruel portrayal of his affair with Sunday – charts emotions deep and fierce, unappeased by time. *Paradise Garden* is an act of revenge administered as public violation. Interestingly, Nolan dedicated it to Cynthia. Its title refers to the first cultivated gardens, those of ancient Persia ('paradise' was Persian for enclosure) but it can also refer to the Garden of Eden, a place of beauty, temptation and banishment, an archetypal symbol of loss.

A handsome and expensive book, published in a limited edition by Lord Alistair McAlpine, one of Nolan's patrons, it contains illustrations by Nolan and an introduction by Robert Melville. In the poems, Nolan presents himself as the duped innocent, the naive young artist lured to Heide where he 'fatally hooked' the 'baited wife'. But it was Sunday, not John, from whom Nolan desired to exact retribution. John was merely 'the usual lawyer/sleeping by' while Sunday was Lady Macbeth, the 'subtle angel, subtle tart' whose 'old plumbing' Nolan 'steeled' himself to enter with 'a noon whisky'. He makes a brutal joke about Sunday's infertility – Quinn cashed 'a dud cheque' on her fallopian tubes – and comments on her 'uncanny calmness' in bed. The Heide garden was Sunday's domain where she moved 'just like a bee/stripping souls'. Even Gethsemane was included – 'stuffed/in the hole/above the knee'.[3]

Nolan's disgust is equally self-disgust: he had entered into a liaison that was transformative and unconventional but that, in retrospect, made him feel ashamed and betrayed. The very passion that fuelled the involvement was subject to such severe treatment because it triggered guilt and self-loathing. Nolan needed to blame someone for his turbulent feelings, his sense of loss, his travail in the paradise garden. Sunday once more provided inspiration – *Paradise*

Garden is Nolan's only published collection of verse – but this time his muse gave birth to a monstrous expression. Nolan could not control his feelings about Sunday: he needed to announce he despised her, that she physically disgusted him, that she had wrecked his first marriage, stolen his paintings and broken his heart.

Cynthia was the ideal audience for *Paradise Garden*. After all, she had eviscerated her nearest and dearest in *Daddy Sowed a Wind!* She loathed Sunday, partly because she lived in fear of losing Nolan. As a wordsmith, Cynthia may have even assisted in crafting the poems, whose careful, dagger-sharp rhythms and metaphors bear the marks of time and effort. As Nolan's secretary, she would have typed them out. Formally, the poems have the same light touch and short stanzas as the delicate offerings Nolan sent to Sunday from the Wimmera, a connection he no doubt intended her to make. While the poems were a public act, and dedicated to Cynthia, their barbs were meant for Sunday. But Cynthia was no fool. While *Paradise Garden* advertises the gulf between the former lovers, Cynthia must have recognised it also revealed Nolan's enduring, unbridled obsession with Sunday.

Sunday struggled to understand the attack. She told Jean Langley, 'thank God you have not had an evil book written about you, bound in thick leather to preserve it for the library shelves and so to slowly poison me in my lifetime as well as my death'. But Sunday neither hated nor rejected Nolan. 'A great river of love and tenderness pours over this consuming darkness.' She tried to distract herself. There was 'joy at Heide', she told Langley, with 'persimmon coloured sunsets behind the red gums . . . and the wintersweet on the river bank is in flower. When we walk in the evening its sweet swooning scent meets us at the fence and trails of blue fog wrap around our shoulders'.[4]

Sunday sought to balance Nolan's antagonism with a benevolent gesture, one that specifically honoured him. In 1961 Doodie Pitblado, who had worked for the Baillieu family as Sunday's companion, died and left a bequest. In 1972, Sunday decided to use the money to buy Nolan's *Burke and Wills at the Gulf* (1961), a lyrical evocation of the doomed explorers, and donate it to the National Gallery of Victoria. Seeing the painting at the NGV, its plaque bearing Pitblado's name, Sunday told Langley that 'my Nolan is happy' and hoped 'Doodie is smiling away in heaven'.[5]

But it did not requite Sunday's pain, or her own obsession with Nolan. In order to heal the wounds that his words had inflicted, Sunday took Nolan's love letters from the Wimmera, and began to laboriously type them out. Sometimes she forgot she had already transcribed a letter, and did it twice. Her typing is neat and accurate, almost error-free. Every comma and full stop of Nolan's is there – so are the little poems and affectionate nicknames he invented for her, the intimate, almost daily, record of his art and life. Sunday's copies are a boon for the historian when Nolan's handwriting proves difficult to decipher but they are also a strange document. It is as though Sunday is attempting to recreate the power and beauty of the affair by repeating Nolan's words like an incantation that will restore him, and the past, to her. Worrying the ghosts of their old love was a compulsion Nolan and Sunday shared.

After discussing Nolan with Langley, Sunday felt 'quite blind with sadness. I would die and be lost forever if I tried to repress these thoughts. The only way I find strength is to face it all and let everything filter through me and on and on … In all the 25 years or whatever it is since Nolan went away I have never ever received one tiny spec of a message of love – not from Nolan, not from anyone. Not one spec of hope of anything. It is a long time to wait.

Can you understand. I beg you please always always tell me everything you know. Everything.'[6] Sunday told Langley, 'Nolan is often
in Melbourne so next time will you go and find him and bring him
to me. Every day I think it will be today. He will come today.'[7]

Langley offered Sunday two of her greatest pleasures – the solace
of friendship and adventures in nature. 'We try to get away to the
bush every spring,' John told Sam Atyeo.[8] Not only was it wildflower season, it was was also a treat marking Sunday's birthday on
15 October. The trips, which included Mt Buffalo, the Flinders
Ranges, the Grampians and Little Desert, were usually made with
Langley who had become an excellent wildflower painter. John felt
he and Sunday needed 'the stimulus' of Langley's enthusiasm 'to
spur us to overcome all the practical difficulties which stand in the
way of anything more than a day trip'. If they did go to the bush
without Langley 'we certainly do miss you and it makes a big difference to our day'.[9]

The Reeds provided 'the most marvellous help' for Langley's
work. 'Because I had to write about [the wildflowers] as well [as
painting them], there was an awful lot of research and they put that
together.' The Reeds were instrumental in organising the publication of Langley's *Australian Bush Flowers* with Lansdowne Press in
1970, acting as her agent and negotiating her contract.

The Reeds took Langley 'all over the country' searching for
specimens. Sunday didn't like to fly, so the trips were done by car
and the Reeds bought one for the purpose, a pale blue Volvo station
wagon, Sunday's favourite colour. Langley recalled 'they responded
to my visual response to the world . . . I could see what they could
see . . . In the bush we shared our love of all the creatures. [The
Reeds] seemed to wear very soft shoes and they were very light in
the bush, two elegant figures in their funny old trousers and jumpers

and funny old bush hats. They walked so beautifully in the bush. They were like a pair of Red Indians ahead of me.' But it was not all plain sailing. Sunday was 'terrified of being alone in the bush for even a second. If John went to have a wee, "Don't leave us John! Don't leave us!" We'd get bogged in the middle of a stream, twenty miles from civilisation and John was seventy or something. She was crying. She was terrified of anything happening. She was very nervous.'[10]

Langley's wildflower project lead Sunday to begin one of her own. Ludwig Leichhardt had written a journal of his 1844 expedition from Queensland's Moreton Bay to Port Essington, 300 kilometres from Darwin.[11] Sunday conceived 'the lovely idea of putting together a book of the flowers [Leichhardt] talks about.' It was to be 'quite a monumental task as he mentions them in nearly every diary entry. Identification itself is a problem and then there will be the process of selection, which will also involve the tracking down of early illustrations [Sunday] would want to incorporate in the book.'[12]

Leichhardt was a controversial, enigmatic character who had inspired Patrick White's novel *Voss*, published in 1957 to international acclaim. At White's request, Nolan designed the dust-jacket. Tucker had also been interested in Leichhardt, reading accounts of his travels. In 1848, on his fourth expedition, Leichhardt and his entire party vanished somewhere near the Maranoa River in central Queensland. Tucker, Nolan and White created major works by examining ill-fated Australian heroes – in the case of Tucker and Nolan, their subjects included Kelly as well as Burke and Wills. The harsh profiles of Tucker's Explorers, with their grimly closed mouths, depict the fate of men engulfed by their deeds, by their hubris and by the land itself.

Sunday's reading of Leichhardt was different. She was drawn to

Leichhardt's first and most successful expedition where he and his party travelled overland to Port Essington, a journey of nearly 5000 kilometres. She was interested in Leichhardt's relationship with the landscape, not as a site for an epic of masculine defeat but as a place of respectful scientific observation, mirroring her own reverence for the natural world. Her project unpicks masculinist narratives about the landscape involving death, pride and failure. She follows the example of many Australian women artists who addressed the landscape in miniature rather than focusing on its magnitude, concentrating on the fragile and fleeting beauty of flowers. Her project is typified by a 'feminine' attention to detail, a lack of concern with heroics or tragedy (the latter implying finality, death and closure), a refusal to identify with male mythology and hubris and, further, with the suicidal message implicit in the disaster stories of Australian explorers.

Unfortunately, the project petered out. Perhaps it was because, unlike research for Langley's book or Susie Brunton's herb business, there was no-one to share it with.

The Reeds' journeys into the bush were motivated not only by their love of wildflowers and their eagerness to help Langley but because the visits formed their prime connection with nature, apart from Heide. By the mid-'70s, visits to Aspendale were rare.

Firstly, the Reeds believed Port Philip Bay was so badly polluted, it was dangerous to swim there. Sunday no longer swam in the Yarra for the same reason. Secondly, with the end of the Moras' marriage, the convivial summers had come to an end. Mary Boyd, John Perceval and their children had been part of those holidays, too. The Percevals were now also divorced and John had married Anne Hall, a young painter. But Perceval remained 'a hopeless alcoholic', rotating between 'home and hospital with unfailing regularity'.[13]

Aspendale was for special occasions like Christmas and New Year when Sunday would make a huge tureen of delicious, pale purple borscht. The rest of the time the house was loaned to friends. Russell Deeble, a poet and close friend of Sweeney's, lived there after his return from India and turned it into a 'Buddhist shrine'.[14] At least, John reflected, it was being used. Finally, the maintenance of Heide kept the Reeds at home. Sunday trusted only Susie Brunton to care for the cats: if she was unavailable, the Reeds would not leave.

To provide relief from the summer heat, the Reeds asked Susie's architect husband, Robert, to design a swimming pool. As usual, it was Sunday's idea. Part of the paddock was closed off and the pool was positioned 'on the hillside about 50 yards from the house and [it] really looks quite like a dam – which is what we wanted – and fits into the landscape quite happily'.[15] On hot days Sunday alternated 'between work in her nearby kitchen garden and swims in the pool'.[16] But the pool was unheated and only the hardy could venture into its freezing depths for a dip. However, it did provide a playground for Sweeney's sons, Mishka and Danila, born in 1971 and 1973. The children were 'a great joy' to Sunday, especially Mishka who was 'always called Mu Mu' and 'who cannot yet say "S" and calls her "Hunday".' Mishka was 'delightful and indefatigable and wears everyone out'.[17]

In August 1972, Sweeney Reed Galleries opened in smart, refurbished premises at 266 Brunswick Street, Fitzroy. Sunday and Sweeney had put their heads together and started the gallery but this time Sweeney was in partnership with Julian Stirling. The Reeds hoped Stirling, an older, accomplished dealer, would act as a brake and a guide for Sweeney and assist him in managing the venture. Sweeney had been employed at Stirling's Southern Cross

Sidney Nolan. *Railway Guard, Dimboola.* 1943. Ripolin
enamel on canvas. 77 x 64 cm. *National Gallery of Victoria.*

Sidney Nolan. *The Trial.* 1947. Ripolin enamel on composition board.
90.7 x 121.2 cm. *National Gallery of Australia.*

Sidney Nolan. *The defence of Aaron Sherritt.* 1946. Ripolin enamel on composition board. 121.2 x 90.7 cm. *National Gallery of Australia.*

Sidney Nolan. *Quilting the armour.* 1947. Ripolin enamel on composition board. 90.4 x 121.2 cm. *National Gallery of Australia.*

Sidney Nolan. *For the one who paints such beautiful squares.* c. 1946–47. Watercolour on paper. 10.5 x 11.6 cm. *Heide Museum of Modern Art.*

Charles Blackman. *Prone Schoolgirl.* c. 1953. Enamel on cardboard. 79.0 x 93.5 cm. *Heide Museum of Modern Art.*

Left: Charles Blackman. *Alice*. 1956.
Oil on composition board.
189.9 x 133.0 cm.
Heide Museum of Modern Art.

Below: Laurence Hope. *Lovers*. 1952.
Oil on canvas. 66.0 x 59.0 cm.
Heide Museum of Modern Art.

Mirka Mora. *The sky is full with stars*. 1958. Enamel on composition board. 91.5 x 60.8 cm.
Heide Museum of Modern Art.

Ian Sime. *Painting I*. 1955. Enamel on composition board. 91.5 x 122.0 cm.
Heide Museum of Modern Art.

Asher Bilu. *Abstract*. 1958. Synthetic polymer on paper. 39.0 x 56.0 cm.
Heide Museum of Modern Art.

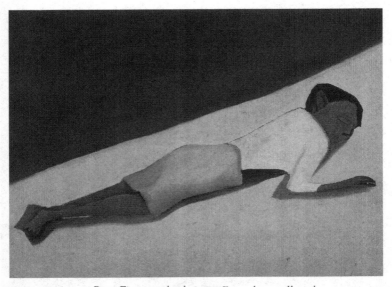

Robert Dickerson. *Prone Figure on a beach.* 1955. Enamel on cardboard.
67.4 x 91.0 cm. *Heide Museum of Modern Art.*

Fred Williams.
The Boyfriend.
1956. Hand-
touched etching
on paper.
21.8 x 18.1 cm.
*Heide Museum of
Modern Art.*

Ron Upton. *Three Forms*. 1964. Ciment fondu. 229.0 x 139.0 x 75.0 cm.
Heide Museum of Modern Art.

Left: Les Kossatz. *Love Kite*. 1967. Oil, enamel, tin and composition board.
166.0 x 93.0 cm. *Heide Museum of Modern Art.*

Right: Jean Langley. Left: Purple Eyebright (*Euphrasia collina*) and right: Fairies
Aprons or Purple Bladderwort (*Utricularia dichotoma*). c. 1970. 22.4 x 25 cm.
Watercolour. Sunday was delighted to find the rare Fairies Aprons that grows in
shallow swampy water. *Collection the artist.*

John Sinclair. Sunday and *Rosa mutabilis*. c. 1974.
Courtesy Jean Langley / Heide Museum of Modern Art.

Galleries, dealing in the work of Tucker, Boyd, Nolan and Vassilieff. Though respected in the art world, Sweeney was also acquiring a reputation for being erratic and unreliable. Alan McCulloch sounded a warning. While Sweeney had opened 'the glamour gallery . . . it now behoves the unpredictable Sweeney to live up to the standard of the architecture.'[18]

Sweeney had some triumphs. In October 1976, he showed the full series of Tucker's Images of Modern Evil for the first time. It was a critical and popular success, vindicating Tucker's early calibre as an artist and introducing him to a younger generation. It seemed Sweeney was living out the Reeds' heritage by advancing, not only contemporary art but art whose promise the Reeds had discerned decades before. Patrick McCaughey, the *Age*'s influential art critic, described Images of Modern Evil as 'myths themselves in the story of Australian art'. McCaughey could 'only commend the importance of this exhibition as it marks the turning of the Australian myth from innocence to experience, from the bush idyll to the city of dreadful night, from extrovert diversion to inward desperation'.[19] Such a commendation must have been enormously satisfying for Sweeney, Tucker and the Reeds.

As far as current art, Sweeney continued to exhibit Les Kossatz and attracted a new group including Alan Mitelman, Jeff Makin and Sydney pop artist Ken Reinhard. But, unfortunately, the gallery's bright prospects dimmed and, within eighteen months, it was faltering.

Peregrine Smith, Sweeney's half-brother and Hester's son to Gray Smith, worked for Sweeney in the gallery's final year. He found Sweeney was 'totally irresponsible with money. It was fine if everyone used cheques but as soon as it was cash money, it went into his pocket. If he got paid $18,000 for something in cash, it went straight into his pocket. It never came back out. Cash money was cash money, it was to be spent.' When Peregrine complained to Sweeney that he was owed seventeen weeks' salary, Sweeney told him, 'Take some stock.'

Other, equally disturbing signs began to emerge. Peregrine observed that 'Sweeney's mood would go up, then he'd go down . . . When he was down, he wouldn't stay in the gallery. He'd disappear. I never knew where he was.'[20] The gallery closed without warning in 1975, in the middle of Les Kossatz's exhibition. Kossatz arrived at the gallery to find the doors locked. He negotiated with Sweeney – who seemed blithely unconcerned about the situation – to keep the gallery open, offering to cover rent and other costs himself.

One of Sweeney's chief problems was his inability to complete a project. At the outset of any plan, he was optimistic, encouraging and full of ideas but when it came to the daily grind, to life's tedious, repetitive details, his interest fluttered away to another scheme. Despite his chaotic business practices, Sweeney inspired enduring loyalty and love in many of the artists he exhibited. He continued to deal privately, negotiating the sale of many of Tucker's major works to the National Gallery of Australia. He then hoped to find a position in a public gallery. John wore a brave face about the latest setback, telling friends that Sweeney believed 'the dealer world out there stinks so badly that he will be glad to get out of it'.[21]

Sweeney's marriage was also under strain and the Reeds saw little of him or Pamela, John observing, 'Sweeney turns up periodically but for the most part the two establishments [Heide I and Heide II] are very much apart – it must be at least 3 months since Pamela was down here.' Sweeney and Pamela were planning to leave Heide and move into a renovated terrace house at Gore Street, Fitzroy, where, as John understood it, they would 'live separate lives'.[22] The

Reeds were despondent about the prospect of losing close touch with the family and increasingly worried about Sweeney's state of mind and his future. Sunday was 'deeply distressed about his behaviour, about how to make him happy and what was to become of him'.[23] At the same time, Peter Hobb was travelling through Turkey and India, making for lonely times at Heide.

It was not only Sweeney's future that weighed on the Reeds. Ever since moving to Heide, they had planned for it to become a public park. In 1976, they began discussions with the State Government about the sale of Heide and their collection. They recognised Sweeney would not be competent, nor was he interested, in managing the property. Though Sweeney 'loves the place . . . it would be a burden for him', John reflecting, 'his temperament is so very different to ours'.[24] Though sentimentally attached to Heide I, Sweeney showed no inclination for gardening, bird-watching or the bush.

But the negotiations proved a long, slow, exhausting business, taking four years, and making the Reeds 'almost despair'.[25] It was the active support of future premier Rupert (Dick) Hamer that made the entire project possible. In 1969, Hamer was minister for local government when John contacted him about the City of Doncaster's plan to reclassify Heide as a farm. It meant the rates would skyrocket. John, as a member of the Yarra Valley Conservation League, appealed to Hamer. 'My basic concern is to try and preserve this property in its present [form] as part of the Yarra Valley.'[26] The council rescinded its decision.

Hamer, an active conservationist, was involved in framing government policy that lead to increasing public land along the Yarra River, as well as the continuous planting of trees along its banks. When he became premier in 1972, Hamer also supported

Neil Douglas's vocal campaigns to curb the destruction of native trees in the Yarra Valley.

Hamer was also minister for the arts and he was keen to meet the Reeds whose history he admired. Heide II was 'an extraordinary house. It seemed built for the display of paintings. They were living in a gallery.' Hamer was also impressed by Sunday's energy. 'She worked every day in that garden. She was glad to know it was going to be looked after and open to the public.'[27]

Part of Heide's appeal was that the property extended right down to the river. John and Hamer agreed that 'specified land in the Yarra Valley should be gazetted for permanently restricted use only'.[28] The State Government also bought the land adjoining Heide and created Banksia Park. But even Hamer's unqualified support and his powers as premier did not speed the wheels of bureaucracy, and negotiations dragged on through the '70s.

As part of the same process of divesting themselves of their property and preserving it for perpetuity, Sunday decided to donate the twenty-five Kelly paintings, and the accompanying drawings, to the National Gallery of Australia. As with Hamer, the matter depended on personal trust and esteem. But it was also the Reeds' opportunity, after the slings and arrows exchanged with Eric Westbrook, to snub the National Gallery of Victoria. Though *Evening with Bathers* went to the NGV, the Reeds chose to sell their other key Streeton, *Gorse in Bloom*, to the Art Gallery of South Australia. The Reeds avowed that no-one had approached them from the NGV. That was probably true. Equally, they felt personally wounded by the gallery and its director.

John had first met James Mollison, then a director of Gallery A, when he was invited to judge a 'Young Minds' exhibition at MoMAA. In his new role as director of the National Gallery of

Australia, Mollison was making waves, purchasing Pollock's *Blue Poles* and Picasso's *Grand Nu*, which caused heated debate about the works' value, both aesthetic and monetary. The Reeds admired Mollison's courage and his commitment not only to international art but also to contemporary Australian art. But it was more than that. John felt Mollison was doing 'a wonderful job . . . and is, in fact, reserving a special place where the Kellys can be permanently shown. He seems to love them and has said so in one of the papers and Sunday likes him very much.'[29]

When discussions about the Kellys began in 1972, it was announced in the media, making Sunday feel 'so nervous and exposed'.[30] When the series was delivered to the NGA in 1977, Sunday decided the wall label accompanying the series should read 'with love from Sunday Reed'. The choice of words infuriated Nolan. Jean Langley felt 'a little sad that [the Kellys] are not going to live at Heide not only tomorrow but a hundred years from now, they really belong at Heide . . . Heide is the perfect setting and historically right . . . I certainly shall miss them at Heide even though one didn't see them all . . . It is always a luxury to be able to sit in a big chair at Heide and look.'[31]

Art was not entirely forgotten during the '70s but it took second place to the Reeds' bigger plans and worries. As usual, the Reeds were attracted to the most contemporary art. In 1971, environmental sculptor John Davis approached John with the idea of creating a 'process work' in the paddock that involved placing polythene sheeting over grass. The grass grew through holes in the sheeting. Davis's work, its roots in '60s earthworks and Italian *arte povera* movement, proved ideal for the Heide park. Once Davis had assured John the grass would not be damaged, the project went ahead.

The '60s and '70s were an age of spectacle where three-dimensional art was concerned. The Reeds had travelled to Sydney to witness Christo take on the massive task of wrapping Little Bay in millions of metres of plastic and rope. They also enjoyed English performance artists Gilbert and George and attended their witty peformances at the National Gallery of Victoria, singing 'Underneath the arches' wearing suits and painted faces. John congratulated arts patron John Kaldor, who brought Gilbert and George to Australia, telling him of the 'immense pleasure' he and Sunday gained from the artists' 'sculpture'.[32] Kaldor had also funded Christo's wrapping of Little Bay.

Despite such interests, the Heide grounds, so ideally suited to the location of sculpture, were rarely used in this way. Sunday's taste in sculpture was a distinct area of limitation for her. Aside from the purchase of Ron Upton's *Three forms* in 1965, Sunday collected sculpture for the interior not the exterior of Heide II. She particularly admired Vassilieff's compact, limestone, figurative works like *Stenka Razin* (1950) and displayed them in Heide II. She also bought Les Kossatz's *Love kite* (1967, Heide Museum of Modern Art) and Syd Ball's *Khamsa blue* (1966–67, Heide MoMA), both wall pieces that functioned more as paintings than sculpture. There was an explosion of sculptural activity in Australia in the 1970s but Sunday chose to ignore it, just as she had during the 1950s. She responded to two-dimensional, not three-dimensional, art.

On his own, John visited the Ewing and George Paton Galleries at the University of Melbourne Union, a centre for experimental art. Director Kiffy Rubbo (then Carter) invited John to participate in The Letter Show, one of the many theme-based exhibitions she devised with assistant director Meredith Rogers. Rubbo was one of the few younger gallery directors who recognised John's significance and sought to include him in her activities. The Reeds also regularly visited Realities, whose flamboyant director, Marianne Baillieu, was married to Ian, the son of Darren, Sunday's older brother. Realities, in Toorak, was Melbourne's most stylish commercial gallery.

By 1977, when Sunday donated the Kellys to the National Gallery of Australia, the Reeds' relations with Nolan had deteriorated further, if that was at all possible. There were two reasons for this. In November 1976, Cynthia had committed suicide and, soon after, Nolan began living with Mary Boyd. It is difficult to know which incident produced the most pain and confusion for Sunday: the sudden death of her sister-in-law or the loss of one of her closest friends to her obsession.

The circumstances of Cynthia's death were disquieting. On that day, she and Nolan had travelled into London from their Putney home. They had lunched together and, after agreeing to meet for afternoon tea, Nolan set off for Marlborough Galleries. Cynthia then visited a woman friend who registered nothing amiss. Afterwards, Cynthia checked into a hotel in Piccadilly and took a quantity of prescription drugs. She left two notes: one for whoever found her and one for the coroner 'giving very exact descriptions of what she had taken and in what order'. She had also sent letters to Patrick White, Maie Casey and Elwyn and Lily Lynn.

When Cynthia did not arrive for their appointment, Nolan waited and then went home, where he found a telegram from her that read, 'Proceeding by easy stages to the Orkneys'. Nolan had no idea what it meant. The next morning, the police arrived.

According to Charles Osborne, a friend of the Nolans and Barrett Reid, Nolan was 'shattered'.[33]

There had been no contact between the Reeds and Cynthia since she and Nolan visited Heide in March 1948 as newlyweds. They were aware of her hostility towards them, not only from her stony silence, but because of rumours that had reached them. Jean Langley, on her first visit to London in 1960, discovered that 'Nolan and Cynthia were saying that Sunday had sent me to spy on them'. It was 'the story that went around the Australian group'.[34]

Not only did Cynthia's death stun and mystify the Reeds, so did her previous behaviour. 'What went wrong? What destroyed our relationship . . . and made Cynthia so frighteningly bitter?' John asked Atyeo. 'Why did she set out to "punish" Sunday and me over so many years, doing all she could to hurt us? . . . While she lived there could the germ of a hope somewhere in oneself that one day all would be well. Now that can never be.'[35]

If John had read Cynthia's *Open Negative: An American Memoir*, published in 1967, perhaps he would have found some answers. Set in 1958–59, when Nolan had a Harkness fellowship to New York, the book's first section covers the Nolans' road trip across America with Jinx, while the second describes Cynthia's hospitalisation for tuberculosis in New York. *Open Negative* presents a series of anguished portraits – of physical illness, of the Nolans' marriage, of Cynthia herself. Nolan dominates, a magnificently relentless, uncaring and optimistic individual, who exhorts the delicate Cynthia, 'Never tell me that you're too tired to walk. Energy! Energy!'[36]

From the beginning, Cynthia is beset with illness. Excruciating back pain means she has to lie flat in the rear of the car. Then she succumbs to a mysterious allergy. All the while Nolan keeps her on the move, making her comment, 'this continual moving about would kill me'.[37] There are ghastly social occasions where she has to cope with wealthy philistines and svelte blondes who make a beeline for Nolan. She observes it is a futile lifestyle, one that is damaging her. When she is diagnosed with TB and placed in hospital, her relief, despite her fears about the disease, is palpable. 'All I want is to be quiet.'[38]

As Cynthia's early letters to John reveal, she had been battling her demons for many years. Despite external successes, doubt and torment continued to rage. There had been many crises in the Nolans' marriage, often triggered by Nolan's infidelities, and Cynthia had left him on several occasions. Not long before she died, Cynthia asked Charles Osborne to store paintings of Nolan's that he had given to her. Barrett Reid quoted him as saying that Cynthia 'wanted to leave Nolan but she didn't have any money'.[39] Unwillingly, Osborne agreed and placed the paintings on short-term loan in several provincial galleries. Cynthia had also persuaded Nolan to sell their Putney home and the couple were in the process of buying an apartment in Westminster.

Osborne also told Barrett that 'Cynthia loved Nolan more than life itself and ... had persuaded herself that she was not necessary to his life any longer.'[40] Dispersing the paintings, an act which John understood were 'gifts rather than loans', meant that Nolan was financially disadvantaged. He was forced to 'start again from the beginning'.[41] With their home sold, he also had nowhere to live.

Cynthia's last book, *Paradise, And Yet*, about Papua New Guinea, was published in 1971, the same year as *Paradise Garden*, and, oddly, with a not dissimilar title. In her four books of travel writing, Cynthia casts Nolan as the purpose of her travels, her destination, her narrative. In *Paradise, And Yet*, her impressions are located around Nolan, a troubling centre of attraction from which her gaze never strays. A growing melancholy can be discerned in *Paradise, And Yet*; a disconnected quality that, like light altering at sunset, is hard to catch, but pervasive, encompassing. Adding to Cynthia's unhappiness was the news that a new manuscript had been rejected by a publisher.

As her depression deepened, she wrote to Albert Tucker in a scrawling hand, letters where she confused Barbara, Tucker's second wife, with Mary Dixon, his former companion, though Mary and Tucker had separated years before. Cynthia also made acidic comments to Tucker about Nolan, hinting at heinous behaviour. It seemed the great love of Cynthia's life had turned to hatred, despair and paranoia, making the threats about suicide in her early letters to John a horrible prophecy.

Nolan turned to Arthur and Mary Boyd, two of his oldest friends, for comfort. Soon Mary wrote to the Reeds advising them Nolan was staying with her. In 1976 Mary, who had trained as a cattle breeder, bought Ruthland, a property on the Welsh border. When she first moved there, the Reeds were delighted that she was taking steps towards a new life. Through an English nursery, Sunday arranged to send Mary many of her favourite roses. She and John also gave advice about the specifics of gardening in a cold climate. Mary, intense and sensitive, had continued to recount in her many letters to Sunday her problems adjusting to the end of her marriage to Perceval.

Mary was quick to reassure the Reeds that, despite the changed circumstances, her friendship with them would remain unaltered. Nolan even declared that *Paradise Garden* was 'a terrible book'. ('Well, why did he write it?' John wondered.)[42] Sunday, concerned for Nolan after Cynthia's death, was eager to send him 'a message of love'.[43] Perhaps now an understanding with Nolan could be reached and a reconciliation effected. But, at the same time, Sunday was 'overwhelmed with fear'[44] that 'Mary might now have to forsake us all in some way.' *Paradise Garden* was still 'burning in [Sunday's] heart'.[45]

When Mary arrived in Australia, she rang from Sydney, expressing her desire to come to Heide. John explained to Langley that 'this might not be a good idea as Sun does not feel she could carry a relationship with Mary (for whom she feels so deeply) from which, in effect, Nolan excluded himself'. Sunday was experiencing 'the breakdown of her nervous system' over the matter and it caused her to be 'in an almost constant state of fear'.[46]

Langley, also a close friend of Mary's, had met with her and Nolan in London. Langley's appraisal of Nolan, and the troubled situation, was frank, astute and earthy. 'Is this man Nolan worth all this sadness and heartache and trouble and horror?' she asked Sunday. 'He wasn't so very impressive. I liked him but I can't say I was greatly impressed. He doesn't look very interesting any more, he looks small and old and rather more like an actor in appearance than an artist, his face doesn't seem to have developed strength ... I am so used to serious people that I got a bit of a shock to find this man, your Nolan, such a big performer, such a talker, such a maker of laughs and light thoughts and I couldn't see him in the Heide world very clearly ... I do hope you and John have not wasted all your love and heartache on someone unworthy ... I was shocked to see our great Nolan look like an Irish scallywag.'[47]

When Mary wrote on 20 January 1978 telling the Reeds she and Nolan had married that day, it must have recalled Nolan's telegram thirty years before, saying he had married Cynthia. Mary and Nolan visited Australia the following month but would be in Melbourne for only one day. Being unable to visit Heide was, Mary told the Reeds, 'the only thing' marring her 'great happiness'. She believed Nolan felt 'true love' for Sunday and John but was 'overwhelmed' at the thought of seeing them.[48] John gallantly responded, 'let us all be overwhelmed together'.[49] But Sunday told Jean Langley that she was 'overwhelmed with fear of [Mary's] visit and the dread of how it may affect me in some awful way'.[50] She wished Langley could be at her side.

The Reeds were not the only ones surprised by Nolan's union. Patrick White, in his 1981 memoir *Flaws in the Glass*, railed against Nolan for 'flinging himself on another woman's breast when the ashes were scarcely cold'. He also criticised Nolan's 'chase after recognition . . . the cameras, the public birthdays, the political hanky-panky'. As far as White was concerned, 'the best of [Nolan] will never die, nor will Cynthia, because the best of Nolan was their collaboration'.[51] Nolan's reply was *Nightmare* (1982, Private Collection), a caricature of a grim-faced White with Manoly Lascaris, White's partner, represented as a bloated dog.

Sunday's wish to make contact with Nolan was finally granted. But it was fruitless and frustrating. In 1978, Mary visited Heide, 'for one brief hour' but Nolan remained sitting outside in the car, which the Reeds did not know.[52] Mary recalled, 'Sunday tore me to pieces because I didn't bring Sid.' Nolan had warned her the visit would be 'horrendous'.[53] Back at their hotel, Mary persuaded Nolan to ring Sunday. To Sunday's frustration, Nolan kept the conversation light and playful, parrying her remarks and refusing to be drawn. Distraught and disappointed, Sunday found all her letters to him and burned them. After that, contact between Mary and the Reeds virtually ceased. But if destroying the letters was meant to be a final act, a cleansing ritual, it did not succeed. Sunday's feelings for Nolan did not change. Surely it would not have surprised Nolan who once declared to John that 'love for Sun is final'.

In 1977, after years of trying to combat his alcoholism, Perceval had himself committed to Larundel psychiatric hospital in Parkville and surrendered his affairs to the public trustee. He stayed there for the next nine years. The Reeds regularly visited him, though it was 'gruelling'. As Barrett Reid recalled, they had to walk 'through a series of locked doors to a crowded ward. Perceval could not work at Larundel, not because he did not want to, but because of the noise and intrusion of other patients.'[54]

Early in 1978, there was more bad news when Greenhill, Barrett and Philip Jones's home, an old, converted hotel at St Andrews that the Reeds had bought them, burned down. The fire started in the bedroom, next to Barrett's library, and, John wrote, 'almost all [Barrett's] poems – he has no copies – were lost, and the whole of his library'.[55] Fortunately, Les Kossatz was driving past and assisted the local fire brigade. 'We saved most of the art – the Hester, the Nolan. We just threw everything onto the road.'[56] At the Reeds' invitation, Barrett and Jones moved to Aspendale while the task of rebuilding Greenhill began.

Under these pressures, Sunday and John's health began to deteriorate. Prior to Cynthia's death, both endured a bout of influenza. It affected Sunday particularly badly, John noting that 'her nervous system had a real knock out blow and recovery is a slow business'.[57] Her weight dropped to forty kilos. After the call from Nolan, Sunday contracted shingles, a skin disease characterised by a rash that can permanently damage the eyes. It is an illness usually associated with stress.

In September came another shock. John, who had gone into hospital with a blocked bowel, was diagnosed with a malignant tumour. With typical self-effacement, John told John Sinclair that 'the whole business is so much worse for Sunday than for me, not that I am a stoic as you suggest, and I thoroughly dislike pain; but Sunday's empathy penetrates all barriers and takes on all the most subtle distresses of my own troubles so that her suffering is a continuous and total experience which allows her little respite'.[58] Perhaps John meant he not only had to bear his own illness but Sunday's anxieties, too.

John was optimistic about his chances for a full recovery, telling Atyeo that his operation was 'a 3-hour affair but all went well and the surgeon was able to make a clean job of it and said that in all other respects my insides were those of a young man . . . I am home again with a big cut down my front and a bit slow on my feet but with the prospect of being pretty well back to normal in a couple of months.' Sunday took John's illness as a personal insult. 'She has always believed that such an evil as this could be avoided if one lived and ate sensibly, and in terms of emotional shock it has all been much worse for her than for me and her recovery is really a more different one than mine.'[59]

As he had hoped, John made excellent progress, allowing the Reeds to concentrate on the sale of Heide to the government and the changes it would mean for them. They would vacate Heide II, in order for it be refurbished as an art gallery, and move back to Heide I, which was in need of repairs.

In the midst of these plans, came an 'almost mortal blow'.[60] In March 1979, Sweeney committed suicide at Les Kossatz's Carlton studio. At the time, Kossatz was in London. Sweeney's composure was eerily reminiscent of Cynthia's. That afternoon he called past Russell Deeble's, a short distance away in Pitt Street. He was carrying two hamburgers, one in each hand, for Deeble and himself.

Deeble knew something was wrong 'but I was used to things being wrong. In retrospect, Sweeney was at his calmest and that's what was wrong.'[61] After they'd discussed the football and eaten the hamburgers, Deeble told Sweeney he had to get ready for a dinner engagement.

Sweeney said goodbye, then returned to Kossatz's studio and barricaded himself in. He tidied everything in his usual fastidious manner, then he got into bed and took 79 tryptanol tablets, 30 valium and 25 sinequan, washed down with whisky. His body was found on 29 March. Over that weekend, several people tried to ring him including Deeble and Tucker.

Tucker was trying to apologise for a misunderstanding. In January, Sweeney had delivered to the National Gallery of Australia many of the Tuckers they would subsequently buy. Tucker pointed out to Sweeney, 'Now there's going to be [a] tax problem for me. I'm going to have a problem with provisional tax. And Sweeney's voice went flat and dead; he'd forgotten about the tax thing. Then he hung up and that was that ... I kept trying to ring him after that and so while I'd been ringing, the phone had been going with him lying there dead in bed.'[62]

Sweeney left notes for Pamela, Tucker, Kossatz and a former girlfriend in London, but not for Sunday and John. The last time Sunday had seen Sweeney was at Heide. She glanced up from working in the kitchen garden to catch sight of him standing on the crest of the hill. When she looked again, he was gone. That weekend, Pamela returned home to find Sweeney's final gesture had been to deck her bedroom with photographs and mementos, including strips of paper typed with quotations from Buddhist texts.

Pamela had tried to make Sweeney see a psychiatrist but, when they had to wait for the appointment, Sweeney upended a vase of flowers and threw magazines around before storming out. Shortly after, Sweeney made a suicide attempt, but was found by Pamela and his sons. He was furious with her for ringing an ambulance and saving him. Pamela was convinced by a friend not to tell John and Sunday about the incident. He had also physically attacked Pamela.

Sweeney's friends were aware his behaviour was becoming reckless, extreme and aggressive. He would arrive at Susie and Robert Brunton's in the middle of the night until 'we couldn't take it any more. We had a family. We couldn't sit there listening to Sweeney raving until 5 am. We just didn't answer the door.'[63] Late one night he arrived at Russell Deeble's and broke in, terrifying Deeble and his partner Jacqueline Mitelman. Deeble confronted him. 'I told him to get out, never to do that again.'[64]

Yet the last two years of Sweeney's life saw an astonishing creative flowering. In 1977, he enrolled at the Victorian College of the Arts as a mature-age student in the printmaking course. He needed academic qualifications if he was to start a new career in a public gallery. It was not Sweeney's first foray into making art. Since his time in London in the '60s, he had been involved in the concrete poetry movement. Concrete poetry combined poetry and typography, using the poem both as text and visual display, creating rhythms with spaces and words. Sweeney exhibited his cool, stylish 'visual poems' at Georges Mora's Tolarno Galleries in 1977.

At the VCA, Sweeney developed a new expression that combined exquisitely delicate, embossed etchings with his tender, elliptical, haiku-like poems. His vocabulary as a poet is similar to Hester's where love, the heart and the natural world are used to moving effect. 'True love like no love/boundless space/in the eye of a lonely bird'. The works showed Sweeney to be, as John wrote to Atyeo, 'a superb and meticulous craftsman of the utmost sensitivity'.[65]

Sweeney successfully completed two years of his course, then, at the beginning of his third year, he withdrew, citing the breakdown of his marriage. The weight of his fractured past was proving a tremendous strain. For Sweeney, two marriages and three businesses had failed. He was the father of three children. There was also the vexed matter of his parentage.

After the Reeds had adopted him, Hester had convinced them Tucker was not Sweeney's father. She believed he was the son of Billy Hyde, a drummer, with whom she had been having an affair. Sweeney's attitude to the story was confused. He told Peregrine unequivocally, 'Bert is not my father'[66] but to Pamela his attitude was, 'it's who you live with, it's not a story that you can ever authenticate. Who cares? [Hyde] wasn't part of my life. Bert, Joy, Sun and John were.'[67]

Tucker shared Sweeney's ambivalence. Publicly, Tucker avowed Sweeney was his son. During the course of writing *Australian Gothic: A Life of Albert Tucker*, Bert told me several times, 'I have never seen anything of myself in Sweeney.' In December 1976, when Billy Hyde died, Sunday handed Sweeney the obituary, saying, 'Your father is dead.' The matter had been discussed with Sweeney since he was a young man. It made his attitude towards Hester, Tucker and the Reeds increasingly complex. Pamela recalled, 'Bert was white and Joy was black. She is the one who left and Bert did what he could. He talked a lot about that.'[68]

Nor did Sweeney develop an easy, trusting relationship with Tucker. Though he admired Tucker and wanted to act as his agent, Sweeney had conflicting feelings about him, of which Kossatz and Deeble were aware. Tucker, tough-minded and opinionated, did not fit the mould of a kindly father figure. But Sweeney upheld an attitude adhered to by Sunday and John: no matter how difficult or demanding a good artist – and the Reeds had endured more than their share of problems with Tucker – commitment was always maintained. It was the same with Hester: Sweeney respected her as an artist while regarding her as a careless mother and an intemperate woman.

But even the complexities of Sweeney's past and his dilemma about his marriage break-up do not wholly explain his suicide. It is tragic that Sweeney, bedevilled by an inability to finish a task, was able, with deliberation and exactitude, to finish his own life.

Sunday was devastated and inconsolable, demanding of Deeble, 'You're his friend. Why did he do it?' When Kossatz returned from London, he went to Heide. 'I got abused as though it were my fault. Sunday was really heavy on me.'[69] Kossatz knew about the other suicide attempt and the Reeds felt they should have been informed. John told Gil Jamieson that 'in a way it means the end of our lives, too. Sweeney meant everything to us and was so deeply embedded in our lives that they seem to stand still without him.'[70] Later that year, when Georges Mora had an exhibition of Sweeney's work, the Reeds had the chance to view the quality and originality of his etchings. John found the show 'so beautiful, and so terribly, terribly sad . . . [Sweeney] took many mysteries with him when he ended his life and there will never be any answer to the simple question of why he made the decision. It is a blow from which Sunday and I will never recover.'[71]

Meanwhile, the Reeds were involved in the task of cleaning up Heide I. John told Laurence Hope, now living in London, 'the old house has been full of carpenters, plumbers and painters and the mess has been indescribable . . . Basically it will be just as it used to be, with a few changes of colour and minor details', including restoring the cattery at the rear of the house. 'The outside of the house will be painted a palish stone colour with the windows white and the roof will be white as well.'[72] But they were still waiting for the sale to be confirmed by the government, finding that 'the destiny of Heide' was now subject to 'political considerations and bureaucratic interference', making Sunday feel 'very insecure'.[73]

Late in 1979, in a burst of publicity, the State Government announced it was buying Heide for nearly one million dollars, even though negotiations were continuing. 'I hope they don't pull out the roses,' Sunday told a journalist, 'and they make the swimming pool into a pond for the ducks.' She reflected, 'it feels so strange to be moving back to where you started at our time of life. Maybe they'll make us a little gate to look out of.'[74]

By July 1980, John could announce that 'at last the government has come good and signed the document and paid the deposit'.[75] Immediately the Reeds moved back into Heide I but it proved a traumatic experience. There was not only the wrench of quitting Heide II, their home for thirteen years, 'into which we had put so much of ourselves', but for Sunday 'the loss of her special creation, her kitchen garden' was 'almost unbearable . . . and even now [she] cannot go down there'.[76]

The most painful aspect, however, was the memory of Sweeney who had 'lived here for so many years'.[77] 'Heide carries so many memories and ghosts,' John wrote to Atyeo, 'with which we have to come to terms but we sit in the library and think of you painting your *Dancing Girl* there and, as Sun says, with not one drop of paint falling on the floor. And the jazz records going all the time.'[78] John reminded Atyeo that 'the porch you designed is still there and your angel is again pinned to our bedroom door'.[79]

The connection with Atyeo, revived in the late '60s, provided enormous support during the awful events of the Reeds' later years.

They were delighted that his retrospective exhibition was being planned with Jennifer Phipps, curator of Australian art at the National Gallery of Victoria, and there was also the chance of a commercial show in Melbourne.[80] They longed to have him stay with them at Heide.

Cynthia's death weighed heavily on Atyeo, too. They had collaborated closely in the 1930s and, in 1939, she had stayed with him and Dyring in the south of France. Then she followed Atyeo to the West Indies where they'd had an affair. But Atyeo had earned Cynthia's disfavour and there was no further contact. After her death, Atyeo got in touch with Jinx, her daughter, who corresponded with him and visited him in Provence.

Almost as soon as the Reeds were settled in Heide I, there was another disaster. Sunday was busy getting the garden back in order. She was 'carrying a bucket of compost in one hand and a full watering can in the other,' when she 'tripped and crashed on to a brick path' but 'being Sunday went on working for half an hour'.[81] Finally, the pain forced her indoors and John got the doctor who diagnosed a fractured hip. In the first doctor's opinion, 'she would have to be operated on at once and have a steel pin inserted' but the surgeon did not agree.[82] Anyway, Sunday 'refused point blank to stay in hospital' and was 'getting around the house on a walking frame'.[83] The rest of the time she was confined to bed.

John recognised that 'Sunday cannot work at a normal pace: she gets carried away and goes frantically at whatever she is doing'.[84] She was 'having a terrible time and just does not know how she is going to stare out of the French windows for three months'.[85] There was some comfort in reading *Wealth Within* and *Strange Places and Simple Truths* by Melbourne psychiatrist Ainslie Meares, self-help manuals for healing that espoused natural methods like meditation, books loaned to her by John's sister, Margaret. The Reeds had known Meares when he visited MoMAA. Fortunately, Sunday's hip knitted perfectly.

At Christmas, Barrett Reid and Philip Jones moved back to Greenhill, now rebuilt. A few days later, Barrett was rushed to hospital with a suspected heart attack. It was discovered he had Hodgkin's disease which, as John noted, 'inevitably brought back floods of our dear Joy'.[86] John, too, had just received a fresh and terrible diagnosis: a secondary cancer had appeared in his liver. 'Now Barrie and I face the possibility of death together . . . The implications of the loss of Barrie, following the loss of Sweeney, are just too great for us to contemplate calmly . . . for us he is part of the very core of our lives.'[87]

John's cancer was inoperable. Though he got a 'gloomy prognosis' from his doctor, he initially responded to treatment. He felt he was 'one of the lucky ones' and, by June, 'the malignancy subsided and is being kept under control as a low level [of chemotherapy]'.[88] Sunday responded to the crisis by reading books about special diets for cancer and experimenting with Vitamin C. But she became ill with sciatica which was like 'having an acute toothache all down your leg . . . It was brought on by overworking in the garden and aggravating a faulty disk in her spine . . . nothing to be done except rest, and she finds that very difficult.'[89]

For Barrett, there was good news. After undergoing treatment for Hodgkin's, he went into a complete remission though he had been 'at first convinced he had only a few months to live'.[90] By September, however, John's condition had once again deteriorated and he begged Laurence Hope to 'please keep our own bad news to yourself as we don't talk about it anymore than we can help'.[91]

During that difficult period, Darren, Everard and Sunday

came into closer contact, the brothers and sister putting aside the differences that had separated them over the years. Sunday visited Everard's country property and Everard would bring 'a bucketful of roses' when he came to Heide, pleasing Sunday because 'they were the same old-fashioned roses she liked'.[92]

For some time, John had been discussing strategies for euthanasia with his brother, Dick. He and Sunday had stored a large quantity of prescription pills but they were worried that 'they might lose their effectiveness with time and we could not get any more'. John thought that 'many common drugs' would probably 'do the trick if taken in large quantities' but the problem was to have one that would 'be effective in reasonably small quantities and will work rapidly and without distressing effects, such as violent vomiting. Sunday is very scared of this . . . The worst thing of all would be to bungle it and get carted off to hospital and given a stomach pump.'[93] John and Sunday had discussed it with two doctors but 'we finally have to rely on our resources'.[94]

It is disquieting to read of the Reeds' plans, so soon after the deaths of Cynthia and Sweeney. John was calm at the prospect. 'If the moment comes when I feel I do not want to wait any longer, I will take my own life. It is more difficult for Sunday than it is for me, partly because of the nature of her temperament . . . We have, of course, thought of the end of our lives and always hope they will end together, and perhaps that will be so. I think neither of us fear the fact of death as such but the process of dying is a different thing.'[95]

Despite the shadows gathering around them, 1981 was a busy and important year for the Reeds. A retrospective of Hester's opened at the National Gallery of Victoria in September, Richard Haese's *Rebels and Precursors: The Revolutionary Years of Australian Art* was published in October and Heide Park and Art Gallery opened to the public in November.

The Reeds admired the thoroughness and perception that Haese brought to his groundbreaking research on Australian culture in the 1930s and '40s, that privileged the role of the Reeds, Nolan, Tucker and the Heide circle. But old enmities died hard. John baulked at what he considered the importance Haese gave to the 'communist-social realist element' which was 'vastly over stressed, to the detriment of the book as a whole . . . Counihan, I note, has more space in the index than anyone else.' John also noted Counihan's name graced the front cover while his and Sunday's did not.[96]

In 1977 I began my master's thesis on Joy Hester and, in 1981, curated her retrospective. Sweeney generously involved himself in my research and we became friends. We met at the Victorian College of the Arts when he was a student and I was the art history lecturer. When I interviewed the Reeds for my research, he insisted on accompanying me to Heide, predicting it would be distressing for Sunday. It was not my first visit; I'd interviewed John previously, but it was the first time I was to meet Sunday.

Sweeney and I sat at the table in the living room, filled with autumn light, while John made coffee and produced a plate of biscuits. He told me Sunday didn't want to be interviewed about Joy, that she was uncomfortable about the formality and perhaps would not join us. We had decided to begin without her when she appeared at the top of the stairs and slowly made her way down.

I felt anxious. How was this going to go? To break the ice, Sweeney began making conversation. Sunday didn't meet my eyes. I switched on the tape recorder. Sunday's hearing problem meant she would talk over – or under – John, Sweeney or me, counter-pointing questions and comments in a frail, clear, insistent voice.

Now that she had decided to be part of the interview, Sunday was keen to help, asking exactly what I needed to know, warning me not to let her ramble, and seeking John's corroboration when dates and facts eluded her. Sunday's memory was, however, sharper than his. Her manner was diffident and courteous – she seemed shy – but she was confident about her views and put them succinctly. Yet there were undercurrents, and even a sense of contest.

Sunday remained guarded and I sensed I had not won her trust. Nor was I was sure whether she approved of me, or my research. After all, Joy was her treasured friend. I had the feeling that my tape recorder and my questions were unsettling a previously established balance for Sunday between herself and Joy, a dialogue she did not wish to be interrupted. Sunday seemed tuned to inner realities of time and place that intersected with the room we were in. Hers was a compelling, disquieting presence, the focus of the interview, of its mood and flow. In a flash, Sunday could exert emotional pressures that were subtle, forceful and very much under her control. And, so, I felt, were we. I pushed on with my questions until, after nearly an hour, the memories overwhelmed Sunday and she wept.

The next time Sunday and I met was in 1981 at Heide I. By then the Reeds had returned and I was in the process of selecting Hester's works for the show. In the interim, Sweeney had died. I sent Sunday and John a short, inadequate note; I barely knew what to say or how to address their grief. But I refrained from contacting them about my research, feeling that whatever distress Sunday experienced about Joy would only be magnified by Sweeney's death. Barrett, whom I saw regularly, kept them informed of my progress.

We were in the dining room, looking at Hester's hand-written poems, which I was keen to include. Sunday was happy to lend them but she had another idea: I should include *Face* VI (c.1947–48,

Heide MoMA) which she had propped against the wall for me to view. Sunday told me it was her favourite work of Hester's, an imaginary portrait of Elizabeth, the ill-fated heroine from Julien Green's gothic novel *Midnight*, a book Hester and Sunday both loved. I hesitated for a moment, wondering aloud if I had already selected enough from the Faces series. Privately, I felt a little peeved. There had been no discussion: Sunday just expected me to obey her.

'Johnny,' Sunday suddenly wailed, 'Johnny, she doesn't want to include it.' 'No, I didn't say that,' I countered, mortified. 'I'm just not sure . . .' 'What's the girl saying?' she demanded of John. 'What does she say? I can't hear her.' Up until then Sunday seemed perfectly able to hear me. John, who must have witnessed such scenes many times, remained unfussed. 'Now Sun, now Sun,' he said mildly, shaking his head. As I continued to bluster, Sunday continued to wail. 'I'll include it,' I said and, magically, the atmosphere cleared.

Later we had coffee and I stayed on, discussing the show. Sunday was sitting on the dining room table, resting her feet on a chair. She did not move with the stiffness or fraility of an older woman: she was lithe and sure. John was standing nearby. Suddenly, she leaned forward, hooked a finger into his belt and tugged him towards her, so he rested between her knees. It was a cheeky, sexy, possessive gesture, and John's face lit up with pleasure. I felt surprised and slightly embarrassed, naive as I was, to see older people demonstrate such feelings. In a playful, unself-conscious way, Sunday revealed their intimacy, a bond undiminished by time.

Sunday did not attend the opening by Dick Hamer of Heide Park and Art Gallery on 8 November. She went to the movies instead, fleeing not only the prospect of visitors calling by Heide I afterwards, but the disquiet of seeing her home transformed into a public gallery, filled with strangers. The opening exhibition was Nolan's Kelly series. Friends were astonished. 'Is Sunday really truly out?' enquired David McGlashan.[97]

John attended the opening briefly, recognising 'it was the climax of years and work and frustration and now everything has gone full steam ahead'. He was full of praise for Hamer. 'He has been right behind it all the way, and without his active interest it would never have come off.' But, as far as the gallery went, the Reeds had decided 'not [to] take any part in what goes on, as we think that is best'.[98] Though John frequently took walks in the park, Sunday never went near Heide II. It saddened Maudie Palmer, the newly appointed director. Palmer had great plans for Heide. The kitchen garden was already in the process of being restored. Then Heide II was converted into a public gallery, the collection catalogued and the opening planned. Also on Palmer's agenda was the creation of a sculpture park.

In fact, Sunday was not only miserable about quitting her garden but annoyed, too. When John Sinclair remarked that 'now the State Government owned Heide, people were saying what a wonderful garden it had', Sunday fulminated 'they say that now, but nobody said it then'.[99] Since her beloved home had become a state institution, it might have made Sunday even more aware of the lack of official recognition accorded to her and John: they received no public honours, were not appointed to the boards of arts institutions, invited to judge awards or sit on committees, roles that signify public prestige, peer respect and professional acknowledgement. The Reeds liked their privacy. Equally, they wanted to be thanked. It seemed that the establishment they had once rejected had not forgotten them.

Georges Mora, as a board member, kept the Reeds informed about the gallery's progress. But Sunday had retreated from Georges, too, prompting him to write that he knew she was depressed about Sweeney. While they would always mourn Sweeney, she must not blame herself because 'somehow we are all to blame' and it was 'part of Sweeney's tragic gesture' to make them feel guilty. 'But we are not, you the least. You loved him, maybe you didn't understand him.' Georges chided her, encouraging her to become 'a hardened warrior like me!'[100] John tried to protect Sunday, rebuffing the overtures of friends like Susie Brunton and Ron Upton, telling them Sunday was too upset to have visitors.

Perhaps John was trying to protect himself, too. His condition was deteriorating rapidly and he no longer responded to treatment. He summoned Maudie Palmer and told her 'that while he knew Heide Park and Art Gallery was a beautiful place, he didn't want it to be just another beautiful place for people to visit . . . He wanted it to retain some sense of its special creative quality, a sense of always seeking that thin edge.' Palmer resolved 'that is what we will try to do'.[101]

Nadine Amadio was aware of how ill John was. As music critic for the *Financial Review*, she was interviewing Nolan, in Sydney at the time, for his plans to design sets for Wagner's Ring cycle. When Amadio asked Nolan, 'Did you know that John Reed is dying?', he replied, 'I don't want to know about that.' Amadio responded, 'I want to tell you. Don't you think it's time that all this finished and you rang and wished John godspeed? I mean, your lives were very close once. "It's too late for that", he said.' When Amadio rang John and told him, he was furious. 'He said, "How dare you say things like that to Sid? That doesn't mean anything if he rings now you told him to."' Amadio was 'devastated. He really told me off.' But

John rang back and apologised, saying 'I know you only were doing what you thought was right.' But Amadio 'could tell that it had affected [Nolan] that I'd said John was dying . . . He was very quiet, very subdued . . . He was diminished by that news but he didn't ring.'[102]

On Friday 4 December, John reported, 'I have become very weak and extremely sluggish in my movements, and it would seem that the therapy has done as much as it can.'[103] The following evening, John died peacefully, six days short of his eightieth birthday. He was cremated in a private ceremony and his ashes strewn under the canoe tree.

In the week that followed, Sunday made plans to follow John. She was not ill, there was nothing wrong with her, but the terrible blows of the '70s had taken their toll, Sweeney's death the most gruelling of all. Brunton recalled that Sunday 'had always said, "I can't manage without John." Her life was so involved with him.' When Sunday had rung Brunton and told her, 'I can't stay here', meaning Heide, they made plans to visit Aspendale together.[104] Nadine Amadio was preparing to come down from Sydney. Jean Langley, too, was arranging to see Sunday.

On 6 December, the Hester retrospective had closed and, a few days later, I went out to Heide to return *Face* VI and Hester's poems to Sunday. We had afternoon tea in the library. Sunday was abstracted and strangely calm. Though Barrett, now in remission from Hodgkin's disease, was at her side, she seemed utterly alone and the house, empty. The unease that had marked our previous meetings, my uncertainty about her support for my research and my hesitancy in her presence were gone. Whatever resistance we had met, and recognised, in one another dissolved that afternoon.

To my surprise, knowing how ill John was, the Reeds had

attended the opening of Hester's retrospective. They had arrived late, missing the speeches, both dressed in white and holding hands, a dapper, handsome couple. I was nervous about Sunday's response to the show. Sunday, I noticed, didn't bother socialising but went straight to the works and studied them. (She was right: *Face* VI was an important addition.)

When Sunday finished, she walked up to me. She was beaming. 'You clever girl', she said. I melted with relief and pleasure. For the first time, I glimpsed the radiant, unequivocal approval Sunday's friends and favoured artists had described, the bright beam of encouragement and delight that made one feel one's work was recognised and valued by a very special intelligence.

That last time, at Heide, we said our farewells at the front door. On each side of the door were the glass panels, etched with the roses Joy had designed. Sunday said she knew that the exhibition would lead to greater interest in Joy's work. Did I kiss her goodbye? I can't remember. She was smiling as I left.

On Tuesday 15 December, Sunday took her life. Her death notice explains it best: 'Love follows swiftly'. Barrett Reid assisted her. After the funeral, her ashes were scattered on the Heide earth, beneath the old river red gum.

Afterword

In December 2001, Heide I opened to the public as a house museum and art gallery, part of the Heide Museum of Modern Art. As a member of the Heide MoMA board, I was on the committee, chaired by Sarah McKay, Everard's daughter, that oversaw the restoration of the house and garden.[1]

After Sunday died, Barrett lived at Heide I until his death in 1995. He had retired from the State Library of Victoria but pursued a vigorous career as editor of *Overland*, a literary journal, which was produced in the Heide dining room. Artists, poets and writers continued to visit, and Barrett maintained the tradition of cultural conviviality established by the Reeds.

Barrett also became a fierce guardian of the Reeds' reputation and though he usually showed generosity to all who required assistance, he made exceptions. One was Bernard Smith. Remembering old antagonisms with the Reeds (Smith also had some reservations about Haese's *Rebels and Precursors*), Barrett refused Smith access to the Reed Papers when he was writing *Noel Counihan: Artist and Revolutionary*. While Barrett enjoyed the book and regarded Smith as an 'impressive figure', he felt there was a 'contradiction between [Smith's] Communist ideology and a more complex aesthetic he later learnt.'[2]

Barrett himself had two major projects underway. He was in the process of selecting the first collection of his poetry, as well as tackling the enormous job of editing John's letters. Both *Making Country*, his volume of poetry, and *Letters of John Reed* would be published posthumously.[3] Since his first bout of cancer in 1980, Barrett's health remained uncertain: he went through long periods of remission but, eventually, illness overtook him. He remained courageous and clear-headed until the end. Barrett died on 6 August 1995 at Heide I, surrounded by close friends Maudie Palmer, poet Shelton Lea and Beryl Glasson, his housekeeper and carer.

It seemed Heide was destined to remain a centre for old loves, feuds and yearnings. Though Sunday had left the house equally to Barrett and Philip Jones, Barrett had persuaded Philip to allow him to take sole possession, while Philip remained at Greenhill. After Barrett's death, the situation lead to a legal wrangle between Jones, the trustees of the Reed estate and Heide MoMA. Jones believed it was his right to return to Heide after Barrett's death. William Forrest and Richard Llewellyn, Reed estate trustees, and the Heide MoMA board, negotiated with Jones about the matter. The dispute was resolved when Jones accepted a cash settlement, two paintings from the Heide MoMA collection and a selection of books from the Heide library. Heide I then became the property of Heide MoMA.

Nolan, in the company of Mary, visited Heide soon after the

Reeds' deaths in 1982. Over lunch with critic Susan McCulloch around that time, Nolan told her an extraordinary story. He said that, unknown to Mary, he had secretly visited Heide where he saw Sunday and John. 'It was weird,' he said, 'they wanted it all to start again.' McCulloch asked, 'What to "start again"?' 'The whole thing,' Nolan replied, 'the whole relationship.' McCulloch regarded Nolan's story as 'bizarre'.[4] It was not only bizarre, it was untrue. Nolan did not visit Heide or see the Reeds. But in Nolan's mind, it seemed, the fantasy continued to play, so real that he believed he had returned to Heide where Sunday and John begged him to re-enter their lives.

While the dispute between Jones, Heide MoMA and the Reed estate trustees continued, several people, including John Brereton, lecturer at Burnley Horticultural College, stayed at Heide I, acting as caretakers, but the house and garden became progressively neglected. In 1998, Heide MoMA was awarded a $2.5 million grant from the Federal Government's Centenary of Federation Cultural and Heritage Fund to cover the costs of refurbishment.

Though Barrett was a keen gardener, he did not have the funds to adequately maintain the property. It needed extensive restoration, including restumping. The walls were filled with white ant. If the house was to be open to the public and artworks shown there, it needed to be upgraded to international museum standard. Without IMS and adequate security, public collections would not loan their works.

Though Heide I's pristine art gallery appearance bears no resemblance to the way the Reeds lived, the gains are significant. Research was carried out to discover and restore the rooms' original colour schemes. Ugly worn carpets were removed revealing the original floorboards. An investigation was made into Mike Brown's mural in the dining room which had been painted over. Unfortunately, it was in such a bad state it could not be repaired. The beautiful rose wallpaper Sunday chose for the bedroom has been replaced.

Some of Sunday's favourite pieces of furniture are there, though few original pieces remain. In the bedroom is Sunday's cheval mirror plus the Louis XIV-style writing desk with its pink velvet top. There is also the nineteenth-century Wellington desk, bought by Sunday's father. In the hall is the Georgian chest Sunday not only stripped of its shellac but scrubbed with a wire brush. The library is the most atmospheric room, with its books, sofa, chairs and John's desk facing the window. It is painted in the same warm terracotta tones Nolan and Sunday used in the 1940s. The house entertains a series of exhibitions both historical and contemporary.

Landscape architect Elizabeth Peck, who restored the garden, felt 'Sunday's spirit is still very much there'. Peck believed 'there was an overlaying of gardening styles from different occupants. I've tried to retain the simplicity, the sense of a working, practical garden, small pieces of the overlay so we didn't lose the whole story.'

Peck also re-planted the orchard, consulting 1930s and '40s catalogues to identify the correct species of apple and pear trees, then sourced them from a nursery in Gippsland. Sunday's English lavender hedge along the drive has also been re-planted. Peck restored Sunday's taste for regularity by using original materials for the paths 'so you can still see the old patterns'.[5] The wild garden remains, as do ferns and casuarinas planted by Barrett. In 2004, to celebrate the publication of this book, the Heart Garden was recreated.

Despite Sunday's obsession with Nolan, and the provocation and inspiration he inspired, he was not the love of her life. In her life's final act, she recognised John as the ground on which her creativity flourished. Obsession implies yearning, dominance, even illness.

Its Latin root means 'besieged' or 'beset'. Being obsessed with another person is not the best way to understand them: reality tends to be extinguished by fantasy. It seemed Sunday never understood the dark, complex and hostile strands of Nolan's character; never accepted, trapped within her own obsession and egotism, that all he desired, after he had left, was to hurt her.

John's life project was Sunday: everything revolved around her. The tragedy of their marriage was also its strength: their mutual willingness to invite others into their intimacy. John encouraged Sunday to develop her full potential as a modernist patron, as a collaborator in the production of art, as a gardener, a publisher, as the directing force of Heide and its chief designer.

Sunday interpreted modernism as a very personal enterprise, a dialectics of feeling that involved friendship as well as formalism. Space, shape and structure – the elements of art that modernism challenged and changed – were life matters for Sunday, represented by relationships that occurred, not only in a painting or poem, but in her garden, her kitchen and her bedroom; sites of her creativity, that, in turn, inspired others.

Modernism destroyed many of art's long-cherished illusions by revealing them as pictorial tricks or subterfuges, like the illusion of three-dimensional space on a two-dimensional surface. To be modern meant to spurn such fallacies as old-fashioned and un-necessary. For Sunday, modernism also meant reinterpreting the accepted structures of a woman's life and the essence of 'women's work'. She challenged ideas about marriage, fidelity, family and domesticity, transforming them with her own personal, and very modern, touch.

Enduring creative achievements arise not only from strengths but limitations, too. Sunday needed to act in collaboration with others to realise her vision. It could make her difficult and demanding as well as munificent, loyal and inspiring. The result is Heide, a gallery, a collection, a park and a garden founded on webs of passionate, personal connections.

Goodness knows how Sunday would feel about strangers wandering through her private domain but Heide's destiny was always meant to be a gift, shared and preserved by the energy of others.

The ghosts remain, aware of new voices in the rooms, new footsteps in the hall, lingering as witnesses to what Sunday honoured most – creativity and change.

Acknowledgements

I AM INDEBTED TO NADINE AMADIO, Susie Brunton, Peter Hobb, Philip Jones and Jean Langley who shared their memories, loaned archival material, answered endless queries and showed a constant warmth and openness. For the same reasons, I am also grateful to Peter Burns, Neil Douglas, Laurence Hope, Les Kossatz and Ron Upton.

Bernard Smith kindly agreed to read the manuscript and his wisdom and encouragement had a beneficial effect. The Literature Board, Australia Council, awarded me a grant that greatly assisted.

I would also like to thank Ian Baillieu; Asher and Luba Bilu; Gay Cuthbert; Peter Dwyer, St Paul's Cathedral; Ann Galbally; Jane Grant; Sir Rupert Hamer; Deborah Hart, National Gallery of Australia; Richard Heathcote, National Trust; Wendy Hitchmough, Charleston; Jill Kitson; Terence Lane, National

Gallery of Victoria; Bruce Lorimer; Mary McBride; Eve McGlashan; Ken McGregor; Neil Martin; Andrea May, Mornington Peninsula Art Gallery; Maudie Palmer; Elizabeth Peck; Antony Penrose, Farley's Farm; Jennifer Phipps, National Gallery of Victoria; Peter Redlich; Cathie Shelton, Ballarat Genealogical Society; Janet South and Barbara Stephenson, Nepean Historical Society; Geoffrey Smith, National Gallery of Victoria; Peter Struthers; Gordon Thomson; Nicholas Usherwood; Henry von Bibra; Pamela Warrender; Terry Whelan; Lyn Williams. I would also like to thank the trustees of the John and Sunday Reed Estate and the Barrett Reid Estate.

In Tasmania, I would like to thank Gary Austin, Helen Bond, Max Cameron and Ross James. Peter and Sally Holyman and Kenneth and Berta von Bibra generously took me on a guided tour of Mt Pleasant while Daniel Thomas orchestrated the entire trip. Staff at Heide Museum of Modern Art, including director Lesley Alway, assisted this project in a variety of ways. I'm particularly grateful to Jennifer Ross, Registrar, Exhibitions.

It's a lucky writer who has a publisher like Jane Palfreyman and an editor like Nadine Davidoff, staunch friends and consummate professionals.

JB

Endnotes

INTRODUCTION

1.   Jean Langley, taped interview, 3 September 1997, Safety
     Beach.
2.   Jean Langley, taped interview, 2 December 2002, Safety
     Beach.
3.   Jane Brown, *Gardens of a Golden Afternoon: A Social History of
     Gardens and Gardening*, Penguin, Harmondsworth, 1985,
     p. 50.
4.   In later years, the whole area outside the kitchen would
     become known as 'the Heart Garden'. In the early 1970s,
     Sweeney Reed paved and fenced the area to make it safe
     for his sons Mishka and Danila. Susie Brunton recalled it
     was 'just the heart of the house . . . we used to sit out there

and have afternoon tea a lot.' (Taped interview, 17 July 1999, Frankston.)

CHAPTER 1: TROUBLED PRINCESS

1. James Paxton, *Toorak As I Knew It*, Prahran Historical and Arts Society, Prahran, 1983, p. 18.

2. Sunday Reed to John Reed, 4 January 1933, Reed Papers, State Library of Victoria.

3. J.D. Poynter, in Bede Nairn and Geoffrey Serle (ed.), *Australian Dictionary of Biography*, vol. 7, Melbourne University Press, Melbourne, 1979, p. 139.

4. Terry Whelan, taped interview, 27 June 2002, North Fitzroy.

5. Michael Cannon, *The Land Boomers*, Nelson, Melbourne, 1976, p. 196.

6. Barrett Reid, taped interview, 19 August 1994, Bulleen. I am also grateful to the Queenscliffe Historical Society for supplying me with information about James Baillieu.

7. Nairn and Serle, *Australian Dictionary of Biography*, p. 139.

8. Nairn and Serle, *Australian Dictionary of Biography*, p. 139.

9. Cannon, *Land Boomers*, p. 204.

10. Barrett Reid, taped interview, 19 August 1994, Bulleen.

11. Sunday Reed to John Reed, 4 January 1933, Reed Papers, State Library of Victoria.

12. Jean Langley, taped interview, 25 October 1994, Safety Beach.

13. J.S. MacDonald, *The Art of Fred McCubbin*, Lothian, Melbourne, 1916. Clive Baillieu, Alfred Deakin, Edward

Dyason and members of the Syme and Manifold families also contributed.

14. Ann Galbally and Anne Gray (eds.), *Letters from Smike: The Letters of Arthur Streeton*, Oxford University Press, Melbourne, 1989, p. 176.

15. Terry Whelan, taped interview, 27 June 2002, North Fitzroy.

16. Janine Burke (ed.), *Dear Sun: The Letters of Joy Hester and Sunday Reed*, William Heinemann, Port Melbourne, 1995, p. 151.

17. Galbally and Gray, *Letters from Smike*, p. 144.

18. Barrett Reid, taped interview, 19 August 1994, Bulleen.

19. Nadine Amadio, taped interview, 1 June 2002, Sydney.

20. Sunday gave the book to Mirka Mora in the 1950s. Mirka Mora, *Wicked but Virtuous: My Life*, Viking, Ringwood, 2000, p. 150.

21. Jean Langley, taped interview, 25 October 1994, Safety Beach.

22. Burke, *Dear Sun*, p. 171.

23. Jean Langley, taped interview, 25 October 1994, Safety Beach.

24. Paxton, *Toorak*, p. 18.

25. I am indebted to James Paxton's *Toorak As I Knew It* for impressions of Toorak in these years.

26. Michael Cannon, *The Long Last Summer*, Nelson, Melbourne, 1985, p. 5.

27. Barrett Reid, taped interview, 19 August 1994, Bulleen.

28. St Catherine's was founded in Castlemaine and in 1903 it

was taken over by Ruth, Aphra and Nora Langley, the daughters of Henry Langley, the Anglican bishop of Castlemaine. In 1911, the sisters named it after St Catherine's School, Sydney, which they had attended.

29. Peter Hobb, taped interview, 3 December 2002, Tootgarook.

30. Jane Brown, *Gardens of a Golden Afternoon: A Social History of Gardens and Gardening*, Penguin, Harmondsworth, 1985, p. 33–34.

31. Burke, *Dear Sun*, p. 143.

32. Axel Clark, *Henry Handel Richardson*, Simon and Schuster, St Peters, 1990, p. 136.

33. Cannon, *Long Last Summer*, p. 5

34. Terry Whelan, taped interview, 27 June 2002, North Fitzroy.

35. Nairn and Serle, *Australian Dictionary of Biography*, p. 140.

36. Peter Hobb, taped interview, 3 December 2002, Tootgarook.

37. Jean Langley, taped interview, 25 October 1994, Safety Beach.

38. Barrett Reid, taped interview, 19 August 1994, Bulleen.

CHAPTER 2: THE WIDE WORLD

1. Angela Woollacott, *To Try Her Fortune in London*, Oxford University Press, New York, 2001, p. 28.

2. Nina Murdoch, *Seventh Heaven: A Joyous Discovery of Europe*, Angus and Robertson, Sydney, 1930, p. 1.

3. Sunday Reed to John Reed, 1943, Reed Papers, State Library of Victoria.

4. Michael Cannon, *The Long Last Summer*, Nelson, Melbourne, 1985, p. 7.

5. Murdoch, *Seventh Heaven*, p. 177.

6. Barrett Reid, taped interview, 19 August 1994, Bulleen.

7. Murdoch, *Seventh Heaven*, p. 253.

8. Gertrude Stein, *Paris France*, Liveright, New York, 1970, p. 11.

9. Sunday Reed to Jean Langley, 26 November 1960, Langley Papers.

10. Janine Burke, *Australian Women Artists, 1840–1940*, Greenhouse Publications, Richmond, 1980, p. 83.

11. Stein, *Paris France*, p. 11. In her later years, Stein wore clothes designed by Pierre Balmain.

12. M.B. Ginsburg, *Fashion: 1900–1939*, Scottish Arts Council/Victoria and Albert Museum, London, 1975, p. 11.

13. Burke, *Australian Women Artists*, p. 40.

14. Barret Reid, taped interview, 19 August 1994, Bulleen.

15. Leonard Quinn returned to Massachusetts, dying at North Attleboro, Bristol County, in June 1972.

16. Henry James, *The Bostonians*, Macmillan, London, 1921, p. 202.

17. James, *The Bostonians*, p. 276.

18. Nadine Amadio, taped interview, 1 June 2002, Sydney.

19. Jean Langley, taped interview, 2 December 2002, Safety Beach.

20. Ronald Hutton, *The Triumph of the Moon: A History of Modern Pagan Witchcraft*, Oxford Univeristy Press, Oxford, 1999, p. 53.

21. Edmund Campion, *Australian Catholics: The Contribution of Catholics to the Development of Australian Society*, Viking, Ringwood, 1985, p. 118.

22. As were Edmund Barton, George Reid, Joseph Cook, Earle Page, Robert Menzies, Arthur Fadden, John McEwen, John Gorton and William McMahon. Gerard Henderson, 'The secret we should all be let in on', *Age*, 2 September 2002.

23. Campion, *Australian Catholics*, p. 87.

24. James Paxton, *Toorak As I Knew It*, Prahran Historical and Arts Society, Prahran, 1983, p. 36.

25. Naomi Turner, *Catholics in Australia: A Social History*, vol. 2, Collins Dove, North Blackburn, 1992, p. 47.

26. Philip Jones, telephone interview, 30 September 2002, Melbourne.

27. Arthur Baillieu to Sunday Reed, 1 March 1928, Reed Papers, State Library of Victoria.

28. Carl Rollyson, *Beautiful Exile: The Life of Martha Gellhorn*, Duffy and Snellgrove, Sydney, 2001, p. 23.

29. Nancy Mitford, *Zelda Fitzgerald*, Penguin, Harmondsworth, 1970, p. 155.

30. Michael Keon, *Glad Morning Again*, Imprint, Watsons Bay, 1996, p. 116.

31. Francis Miltoun, *Rambles in Provence and on the Riviera*, Sisley's, London, 1907, p. 237.

32. Zelda Fitzgerald, *Save Me the Waltz*, Penguin, Harmondsworth, 1971, p. 86.

33. Fitzgerald, *Save Me the Waltz*, p. 104.

34. Keon, *Glad Morning Again*, p. 85.

35. Sunday Reed to Gray Smith, 30 June 1949, Reed Papers, State Library of Victoria.

36. Scott Fitzgerald, *Tender is the Night*, Penguin, Harmondsworth, 1970, p. 92.

37. Keon, *Glad Morning Again*, p. 83.

38. David Piper, *Vincent Van Gogh: Portrait of Provence*, The Folio Society, London, 1959, n.p.

39. Jean Langley, taped interview, 2 December 2002, Safety Beach.

40. Shari Benstock, *Women of the Left Bank: Paris 1900–1940*, Virago, London, 1987, p. 68.

41. The Cotswolds cover an area that stretches west from Oxford to the Welsh borders, from Bath in the south and Worcester in the north. See Garry Hogg, *The Cotswolds*, Batsford Ltd, London, 1973, p. 56.

42. Jill Duchess of Hamilton, Penny Hart and John Simmons, *The Gardens of William Morris*, Hodder and Stoughton, Rydalmere, 1998, p. 56. Kelmscott Manor, Morris's home, was not open to the public in the late 1920s and it is unlikely that Sunday viewed it. Like Vanessa Bell and Duncan Grant who spent part of each year at Charleston in Sussex, Morris rented Kelmscott Manor. It was part of an estate, later bought and restored by the Society of Antiquaries.

43. Brenda Maddox, *The Married Man: A Life of D.H. Lawrence*, Sinclair-Stevenson, London, 1994, p. 487.

44. Mervyn Levy (ed.), *Paintings of D.H. Lawrence*, Cory, Adams and Mackay, London, 1964, p. 64.

45. Reed, 'Autobiography', Reed Papers, State Library of Victoria, n.p. John remarked that 'Sunday's contact with the art world was probably limited to Arthur Streeton, a friend of her father's, Alice [sic] Goodsir who painted her portrait in Paris and D.H. Lawrence's supposedly erotic watercolours which she saw in London and conventional paintings she saw in conventional homes.'

46. Michael Keon, *Glad Morning Again*, p. 119.

47. Sunday Reed to Jean Langley, 16 July 1960, Reed Papers, State Library of Victoria.

48. Nadine Amadio, taped interview, 1 June 2002, Sydney.

49. Jean Langley, taped interview, 3 September 1997, Safety Beach.

50. Nadine Amadio, taped interview, 1 June 2002, Sydney.

51. Jean Langley, taped interview, 3 September 1997, Safety Beach.

52. Arthur Baillieu to Sunday Reed, c.1931, Reed Papers, State Library of Victoria.

53. Karen Quinlan, *In a picture land over the sea, Agnes Goodsir, 1864–1939*, Bendigo Art Gallery, Bendigo, 1998, p. 45.

54. Muriel Segal, 'Archibald Memorial is Superb Statuary', *Herald*, 3 July 1930.

CHAPTER 3: JOHN

1. John Reed, 'Autobiography', Reed Papers, State Library of Victoria.

2. Reed, 'Autobiography'.

3. Cynthia Reed, *Daddy Sowed A Wind!*, Shakespeare Head, Sydney, 1947, p. 9.

4. Helen Bond, telephone interview, 10 September 2002, Launceston.

5. Henry Reed to John Reed, 30 June 1926, Reed Papers, State Library of Victoria.

6. Patrick White, 'The Cynthia I Knew', *Australian*, 7 December 1976.

7. Henry Reed to John Reed, 25 November 1929, Reed Papers, State Library of Victoria.

8. Kenneth von Bibra, taped interview, 10 September 2002, Mt Pleasant.

9. Reed, 'Autobiography'.

10. John Reed to Margaret Reed, 1920, Reed Papers, State Library of Victoria.

11. Barrett Reid, 'Making it New in Australia', *Angry Penguins and Realist Painting in Melbourne in the 1940s*, Hayward Gallery, London, 1988, p. 28.

12. John Reed to Sunday Reed, April 1931, Reed Papers, State Library of Victoria.

13. John Reed to Sunday Reed, April 1931, Reed Papers, State Library of Victoria.

14. Reed, *Daddy*, p. 5.

15. John Reed to Sunday Reed, 1931, Reed Papers, State Library of Victoria.

16. David Marr, *Patrick White: A Life*, Vintage, Sydney, 1991, p. 70.

17. Reed, 'Autobiography'.

18. Michael Cannon, *The Long Last Summer*, Nelson, Melbourne, 1976, p. 162.

19. John Reed to Mary Christina Sewell, 4 December 1981, Reed Papers, State Library of Victoria.

20. Robin Roberts to John Reed, 30 November 1924, Reed Papers, State Library of Victoria.

21. Robin Roberts to John Reed, 30 November 1924, Reed Papers, State Library of Victoria.

22. Joseph Conrad, *Victory*, Penguin, Harmondsworth, 1966, p. 87.

23. Henry Reed to John Reed, 8 March 1925, Reed Papers, State Library of Victoria.

24. Henry Reed to John Reed, 28 October 1928, Reed Papers, State Library of Victoria.

25. Henry Reed to John Reed, 8 March 1925, Reed Papers, State Library of Victoria.

26. Reed, 'Autobiography'.

27. Reed, 'Autobiography'.

28. Ross McMullin, *Will Dyson*, Angus and Roberston, Sydney, 1984, p. 259.

29. Reed, 'Autobiography'.

30. Reed, 'Autobiography'.

31. McMullin, *Dyson*, p. 252.

32. Reed, 'Autobiography'.

33. Judith O'Callaghan, 'Fred Ward and Life Before Canberra', in Michael Bogle (ed.), *Designing Australia*, Pluto Press, Annandale, 2002, p. 155.

34. Reed, 'Autobiography'.

35. Robin Boyd, *Victorian Modern: One Hundred Years of Modern Architecture*, Architecture Students' Society of the Royal Victorian Institute of Architects, Melbourne, 1947, p. 20.

36. Reed, 'Autobiography'.

37. Fred Ward, 'The Problems of Furniture Design', in Bogle (ed.), *Designing Australia*, p. 149.

38. Ward, 'Furniture Design', in Bogle (ed.), *Designing Australia*, p. 152.

39. Frank Whitford, *Bauhaus*, Thames and Hudson, London, 1994, p. 206.

40. Whitford, *Bauhaus*, p. 206.

CHAPTER 4: TOGETHER

1. Reed Papers, State Library of Victoria.

2. John Reed, 'Autobiography', Reed Papers, State Library of Victoria.

3. Jean Langley, taped interview, 3 September 1997, Safety Beach.

4. Jean Langley, taped interview, 3 September 1997, Safety Beach.

5. Reed, 'Autobiography'.

6. Michael Keon, *Glad Morning Again*, Imprint, Watsons Bay, 1996, p. 126.

7. Abigail Heathcote, *A Far Cry: Spinning Yarns with Neil Douglas*, Karella Publishing, n.d., p. 70.

8. Reed, 'Autobiography'.

9. Sunday Reed to John Reed, Undated, Reed Papers, State Library of Victoria.

10. Sunday Reed to John Reed, c.1932, Reed Papers, State Library of Victoria.

11. Sunday Reed to John Reed, c.1931, Reed Papers, State Library of Victoria.

12. Sunday Reed to John Reed, late 1930, Reed Papers, State Library of Victoria.

13. John Reed to Sunday Reed, late 1930, Reed Papers, State Library of Victoria.

14. Sunday Reed to John Reed, c.1930, Reed Papers, State Library of Victoria.

15. John Reed to Sunday Reed, c.1930, Reed Papers, State Library of Victoria.

16. Sunday Reed to John Reed, c.1931, Reed Papers, State Library of Victoria.

17. Sunday Reed to John Reed, 4 January 1933, Reed Papers, State Library of Victoria.

18. Sunday Reed to John Reed, c.1931, Reed Papers, State Library of Victoria.

19. Sunday Reed to John Reed, c.1931, Reed Papers, State Library of Victoria.

20. John Reed to Sunday Reed, c.1931, Reed Papers, State Library of Victoria.

21. John Reed to Sunday Reed, c.1931, Reed Papers, State Library of Victoria.

22. John Reed to Sunday Reed, c.1931, Reed Papers, State Library of Victoria.

23. John Reed to Sunday Reed, c.1931, Reed Papers, State Library of Victoria.

24. John Reed to Sunday Reed, c.1931, Reed Papers, State Library of Victoria.

25. John Reed to Sunday Reed, c.1932, Reed Papers, State Library of Victoria.

26. W.H. Hudson, *South American Romances*, introduction by Ruth Tomalin, Duckworth, London, 1926, p. xi.

27. Jean Langley, taped interview, 25 October 1994, Safety Beach.

28. John Cowper Powys, *Wolf Solent*, Jonathan Cape, London, 1929, p. v.

29. John Reed to Sunday Reed, c.1932, Reed Papers, State Library of Victoria.

30. John Reed to Sunday Reed, c.1932, Reed Papers, State Library of Victoria.

31. Hermione Lee, *Virginia Woolf*, Chatto and Windus, London, 1996, p. 320.

32. Lee, *Virginia Woolf*, p. 337.

33. Nadine Amadio, taped interview, 1 June 2002, Sydney.

34. Sunday Reed to John Reed, c.1932, Reed Papers, State Library of Victoria.

35. Sunday Reed to John Reed, c.1932, Reed Papers, State Library of Victoria.

36. Arthur Baillieu to Sunday Reed, 18 June 1931, Reed Papers, State Library of Victoria.

37. Henry Reed to John Reed, 11 October 1930, Reed Papers, State Library of Victoria.

38. Arthur Baillieu to Sunday Reed, 18 June 1931, Reed Papers, State Library of Victoria.

39. Judith O'Callaghan, 'Fred Ward and Life Before Canberra', in Michael Bogle (ed.), *Designing Australia*, Pluto Press, Annandale, 2002, p. 156.

40. John Reed to Sunday Reed, 13 January 1932, Reed Papers, State Library of Victoria.

CHAPTER 5: THE FIRST CIRCLE

1. Reed Papers, State Library of Victoria.

2. Reed Papers, State Library of Victoria.

3. After the Second World War, the house was altered to create one dwelling and remains so today. I am grateful to Neil and Helen Martin, former owners of 27 Marne Street, for allowing me to visit the house and for explaining changes to it both during and prior to the period of their occupancy.

4. John Reed, 'Autobiography', Reed Papers, State Library of Victoria.

5. Gavin Fry, *Adrian Lawlor: A Portrait*, Heide Park and Art Gallery, Bulleen, 1983, p. 2.

6. Reed, 'Autobiography'.

7. George Bell, *Sun*, 9 December 1930.

8. Arthur Streeon, *Argus*, 9 December 1930.

9. Adrian Lawlor, 'By Kind Request', A *Comment*, April 1942, n.p.

10. Connie Smith was a neighbour of Lawlor's, a vivacious and sociable woman who was also an enthusiastic patron of Danila Vassilieff's. She commissioned Vassilieff's *Expulsion from Paradise* (1940, National Gallery of Australia), a multi-panelled screen depicting the banishment from Eden, where a curvaceous Eve and an impudent Adam are menaced by a Russian-style archangel brandishing a fiery sword. Alex, Connie's husband, objected and sent the screen back to the artist on the grounds it was 'blasphemous'. In the mid-'30s, Connie had bought and renovated Penleigh Boyd's old wattle-and-daub studio which stood less than 200 metres from Broom Warren. In 1938, she organised an exhibition at the Boyd studio that included Albert Tucker, together with Bell, Frater, Shore and Harry de Hartog. John Reed gave the opening speech. It provided another chance for *Argus* critic, and John's former friend, Harold Herbert, to sneer that 'the "contemporaries" have banded together and I am glad that they have decided to exhibit at a reasonable distance from Melbourne. City dwellers will not be unduly disturbed ... [It is] shockingly poor art which would make [Penleigh] Boyd turn in his grave.' The studio was Lawlor and Smith's trysting place. The affair lasted many years and was widely known in the little artists' community. Alex Smith, a real estate agent with no interest in the arts, simply turned a blind eye. Though it did not affect the

care with which Lawlor treated his wife Eva, especially during the illness of her later years, it made for strains and tensions. Eva was reserved and homely and, as far as Lawlor was concerned, theirs had not been a love match.

11. Lawlor, 'By Kind Request'.

12. Reed, 'Autobiography'.

13. John Reed to Sam Atyeo, 12 December 1974, Reed Papers, State Library of Victoria.

14. Sam Atyeo to John Reed, 1974, Reed Papers, State Library of Victoria.

15. John Reed quoted in Jennifer Phipps, *Atyeo*, Heide Park and Art Gallery, Bulleen, 1982, p. 8.

16. George Johnston, *My Brother Jack*, Angus and Robertson, Sydney, 1991, p. 95–6.

17. George Bell, *Sun*, 20 December 1932.

18. Clarice Zander, Letter to the Editor, December 1932, Reed Papers, State Library of Victoria.

19. Patrick White, 'The Cynthia I Knew', *Australian*, 7 December 1976.

20. Cynthia Reed to John Reed, 1945, Reed Papers, State Library of Victoria.

21. John Reed to Sunday Reed, March 1932, Reed Papers, State Library of Victoria.

22. Quoted in Jane Grant, 'The Life and Work of Cynthia Reed Nolan', Ph.D thesis, Sydney University, 2002, p. 23–4. I am grateful to Dr Grant for allowing me to read her thesis.

23. Quoted in Kylie Tennant, *Evatt: Politics and Justice*, Angus and Robertson, Sydney, 1970, p. 97. It was not until Henry Reed died in 1956 that his children received their inheritance.

24. Reed, 'Autobiography'.

25. Janine Burke (ed.), *Dear Sun: The Letters of Joy Hester and Sunday Reed*, William Heinemann, Port Melbourne, 1995, p. 171.

26. Sunday Reed to John Reed, c.1932, Reed Papers, State Library of Victoria.

27. Maie Casey, 'George Bell in Bourke Street', *Art and Australia*, September 1966, p. 120.

28. Felicity St John Moore, *Classical Modernism: The George Bell School*, National Gallery of Victoria, Melbourne, 1992, p. 1.

29. June Helmer, *George Bell: The Art of Influence*, Greenhouse Publications, Richmond, 1985, p. 13.

30. Maidie McGowan, taped interview, 8 August 1997, Frankston.

31. Mary Eagle and Jan Minchin, *The George Bell School*, Deutscher Art Publications, Melbourne, 1981, p. 56.

32. Casey, 'George Bell', *Art and Australia*, p. 120.

33. Eagle and Minchin, *Bell School*, p. 174.

34. Eagle and Minchin, *Bell School*, p. 176.

35. Eagle and Minchin, *Bell School*, p. 44.

36. Casey, 'George Bell', *Art and Australia*, p. 120.

37. Janine Burke, 'Special Edition: The Prints of Ethel Spowers and Eveline Syme', *Imprint*, Winter 1993, Part 1, p. 23.

38. Claude Flight, *Lino-Cuts: A Handbook of linoleum colour prints*, London, 1927, p. 3–4.

39. Roger Fry, *Vision and Design*, Chatto and Windus, London, 1920, p. 26.

40. John Reed to Sunday Reed, 1933, Reed Papers, State Library of Victoria.

41. Sam Atyeo to Sunday Reed, 7 January 1933, Reed Papers, State Library of Victoria.

42. Sam Atyeo to John and Sunday Reed, 1933, Reed Papers, State Library of Victoria.

43. Sam Atyeo to John and Sunday Reed, 1933, Reed Papers, State Library of Victoria.

44. Sam Atyeo to Sunday Reed, July 1933, Reed Papers, State Library of Victoria.

45. Sam Atyeo to Sunday Reed, 4 January 1934, Reed Papers, State Library of Victoria.

46. Sam Atyeo to Sunday Reed, January 1934, Reed Papers, State Library of Victoria.

47. Sam Atyeo to Sunday Reed, January 1934, Reed Papers, State Library of Victoria.

48. Sunday Reed to John Reed, 16 July 1933, Reed Papers, State Library of Victoria.

49. Sam Atyeo to John and Sunday Reed, 1933, Reed Papers, State Library of Victoria.

50. Reed, 'Autobiography'. *Sunita*, reproduced from the exhibition in *Art in Australia*, April 1933, p. 9, is not the work the Reeds acquired.

51. Stephen Gardiner, *Epstein: Artist Against the Establishment*, Michael Joseph, London, 1992, p. 261.

52. Basil Burdett, 'Mrs Zander's Exhibition of British Contemporary Art', *Art in Australia*, April 1933, p. 8. Clarice was known as Alleyne Zander professionally.

53. George Bell, *Sun*, 6 June 1933.

54. Sam Atyeo to John and Sunday Reed, 1933, Reed Papers, State Library of Victoria. *Norfolk Island Pine* hung in Vivian Ebbott's consulting rooms which Atyeo had designed.

55. Sam Atyeo to John and Sunday Reed, 1 January 1934, Reed Papers, State Library of Victoria.

56. Jennifer Phipps, *Atyeo*, Heide Park and Art Gallery, Bulleen, 1982, p. 9.

57. 'The Lively Arts', Tony Morphett interviewing John Reed, ABC TV, 1964.

58. John Reed, 'Autobiography'.

59. John Reed to Edwin Tanner, 31 December 1979, Reed Papers, State Library of Victoria.

60. Peter Hobb, taped interview, 2 December 2002, Tootgarook.

61. Herbert Read, *Art Now*, Faber and Faber, London, 1960, p. 43.

62. Read, *Art Now*, p. 60.

63. Sam Atyeo to Sunday Reed, 24 February 1934, Reed Papers, State Library of Victoria.

64. Sam Atyeo to Sunday Reed, c.1934, Reed Papers, State Library of Victoria.

65. Terry Ingram, 'Sam Atyeo – the artist who dressed Doc Evatt lands in a bed of roses', *Australian Financial Review*, 13 October 1980.

66. Tennant, *Evatt*, p. 97.

67. Reed, 'Autobiography'.

68. Reed, 'Autobiography'.

69. Sam Atyeo to John and Sunday Reed, 1936, Reed Papers, State Library of Victoria.

70. Sam Atyeo to John and Sunday Reed, 1933, Reed Papers, State Library of Victoria.

71. Sam Atyeo to John and Sunday Reed, 1933, Reed Papers, State Library of Victoria.

72. John Reed to Sunday Reed, 23 April 1937, Reed Papers, State Library of Victoria.

73. John's relationship with Moya Dyring is examined in Gay Cuthbert, 'Changing the Landscape: The Life and Art of Moya Dyring', Master of Creative Arts, University of Melbourne, 2002.

74. Sam Atyeo to John and Sunday Reed, 1933, Reed Papers, State Library of Victoria.

75. Sam Atyeo to John and Sunday Reed, 1933, Reed Papers, State Library of Victoria.

76. John Reed to Sunday Reed, 1934, Reed Papers, State Library of Victoria.

77. John Reed to Sunday Reed, 1935, Reed Papers, State Library of Victoria.

78. Sam Atyeo to John and Sunday Reed, 1933, Reed Papers, State Library of Victoria.

79. Sam Atyeo to Sunday Reed, 7 January 1933, Reed Papers, State Library of Victoria.

80. Sam Atyeo to John and Sunday Reed, 1933, Reed Papers, State Library of Victoria.

81. Sam Atyeo to Sunday Reed, c.1934, Reed Papers, State Library of Victoria.
82. John Reed to Sunday Reed, c.1934, Reed Papers, State Library of Victoria.
83. Philip Jones, taped interview, 18 October 1994, Elwood.
84. John Reed to Sidney Nolan, 13 October 1964, Reed Papers, State Library of Victoria.
85. Cynthia Reed to Sunday Reed, March 1934, Reed Papers, State Library of Victoria.
86. Moya Dyring to John and Sunday Reed, 14 April 1934, Reed Papers, State Library of Victoria.
87. Marianne Dekoven, 'Modernism and Gender', in Michael Levenson (ed.), *The Cambridge Companion to Modernism*, Cambridge University Press, Cambridge, 1999, p. 175.
88. Richard Haese interview with John Reed, 10 September 1973, Heide, Reed Papers, State Library of Victoria.
89. Burke, *Dear Sun*, p. 228.

Chapter 6: Heide House
1. Moya Dyring to Sunday Reed, 1937, Reed Papers, State Library of Victoria.
2. Neil Douglas, telephone interview, 12 December 1996, Venus Bay.
3. Sunday Reed, 20 July 1981, Reed Papers, State Library of Victoria.
4. Marion Cran, *The Garden of Ignorance: The Experiences of a Woman in a Garden*, Herbert Jenkins, London, c.1924, p. 15.

5. Sunday Reed to John Reed, 4 January 1933, Reed Papers, State Library of Victoria.

6. John Reed to Sunday Reed, July 1933, Reed Papers, State Library of Victoria.

7. Sunday Reed to John Reed, 16 July 1933, Reed Papers, State Library of Victoria.

8. John Reed, 'Heide: Some Background Notes for the Committee of Management of Heide Park and Art Gallery', 8 October 1980, Heide MoMA.

9. Reed, 'Heide', n.p.

10. Ann Galbally, *Arthur Streeton*, Lansdowne, East Melbourne, 1979, p. 14.

11. Sam Atyeo to John Reed, 20 April 1967, Reed Papers, State Library of Victoria.

12. Neil Douglas, taped interview, 25 January 1997, Venus Bay.

13. Reed, 'Heide', n.p. The stone pine (*Pinus pinea*) near the rear of the house, which still stands, was probably planted around 1880.

14. John Reed to Sam Atyeo, 21 June 1974, Reed Papers, State Library of Victoria.

15. John Reed to Sunday Reed, c.1931, Reed Papers, State Library of Victoria.

16. Reed, 'Heide', n.p. John was wrong about the oak: it was Algerian not Mexican.

17. Edna Walling, 'Garden Plan for Mrs A Baillieu', June 1930, Picture Collection, State Library of Victoria.

18. John Reed to Sunday Reed, 1936, Reed Papers, State Library of Victoria.

19. Barrett Reid, taped interview, 19 August 1994, Bulleen.

20. I am grateful to Mary McBride for giving me information about her uncle, Thomas James Heffernan. Mary McBride, taped interview, 13 November 2003, Elwood.

21. John Reed to Sunday Reed, c.1932, Reed Papers, State Library of Victoria.

22. John Reed to Sunday Reed, c.1932, Reed Papers, State Library of Victoria.

23. I am grateful to Peter Struthers who organised the opening exhibition at Heide I in December 2001 for information about the furniture in the house.

24. Peter Hobb, taped interview, 2 December 2002, Tootgarook.

25. Peter Hobb, taped interview, 22 July 1998, Rye.

26. Jean Langley, taped interview, 25 October 1994, Safety Beach.

27. Barrett Reid, taped interview, 19 August 1994, Heide.

28. 'Love Storm', in Barrett Reid, *Making Country*, Angus and Robertson, Pymble, 1995, p. 81.

29. Patrick McCaughey, *Australian Painters of the Heidelberg School*, The Jack Manton Collection, Oxford University Press, Melbourne, 1979, p. 78.

30. Bridget Whitelaw, ' "Plein Air" Painting: The Early Artists' Camps Around Melbourne', *Golden Summers*, National Gallery of Victoria, Melbourne, p. 55.

31. Galbally, *Streeton*, p. 15.

32. Henry von Bibra, telephone interview, 2 September 2002, Melbourne.

33. Kenneth von Bibra, taped interview, 10 September 2002, Mt Pleasant.

34. Sidney Nolan, *Paradise Garden*, Alistair McAlpine, London, 1971, p. 89.

35. Sunday Reed to John Reed, c.1931, Reed Papers, State Library of Victoria.

36. Sunday Reed to John Reed, January 1936, Reed Papers, State Library of Victoria.

37. Sam Atyeo to John and Sunday Reed, 1935, Reed Papers, State Library of Victoria.

38. John Reed to Sunday Reed, 1936, Reed Papers, State Library of Victoria.

39. Abigail Heathcote, *A Far Cry: Spinning Yarns with Neil Douglas*, Karella Publishing, n.d., p. 70.

40. Neil Douglas, taped interview, 22 September 1980, Kangaroo Ground.

41. Heathcote, *A Far Cry*, p. 70.

42. Neil Douglas, taped interview, 22 September 1980, Kangaroo Ground.

43. Neil Douglas, taped interview, 25 January 1997, Venus Bay.

44. Neil Douglas, taped interview, 22 September 1980, Kangaroo Ground.

45. Neil Douglas, taped interview, 25 January 1997, Venus Bay.

46. Heathcote, *A Far Cry*, p. 71.

47. Neil Douglas, telephone interview, 7 July 2002, Dimboola.

48. Neil Douglas, taped interview, 25 January 1997, Venus Bay.

49. Neil Douglas, telephone interview, 12 December 1996, Venus Bay.

50. Neil Douglas, taped interview, 25 January 1997, Venus Bay.

51. Neil Douglas, taped interview, 25 January 1997, Venus Bay.

52. Simon Dickeson, taped interview, 25 September 2000, North Fitzroy.

53. Heathcote, *A Far Cry*, p. 71. Not all the Reeds' gardening books remain in the library at Heide I. Many were lost or given away over the years. Several important books are housed at the Garden Research Centre, Ripponlea, Hotham St, Elsternwick. Ripponlea is administered by the National Trust. See chapter 13, footnote 42.

54. Neil Douglas, taped interview, 25 January 1997, Venus Bay.

55. Claire Joyes, *Monet at Giverny*, Mayflower Books, 1975, New York, p. 37.

56. Monet died in 1926 and left the property to his son Michel, who did not live there. Monet's step-daughter, Blanche, lived there and maintained the property but after the Second World War it fell into disrepair. Though the garden was not open to the public, artists and others did visit. Moya Dyring visited and painted the garden in 1951.

 In 1966, Michel Monet bequeathed the property to the

Académie des Beaux-Arts and in 1977 a curator was
appointed. Sunday told Michael Keon she had visited
Monet's Giverny (Michael Keon, *Glad Morning Again*,
Imprint, Watsons Bay, 1996, p. 84) and she also discussed
it with Douglas. (Neil Douglas, taped interview,
25 January 1997, Venus Bay.)

57. Joyes, *Monet at Giverny*, p. 37.
58. Joyes, *Monet at Giverny*, p. 37.
59. Jane Brown, *Gardens of a Golden Afternoon*, Penguin,
Harmondsworth, 1985, p. 63.
60. William Robinson, *The Wild Garden*, 1977, The Scolar
Press, London, p. 14.
61. Brown, *Gardens of a Golden Afternoon*, p. 25.
62. Frances Jekyll and G.C. Taylor (ed.), *Gertrude Jekyll: A
Gardener's Testament, Selection of Articles and Notes*, Antique
Collector's Club, London, 1982, p. 76.
63. Neil Douglas, taped interview, 25 January 1997, Venus
Bay.
64. Neil Douglas to Sunday and John Reed, c.1936, Reed
Papers, State Library of Victoria.
65. Jekyll and Taylor, *Gertrude Jekyll*, p. 176.
66. Neil Douglas, taped interview, 25 January 1997,
Venus Bay.
67. Marion Cran, *I Know a Garden*, Herbert Jenkins, London,
c.1930, p. 76.
68. Cran, *The Garden of Ignorance*, p. 8.
69. Cran, *The Garden of Ignorance*, p. 25.
70. Cran, *The Garden of Ignorance*, p. 18.

71. Cran, *The Garden of Ignorance*, p. 11.

72. Janine Burke (ed.), *Dear Sun: The Letters of Joy Hester and Sunday Reed*, William Heinemann, Port Melbourne, 1995, p. 254.

73. Eleanour Sinclair Rohde, *The Scented Garden*, Medici Society, London, 1989, p. 138.

74. Susie Brunton, taped interview, 17 April 1999, Frankston.

75. Rohde, *The Scented Garden*.

76. John Reed to Sunday Reed.

77. Sunday Reed to Guy Jackes (or Jacks. Sunday's writing is unclear.), 22 July 1981, Reed Papers, State Library of Victoria.

78. Mary Nolan, telephone interview, 26 June 2000, Presteigne.

79. Burke, *Dear Sun*, p. 241.

80. Rohde, *The Scented Garden*, p. 139.

81. Peter Hobb, taped interview, 22 July 1998, Rye.

82. Susie Brunton, taped interview, 17 April 1999, Frankston.

83. John Reed to Dick Reed, 7 September 1980, Reed Papers, State Library of Victoria.

84. Peter Hobb, taped interview, 22 July 1998, Rye.

85. Jane Brown, *Gardens of a Golden Afternoon*, p. 50.

86. Nigel Nicolson, *Portrait of a Marriage*, Futura, London, 1974, p. 13.

87. Jekyll and Taylor, *Gertrude Jekyll*, p. 198.

88. Cran, *The Garden of Ignorance*, p. 109.

89. David Austin, *Old Roses and English Roses*, Peribo, Mt Kuringai, 2000, p. 15.

90. Quoted in Max Delany, *Sweeney Reed: Artist + Concrete Poet*, Museum of Modern Art at Heide, Bulleen, 1996, p. 7.

91. Heathcote, *A Far Cry*, p. 72.

92. Neil Douglas, taped interview, 25 January 1997, Venus Bay.

93. Heathcote, *A Far Cry*, p. 71.

94. Neil Douglas, taped interview, 25 January 1997, Venus Bay.

95. Sam Atyeo to Sunday Reed, 22 November 1936, Reed Papers, State Library of Victoria.

96. Heathcote, *A Far Cry*, p. 71.

97. D.H. Lawrence, *Lady Chatterley's Lover*, Heinemann, London, 1987, p. 4–5.

98. D.H. Lawrence, *Lady Chatterley's Lover*, p. 27.

99. D.H. Lawrence, *Lady Chatterley's Lover*, p. 83.

100. D.H. Lawrence, *Lady Chatterley's Lover*, p. 87.

101. D.H. Lawrence, *Lady Chatterley's Lover*, p. 195.

102. D.H. Lawrence, *Women in Love*, Penguin, Harmondsworth, 1974, p. 353.

103. John Reed to Sunday Reed, 31 May 1937, Reed Papers, State Library of Victoria.

104. Neil Douglas, taped interview, 22 September 1980, Kangaroo Ground.

105. John Reed to Sunday Reed, 1936, Reed Papers, State Library of Victoria.

106. Sunday Reed to John Reed, 1936, Reed Papers, State Library of Victoria.

107. Sunday Reed to John Reed, 15 May 1937, Reed Papers, State Library of Victoria.

108. Moya Dyring to Sunday Reed, 26 May 1937, Reed Papers, State Library of Victoria.

109. Moya Dyring to Sunday Reed, 24 May 1937, Reed Papers, State Library of Victoria.

110. Sunday Reed to John Reed, 15 May 1937, Reed Papers, State Library of Victoria.

111. Sunday Reed to Jean Langley, 3 May 1956, Reed Papers, State Library of Victoria.

112. Sunday Reed to John Reed, 15 May 1937, Reed Papers, State Library of Victoria.

113. John Reed to Sunday Reed, 16 June 1937, Reed Papers, State Library of Victoria.

114. Moya Dyring to Sunday Reed, 24 May 1937, Reed Papers, State Library of Victoria.

115. George Bell, *Sun*, 25 May 1937.

116. Moya Dyring to Sunday Reed, 26 May 1937, Reed Papers, State Library of Victoria.

117. George Bell, *Sun*, 25 May 1937.

118. Bernard Smith, *Australian Painting*, Oxford University Press, Melbourne, 1962, p. 210.

119. Barrie Reid (ed.), *Modern Australian Art*, Museum of Modern Art of Australia, Melbourne, 1964, p. 20.

120. Gertrude Stein, *Three Lives*, Peter Owen, London, 1970, p. 57.

121. Shari Benstock, *Women of the Left Bank: Paris 1900–1940*, Virago, London, 1987, p. 160.

122. John Reed to Sunday Reed, 16 June 1937, Reed Papers, State Library of Victoria.

123. John Reed to Sunday Reed, 14 June 1937, Reed Papers, State Library of Victoria.

124. John Reed to Sunday Reed, 31 May 1937, Reed Papers, State Library of Victoria.

125. Moya Dyring to John and Sunday Reed, 9 August 1937, Reed Papers, State Library of Victoria.

126. Neil Douglas, taped interview, 22 September 1980, Kangaroo Ground.

127. Peter Hobb, taped interview, 22 July 1998, Rye.

128. Philip Jones, taped interview, 18 October 1994, Elwood.

129. Burke, *Dear Sun*, p. 264.

130. Peter Hobb, taped interview, 22 July 1998, Rye.

131. Anne Cairns, taped interview, January 2003, Merricks.

132. Burke, *Dear Sun*, p. 254.

133. Michael Keon, *Glad Morning Again*, Imprint, Watsons Bay, 1996, p. 84.

134. Jean Langley, taped interview, 3 September 1997, Safety Beach.

135. Barrett Reid, taped interview, 19 August 1994, Heide.

136. Heathcote, *A Far Cry*, p. 70.

137. Neil Douglas, taped interview, 25 January 1997, Venus Bay.

138. D.H. Lawrence, *Lady Chatterley's Lover*, p. 24.

CHAPTER 7: NOLAN

1. Pamela Warrender, taped interview, 3 February 2003, Toorak.

2. Sunday Reed to John Reed, Jan/June 1943, Horsham, Reed Papers, State Library of Victoria.

3. John Reed, 'Artobiography', *Overland*, no. 101, 1985, p. 58.

4. Patrick White, *Flaws in the Glass: A Self Portrait*, Jonathan Cape, London, 1981, p. 234.

5. Reed, 'Artobiography', p. 58.

6. Brian Adams, *Such is Life: A Biography of Sidney Nolan*, Vintage, Sydney, 1989, p. 37.

7. Reed, 'Artobiography', p. 58.

8. Janine Burke, *Australian Gothic: A Life of Albert Tucker*, Knopf, Sydney, 2002, p. 30.

9. Adams, *Nolan*, p. 14.

10. Reed, 'Artobiography', p. 58.

11. John Sinclair, 'Nolan's Student Years', *Art and Australia*, September 1967, p. 436.

12. Enid Rhodes Pechel (trans.), Arthur Rimbaud, *A Season in Hell, The Illuminations*, Oxford University Press, Oxford, 1979, p. 7.

13. Wallace Fowlie, *Rimbaud's Illuminations*, Harvill Press, London, 1953, p. 30.

14. Pechel, *Illuminations*, p. 117.

15. Adams, *Nolan*, p. 42.

16. Michael Keon, *Glad Morning Again*, Imprint, Watsons Bay, 1996, p. 138.

17. Adams, *Nolan*, p. 42.

18. Nadine Amadio, taped interview, 1 June 2002, Sydney.

19. Joan James, taped interview, 2 April 1999, Middle Park.

20. Jane Clark, *Sidney Nolan: Landscapes and Legends*, University of Cambridge, Cambridge, 1987, p. 58.

21. Keon, *Glad Morning*, p. 117.

22. Gay Cuthbert, 'Changing the Landscape: The Life and Art of Moya Dyring', Master of Creative Arts, University of Melbourne, 2002, p. 30.

23. George Bell, *Sun*, 11 June 1940.

24. Richard Haese, *Sidney Nolan: The City and the Plain*, National Gallery of Victoria, Melbourne, 1983, p. 9.

25. Adams, *Nolan*, p. 52.

26. Peter Ross, Sidney Nolan Interview, ABC TV, 1992.

27. Haese, *Sidney Nolan*, p. 12.

28. Adams, *Nolan*, p. 53.

29. Haese, *Sidney Nolan*, p. 9.

30. Sidney Nolan, *Untitled poems*, c.1943, Reed Papers, State Library of Victoria.

31. Sunday Reed, 'Diary', 1943, Reed Papers, State Library of Victoria.

32. Sidney Nolan to Sunday Reed, 25 March 1942, Reed Papers, State Library of Victoria.

33. Sidney Nolan to Sunday Reed, 12 December 1942, Horsham, Reed Papers, State Library of Victoria.

34. Sunday Reed to John Reed, 1943, Horsham, Reed Papers, State Library of Victoria.

35. John Reed to Sunday Reed, c.1942, Reed Papers, State Library of Victoria.

36. John Reed to Sunday Reed, c.1943, Reed Papers, State Library of Victoria.

37. Sidney Nolan to Sunday Reed, 4 May 1942, Dimboola, Reed Papers, State Library of Victoria.

38. Sunday Reed to John Reed, 1943, Horsham, Reed Papers, State Library of Victoria.

39. Sidney Nolan to Sunday Reed, February 1943, Nhill, Reed Papers, State Library of Victoria.

40. Sunday Reed to John Reed, 1943, Horsham, Reed Papers, State Library of Victoria.

41. Sidney Nolan to Sunday Reed, 25 March 1943, Nhill, Reed Papers, State Library of Victoria.

42. Michael Keon, *Glad Morning*, p. 132.

43. Elwyn Lynn, *Sidney Nolan: Myth and Imagery*, Macmillan, London, 1967, p. 11.

44. *Argus*, 17 September 1937.

45. John Reed, 'Danila Vassilieff: Cossack and Artist', *Art and Australia*, September 1966, p. 113.

46. Albert Tucker, taped interview, 5 July 1979, Hurstbridge.

47. Reed, 'Vassilieff', p. 114.

48. John Reed, draft letter to Robert Hughes, c.1965, Reed Papers, State Library of Victoria.

49. Sidney Nolan to Sunday Reed, 18 May 1943, Nhill, Reed Papers, State Library of Victoria.

50. Sidney Nolan to Sunday Reed, 5 August 1942, Ballarat, Reed Papers, State Library of Victoria.

51. Sidney Nolan to Sunday Reed, 17 August 1943, Nhill, Reed Papers, State Library of Victoria.

52. Sidney Nolan to Sunday Reed, 20 May 1943, Nhill, Reed Papers, State Library of Victoria.

53. Barrett Reid and Nancy Underhill (eds.), *The Letters of John*

Reed: *Defining Australian Cultural Life, 1920–1981*, Viking, Ringwood, 2001, p. 283.

54. Reid and Underhill, p. 346.

CHAPTER 8: THE SECOND CIRCLE

1. Max Harris to Sunday Reed, c.1944, Reed Papers, State Library of Victoria.

2. Janine Burke, *Australian Gothic: A Life of Albert Tucker*, Knopf, Sydney, 2002, p. 166.

3. Sunday Reed, taped interview, 5 June 1978, Bulleen.

4. Yvonne Boyd, taped interview, 7 July 2000, Elwood.

5. John Reed to Sam Atyeo, 3 July 1978, Reed Papers, State Library of Victoria.

6. Janet Hawley, 'Travels With My Artist', *Good Weekend*, 4 June 1994, p. 15.

7. Letter from Cynthia Reed to John Reed, quoted in Jane Grant, 'The Life and Work of Cynthia Reed Nolan', Ph.D thesis, Sydney University, 2002, p. 44.

8. Grant, 'The Life and Work of Cynthia Reed Nolan', p. 44.

9. Barrett Reid and Nancy Underhill (eds.), *The Letters of John Reed: Defining Australian Cultural Life, 1920–1981*, Viking, Ringwood, 2001, p. 271.

10. Anne Cairns, taped interview, 26 January 2003, Merricks.

11. Albert Tucker, taped interview, 7 January 1997, St Kilda.

12. Gordon Thomson, taped interview, 18 April 2001, Carlton.

13. Albert Tucker, taped interview, 7 January 1997, St Kilda.

14. Sunday Reed to John Reed, 1944, Reed Papers, State Library of Victoria.

15. Janine Burke (ed.), *Dear Sun: The Letters of Joy Hester and Sunday Reed*, William Heinemann, Port Melbourne, 1995, p. 51.

16. In Hebrew, Gethsemani means oil-press (*gat*, press, and *seman*, oil). Mark (xiv, 32) calls it *chorion*, a 'place' or 'estate', while John (xviii, 1) speaks of it as *kepos*, a 'garden' or 'orchard'. In the East, a field shaded by numerous fruit trees and surrounded by a wall of loose stone or a quickset hedge forms the *el bostan*, the garden. The name 'oil-press' indicates it was planted specifically with olive trees. It was a place where Jesus often went to meditate and, at a point of crisis, to take refuge. 'Gethsemani', Catholic Encyclopaedia, www.newadvent.org.cathen.

17. Barrett Reid, *Making Country*, Angus and Robertson, Sydney, 1995, p. 76.

18. Burke, *Dear Sun*, p. 251.

19. Burke, *Dear Sun*, p. 40.

20. Neil Douglas, taped interview, 22 September 1980, Kangaroo Ground.

21. Neil Douglas, taped interview, 25 January 1997, Venus Bay.

22. Burke, *Australian Gothic*, p. 165.

23. John Perceval, interview, 24 November 1998, Balwyn.

24. Barry Pearce, *Arthur Boyd Retrospective*, The Beagle Press/Art Gallery of NSW, Sydney, 1993, p. 13.

25. Burke, *Australian Gothic*, p. 166.

26. Barrett Reid, taped interview, 19 August 1994, Bulleen.

27. Sunday Reed to John Reed, c.1935, Reed Papers, State Library of Victoria.

28. Burke, *Dear Sun*, p. 257.

29. Jean Langley, taped interview, 25 October 1994, Safety Beach.

30. Sunday Reed to Jean Langley, 24 September 1972, Langley Papers.

31. Sunday Reed to Jean Langley, 3 September 1972, Langley Papers.

32. Jean Langley, taped interview, 25 October 1994, Safety Beach.

33. Burke, *Dear Sun*, p. 257.

34. Joy Hester to Yvonne Boyd, 10 August 1943, Boyd Papers, Bundanon.

35. John Reed, 'Artobiography', *Overland*, no. 101, 1985, p. 56.

36. The Reeds would later allege that Michael Keon had stolen the money and banned him from Heide. Keon denied the charge. John apologised profusely to Bergner.

37. Burke, *Dear Sun*, p. 257.

38. Nadine Amadio, taped interview, 1 June 2002, Sydney.

39. Joy Hester to Albert Tucker, 1942, Tucker Papers.

40. Sunday Reed to Albert Tucker, c.1945, Reed Papers, State Library of Victoria.

41. Gisele Bellew, interview, 2 June 2000, Paris.

42. Albert Tucker, interview, 7 January 1997, St Kilda.

43. John Yule, interview, 12 August 1994, South Melbourne.

44. Quentin Bell and Virginia Nicholson, *Charleston: A Bloomsbury House and Garden*, Hodder and Stoughton, Rydalmere, 1997, p. 12.

45. Wendy Hitchmough, interview, 26 July 2002, Charleston, Sussex.

46. Antony Penrose, taped interview, 26 July 2002, Farley's Farm, Sussex. Antony Penrose is the director of Farley's Farm house museum.

47. Reid and Underhill, p. 189.

48. Reid and Underhill, p. 191.

49. Burke, *Dear Sun*, p. 228.

50. Alister Kershaw, *Hey Days: Memories and Glimpses of Melbourne's Bohemia*, 1937–1947, Imprint, North Ryde, 1991, p. 35.

51. Barrett Reid, taped interview, 19 August 1994, Bulleen. In fact, Sunday did visit Merthon occasionally and took Nadine Amadio there in the 1960s.

52. Reid and Underhill, p. 200.

53. Max Harris to John Reed, March 1943, Reed Papers, State Library of Victoria.

54. Michael Keon, *Glad Morning Again*, Imprint, Watsons Bay, 1996, p. 117.

55. Sunday Reed to John Reed, 1943, Horsham, Reed Papers, State Library of Victoria.

56. *Angry Penguins*, no. 4, 1943, p. 46.

57. Nolan's only painting derived from Rimbaud's *Illuminations* at that time was *Royalty* (1942, Heide MoMA). See Jane Clark, *Sidney Nolan: Landscape and Legends*, University of Cambridge, Cambridge, 1987, p. 40.

58. Graham Robb, *Rimbaud*, Macmillan, London, 2000, p. 60.

59. *Angry Penguins*, no. 4, 1943, p. 42.

60. *Angry Penguins*, no. 4, 1943, p. 43.

61. *Angry Penguins*, no. 4, 1943, p. 42.
62. *Angry Penguins*, no. 4, 1943, p. 42.
63. *Angry Penguins*, no. 4, 1943, p. 42.
64. Robb, *Rimbaud*, p. 59.
65. Enid Rhodes Peschel (trans.), Arthur Rimbaud, *A Season in Hell, The Illuminations*, Oxford University Press, Oxford, 1979, p. 121.
66. *Angry Penguins*, no. 4, 1943, p. 42.
67. Reid and Underhill, p. 206.
68. Max Harris to John Reed, March 1943, Reed Papers, State Library of Victoria.
69. *Angry Penguins*, no. 5, October, 1943, n.p.
70. Burke, *Dear Sun*, p. 57.
71. Max Harris to John and Sunday Reed, c.1953, Reed Papers, State Library of Victoria.
72. Max Harris to Sunday Reed, c.1944, Reed Papers, State Library of Victoria.
73. Reid and Underhill, p. 405.
74. *Angry Penguins*, 1945, n.p.
75. Reid and Underhill, p. 430.
76. Reid and Underhill, p. 440.
77. Reid and Underhill, p. 351.
78. Sidney Nolan to John Reed, 30 September 1946, Reed Papers, State Library of Victoria.

CHAPTER 9: NED

1. Nolan took Kelly's statement from documents about his trial and used it as the title for *Nobody knows anything about my case but myself* (1946, Heide MoMA).

2. David Malouf, *An Imaginary Life*, Picador, Woollahra, 1980, p. 15.

3. Nadine Amadio, taped interview, 1 June 2002, Sydney.

4. Warwick Reeder, 'Nolan at Heide', in *The Ned Kelly Paintings: Nolan at Heide, 1946–47*, Heide Museum of Modern Art, Bulleen, 1997, p. 11.

5. Elwyn Lynn, *Sidney Nolan: Myth and Imagery*, Macmillan, 1967, Melbourne, p. 18.

6. Sidney Nolan to Joy Hester, c.1943, Tucker Papers, State Library of Victoria.

7. Andrew Sayers, *Sidney Nolan's Ned Kelly*, National Gallery of Australia, Canberra, 2002, p. 8.

8. Noel Barber, *Conversations with Artists*, Collins, London, p. 90.

9. T.G. Rosenthal, *Sidney Nolan*, Thames and Hudson, Melbourne, 2002, p. 77.

10. Sayers, *Ned Kelly*, p. 64.

11. Barrett Reid, 'Nolan in Queensland', *Art and Australia*, September 1967, p. 447.

12. Janine Burke, *Australian Gothic: A Life of Albert Tucker*, Knopf, Sydney, 2002, p. 163.

13. Peter Hobb, taped interview, 22 July 1998, Rye.

14. Nadine Amadio, taped interview, 1 June 2002, Sydney.

15. Sidney Nolan to John Reed, 14 January 1948, Reed Papers, State Library of Victoria.

16. Barrett Reid and Nancy Underhill (eds.), *The Letters of John Reed: Defining Australian Cultural Life, 1920–1981*, Viking, Ringwood, 2001, p. 617.

17. Sidney Nolan to Sunday Reed, 10 February 1943, Dimboola, Reed Papers, State Library of Victoria.

18. Michael Keon, *Glad Morning Again*, Imprint, Watsons Bay, 1996, p. 115.

19. Sunday was in Queensland from July–November 1946 and so was absent when Nolan painted *Kelly and Horse* (1946, NGA), *Landscape with Windmill* (1946, NGA), *Ned Kelly* (1946, NGA), *Bush Picnic* (1946, NGA), *The encounter* (1946, NGA), *The chase* (1946, NGA), *Mrs Reardon at Glenrowan* (1946, NGA), *Burning at Glenrowan* (1946, NGA), *Siege at Glenrowan* (1946, NGA) and *Constable Fitzpatrick and Kate Kelly* (1946, NGA).

20. Peter Hobb, taped interview, 2 December 2002, Tootgarook.

21. Sunday Reed to Sidney Nolan, 1942, Dimboola, Reed Papers, State Library of Victoria.

CHAPTER 10: MOTHERHOOD

1. John Sinclair to John Reed, 29 December 1948, Reed Papers, State Library of Victoria.

2. Sunday Reed to Jean Langley, 24 December 1948, Langley Papers.

3. Sidney Nolan to John Reed, 25 September 1947, Reed Papers, State Library of Victoria.

4. For a more detailed discussion of these events see Janine Burke, *Australian Gothic: A Life of Albert Tucker*, Knopf, Sydney, 2002, p. 277–291.

5. Janine Burke (ed.), *Dear Sun: The Letters of Joy Hester and Sunday Reed*, William Heinemann, Port Melbourne, 1995, p. 228.

6. Burke, *Dear Sun*, p. 108.

7. Burke, *Dear Sun*, p. 109.

8. For a more detailed discussion of these events see *Australian Gothic*, p. 260–1.

9. Burke, *Dear Sun*, p. 134.

10. Sidney Nolan to John Reed, 22 August 1947, Reed Papers, State Library of Victoria.

11. Sidney Nolan to John Reed, 25 September 1947, Reed Papers, State Library of Victoria.

12. Barrett Reid, taped interview, 19 August 1994, Bulleen.

13. Cynthia Reed, *Daddy Sowed a Wind!*, The Shakespeare Head, Sydney, 1947, p. 30.

14. Reed, *Daddy Sowed a Wind!*, p. 49.

15. Reed, *Daddy Sowed a Wind!*, p. 73.

16. Cynthia Nolan to John Reed, 1945, Reed Papers, State Library of Victoria.

17. Cynthia Nolan to John Reed, 1944, Reed Papers, State Library of Victoria.

18. Barrett Reid and Nancy Underhill (eds.), *The Letters of John Reed: Defining Australian Cultural Life, 1920–1981*, Viking, Ringwood, 2001, p. 412.

19. Sidney Nolan to John Reed, 3 February 1948, Reed Papers, State Library of Victoria.

20. Barrett Reid, taped interview, 19 August 1994, Bulleen.

21. Reid and Underhill, p. 451.

22. Reid and Underhill, p. 454.

23. Sunday Reed to Jean Langley, c.1960, Reed Papers, State Library of Victoria.

24. Burke, *Dear Sun*, p. 157–8.

25. Burke, *Dear Sun*, p. 162.

26. Burke, *Dear Sun*, p. 172–3.

27. Burke, *Dear Sun*, p. 174.

28. Burke, *Dear Sun*, p. 180.

29. Burke, *Dear Sun*, p. 179.

30. Sunday Reed to Jean Langley, 24 December 1948, Langley Papers.

31. Burke, *Dear Sun*, p. 186.

32. Sunday Reed to Jean Langley, 24 December 1948, Langley Papers.

33. Burke, *Dear Sun*, p. 186.

34. Sunday Reed to Jean Langley, 24 December 1948, Langley Papers.

35. John Reed to Pablo Picasso, 1949, Reed Papers, State Library of Victoria. John would later regard this letter as 'a complete fiasco'. It taught him 'that one should never indulge in pilgrimages to one's heroes' though, he considered, 'it would have been nice to just meet [Picasso] in the street'. John Reed to Laurence Hope, 8 August 1967, Reed Papers, State Library of Victoria.

36. Burke, *Dear Sun*, p. 187.

37. Burke, *Dear Sun*, p. 178.

38. John Reed to Albert Tucker, April 1950, Tucker Papers, State Library of Victoria.

39. Burke, *Dear Sun*, p. 178.

40. Burke, *Dear Sun*, p. 194.

41. Burke, *Dear Sun*, p. 182.

42. Burke, *Dear Sun*, p. 178.

43. Sunday Reed to Joy Hester, 19 January 1949, Smith Papers.

44. Joy Hester to Sunday Reed, 1 February 1949, Reed Papers.

45. Burke, *Dear Sun*, p. 203.

46. Albert Tucker, taped interview, 7 January 1997, St Kilda.

47. Reid and Underhill, p. 449.

48. Burke, *Dear Sun*, p. 180.

49. Nadine Amadio, taped interview, 1 June 2002, Sydney.

50. Gordon Thomson, taped interview, 18 May 2001, Carlton.

51. Neil Douglas, telephone interview, 7 July 2002, Dimboola.

52. Jean Langley, taped interview, 25 September 1997, Safety Beach.

53. Burke, *Dear Sun*, p. 180.

54. Madame Mosser to Sunday Reed, April/May 1949, Reed Papers, State Library of Victoria.

55. Burke, *Dear Sun*, p. 213.

56. Reid and Underhill, p. 465.

57. Jean Langley, taped interview, 2 December 2002, Safety Beach.

58. Jean Langley, taped interview, 25 October 1994, Safety Beach.

59. Burke, *Dear Sun*, p. 222.

60. Jean Langley, taped interview, 25 September 1997, Safety Beach.

61. Jean Langley, taped interview, 25 October 1994, Safety Beach.

62. Anne Cairns, taped interview, 26 January 2003, Merricks North.

63. Burke, *Dear Sun*, p. 228.

CHAPTER 11: THE THIRD CIRCLE

1. Barrett Reid, 'Making it New in Australia', in *Angry Penguins and Realist Painting in Melbourne in the 1940s*, Hayward Gallery, London, 1988, p. 47.

2. Reid, 'Making it New in Australia', p. 47.

3. Reid, 'Making it New in Australia', p. 48.

4. Sidney Nolan to John Reed, 28 February 1948, Reed Papers, State Library of Victoria.

5. Nadine Amadio, taped interview, 1 June 2002, Sydney.

6. Barrett Reid, taped interview, 19 August 1994, Bulleen.

7. Reid, 'Making it New in Australia', p. 48.

8. Laurence Hope, taped interview, 27 July 1980, Sydney.

9. Janine Burke (ed.), *Dear Sun: The Letters of Joy Hester and Sunday Reed*, William Heinemann, Port Melbourne, 1995, p. 110.

10. Barrett Reid, *Making Country*, Angus and Roberston, Pymble, 1995, p. 105.

11. Mirka Mora, *Wicked but Virtuous: My Life*, Viking, Ringwood, 2000, p. 54.

12. Simon Dickeson, taped interview, 25 September 2000, North Fitzroy.

13. Barrett Reid to John Reed, 30 June 1948, Reed Papers, State Library of Victoria.

14. Barrett Reid to John Reed, 29 July 1947, Reed Papers, State Library of Victoria.

15. Barrett Reid and Nancy Underhill (eds.), *The Letters of John Reed: Defining Australian Cultural Life, 1920–1981*, Viking, Ringwood, 2001, p. 444.

16. Barrett Reid to John Reed, 29 July 1947, Reed Papers, State Library of Victoria.

17. Felicity St John Moore, *Charles Blackman: Schoolgirls and Angels*, National Gallery of Victoria, Melbourne, 1993, p. 15.

18. Barrett Reid to John Reed, 1949, Reed Papers, State Library of Victoria.

19. Barrett Reid to John Reed, February 1951, Reed Papers, State Library of Victoria.

20. Barbara Blackman, *Glass After Glass: Autobiographical Reflections*, Viking, Ringwood, 1997, p. 146.

21. Barbara Blackman, taped interview, 25 September 1980, Paddington.

22. Barbara Blackman, *Glass After Glass*, p. 147.

23. Charles Blackman, interview, 6 August 1979, Melbourne.

24. Charles Blackman to Sunday Reed, c.1953, Reed Papers, State Library of Victoria.

25. Reid and Underhill, p. 483.

26. Charles Blackman, interview, 6 August 1979, Melbourne.

27. Barrett Reid to Sunday Reed, c.1950, Reed Papers, State Library of Victoria.

28. Reid and Underhill, p. 502.

29. Mirka Mora, *Wicked but Virtuous*, p. 53.

30. Mirka Mora, interview, 26 September 1994, St Kilda.

31. Mirka Mora, *Wicked but Virtuous*, p. 53.

32. Georges Mora to John Reed, 5 August 1970, Reed Papers, State Library of Victoria.

33. Mirka Mora, *Wicked but Virtuous*, p. 59.

34. Georges Mora to Sunday Reed, 27 December 1970, Reed Papers, State Library of Victoria.

35. John Reed, 'Streeton Memorial Exhibition: The Decay of an Artist', *Angry Penguins*, December, 1994.

36. Bernard Smith, *Australian Painting*, Oxford University Press, Melbourne, 1971, p. 292; Manning Clark, *A Short History of Australia*, Macmillan, Melbourne, 1981, p. 224.

37. R.H. Croll (ed.), *Collected Poems of John Shaw Neilson*, Lothian, Melbourne, 1949, p. 40.

38. Barrett Reid, *Making Country*, p. 55.

39. Quoted from 'Awake' (1951), 'Try me Again' (c.1952) and 'Take a word like home' (c.1950). Photocopies, collection the author.

40. Robert Gibson, *The Land Without a Name: Alain-Fournier and his World*, Elek, London, 1975, p. 111.

41. Sunday Reed, taped interview, June 1978, Bulleen; Jules Supervielle, 'Child of the High Seas', John Lehmann (ed.), *Orpheus: A Symposium of the Arts*, vol. 1, London, 1948, p. 212.

42. Barrett Reid, 'Joy Hester: Draughtsman of Identity', *Art and Australia*, August 1966, p. 53.

43. Reid and Underhill, p. 471–72.

44. Reid and Underhill, p. 475.

45. Reid and Underhill, p. 503.

46. Reid and Underhill, p. 510.

47. Reid and Underhill, p. 517.

48. Reid and Underhill, p. 470.

49. Reid and Underhill, p. 522.

50. *CAS Broadsheet*, 1954, n.p.

51. Jean Langley, taped interview, 2 December 2002, Safety Beach.

52. John Reed, Foreword, CAS *Exhibition catalogue*, April 1954; CAS *Broadsheet*, 1954.

53. John Reed, CAS *Broadsheet*, November 1955.

54. Peter Burns, taped interview, 20 May 2003, Kangaroo Ground. The Reeds honoured Burns by giving him a Sime abstract as a birthday present.

55. John Olsen, 'John Howley', *Art and Australia*, March 1971, p. 335.

56. Janine Burke, 'Don Laycock', *Art and Australia*, March 1976, p. 57.

57. Janine Burke, 'The Impact of Post-War American Painting on Melbourne Painting, 1953–1968', B.A. (Hons.) thesis, University of Melbourne, 1974, p. 7.

58. Ian Sime, CAS *Broadsheet*, December 1954, n.p.

59. Burke, *Dear Sun*, p. 236–37.

60. Burke, *Dear Sun*, p. 241. Hester did produce a type-written selection of her poetry. Original now lost. Photocopy, collection the author.

61. Barrett Reid, 'New Time, New Place', *Ern Malley's Journal*, vol. 1, no. 1, November 1952, p. 44.

62. Burke, *Dear Sun*, p. 246.

63. Elizabeth Vassilieff, 'Inside-Outside', *Ern Malley's Journal*, vol. 1, no. 3, October 1953, p. 4.

64. Burke, *Dear Sun*, p. 238.

65. Jennifer Dickerson, *Robert Dickerson, Against the Tide*, Pandanus Press, Brisbane, 1994, p. 46.

66. Dickerson, *Against the Tide*, p. 60.
67. Dickerson, *Against the Tide*, p. 26.
68. Dickerson, *Against the Tide*, p. 32.
69. Burke, *Dear Sun*, p. 255–56.
70. John Reed to Albert Tucker, 23 August 1953, Tucker Papers.
71. John Reed to Albert Tucker, 24 November 1953, Tucker Papers.
72. John Reed to Albert Tucker, 23 August 1953, Tucker Papers.
73. Barrett Reid, taped interview, 19 August 1994, Templestowe.
74. Burke, *Dear Sun*, p. 251.
75. Reid and Underhill, p. 504–5.
76. Pamela McIntosh, taped interview, 8 February 1999, Warrion.
77. Joy Hester to Sunday Reed, c.1954, Reed Papers, State Library of Victoria.
78. Joy Hester 'Untitled', c.1954, Reed Papers, State Library of Victoria.
79. Barrett Reid, taped interview, 19 August 1994, Templestowe.
80. Burke, *Dear Sun*, p. 241.
81. Susie Brunton, taped interview, 14 April 1999, Frankston.
82. Burke, *Dear Sun*, p. 248.
83. Alannah Coleman to Sunday Reed, 22 June 1950, Reed Papers, State Library of Victoria.
84. Susie Brunton, taped interview, 14 April 1999, Frankston.

85. Sunday Reed to Jean Langley, c.1971, Reed Papers, State Library of Victoria.

86. Susie Brunton, taped interview, 14 April 1999, Frankston.

87. Sunday Reed to Jean Langley, 16 July 1960.

88. Burke, *Dear Sun*, p. 238.

89. John Reed, 'Heide: Some Background Notes for the Committee of Management of Heide Park and Art Gallery', 8 October 1980, Heide MoMA.

90. Jean Langley, taped interview, September 1997, Safety Beach.

CHAPTER 12: NOW WE'VE GOT OUR GALLERY

1. John and Sunday Reed, 'Gallery Report', Contemporary Art Society Minutes, Annual General Meeting, 29 November 1957, State Library of Victoria.

2. CAS Minutes, Annual General Meeting, 25 November 1955, State Library of Victoria.

3. Erica McGilchrist, interview, 1976, Caulfield.

4. Peter Burns, taped interview, 20 May 2003, Kangaroo Ground.

5. Alan McCulloch, *Herald*, 11 May 1955.

6. *CAS Annual Exhibition catalogue*, Preston Motors, May 1955.

7. CAS Minutes, 6 March 1956, State Library of Victoria.

8. CAS Minutes, 20 February 1956, State Library of Victoria.

9. CAS Minutes, 25 July 1956, State Library of Victoria.

10. Janine Burke (ed.), *Dear Sun: The Letters of Joy Hester and*

Sunday Reed, William Heinemann, Port Melbourne, 1995, p. 266–67.

11. Barrett Reid and Nancy Underhill (eds.), *The Letters of John Reed: Defining Australian Cultural Life*, 1920–1981, Viking, Ringwood, 2001, p. 509.

12. John and Sunday Reed, 'Gallery Report', CAS, 29 November 1957, State Library of Victoria.

13. Alan McCulloch, *Herald*, 6 June 1956.

14. Alan McCulloch, *Herald*, 14 November 1956.

15. Alan McCulloch, *Herald*, 27 November 1957.

16. John and Sunday Reed, 'Gallery Report', CAS, 29 November 1957, State Library of Victoria.

17. There was some refurbishment when GCA opened as MoMAA carried out by architects working for Kurt Geiger that included creating a stock room on the first floor and placing lights on the stairwell leading to the display room on the second floor. (Peter Burns, telephone interview, 24 July 2003.)

18. Museum of Modern Art and Design of Australia, Permanent Collection catalogue, 1962.

19. At the start, John negotiated for a salary of twenty pounds a week, adding, 'I would not like twenty pounds to be regarded as an appropriate salary for a Director, but rather as something as personal to myself, and of a temporary nature.' John Reed to William Shmith, 26 June 1958, Reed Papers, State Library of Victoria.

20. Sunday Reed to Jean Langley, 16 July 1960, Langley Papers.

21. Janine Burke, 'The Museum of Modern Art of Australia', *Art and Australia*, September 1977, p. 70–72.

22. Sunday Reed to Jean Langley, 16 July 1960, Langley Papers.

23. John Reed, taped interview, 22 May 1974, Templestowe.

24. Barrett Reid, taped interview, 5 August 1974, St Andrews.

25. John Reed, taped interview, 22 May 1974, Templestowe.

26. MoMAA Minutes, 31 August 1959, MoMAA Papers, State Library of Victoria.

27. The Boyd retrospective was not organised by MoMAA but the Adelaide Cultural Centre.

28. MoMAA Minutes, 20 April 1961, MoMAA Papers, State Library of Victoria.

29. On 23 March 1959, John terminated McNicoll's employment. He felt the cause was her 'extremely critical attitude of me both personally and as Director of the Museum'. John Reed to Ruth McNicoll, 23 March 1959, MoMAA Papers, State Library of Victoria.

30. Philip Jones, taped interview, 12 April 2000, Melbourne.

31. Asher Bilu, taped interview, 22 July 2003, Brighton.

32. Pamela Warrender, taped interview, 3 February 2003, Toorak.

33. Bryan Robertson to Sunday Reed, 11 January 1957, Reed Papers, State Library of Victoria.

34. Reid and Underhill, p. 515.

35. Sunday Reed to Sidney Nolan, cable dated 25 September 1958, Reed Papers, State Library of Victoria.

36. Barrett Reid, taped interview, 19 August 1994, Templestowe.

37. Lyn Williams, telephone interview, 18 August 2003, South Yarra. Fred Williams restored other works for the Reeds during 1963–64 including Blackman, Coburn, Tipper, Hester and several other Nolans.

38. John Reed to Robert Hughes, 15 February 1964, Reed Papers, State Library of Victoria.

39. Pamela Warrender, taped interview, 3 February 2003, Toorak.

40. Reid and Underhill, p. 616.

41. Reid and Underhill, p. 617–19.

42. Pamela Warrender, taped interview, 3 February 2003, Toorak.

43. Sunday Reed to Jean Langley, 16 July 1960, Langley Papers.

44. Lewis Carroll, *Alice's Adventures in Wonderland* and *Through the Looking Glass*, Signet Classics, New York, 1960, p. 63.

45. Felicity St John Moore, *Charles Blackman: Schoolgirls and Angels*, National Gallery of Victoria, Melbourne, 1993, p. 19.

46. Nadine Amadio, taped interview, 1 June 2002, Sydney.

47. 'Antipodean Manifesto', Victorian Artists Society Gallery, East Melbourne, August 1959.

48. John Reed, taped interview, 22 May 1974, Bulleen.

49. 'Letters to the Editor', *Modern Art News*, vol. 1, no. 1, 1959, p. 4.

50. Reid and Underhill, p. 501.

51. John Reed to Albert Tucker, 5 April 1958, Tucker Papers.

52. Danila Vassilieff Memorial Exhibition, MoMAA, Melbourne, June 1959.
53. Sunday Reed to Jean Langley, December 1960, Langley Papers.

CHAPTER 13: HEIDE II

1. David McGlashan was in partnership with Neil Everist; Barrett Reid and Nancy Underhill (eds.), *The Letters of John Reed: Defining Australian Cultural Life, 1920–1981*, Viking, Ringwood, 2001, p. 666.
2. Sunday Reed to Jean Langley, 26 November 1960, Langley Papers.
3. Peter Burns, taped interview, 20 June 2003, Kangaroo Ground. The Mora House and Reed House have been joined by current owner Caroline Williams, Georges Mora's second wife. The Mora House has had a second storey added.
4. Eve McGlashan, taped interview, 22 October 2003, St Kilda.
5. Reid and Underhill, p. 568.
6. Eve McGlashan, taped interview, 22 October 2003, St Kilda.
7. Reid and Underhill, p. 666–67.
8. Quoted in Janine Burke (ed.), *Dear Sun: The Letters of Joy Hester and Sunday Reed*, William Heinemann, Port Melbourne, 1995, p. 43.
9. John Reed to Mervyn Horton, 22 May 1968, Reed Papers, State Library of Victoria.
10. Neil Clerehan, 'Heide II', *Art in Australia*, September 1968, p. 140.

11. Reid and Underhill, p. 667.

12. Reid and Underhill, p. 602.

13. Pamela Warrender, taped interview, 3 February 2003, Toorak.

14. John Reed to Pamela Warrender, 3 June 1965, MoMAA Papers, State Library of Victoria.

15. Reid and Underhill, p. 569.

16. Philip Jones, interview, 30 July 2003, St Kilda.

17. Jean Langley, taped interview, 25 September 1997, Safety Beach.

18. Alice T. Friedman, 'Domestic Differences: Edith Farnsworth, Mies van der Rohe, and the Gendered Body' in Christopher Reed (ed.), *Not at Home: The Suppression of Domesticity in Modern Art and Architecture*, Thames and Hudson, London, 1996, p. 185. The house became a controversial project when Mies sued Dr Farnsworth for unpaid bills. During the courtcase, the house became an object of public scrutiny, Farnsworth commenting on her discomfort with its lack of private, self-contained spaces.

19. Neil Clerehan, 'Heide II', *Art in Australia*, September 1968, p. 140. American architect John Johansen employed fragmented and geometric forms in his designs.

20. John Reed to Robert Dickerson, 17 December 1966, Reed Papers, State Library of Victoria.

21. Reid and Underhill, p. 620.

22. Susie Brunton, taped interview, 27 August 2003, Elwood.

23. Neil Clerehan, 'Heide II'.

24. Reid and Underhill, p. 681.

25. Reid and Underhill, p. 681.
26. Reid and Underhill, p. 683.
27. Susie Brunton, taped interview, 27 August 2003, Elwood.
28. Neil Clerehan, 'Heide II'.
29. Reid and Underhill, p. 688.
30. Susie Brunton, taped interview, 27 August 2003, Elwood.
31. Philip Jones, interview, 30 July 2003, St Kilda.
32. Le Corbusier, *Towards a New Architecture*, (trans. F. Etchell), Architectural Press, London, 1927, p. 18.
33. Christopher Reed, 'Introduction', in Christopher Reed (ed.), *Not at Home: The Suppression of Domesticity in Modern Art and Architecture*, p. 8.
34. Robin Boyd, *The Australian Ugliness*, Cheshire, Melbourne, 1980, p. 129.
35. Peter Hobb, taped interview, 22 July 1998, Rye.
36. Reid and Underhill, p. 606–67; p. 735.
37. Peter Hobb, taped interview, 22 July 1998, Rye.
38. Susie Brunton, taped interview, 17 May 1999, Frankston. After the Reeds moved to Heide II, Brunton established her own herb garden at Heide I.
39. Sunday Reed to Jean Langley, November 1972, Langley Papers.
40. John Reed, 'Heide: Some Background Notes for the Committee of Management of Heide Park and Art Gallery. c.1981; Sunday Reed to Guy Jackes (?), 20 July 1981, Reed Papers, State Library of Victoria. Sunday appended a list of roses in the kitchen garden to this letter.

41. See Frank Cannata and Noel O'Keefe, *Heide Roses*, Heide MoMA, Bulleen, Victoria, 2003 for a current listing of rose varieties in the kitchen garden.

42. Sunday's list remains in Gertude Jekyll, *Home and Garden: Notes and Thoughts Practical and Critical, of a Worker in Both*, Longmans, Green and Company, London, 1900. Collection Garden Research Centre, National Trust, Ripponlea. Sunday bought the book from a secondhand dealer at an unknown time. I am grateful to Rosalie Dance, Heide MoMA, for drawing my attention to former garden books from the Heide library now in the collection of the National Trust; and to Richard Heathcote, National Trust, for making the books available. Other books from the Heide library now in the Garden Research Centre at the National Trust Ripponlea are Gertrude Jekyll and Edward Mawley, *Roses for English Gardens: Country Life*, Covent Garden, 1902; J.C. Loudon, *Aboretum et Fruticetum Brittanicum*, (8 vols), Longman, Brown, Green and Longmans, London, 1844; and Ellen Wilmott, *The Genus Rosa*, (2 vols) John Murray, London, 1914. In 1981 Guy Jackes (?) made a list of all herbs and flowers in the Heide II kitchen garden. Reed Papers, State Library of Victoria.

43. Peter Hobb, taped interview, 22 July 1998, Rye.

44. Susie Brunton, taped interview, 17 May 1999, Frankston.

45. John Reed to Paul Boston, 21 June 1975, Reed Papers, State Library of Victoria.

46. Susie Brunton, taped interview, 17 May 1999, Frankston.

47. Peter Hobb, taped interview, 22 July 1998, Rye.
48. Susie Brunton, taped interview, 17 May 1999, Frankston.
49. Asher Bilu, taped interview, 22 July 2003, Brighton.
50. Peter Hobb, taped interview, 22 July 1998, Rye.
51. Susie Brunton, taped interview, 17 May 1999, Frankston.
52. Sunday Reed to Jean Langley, 4 August 1969, Langley Papers.
53. Sunday Reed to Jean Langley, 12 August 1969, Langley Papers.
54. Susie Brunton, taped interview, 17 May 1999, Frankston.
55. Philip Jones, interview, 30 July 2003, St Kilda.
56. Sunday Reed to Jean Langley, 9 October 1969, Langley Papers.
57. Philip Jones, interview, 30 July 2003, St Kilda.
58. Peregrine Smith, taped interview, 1 September 1999, Malvern.
59. Ron Upton, 'Some Thoughts and Recollections Relating to Sun and John', August 2003, Ron Upton Papers.
60. Les Kossatz, taped interview, 20 August 2003, Carlton.
61. Ron Upton, 'Some Thoughts and Recollections relating to Sun and John'.
62. Les Kossatz, taped interview, 20 August 2003, Carlton.
63. Alex Selenitsch, taped interview, 15 January 2001, Clifton Hill.
64. Asher Bilu, taped interview, 22 July 2003, Brighton.
65. Mary Boyd to Sunday Reed, undated, Reed Papers, State Library of Victoria.
66. Sunday Reed to Jean Langley, 25 August 1969, Langley Papers.

67. Sunday Reed to Jean Langley, undated, Langley Papers.

68. Peter Hobb, taped interview, 22 July 1998, Rye.

69. Mary Lord, *Hal Porter: Man of Many Parts*, Random House, Sydney, 1993, p. 212.

70. Hal Porter to Sunday Reed, 4 February 1964, Reed Papers, State Library of Victoria.

71. Hal Porter to Sunday Reed, 19 April 1964, Reed Papers, State Library of Victoria.

72. Hal Porter to Sunday Reed, 20 December 1965, Reed Papers, State Library of Victoria.

73. Quoted in Lord, *Porter*, p. 213.

74. Russell Deeble, taped interview, 10 January 2001, Elsternwick.

75. Reid and Underhill, p. 720.

76. Susie Brunton, taped interview, 17 May 1999, Frankston.

77. As editor of *Overland*, Barrett Reid published part of the manuscript in *Overland*, no. 10, 1985, p. 53–60.

78. Reid and Underhill, p. 861.

79. Sunday Reed to Jean Langley, 1973, Langley Papers.

80. Patrick McCaughey, *Australian Painters of the Heidelberg School: The Jack Manton Collection*, Oxford University Press, Melbourne, 1979, p. 78.

81. Dorothy Foster, 'Colourful man of cats and canvas', *Herald*, 26 April 1968.

82. John Reed, 'Autobiography'; John Reed to Alannah Coleman, December 1969, Reed Papers, State Library of Victoria.

83. Foster, 'Colourful man of cats and canvas'.

84. Sunday Reed to Jean Langley, 16 July 1960, Langley Papers.
85. Sunday Reed, taped interview, 5 June 1978, Bulleen.
86. Sunday Reed to Jean Langley, undated, Langley Papers.
87. Les Kossatz, taped interview, 20 August 2003, Carlton.
88. Reid and Underhill, p. 852.
89. John Reed to Mary Christina Sewell, January 1970, Reed Papers, State Library of Victoria.
90. John Reed to Mervyn Horton, 8 July 1968, Reed Papers, State Library of Victoria.
91. Les Kossatz, taped interview, 20 August 2003, Carlton.
92. Ron Upton, 'Some Thoughts and Recollections relating to Sun and John'.

CHAPTER 14: FULL CIRCLE

1. Janine Burke (ed.), *Dear Sun: The Letters of Joy Hester and Sunday Reed*, William Heinemann, Port Melbourne, 1995, p. 215.
2. John Reed to Sidney Nolan, 12 October 1964, Reed Papers, State Library of Victoria.
3. Sidney Nolan, *The Paradise Garden*, Alistair McAlpine, London, 1971: 'Snagging', p. 45; 'Quartet, p. 33; 'By the Stile', p. 109; 'Love Manque', p. 97; 'Foyer', p. 30; 'Corked', p. 105; 'Dead Heading', p. 81.
4. Sunday Reed to Jean Langley, 1972, Langley Papers.
5. Sunday Reed to Jean Langley, 1972, Langley Papers.
6. Sunday Reed to Jean Langley, c.1975, Langley Papers.
7. Sunday Reed to Jean Langley, c.1972, Langley Papers.

8. John Reed to Sam Atyeo, 5 November 1975, Reed Papers, State Library of Victoria.

9. John Reed to Jean Langley, 24 October 1969, Reed Papers, State Library of Victoria.

10. Jean Langley, taped interview, 25 October 1994, Safety Beach.

11. See Ludwig Leichhardt, *Journal of an overland expedition from Moreton Bay to Port Essington, a distance of upwards of 3000 miles, during the years 1844–1845*, T&W Bone, London, 1847.

12. John Reed to Sam Atyeo, 1 June 1975, Reed Papers, State Library of Victoria.

13. John Reed to Sam Atyeo, 1 June 1975, Reed Papers, State Library of Victoria.

14. John Reed to Marshall Sumner, 18 November 1977, Reed Papers, State Library of Victoria.

15. John Reed to Sam Atyeo, 9 January 1974, Reed Papers, State Library of Victoria.

16. John Reed to Gray Smith, 9 April 1974, Reed Papers, State Library of Victoria.

17. John Reed to Leslie Stack, 10 April 1975, Reed Papers, State Library of Victoria.

18. Alan McCulloch, *Herald*, 30 August 1976.

19. Patrick McCaughey, 'Tucker's Images the myths of our art', *Age*, 21 November 1972.

20. Peregrine Smith, taped interview, 1 September 1999, Malvern.

21. John Reed to Alannah Coleman, 19 May 1976, Reed Papers, State Library of Victoria.

22. John Reed to Peter Hobb, 10 August 1976, Reed Papers, State Library of Victoria.

23. Susie Brunton, taped interview, 27 August 2003, Elwood.

24. John Reed to Mary Christina Sewell, 9 October 1970, Reed Papers, State Library of Victoria.

25. John Reed to Marshall Sumner, 1 January 1978, Reed Papers, State Library of Victoria.

26. John Reed to the Honorable Rupert Hamer, 24 March 1969, Reed Papers, State Library of Victoria.

27. Sir Rupert Hamer, taped interview, 21 July 2003, Hawthorn.

28. John Reed to the Honorable Rupert Hamer, 14 July 1969, Reed Papers, State Library of Victoria.

29. John Reed to Jean Langley, 3 June 1977, Reed Papers, State Library of Victoria.

30. Sunday Reed to Jean Langley, November 1972, Langley Papers.

31. Jean Langley to Sunday Reed, 30 May 1977, Reed Papers, State Library of Victoria.

32. Sam Hunter, *American Art of the 20th Century*, Thames and Hudson, London, 1973, p. 370.

32. John Reed to John Kaldor, 12 February 1974, Reed Papers, State Library of Victoria.

33. Barrett Reid to John Reed, 19 April 1977, Reed Papers, State Library of Victoria.

34. Jean Langley, taped interview, 25 October 1994, Safety Beach.

35. John Reed to Sam Atyeo, 25 January 1977, Reed Papers, State Library of Victoria.

36. Cynthia Nolan, *Open Negative: An American Memoir*, Macmillan, London 1967, p. 5.

37. Nolan, *Open Negative*, p. 56.

38. Nolan, *Open Negative*, p. 118.

39. Barrett Reid to John Reed, 19 April 1977, Reed Papers, State Library of Victoria.

40. Barrett Reid to John Reed, 23 April 1977, Reed Papers, State Library of Victoria.

41. John Reed to Barrett Reid, 30 April 1977, Reed Papers, State Library of Victoria.

42. John Reed to Barrett Reid, 27 May 1977, Reed Papers, State Library of Victoria.

43. Barrett Reid to John Reed, 16 June 1977, Reed Papers, State Library of Victoria.

44. Barrett Reid to John Reed, 27 June 1977, Reed Papers, State Library of Victoria.

45. John Reed to Barrett Reid, 27 May 1977, Reed Papers, State Library of Victoria.

46. John Reed to Jean Langley, 29 April 1977, Reed Papers, State Library of Victoria.

47. Jean Langley to Sunday Reed, April 1977, Reed Papers, State Library of Victoria.

48. Mary Boyd to Sunday and John Reed, 20 January 1978, Reed Papers, State Library of Victoria.

49. John Reed to Mary Boyd, January 1978, Reed Papers, State Library of Victoria.

50. Sunday Reed to Jean Langley, 19 April 1977, Reed Papers, State Library of Victoria.

51. Patrick White, *Flaws in the Glass: A Self Portrait*, Jonathan Cape, London, 1981, p. 237.

52. John Reed to Sam Atyeo, 3 July 1978, Reed Papers, State Library of Victoria.

53. Mary Boyd, telephone interview, 25 May 2000, Presteigne.

54. Barrett Reid, *Of Dark and Light: The Art of John Perceval*, National Gallery of Victoria, Melbourne, 1992, p. 31.

55. John Reed to Alannah Coleman, 8 March 1978, Reed Papers, State Library of Victoria.

56. Les Kossatz, taped interview, 20 August 2003, Carlton.

57. John Reed to Sam Atyeo, 25 January 1977, Reed Papers, State Library of Victoria.

58. John Reed to John Sinclair, 1978, Reed Papers, State Library of Victoria.

59. John Reed to Sam Atyeo, 29 October 1978, Reed Papers, State Library of Victoria.

60. John Reed to Mary Christina Sewell, 9 January 1981, Reed Papers, State Library of Victoria.

61. Russell Deeble, taped interview, 10 January 2001, Elsternwick.

62. Barbara Blackman, National Library Oral History Project: Albert Tucker, taped interview, 14 July 1988.

63. Susie Brunton, taped interview, 27 August 2003, Elwood.

64. Russell Deeble, taped interview, 10 January 2001, Elsternwick.

65. John Reed to Sam Atyeo, 29 October 1979, Reed Papers, State Library of Victoria.

66. Peregrine Smith, taped interview, 1 September 1999, Malvern.

67. Pamela McIntosh, taped interview, 8 February 1999, Warrion.

68. Pamela McIntosh, taped interview, 8 February 1999, Warrion.

69. Les Kossatz, taped interview, 20 August 2003, Carlton.

70. John Reed to Gil Jamieson, 16 July 1979, Reed Papers, State Library of Victoria.

71. John Reed to Sam Atyeo, 29 October 1979, Reed Papers, State Library of Victoria.

72. John Reed to Laurence Hope, 10 March 1980, Reed Papers, State Library of Victoria.

73. John Reed to Sam Atyeo, 4 June 1979, Reed Papers, State Library of Victoria.

74. Wendy Harmer, 'A $1m art haven', *Herald*, 6 December 1979.

75. John Reed to Dick Reed, 14 July 1980, Reed Papers, State Library of Victoria.

76. John Reed to Mary Christina Sewell, 9 January 1981, Reed Papers, State Library of Victoria.

77. John Reed to Alannah Coleman, 14 August 1980, Reed Papers, State Library of Victoria.

78. John Reed to Sam Atyeo, 22 December 1980, Reed Papers, State Library of Victoria.

79. John Reed to Sam Atyeo, July 1980, Reed Papers, State Library of Victoria.

80. The Atyeo retrospective, curated by Jennifer Phipps, opened at Heide Park and Art Gallery on 23 November 1982.

81. John Reed to Dick Reed, 1 September 1980, Reed Papers, State Library of Victoria.

82. John Reed to Marshall Sumner, 28 February 1981, Reed Papers, State Library of Victoria.

83. John Reed to Dick Reed, 1 September 1980, Reed Papers, State Library of Victoria.

84. John Reed to Mary Christina Sewell, 9 January 1981, Reed Papers, State Library of Victoria.

85. John Reed to Dick Reed, 7 September 1980, Reed Papers, State Library of Victoria.

86. John Reed to Laurence Hope, 13 January 1980, Reed Papers, State Library of Victoria.

87. John Reed to Mary Christina Sewell, 9 January 1981, Reed Papers, State Library of Victoria.

88. John Reed to Margaret Reed, 29 May 1981, Reed Papers, State Library of Victoria.

89. John Reed to Mary Christina Sewell, 9 January 1981, Reed Papers, State Library of Victoria.

90. John Reed to Mary Christina Sewell, 3 August 1981, Reed Papers, State Library of Victoria.

91. John Reed to Laurence Hope, 25 October 1981, Reed Papers, State Library of Victoria.

92. Barrett Reid, taped interview, 19 August 1994, Bulleen.

93. John Reed to Dick Reed, 7 September 1980, Reed Papers, State Library of Victoria.

94. John Reed to Dick Reed, 14 July 1980, Reed Papers, State Library of Victoria.

95. John Reed to Mary Christina Sewell, 9 January 1981, Reed Papers, State Library of Victoria.

96. John Reed to Richard Haese, 22 October 1981, Reed Papers, State Library of Victoria.

97. Barrett Reid to Sunday and John Reed, 8 November 1981, Reed Papers, State Library of Victoria.

98. John Reed to Dick Reed, 8 November 1981, Reed Papers, State Library of Victoria.

99. Deborah Forster, 'The love of two lives', *Age*, 6 January 1982.

100. Georges Mora to Sunday Reed, 14 September 1980, Reed Papers, State Library of Victoria.

101. Peter Ward, 'Greatness is born', *Australian*, 6 January 1982. Originally called Heide Park and Art Gallery, it is now named Heide Museum of Modern Art.

102. Nadine Amadio, taped interview, 1 June 2002, Sydney.

103. John Reed to Mary Christina Sewell, 4 December 1981, Reed Papers, State Library of Victoria.

104. Susie Brunton, taped interview, 27 August 2003, Elwood.

AFTERWORD

1. Other committee members included Heide MoMA board member Janne Faulkner; Catherin Bull, RMIT lecturer in landscape architecture; and Heide staff, including former

director Warwick Reeder and former curators Max Delany, Ted Gott and Murray White. Anick Houle and Stephen O'Connor, project architects, were also on the committee. Project manager was Russell Smith.

2. Barrett Reid to the author, 10 November 1993, Burke Papers.

3. *Making Country* was published by Angus and Roberston in 1995. *Letters of John Reed: Defining Cultural Change, 1920–1981* was published by Penguin Books in 2001. In 1995, Reid had enlisted Nancy Underhill as co-editor to help complete the research.

4. Susan McCulloch, taped interview, 2 December 2002, Shoreham.

5. Janine Burke, 'Art house', *Age* Saturday Extra, 1 December 2001.

Select bibliography

Brian Adams, *Such is Life: A Biography of Sidney Nolan*, Vintage, Sydney, 1989.

David Austin, *Old Roses and English Roses*, Peribo, Mt Kuringai, 2000.

Quentin Bell and Virginia Nicholson, *Charleston: A Bloomsbury house and garden*, Hodder and Stoughton, Rydalmere, 1997.

Shari Benstock, *Women of the Left Bank, Paris: 1900-1940*, Virago, London, 1987.

Michael Bogle (ed.), *Designing Australia*, Pluto Press, Annandale, 2002.

Robin Boyd, *The Australian Ugliness*, Cheshire, Melbourne, 1980.

Jane Brown, *Gardens of a Golden Afternoon: A Social History of Gardens and Gardening*, Penguin, Harmondsworth, 1985.

Janine Burke, *Australian Gothic: A Life of Albert Tucker*, Knopf, Sydney, 2002.

– (ed.), *Dear Sun: The Letters of Joy Hester and Sunday Reed*, William Heinemann, Port Melbourne, 1995.

– 'Don Laycock', *Art and Australia*, March 1976.

– *Joy Hester*, Greenhouse, Richmond, 1983.

– 'Special Edition: The Prints of Ethel Spowers and Eveline Syme', *Imprint*, Winter 1993.

– 'The Impact of Post-War American Painting on Melbourne Painting, 1953–1968', BA (Hons.) thesis, University of Melbourne, 1974.

– 'The Museum of Modern Art of Australia', *Art and Australia*, September 1977.

Edmund Campion, *Australian Catholics: The Contribution of Catholics to the Development of Australian Society*, Viking, Ringwood, 1985.

Michael Cannon, *The Land Boomers*, Nelson, Melbourne, 1976.

– *The Long Last Summer*, Nelson, Melbourne, 1985.

Lewis Carroll, *Alice's Adventures in Wonderland* and *Through the Looking Glass*, Signet Classics, New York, 1960.

Maie Casey, 'George Bell in Bourke Street', *Art and Australia*, September 1966.

Jane Clark, *Sidney Nolan: Landscapes and Legends*, University of Cambridge, Cambridge, 1987.

Neil Clerehan, 'Heide II', *Art in Australia*, September 1968.

Marion Cran, *I Know a Garden*, Herbert Jenkins, London, c.1930.

– *The Garden of Ignorance: The Experiences of a Woman in a Garden*, Herbert Jenkins, London, c.1924.

R.H. Croll (ed.), *Collected Poems of John Shaw Neilson*, Lothian, Melbourne, 1949.

Scott Cunningham, *Cunningham's Encyclopedia of Magical Herbs*, Llewellyn, St Paul, 2000.

Gay Cuthbert, 'Changing the Landscape: The Life and Art of Moya Dyring', Master of Creative Arts, University of Melbourne, 2002.

Max Delany, *Sweeney Reed: Artist + Concrete Poet*, Museum of Modern Art at Heide, Bulleen, 1996.

Jennifer Dickerson, *Robert Dickerson: Against the Tide*, Pandanus Press, Brisbane, 1994.

Zelda Fitzgerald, *Save Me the Waltz*, Penguin, Harmondsworth, 1971.

Jackie French, *Yates Guide to Herbs*, Angus and Roberston, Pymble, 1997.

Gavin Fry, *Adrian Lawlor: A Portrait*, Heide Park and Art Gallery, Melbourne, 1983.

Roger Fry, *Vision and Design*, Chatto and Windus, London, 1920.

Ann Galbally, *Arthur Streeton*, Lansdowne, East Melbourne, 1979.

Ann Galbally and Anne Gray (ed.), *Letters from Smike: The Letters of Arthur Streeton*, Oxford University Press, Melbourne, 1989.

Jane Grant, 'The Life and Work of Cynthia Reed Nolan', Ph.D thesis, Sydney University, 2002.

Richard Haese, *Sidney Nolan: The City and the Plain*, National Gallery of Victoria, Melbourne, 1983.

Jill Duchess of Hamilton, Penny Hart and John Simmons, *The Gardens of William Morris*, Hodder and Stoughton, Rydalmere, 1998.

Abigail Heathcote, *A Far Cry: Spinning Yarns with Neil Douglas*, Karella Publishing, n.d.

Ronald Hutton, *The Triumph of the Moon: A History of Modern Pagan Witchcraft*, Oxford Univeristy Press, Oxford, 1999.

Claire Joyes, *Monet at Giverny*, Mayflower Books, New York, 1975.

Frances Jekyll and G.C. Taylor (ed.) *Gertrude Jekyll: A Gardener's Testament, Selection of Articles and Notes*, Antique Collector's Club, London, 1982.

Michael Keon, *Glad Morning Again*, Imprint, Watsons Bay, 1996.

Alister Kershaw, *Hey Days: Memories and Glimpses of Melbourne's Bohemia*, 1937–1947, Imprint, North Ryde, 1991.

Le Corbusier, *Towards a New Architecture*, (trans. F. Etchell), Architectural Press, London, 1927.

Ludwig Leichhardt, *Journal of an overland expedition from Moreton Bay to Port Essington, a distance of upwards of 3000 miles, during the years 1844–1845*, T&W Bone, London, 1847.

Margaret Lord, *Decorator's World*, Ure Smith, Sydney, 1969.

Mary Lord, *Hal Porter: Man of Many Parts*, Random House, Sydney, 1993.

Elwyn Lynn, *Sidney Nolan: Myth and Imagery*, Macmillan, London, 1967.

Patrick McCaughey, *Australian Painters of the Heidelberg School*, The Jack Manton Collection, Oxford University Press, Melbourne, 1979.

Ross McMullin, *Will Dyson*, Angus and Roberston, Sydney, 1984.

Brenda Maddox, *The Married Man: A Life of D.H. Lawrence*, Sinclair-Stevenson, London, 1994.

Carol Mann, *Paris Between the Wars*, Vendome Press, London, 1996.

Nancy Milford, *Zelda Fitzgerald*, Penguin, Harmondsworth, 1970.

Felicity St John Moore, *Charles Blackman: Schoolgirls and Angels*, National Gallery of Victoria, Melbourne, 1993.

– *Classical Modernism: The George Bell School*, National Gallery of Victoria, Melbourne, 1992.

Mirka Mora, *Wicked but Virtuous: My Life*, Viking, Ringwood, 2000.

Cynthia Nolan *Open Negative: An American Memoir*, Macmillan, London 1967.

– *Outback and Beyond*, Angus and Roberston, Pymble, 1994.

Sidney Nolan, *Paradise Garden*, Alistair McAlpine, London, 1971.

Susan McCulloch, 'The Heide Feud', *The Australian*, 3 November, 1995.

James Paxton, *Toorak as I Knew it*, Prahran Historical and Arts Society, Prahran, 1983.

Jennifer Phipps, *Atyeo*, Heide Park and Art Gallery, Melbourne, 1982.

Karen Quinlan, *In a picture land over the sea, Agnes Goodsir, 1864–1939*, Bendigo Art Gallery, Bendigo, 1998.

Christopher Reed (ed.), *Not at Home: The Suppression of Domesticity* in *Modern Art and Architecture*, Thames and Hudson, London, 1996.

Cynthia Reed, *Daddy Sowed A Wind!*, Shakespeare Head, Sydney, 1947.

John Reed, 'Artobiography', *Overland*, no. 101, 1985.

— Autobiography manuscript, Reed Papers, State Library of Victoria.

Warwick Reeder, 'Nolan at Heide', in *The Ned Kelly Paintings, Nolan at Heide: 1946–47*, Heide Museum of Modern Art, Bulleen, 1997.

Barrett Reid, *Making Country*, Angus and Robertson, Pymble, 1995.

— 'Making it New in Australia', in *Angry Penguins and Realist Painting in Melbourne in the 1940s*, Hayward Gallery, London, 1988.

— 'Nolan in Queensland', *Art and Australia*, September, 1967.

— *Of Dark and Light: The Art of John Perceval*, National Gallery of Victoria, Melbourne, 1992.

— Barrett Reid and Nancy Underhill (eds.), *The Letters of John Reed: Defining Australian Cultural Life, 1920–1981*, Viking, Ringwood, 2001.

Arthur Rimbaud, *A Season in Hell, The Illuminations*, (trans.) Enid Rhodes Pechel, Oxford University Press, Oxford, 1979.

Graham Robb, *Rimbaud*, Macmillan, London, 2000.

William Robinson, *The Wild Garden*, 1977, The Scolar Press, London.

Eleanour Sinclair Rohde, *The Scented Garden*, Medici Society, London, 1989.

T.G. Rosenthal, *Sidney Nolan*, Thames and Hudson, Melbourne, 2002.

Andrew Sayers, *Sidney Nolan's Ned Kelly*, National Gallery of Australia, Canberra, 2002.

John Sinclair, 'Nolan's Student Years', *Art and Australia*, September, 1967.

Bernard Smith, *Australian Painting*, Oxford University Press, Melbourne, 1971.

Gertrude Stein, *Paris France*, Liveright, New York, 1970.

– *Three Lives*, Peter Owen, London, 1970.

Kylie Tennant, *Evatt: Politics and Justice*, Angus and Robertson, Sydney, 1970.

Naomi Turner, *Catholics in Australia: A Social History*, vol. 2, Collins Dove, North Blackburn, 1992.

E.M. Walling, *The Australian Roadside*, Oxford University Press, Melbourne, 1952.

Patrick White, *Flaws in the Glass: A Self Portrait*, Jonathan Cape, London, 1981.

Angela Woollacott, *To Try her Fortune in London*, Oxford University Press, New York, 2001.

Christopher Wray, *Arthur Streeton*, Jacaranda, Milton, 1993.

ORAL HISTORIES

Nadine Amadio, taped interview, 1 June 2002, Sydney.

Gisele Bellew, interview, 2 June 2000, Paris.

Asher Bilu, taped interview, 22 July 2003, Brighton.

Barbara Blackman, taped interview, 25 September 1980, Paddington.

Charles Blackman, interview, 6 August 1979, Melbourne.

Helen Bond, telephone interview, 10 September 2002, Launceston.

Yvonne Boyd, taped interview, 7 July 2000, Elwood.

Susie Brunton, taped interview, 17 July 1999, Frankston; taped interview, 27 August 2003, Elwood.

Peter Burns, taped interview, 20 May 2003, Kangaroo Ground.

Russell Deeble, taped interview, 10 January 2001, Elsternwick.

Simon Dickeson, taped interview, 25 September 2000, North Fitzroy.

Anne Cairns, taped interview, 26 January 2003, Merricks.

Neil Douglas, taped interview, 22 September 1980, Kangaroo Ground; telephone interview, 12 December 1996, Venus Bay; taped interview, 25 January 1997, Venus Bay; telephone interview, 7 July 2002, Dimboola.

Sir Rupert Hamer, taped interview, 21 July 2003, Hawthorn.

Wendy Hitchmough, interview, 26 July 2002, Charleston, Sussex.

Peter Hobb, taped interview, 22 July 1998, Rye; taped interview, 2 December 2002, Tootgarook.

Peter Holyman, taped interview, 10 September 2002, Mt Pleasant.

Laurence Hope, taped interview, 27 July 1980, Sydney.

Joan James, taped interview, 2 April 1999, Middle Park.

Philip Jones, taped interview, 18 October 1994, Elwood; taped interview, 12 April 2000, Melbourne; telephone interview, 30 September 2002, Melbourne; interview, 30 July 2003, St Kilda.

Jean Langley, taped interview, 25 October 1994, Safety Beach; taped interview, 3 September 1997, Safety Beach; taped interview, 2 December 2002, Safety Beach.

Les Kossatz, taped interview, 20 August 2003, Carlton.

Susan McCulloch, taped interview, 2 December 2002, Shoreham.

Erica McGilchrist, interview, 1976, Caulfield.

Eve McGlashan, taped interview, 22 October 2003, St Kilda.

Maidie McGowan, taped interview, 8 August 1997, Frankston.

Pamela McIntosh, taped interview, 8 February 1999, Warrion.

Mirka Mora, interview, 26 September 1994, St Kilda.

Mary Nolan, telephone interview, 26 June 2000, Presteigne, Wales.

Maudie Palmer, taped interview, 22 March 2004, Box Hill North.

Antony Penrose, taped interview, 26 July 2002, Farley's Farm, Sussex.

John Perceval, interview, 24 November 1998, Balwyn.

Sunday Reed (with John Reed and Sweeney Reed), taped interview, 5 May 1978, Bulleen.

Barrett Reid, taped interview, 19 August 1994, Bulleen.

Alex Selenitsch, taped interview, 15 January 2001, Clifton Hill.

Peregrine Smith, taped interview, 1 September 1999, Malvern.

Gordon Thomson, taped interview, 18 April 2001, Carlton.

Albert Tucker, taped interview, 5 July 1979, Hurstbridge; taped interview, 7 January 1997, St Kilda.

Henry von Bibra, telephone interview, 2 September 2002, Melbourne.

Kenneth von Bibra, taped interview, 10 September 2002, Mt Pleasant.

Pamela Warrender, taped interview, 3 February 2003, Toorak.

Terry Whelan, taped interview, 27 June 2002, North Fitzroy.

Lyn Williams, telephone interview, 18 August 2003, South
Yarra.

John Yule, interview, 12 August 1994, South Melbourne.

Index